Institutions:
The Evolution of Human Sociality

Institutions:
The Evolution of Human Sociality

Edited by
Kaori KAWAI

Translated by
Minako SATO

Kyoto University Press

First published in Japanese in 2013 by Kyoto University Press. This English edition first published in 2017 jointly by:

Kyoto University Press
69 Yoshida Konoe-cho
Sakyo-ku, Kyoto 606-8315
Japan
Telephone: +81-75-761-6182
Fax: +81-75-761-6190
Email: sales@kyoto-up.or.jp
Web: http://www.kyoto-up.or.jp

Trans Pacific Press
PO Box 164, Balwyn North, Melbourne
Victoria 3104, Australia
Telephone: +61-3-9859-1112
Fax: +61-3-8611-7989
Email: tpp.mail@gmail.com
Web: ht:p://www.transpacificpress.com

Copyright © Kyoto University Press and Trans Pacific Press 2017.

Set by Sarah Tuke, Melbourne.

Printed by Focus Print Group, Burwood, Victoria, Australia.

Distributors

USA and Canada
International Specialized Book Services (ISBS)
920 NE 58th Avenue, Suite 300
Portland, Oregon 97213-3786
USA
Telephone: (800) 944-6190
Fax: (503) 280-8832
Email: orders@isbs.com
Web: http://www.isbs.com

Asia and the Pacific (except Japan)
Kinokuniya Company Ltd.

Head office:
38-1 Sakuragaoka 5-chome
Setagaya-ku, Tokyo 156-8691
Japan
Telephone: +81-3-3439-0161
Fax: +81-3-3439-0839
Email: bkimp@kinokuniya.co.jp
Web: www.kinokuniya.co.jp

Asia-Pacific office:
Kinokuniya Book Stores of Singapore Pte., Ltd.
391B Orchard Road #13-06/07/08
Ngee Ann City Tower B
Singapore 238874
Telephone: +65-6276-5558
Fax: +65-6276-5570
Email: SSO@kinokuniya.co.jp

The translation and publication of this book was supported by a Grant-in-Aid for Publication of Scientific Research Results (Grant Number 15HP6007), provided by the Japan Society for the Promotion of Science, to which we express our sincere appreciation.

All rights reserved. No reproduction of any part of this book may take place without the written permission of Kyoto University Press or Trans Pacific Press.

ISBN   978-1-925608-90-8

Contents

Figures	vii
Photographs	viii
Contributors	ix

Introduction—From "Groups" to "Institutions": In Pursuit of an Evolutionary Foundation for Human Society and Sociality
Kaori Kawai   1

Part I: The Mechanism of the Formation of Institutions

1 The Formation of Institutions   *Toru Soga*   19

2 An Institution Called Death: Towards Its *Arche*
Motomitsu Uchibori   39

3 Institution and Ritualization   *Masakazu Tanaka*   59

4 Children, Play, Rules: Places of Expression of Institution
Hitoshige Hayaki   79

5 The Day Teaching Becomes Institution: An Evolutionary Horizon From Apes to Humans   *Hideaki Terashima*   95

Part II: Concrete Phases of the Emergence of Institutions

6 Who is the Alpha Male? The Institutionality of Dominance Rank in Chimpanzee Society   *Hitonaru Nishie*   121

7 Duality of the Mode of Coexistence and Action Selection: Groups and the Emergence of "Institutions" in Chimpanzees
Noriko Itoh   141

8 When Keeping One's Ears Open for the Distant Voices of Others: The Process-Oriented Convention in Chimpanzees and Institution   *Shunkichi Hanamura*   165

9 Peace Building in the Wild: Thinking about Institutions from Cases of Conflict and Peace in Sulu   *Ikuya Tokoro*   197

10 Institutionalized Cattle Raiding: Its Formalization and Value Creation Amongst the Pastoral Dodoth   *Kaori Kawai*   219

Part III: Theory for the Evolution of Institutions

11 What Connects and Separates Pre- and Post-Institution
    Koji Kitamura   241
12 Living One's Role Under Institution: Ecological Niches and
    Animal Societies   *Kaoru Adachi*   265
13 Proofs in Mathematics and the Performance of Institutions:
    A Study of Evolution Starting from Kepler's Equation
    Naoki Kasuga   287
14 Basic Components of Institution: Understanding
    Institution According to Triangular and Tetrahedral Models
    Takeo Funabiki   309

Part IV: The Expansion of Institution Theory

15 The Ontology of Feeling: The Evolutionary Basis of "Natural
    Institutions" in Inuit Extended Family Groups   *Keiichi Omura*   327
16 The Institution of "Feeling": On "Feeling Inside" and
    "Institutionalized Envy"   *Yuko Sugiyama*   349
17 Was the Old Woman's Death a Suicide? A Discussion on the
    Basis of Institutions   *Ryoko Nishii*   371
18 The Evolutionary Foundations of Institutions: Rule, Deviation,
    Identity   *Suehisa Kuroda*   393

Notes   413
Bibliography   423
Name Index   451
Subject Index   452

Figures

1.1	The segmentary lineage system of the Nuer	27
3.1	*Chika engeki*	62
7.1	*Ilombo* fruiting and feeding pattern (1997–1998)	146
7.2	Breakdown of episodes per target individual (interacted and did not interact)	153
7.3	Frequency distribution of the length of time the target individual spent with another individual in visual contact	154
9.1	Relationships	211
12.1	Seasonal food variations in guenon mixed species associations	269
12.2	Seasonal feeding overlap variations in guenon mixed species associations	276
13.1	True anomaly f and eccentric anomaly u in an elliptical orbit	291
14.1	One-to-one human relationship	313
14.2	One-to-one relationship and mediation by a third party (p)	313
14.3	Tripartite relationship	315
14.4	Expansion of a one-to-one relationship	317
14.5	Tripartite relationship and tetrahedral model	321
16.1	A man (Villager C) retelling the story of a witchcraft case	366

Photographs

1.1	Milking camels in the morning	36
2.1	Male menhirs (1) (*Vato lahi*)	46
2.2	Male menhirs (2) (*Vato lahi*)	46
4.1	Juvenile Japanese macaques play-fighting at Funakoshiyama, Hyogo	86
4.2	Juvenile chimpanzees play-fighting, showing play faces with their mouths wide open, at Mahale Mountains National Park, Tanzania	86
5.1	A chimpanzee watching an older sister ant fishing	99
5.2	An Efe Pygmy daughter watching her mother preparing food	99
6.1	Fanana (right) receiving grooming from Kalunde (left), an old male	126
6.2	Alofu	126
7.1	*Ilombo* (*Saba comorensis*, Apocynaceae) fruit	145
7.2	Various forms of social interaction: Grooming, peering, meat-sharing (from top)	152
8.1	Zola (adult female) and her daughter Zuhura, turn toward the sound of a pant-hoot from outside the visible range	171
9.1	A reconciliation ritual where previously antagonistic parties ask for forgiveness from one another	209
10.1	A Dodoth girl hugging her little sister	223
10.2	Evening in Dodothland	237
14.1	Exchanging a woman for pigs at a wedding in the Mbotgote society where the author conducted a field study	318
15.1	An Inuit extended family group	333
15.2	Inuit food sharing	333
16.1	Married women share snuff while discussing arrangements for a ritual	355
16.2	Male villagers on their way to a net-hunting location	363

Contributors

Kaori Kawai (Introduction, Chapter 10)
Professor, Research Institute for Languages and Cultures of Asia and Africa, Tokyo University of Foreign Studies

Toru Soga (Chapter 1)
Professor, Faculty of Humanities and Social Sciences, Hirosaki University

Motomitsu Uchibori (Chapter 2)
Professor, The Open University of Japan

Masakazu Tanaka (Chapter 3)
Professor, Institute for Research in the Humanities, Kyoto University

Hitoshige Hayaki (Chapter 4)
Professor, Faculty of Humanities and Sciences, Kobe Gakuin University

Hideaki Terashima (Chapter 5)
Professor, Faculty of Humanities and Sciences, Kobe Gakuin University

Hitonaru Nishie (Chapter 6)
Postdoctoral Research Fellow, Japan Society for the Promotion of Science

Noriko Itoh (Chapter 7)
Researcher, Wildlife Research Center, Kyoto University

Shunkichi Hanamura (Chapter 8)
Researcher, The Center For African Area Studies, Kyoto University

Ikuya Tokoro (Chapter 9)
Professor, Research Institute for Languages and Cultures of Asia and Africa, Tokyo University of Foreign Studies

Koji Kitamura (Chapter 11)
Emeritus Professor, Okayama University

Kaoru Adachi (Chapter 12)
Lecturer, Kyoto Sangyo University

Naoki Kasuga (Chapter 13)
Professor, Graduate School of Social Sciences, Hitotsubashi University

Takeo Funabiki (Chapter 14)
Emeritus Professor, Graduate School of Arts and Sciences, The University of Tokyo

Keiichi Omura (Chapter 15)
Associate Professor, Graduate School of Language and Culture, Osaka University

Yuko Sugiyama (Chapter 16)
Professor, Faculty of Humanities and Social Sciences, Hirosaki University

Ryoko Nishii (Chapter 17)
Professor, Research Institute for Languages and Cultures of Asia and Africa, Tokyo University of Foreign Studies

Suehisa Kuroda (Chapter 18)
Emeritus Professor, The University of Shiga Prefecture

Introduction

From "Groups" to "Institutions": In Pursuit of an Evolutionary Foundation for Human Society and Sociality

Kaori Kawai

In the context of the evolution of human sociality

This volume attempts to approach matters and phenomena called "institutions" from the perspective of the evolution of human society and sociality—the longest possible time-span as far as human existence is concerned.

It is not easy to talk about institutions in the context of evolution. If we are to understand the evolution of the human psyche and society without the luxury of fossilized remains, we must conduct comparative studies of present-day humans and non-human primates, especially great apes such as chimpanzees and bonobos, two species in the genus *Pan*, which are our close relatives and diverged from us about seven million years ago. For this reason, the contributing authors to this volume are assembled from the field of anthropology in a broad sense, including primate sociology, ecological anthropology and social/cultural anthropology. Each co-author identifies, describes and analyzes institutions and institutional phenomena commonly found or not found in human and non-human primate societies to explore the processes/mechanisms and foundations for the formation of what we call institutions in an attempt to explain the primordial and essential characteristics of the social phenomenon of institutions from an evolutionary perspective.

It must be quite clear from the table of contents that this collection of papers carrying the grand title of *Institutions: The Evolution of Human Society* presents substantially different views from many discourses on institutions produced by the social sciences in a narrow sense, such as political science and economics. Firstly, this volume is not trying to find an answer to the question of the definition of "institution"—"What is an institution?"—or the principles of institution, so to speak. We avoid tackling the definitional issue head-on because the usage of the term "institution" in Western languages (e.g., English) covers a very wide range of meanings, and trying to formulate a strict definition in a large framework including non-human primates will likely diminish its semantic reach and utility.

Let me briefly explain how this book has come about. In a sense, this is a sequel to *Groups: The Evolution of Human Sociality*, published in 2013 (the Japanese edition, *Shudan—Jinrui shakai no shinka*, was published in December 2009). Just as with *Groups*, this volume is the fruit of a joint research project at the Research Institute for Languages and Cultures of Asia and Africa (ILCAA) at the Tokyo University of Foreign Studies. The project began its endeavor to explain human society and sociality in the context of human evolution in April 2005. The joint project was named "Human Society in Evolutionary Perspectives (1)". The suffix (1) expresses our intention to continue this project on a series of themes as an ongoing joint research project. The participants in the first phase of the project met twenty-one times over a period of four years to work on the subject of "groups" (the Groups Research Project: GRP). The participants in "Human Society in Evolutionary Perspectives (2)" on the subject of "institutions" (the Institutions Research Project: IRP) met sixteen times over three years to lay the groundwork for this publication. The third phase of the joint project on the theme of "others" (the Otherness Research Project: ORP) began in April 2012. Accordingly, many of the contributors to this volume have been members of the GRP and ORP as well as co-authors of *Groups*.

In this volume, the scope of our discussion has broadened or advanced from the questions of the "shape" of groups and "how they assemble", which were discussed intensely at the GRP, to the substance or contents of the behaviors of people, apes and monkeys, i.e., "what they do" by *forming groups* or *in groups*. It is thought that when these "behaviors" are replaced and given more abstract names in a generalized framework, they must cover the scope delineated by the term "institutions". A majority of these "behaviors" are things "routinely" or repeatedly performed within groups rather than one-off occurrences, and this gives rise to the question of the subjectability of "behaviors" to rules, that is, behaving according to rules. We would like to examine the institutions in a very loose (broad) sense that are found in collective living by reference to this recurrence and rule dependence.

Why primatology has not addressed "institutions"

Anthropology is an academic discipline that studies the evolution of human society and one of its branches, primatology, studies primates, which have followed the long path of evolution side by side with humans. I shall set aside the relationship between institution theory and social/cultural anthropology that studies human society and culture and first address the way primatology relates to the evolution of human society. In this volume, the younger generation of primatologists in particular is earnestly seeking to engage with this theme.

The Japanese discipline of primatology (a rather unique brand of primatology developed in Japan and commonly known as *saru-gaku*, that is "monkey study"), which began in the 1940s, has since its earliest days studying Japanese macaques traditionally been interested in a space called "society" that extends beyond the individuals comprising a troop (social group)[1]. One of the social phenomena discovered in Japanese macaque troops during the early stages of Japanese primatology, "dominance hierarchy", is particularly reminiscent of a human institution. This phenomenon is based on the dominant-subordinate relationship between individual members of a troop and commonly manifests in all Japanese macaque troops, although the degree of rigidity of the relationship varies somewhat depending on the habitat region. More specifically, there is a clear dominant-subordinate relationship between any pair of individuals within a troop and when these relationships are pieced together they form a social structure where all individuals in the troop are ranked in a linear fashion. However, the way of interpreting a troop with terms such as "dominance hierarchy", i.e., the perspective and approach, was criticized as being overly anthropomorphic. For this reason, together with the arrival of sociobiology, this phenomenon came to be discussed in *biological* terms along with "consanguinity", which was another topic for debate at the time. Thus, institutional phenomena found in non-human primates were either ignored or absorbed into biology and "institutions" were locked in the realm of exclusively human cultural phenomena.

It is small wonder that Western primatology with a tradition of individual-centered ethology has hardly addressed the question of institutions. By contrast, it must have been a key theme in the Japanese primatology tradition, which has developed with a unique emphasis on a comprehensive view of the social group that is the "troop" rather than the individual. Yet, other than Jun'ichiro Itani (1981), who used the rigid term "*kiku*" (certain customary norms) in his attempt to explain something institutional in non-human primates, Suehisa Kuroda (1999), the author of the final chapter here, has largely been a lone voice on the subject.

It is possible to say that the origins of the human family was initially more or less the sole target of the debate about institutions in Japanese primatology. Elucidation of the formation of the primordial family or the origins of the human family is said to have been the primary goal of the Kyoto University African Primate Expedition, led by Kinji Imanishi in the 1960s. Imanishi selected four criteria for the formation of the human family: exogamy, incest taboo, community and the sexual division of labor. Field research on African great apes was undertaken to verify this hypothesis. In the end, Imanishi's hypothesis was rejected because the existence of community could not be established and subsequently the study of the origins of the human family lost its popularity. Besides Itani and Kuroda, Juichi Yamagiwa has continued to pursue this theme. Yamagiwa is a primatologist specializing in research on gorillas who counts *Kazoku no kigen—Fusei no tojo* (Origins of the family: Establishment of paternity) (1994) and *Kazoku shinka ron* (Evolutionary history of human family) (2012) among his list of publications. Family is undoubtedly an institution. However, very few scholars have looked into the origins and evolution of institutions in general, which Itani called "*kiku*" (certain customary norms) and Kuroda termed "natural institutions".

The principal reason for this is the fact that non-human primates do not have human language. For instance, Masao Kawai declares in *Ningen no yurai* (Human origins) (1992) that family is an institution and defines institution as "a form of culture that is only possible for primates with language or linguistic abilities". It is possible to say that even for Itani, who led Japanese primatology and discovered society among non-human primates, the obstacle of the absence of language was insurmountable. While Itani did not define "institution", according to Kuroda (1999) his view can be summarized as "a culture that has the force of constraint on the behaviors of the individual". Itani appears to have considered language as a necessary prerequisite for institutions that generates rigorous rules dictating behavior and custom. Kuroda nominates *Kokoro no oitachi—Shakai to kodo* (The upbringing of the mind: Society and behavior) (Itani 1981) as the thesis that best represents Itani's view of institutions and argues that Itani's definition of institution was as follows: "institutions are behavioral regulations that are verbalized and shared by members of social groups and function as their identities, and social sanctions are imposed on deviation from them". According to Kuroda, Itani importantly stated that "non-human primate culture lacks something to *control* the behaviors of group members, in other words, it has no institution" (emphasis added). However, as Kuroda points out, this logic becomes trapped in the tautology that institutions are created by institutions if language is regarded as an institution as well. From this standpoint, we would not be able to delve into the question of the formation and origin of institutions.

Itani stated that "in the end we have no choice but to use language in order to understand primate behaviors, that is, to describe and classify their behaviors" and from that period, his writings began to mention institutions in the same breath as culture. For example, he defines culture and institution as follows:

> *Culture and institution* are in a sense the behavioral *kiku* (certain customary norms) for the individuals who share them, and describing such *culture and institution* means none other than describing the normative patterns of behavior in a greater number of individuals belonging to a particular society. Thus, the mainstream of ethnology has forgotten the behaviors of individuals while concentrating solely on describing their social standards. (Itani 1981; emphasis added)

Itani left us without explaining the exact meaning of the rigid term "*kiku*" he used in the above passage. Consequently, my argument below remains speculative, but I venture to dwell on this term because *kiku* is thought to be an important concept in relation to institutions that is also used in the context of human society.

Firstly, Itani distinguishes the concept of "institution" from that of "*kiku*" in that the former manifests in society while the latter manifests in individuals. Let's just say that *kiku* is a frame of reference for individual actions and behaviors. In that case, it is considered to correspond to the "internalization of customs and rules" in humans. It seems possible to find institutions in their embryonic form in non-human primates in the realm of things exerting control on some social behaviors. I suspect that Itani chose *kiku* as an equivalent term. In this sense, Itani's *kiku* is similar to the notion of "natural institution" proposed by Kuroda (1999; Chapter Eighteen).

I do not believe that Itani neglected institutions. However, an investigation into the evolution of social structure in primates as a whole was probably a more pressing issue for him. It appears that the debate surrounding the behaviors of individuals has been overlooked by primatology for years, as it was subsequently taken over by the new disciplines of behavioral ecology and sociobiology, and no other primatologists have been willing to contribute to the theory that individuals follow certain types of engagements (*kiku* and "natural institutions") called "institutions".

Background to the Institutions Research Project

From *Groups* to *Institutions*
What we wanted to assert in *Groups* was the resolve that we would begin our discussion of the evolution of human society from the very simple fact that

humans and non-human primates "gather" (assemble), along with the belief that we could depend on the solidity of the visible phenomenon of "groups". This was to avoid the risk of falling into the tautological trap that opens up when the argument is absorbed by highly abstract and semantically broad words such as "society". We hoped to discuss the "collectivity" of groups, or "coexistence" to be more exact, while precluding such a situation. Not that there is anything wrong with tautological arguments. We chose "groups" because we wished to position human society on the same horizon as all other primates based on the evolutionary premise that humans belong to the order primates and at the same time because we wanted to provide a "temporal axis" for the phenomenon of "groups" with its origin and evolution. Moreover, this approach was inevitable if we were to accomplish our objectives.

I shall touch on two points about the argument we presented in *Groups*, the result of the GRP's endeavor, that are relevant to our discussion in this volume.

The first point is the importance of the "non-structure concept". The aspect of the group phenomenon highlighted and addressed in many of the theses in *Groups* was not a structured group, but rather a non-structured assemblage. The discussion was aimed at what emerges from the tangible relationships between individual members of a group, i.e., "social bonds" and the like, rather than the structure of a group as a whole, such as the linear dominance hierarchy[2] observed in Japanese macaque troops. In past discourses on groups, the non-structured part of groups was not only overshadowed by the more holistic research on social structure, but was also excluded as deviation from the (structured) group phenomenon. By contrast, groups here are often depicted with a focus on their activities and behaviors and discussed as non-structured assemblages—in Hitoshi Imamura's terms, "the social" based on social bonds rather than the structured and institutionalized "society". Common characteristics among these groups include: being loose and free assemblies of autonomous individuals, i.e., individuals not tightly controlled by institutions, and being dynamic and fluid due to their transient nature. Although these non-structured assemblages have received little attention in the past, they deserve more recognition in consideration of groups as they account for a substantial share of our daily lives. It should have been more positively appreciated that in both humans and other primates, the structured form of group is merely one aspect and that the reality of the group phenomenon does include some degree of non-structure.

The second point is that "We humans have acquired representational abilities". This is an argument about our acquisition of the ability to perceive even absent and invisible others as friends or enemies as well as the linguistic representational ability to make perception beyond "the here and now" possible. The former is facilitated by the representational function of "We", ready examples of which include cultural categories such as patrilineal descent groups and groups such as ethnic groups and states. In reality, many of them have blurred boundaries and their members often do not know each other. This situation is made possible by the latter ability to make linguistic representations such as "such-and-such patrilineal descent group" or "such-and-such ethnic group" or "such-and-such nation", which represent the mode of being of groups peculiar to humans or "invisible groups" in a way. This would be extremely difficult to do for non-human primates, which are very unlikely to be able to perceive unseen individuals, others they have never met face-to-face, as friends or enemies using the imagination alone, so to speak. The question of the language and imagination or representation involved in group formation demonstrates that human groups are bound together by institutions. "This is because while the workings of representation that make those things that are invisible visible is certainly at play within institutions, it is also at work constructing them" (Uchibori 2013). Thus, institutions in human society came to the foreground and became our next theme as the IRP took up the next phase of this endeavor.

The IRP's approach

In all primate groups, principles for their formation and maintenance exist such as the equality and inequality principles (Itani 1986). Conversely, the very fact that multiple conspecifics exist sympatrically, that is, live collectively as a group, points to the operation of principles (dynamics) of coexistence. We are attempting to locate the origin of institutions and the embryonic state of institutions in this context.

This does not necessarily mean that the extent of control in institutions is clearly articulated in language as in written law or that sanctions are imposed on violators. Such codified institutions, in terms of written language, only began at the dawn of human history five to six thousand years ago at the earliest. As we confront "institutions" in a series of joint studies on "Human Society in Evolutionary Perspectives" to trace their origins, our time-span must have an "evolutionary historical" length rather than be simply "historical".

From the outset, the definition of "institution" was an ongoing issue for the IRP. We found ourselves in a situation where the definition varied from one dictionary or academic discipline to another. We have tried to make the definition as loose, broad and large as possible because our theme also covers non-human primates, in which we did not know whether or not institutions existed. Both humans and non-human primates alter and adjust their own behaviors in accordance with the various natural and social conditions and environments around them. We argue that this fact can be regarded as the first step toward institutionalization.

In considering the primordial form of institution, we perhaps do not need to assume any external existence (what Imamura calls the excluded third term) as necessary, even though such a transcendental existence, be it God or Law, has been mentioned or defined in relation to institutions in the past. To us, it seems sufficient to consider the potentialities of the behaviors of individuals existing on the same plane. As a case in point, some raised the argument that we should look at the fact that people's everyday social interactions wield considerable influence over laws and institutions in human societies. This is easy to see if we remember that laws are revised when our everyday interactions stop working smoothly. As Ikuya Tokoro argues in Chapter Nine, human society is not always controlled and constrained by formal institutions; informal and broadly defined institutions and conventions achieve relative dominance in some situations.

Based on these arguments, should we pay attention to more everyday interactions—including those normally not regarded as interactions, such as eating with others—in our consideration of institutions? We change the way we interact with "others" depending on environmental conditions, in other words, we base our behaviors on those of "others". This is a common phenomenon to both humans and non-human primates. Can we consider that something institutional (an institution in its embryonic stage) emerges in a place like this? What is important in substantiating this point is that the "habit" of the individual may be regarded as mere preferences or ways of doing things, but when "interactions" including joint activities with others are repeated and conventionalized, they can evolve to become "rules" or "customs" and eventually "institutions". On the other hand, it is possible to say that individual "habits" can become customs and institutions when they are shared with others.

As above, the contents of our discussion at the IRP involved tracing back to the origins of institutions through redefining their foundation, whether theoretically or empirically. Its goal was to discover the mechanism by which humans, apes

Introduction

and monkeys live their lives together with other conspecific individuals in the same social group as a process of generating, effecting and changing their own everyday lives. In other words, it was a discourse on the fact that we, and probably apes and monkeys as well, lead our lives in accordance with institutions in the broadest sense, or something institutional (i.e., organizing our behaviors in an orderly manner, including eating, sleeping, moving and dealing with others), to bring social groups into existence, whether we are aware of it or not, as well as on the conditions of such social groups.

Terminology

Before we move on to introduce the contents of each part and chapter in the next section, I would like to discuss terminology.

As is evident from the title, this volume aims to discuss the behaviors of humans, apes and monkeys surrounding "institutions" in the context of the evolution of human society and sociality theoretically or empirically or both. The Japanese term *seido* that is the title of this book is normally translated as "institution" in English. However, "institution" has a broader meaning than *seido* and includes (institutionalized) conventions, practices and systems besides sociological meanings such as laws, regulations and ordinances that are normally used in the Japanese language.

On the other hand, the term "institutions" in the overview of this book below is often used to mean conventions, including traditions, normative examples, customs, habitual practices, conventionalities, rules, traditional procedures and so on, and many of the chapters approach "institutions" from these phenomena with subtly different nuances. These concepts that can be denoted by the term "conventions" are capable of wielding social force. This might have been what Itani meant when he used the rigid term "*kiku*" (certain customary norms). If so, it is possible to say that "institutions" cover all (a bundle or assembly) methods (modes and manners) of leading a collective life with others.

The term "convention" here is of course deeply related to D. Hume's analysis of convention. Or perhaps it is the same as the convention defined by Hume. In Japan, as there is no established translation for Hume's convention, it has instead been translated into various Japanese words, including customary practice, agreement and tacit consent, and these days it is often transliterated. This term is thought to connote not only "customary practice" but also "agreement" and "a general sense of common interest" (see Chapter Six). Meanwhile, Hume made the following comment about "custom".

> Now as we call every thing CUSTOM, which proceeds from a past repetition, without any new reasoning or conclusion, (...) that the past experience, on which all our judgments concerning cause and effect depend, may operate on our mind in such an insensible manner as never to be taken notice of, and may even in some measure be unknown to us. (...) The custom operates before we have time for reflection. (Hume 2010)

As I mentioned earlier, we deliberately refrain from defining the term "institution" in order to resolve the questions of living in institutions and social groups, and in turn how living in one's own group came about and how it is organized, by keeping its meaning space as expansive as possible. It may be used to mean something close to that of Hume's "custom". The usage of the Japanese term *seido* is left to the judgment of each co-author. Some chapters pursue a semantic expansion of the term by setting a provisional definition and arguing how large a leap is possible, while others adopt the approach of cutting into the definition by accumulating various behaviors that create or disrupt order in social groups.

Might I also add as the editor, we could have discussed "practices" as an intermediate term in deriving mores and customs, i.e., conventions, from an accumulation of behaviors. In anthropology, this term has been used to mean habitual actions, customary practices, normative examples, customs, established practices, habits and so on. These "practices" lack a clear reason for engaging in a certain behavior, or a consciousness or awareness of the process of such behavior. They are behaviors people "do all the time, without thinking, for no special reason". In this sense, they emphasize the behavioral aspect of conventions.

The term "practice" is not used in primatology, and the terms "interaction" and "interactive behavior" are instead widely used to denote behaviors of a social nature. However, since we brought the concept of convention (which is also rarely used in this field) into primatology, we probably should have tracked back to "practice" as well. I say so because it is possible to find a stage where individual behaviors—whether interactive or not—become established as practices in a certain group as part of the process of transition to conventions as accumulated behaviors. Therefore, we could have envisaged the relationship between the more conceptual notion of institution and one's living body and its behaviors as follows.

<Idea> institution ↔ convention ↔ practice ↔ (interactive) behavior <Physical>

It is somewhat regrettable that we could not deepen our discussion on this issue at the IRP, but we will attempt to address this with the ORP in the next phase.

Contents

The topics discussed in the eighteen chapters of this volume are extremely diverse. This perhaps gives the impression of diverging into a wide range of subjects as opposed to a seemingly coherent process of human evolution, an axis terminating with human beings on one end. To use unfavorable terms, it may give the impression of being "incohesive". However, we have no intention of regarding "incohesiveness" as a negative. Rather, as I asserted above, the book directly reflects the orientation of our discussion, which is to propose the location of the problems by expanding the conceptual boundaries of institution as much as possible through interdisciplinary dialogue.

In comparison with the previous volume, this book perhaps comes out strongly in terms of the direction of the argument from the assumption of the existence of groups to the individuals who exist in them, whereas *Groups* displays a strong directionality of thinking from individuals to groups. To be more exact, this is more appropriately conceptualized as a reciprocal movement in two directions. The aforementioned argument on institutions from the perspective of interaction emerges as part of this and consequently many of the theses contained herein emphasize one direction while bearing in mind both momenta. The direction from groups to individuals stands out in this volume only in the context of comparison with *Groups*. We suggest that those who have read *Groups* may be interested in paying attention to different phases of this directionality.

I now provide a brief overview of each part and chapter below.

Part I: The Mechanism of the Formation of Institutions
What is the process of the formation of social phenomena that can be called "institutions"? Part I attempts to depict the formative mechanism under five distinct themes. It undertakes the task of theoretically tracing the path

along which a certain social event is pushed, acquires its directionality to institutionalize, develops into something institutional, then finally becomes established as an institution and either persists or transforms into something else. The five themes include: conventional order created by behaviors engaged in with others face-to-face (Chapter One, Soga); "death" that is distinguished from "dying" as a phenomenon in a physiological or biological dimension, i.e., the grounds for the *arche* of the high-dimensional domain of "death" that is formed by the introduction of meaning (Chapter Two, Uchibori); an institution as a bundle of "practices", including ritualizing and ritualistic behaviors, and its legitimization (Chapter Three, Tanaka); rules as the essence of children's play and the origin of institutions (Chapter Four, Hayaki); and differences between the ape's way of learning and human learning (Chapter Five, Terashima). Each of the theses attempts to theorize the mechanism by which institutions are formed under specific conditions.

Part II: Concrete Phases of the Emergence of Institutions

When, where and how does the existence of an institutional or institution-like thing become visible? By what approach do we observers recognize it as an "institution"? Part II is a collection of theses that deploy theoretical speculation freely based on the detailed description and sound analysis of field data. They attempt to address an overflow of concrete events and phenomena that cannot be absorbed into the term "institution" in a narrow sense as used in the social sciences. Chapter Six by Nishie, Chapter Seven by Itoh and Chapter Eight by Hanamura are supported by detailed data obtained through close observations of wild chimpanzees in the Mahale Mountains National Park, Tanzania. They present three different ways to build a rationale for finding something institution-like in chimpanzees. What they address and depict, namely, a rank order of individuals within a unit group, the condition of coexistence and action selection, auditory communication with other individuals and so on, are in fact the concrete phases of chimpanzee institutions. Chapter Nine by Tokoro and Chapter Ten by Kawai shift their gaze to a maritime people in Southeast Asia and a pastoral people in East Africa respectively and, based on concrete ethnographical materials, describe cases in which agonistic and violent events such as conflict and cattle raiding are dealt with, or not adequately dealt with, as something institutional. This is an attempt to look toward the looseness and broadness of institutions in human society, which cannot remain robust or monolithic all the time.

Part III: Theory for the Evolution of Institutions

Based on the supposition that institutions themselves do evolve, the theses in Part III inquire into the mechanism of this evolutionary process. They deepen their theoretical thinking on the formation of the institutional, using concrete examples corresponding to this question. Chapter Eleven by Kitamura discusses events that happened during the transition from pre-institutional primate society to human society via two distinct routes: "prohibitive rules (adjustment)" and "ritual rules (selection)". Chapter Twelve by Adachi considers the emergence of an institution from an ecological niche as a continuum of routine interactions based on observations of mixed species associations of cercopithecines. Chapter Thirteen by Kasuga approaches institutions by connecting the thinking pattern in mathematics and that in anthropology in an analogical fashion by using the mathematical theory of Kepler's equation that is seemingly unrelated to institutions. Chapter Fourteen by Funabiki speculates on how present-day human groups have been able to attain unprecedented levels of scale and complexity exceeding their biological group composition in both quality and quantity. These four theses can be regarded as theories on the formation of institutions.

Part IV: The Expansion of Institution Theory

The four theses in this final part approach the evolution of institutions from novel angles—the perspectives of flesh-and-blood human conditions and behaviors, including feelings, freedom and ethics, completely at odds with the cold and rigid characteristics emanating from the term "institution" such as stasis, fixity and monotony. Discussions on institutions in Chapter Fifteen by Omura and Chapter Sixteen by Sugiyama revolve around "feelings", which are universal cognitive states common to all humankind although they are seemingly irrelevant to institutions. The former argues that coexistence in the extended family group, which is the basic unit of the Inuit subsistence system, is underpinned by feelings and desires, which are institutionalized and form the foundation of primordial "natural institutions", which in turn are linked to "morals". The latter puts forward the argument that "feelings are institutions" by delving deep into the feeling life of slash-and-burn farmers in Zambia and explains in detail the "emotions" involved in strained relations as well as the way feelings such as anger and envy are institutionalized. Chapter Seventeen by Nishii presents vivid data in the form of narratives told by people surrounding the question of whether or not the death of an elderly woman, from her research field, was suicide, and arrives at the finding that the "death" as a social phenomenon constituted the ethical question of how they should have dealt with the deceased. Chapter Eighteen by Kuroda questions in relation to the evolutionary foundation of institutions the commonly accepted definition that institutions cannot exist without language, and attempts to expose the true identity of institution by exploring different definitions for rule and institution and applying them to non-human primates.

Toward "others"

Now we head for the next phase of the project, which is "others". The term "others" has already made a frequent appearance and become a topic of discussion at both the GRP and the IRP. To be more exact, the existence of "others" has been built into our discourse on groups and institutions as a fundamental and crucial element, and we have decided to adopt it as the next theme. This could become a tautological argument, but we will look into face-to-face interactions at the micro-level and ultimately dyadic relationships from the perspective that society and social groups are "bundles of interactions with others". Further, we will ask how the existence of "others" emerges in relation to, confronts and relates to individuals, and how it engages with and/or becomes involved in the formation and maintenance of "society'.

Ownership, sharing, collaboration, cooperation, co-presence, dominance, confrontation, migration/transfer and reciprocity etc. immediately come to mind as social phenomena in which the supposed others appear. Perhaps the element of "others" is included in all social phenomena in the social groups of humans and non-human primates. We believe that we must leave the gate open as wide as possible if we are to understand society and sociality over the maximum time-span of evolution for the human species, as we have done with the GRP and the IRP. We would like to think that groups, institutions and others maintain their connection with the phenomenon of evolution in the depths of society and sociality.

Part I
The Mechanism of the Formation of Institutions

1 The Formation of Institutions

Toru Soga

Key ideas

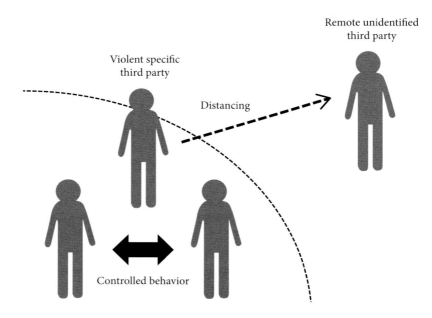

What is "institution"? If we consider that "institution" is a "situation" or "thing" that externally influences a face-to-face interaction, a violent third party is a strong contender for "institution". It takes on a more institutional aspect when a specific violent third party is distanced from the site of interaction and turned into an unidentified third party. This condition is met when the number of people who are interconnected exceeds the individual's cognitive capacity.

Face-to-face behavior and institution

It is generally considered that institution is made explicit by language. For example, institution is represented linguistically in such forms as "must not do ..." or "must do ...". Junichiro Itani (1987) considered that language was a necessary condition for institution and therefore institutions did not exist among non-human primates without language. However, as Suehisa Kuroda (1999) argues, rule making does not necessarily require the precondition of linguistic conceptualization. This chapter will explore the evolutionary bases for institution that are shared by humans and non-human primates.

One evolutionary basis of institution to be examined here is face-to-face behavior. What is important here is, literally, turning one's face towards that of another and detecting and understanding each other's various facial expressions. This face-to-face behavior does not necessarily require language. Non-human primates can easily make such observations. Let us assume that "institutions" are "situations" and "objects" that externally influence face-to-face interactions between two parties. They are not limited to "situations" that are expressed in language. "Objects" can be various "third parties" or "things". For instance, it is easy to imagine that religious things can influence people's face-to-face behavior. However, what is concealed in such religious things and "situations" that is expressed through language are the cultural activities carried out by the people who have created them. It is reasonable to say that the source of these "situations" and "objects (things)" lies in human beings. Consequently, this chapter will focus on various "third parties" instead of looking at "situations" and "objects (things)". By examining various patterns of face-to-face behavior, we attempt to discover the "third parties" that constitute external influences in interactions between two parties. The purpose of this chapter is to consider the formative process of "institution" using "third parties" as stepping-stones.

One primate genus and two human political organizations have been selected to facilitate the exploration of various "third parties" in this chapter. The genus in question is *Macaca*, which includes species such as *M. fuscata* (Japanese macaque), *M. arctoides* (Stump-tailed macaque) and *M. mulatta* (Rhesus macaque). It is more common to choose larger anthropoids such as chimpanzees and gorillas when examining human evolution due to their genetic similarity. However, I am inclined to think that an evolutionary basis for the formation of institutions exists in *Macaca*.

The two types of human society that are examined here are the hunter-gatherer societies of the Bushmen and Pygmies and pastoralist society. Fortes and Evans-Pritchard (2015: 5–7) categorized African societies into three types according to political organization. The first type entails "very small societies" in which even the largest political unit is comprised of members interconnected by kinship ties. The second type includes societies whose political systems are built on a lineage structure. They are "societies without central government" in which no centralized authority, administrative organization or judicial system exists. The third type includes "societies with central government" whose political structure is built on some form of centralized authority, administrative organization and judicial system and whose population tends to be far greater in number than the second type.

As societies move from the first type toward the third type, they experience the advent of different "third parties". The three types of societies differ significantly not only in their political systems, but also in terms of the importance of institution. For instance, the importance of institution is very low in Type 1 societies. In Type 2 societies, some forms of institution may exist, but people's behavior in relation to them tends to vary widely. On the other hand, institution has major social significance in Type 3 societies where people rely on centralized authorities, administrative organizations and judicial systems in organizing their social lives.

What are the characteristics of "situations" and "objects (things and people)" that influence people's face-to-face behavior in these societies? These characteristics may provide clues to the formative process of institutions. This chapter will discuss the hunter-gatherer societies of the Southern African Bushmen and the Central African Pygmies as Type 1 societies and the Eastern African pastoralist societies of the Nuer, Turkana and Gabra as examples of Type 2 societies. Type 3 societies are not considered here as institution already occupies an important place in such societies and the purpose of this chapter is to discover how institution comes into existence.

Control over face-to-face behavior by a specific third party

In this section we examine face-to-face behavior that is considered to be an evolutionary basis of institution, mostly in primate societies. Two types of behavior are discussed: one is conventional behavior generated between two parties facing one another and the other is face-to-face behavior under the influence of a specific third party.

Conventional behavior between two parties facing one another

Let us begin by discussing conventional behavior between two parties facing one another. Here we look at rank within a group of Japanese macaques.

Junichiro Itani and his team successfully habituated Japanese macaques on Koshima Island in Miyazaki Prefecture in 1952. As a result of observations of the individually identified macaques, they found an age-based linear rank among five males of the group. They tested dominance rank by placing food at the midpoint between two individuals and observed which would take it. They concluded after repeating the experiment numerous times that the dominant male invariably took the food. Later on, linear rank was confirmed among forty-four male Japanese macaques at Takasakiyama. The existence of stable rank was also identified among females (Itani 1987: 274). Dominance rank among males was also diachronically stable. Itani recorded rank among individuals in a troop in 1955 and 1962. Although the troop split into Group A and Group B in 1959, no change was observed in rank among the males who remained in Group A, aside from a small number of cases of reversals. Dyadic relationships between males appear to be conventionalized and fixed.

While Itani and others used food to test dominance rank, they reported that rank relationships were easily identifiable based on the facial expressions and manners of two individuals when they came into face-to-face contact. In the world of Japanese macaques, the restrained expressions and manners of the subordinate become apparent over the course of a short encounter. These expressions and manners provide important clues in considering face-to-face behavior between two individuals. As Yuko Sugiyama points out in Chapter Sixteen, facial expressions and manners must also be utilized in the formation of conventional face-to-face behavior in human society. Conventionalizing behavioral patterns between two parties by reading one another's facial expressions is an ability shared by humans and other primates.

Face-to-face behavior under the influence of a specific third party

Nevertheless, it is perhaps inappropriate to think that conventional behavioral patterns between two parties will accumulate and eventually become institutions. When conventionalization of dyadic behavior takes place, it is important for the directly interacting individuals to observe each other's reactions. On the other hand, conforming to institution means obeying a "situation/object" external to the interaction, and in extreme cases the other's reaction does not matter. Conforming to institution means focusing one's attention on institution that exists outside of the dyadic interaction and adjusting one's behavior accordingly without identifying with the party in front.

If institution is a "situation" or "object" that externally influences interacting parties, a violent third party falls under the category of "object" in primate societies. Hitoshi Imamura (1992: 20) emphasizes the significance of violence by stating "It is violence that is the medium as well as the driving force for the creation of order in social relationships". This section looks at the influences of a third party in primate societies with a particular focus on violence.

In *Peacemaking Among Primates*, Frans de Waal (1989) reported the phenomenon of less dominant males mating behind their superior's back. One such case involving rhesus macaques was observed at Wisconsin Primate Center. While the alpha male, Spickles, openly mated with females, the beta male, Hulk, never mated in front of his superior and never drew attention to himself when mating (de Waal 1989: 131). Another case involved stump-tailed macaques bred at the same center. Joey, the third-ranked male, was observed sneaking outside for a secret rendezvous with a female named Honey. Stump-tailed males utter grunts when they ejaculate. When Joey produced a grunt, Honey turned her head and threatened him with a stare. De Waal's interpretation of the situation was that Honey was probably concerned that dominant males might notice them mating if Joey produced any sounds (1989: 165).

As these examples show, the dominant male wields influence as a specific and violent third party in the societies of rhesus macaques and stump-tailed macaques. Rhesus and stump-tailed macaques engage in clandestine mating when dominant males are not watching because they would be met with obstruction if their behavior were noticed by the dominant. When lower-ranked males copulate with females, they control their face-to-face behavior with the dominant's violence and obstruction in mind.

The violent third party appears to maintain a certain level of presence even when absent. De Waal reported that during the breeding season for rhesus macaques, alpha male Spickles entered the heated indoor section and remained there for a long period of time. Second-ranked Hulk took the opportunity to mate many times, but he was so concerned with Spickles' whereabouts that he peeked at him through a crack in the door on numerous occasions during mating. De Waal suggested that inhibitions according to social rules are so deeply ingrained in primate societies that concern about the enforcer's reaction persists even in his absence (1996: 105–110). If the violent third party can wield influence for a certain period when he is outside of the field of vision of the two interacting parties, he can be considered highly "institutional". Consequently, I would like to propose that the following two conditions are evolutionary bases for the formation of institutions.

1. Two individuals within a group conduct face-to-face interaction in accordance with an external presence.
2. Influence persists even when the external presence is temporarily out of sight.

Institutional phenomena in humans

In this section, I leave non-human primate societies and examine institutional phenomena in human societies. I examine Type 1 "very small societies" and Type 2 "societies without government", whose political systems are built on a lineage structure according to the aforementioned categorization by Fortes and Evans-Pritchard (2015: 5–7), and examine how social order is formed in each society.

Very small societies: Face-to-face sharing

The Bushmen living in the arid zone of southern Africa and the Pygmies inhabiting the tropical forests of Central Africa form very small social groups. Around the 1960s, the Bushmen lived in highly migratory camps. Tanaka (1971: 113–132) reported that each camp contained ten families (about fifty people) on average, but the size varied frequently as individual family units came and went. However, camp fission-fusion did not occur in a random manner. Those who gathered at a camp were families in close kinship relationships such as parents with their children and siblings. On the other hand, the residential group of the Pygmies was referred to as a "band" as its membership was more stable than that of the Bushmen. An average band comprised fourteen to fifteen families, amounting to sixty to seventy people (Ichikawa 1982). It is clear that both peoples form very small groups within which they closely associate with other members. Members of such societies are limited to close relatives who know each other well.

Bushman and Pygmy societies are known to be egalitarian. Kinship is used as a political system. It appears that there is no such thing as institution, let alone centralized authority. The only institutional phenomenon anthropologists took a strong interest in was sharing behavior as an economic system.

In the case of the Pygmies who carry out net-hunting in groups, the owner of the catch distributes meat to participants according to the roles they played in the hunt. Each participant who receives his share of meat is free to distribute it further. This multi-level distribution practice ensures that all camp residents end up receiving meat equally. In the past, this sharing practice was interpreted as gift giving from one who has meat to one who has none, and it was thought that the giver acquires prestige while the receiver incurs a debt. It was supposed that the process of achieving economic equality gave rise to political inequality, and therefore the hunting-gathering peoples were desperately trying to extinguish this inequality (Ichikawa 1991).

The question is whether these people in kinship relations actually feel honored or indebted through the meat sharing process. According to Tadashi Tanno (1991), this is a misinterpretation stemming from the idea of "egalitarian society" suggested by Woodburn (1982). Woodburn explained that meat sharing amongst the Pygmies was a kind of tax system in which those who lived in the same residential group were obliged to participate. However, Tanno (1991) argued that Woodburn's hypothesis was overly biased toward individualistic interpretation and failed to understand the state of interpersonal relationships in hunter-gatherer societies. Woodburn and other anthropologists in his camp fell in the belief that individualistic people acquired prestige or indebtedness or tried to negate it through the act of gifting meat to others.

According to Tanno, Pygmies form camps through the gathering of those considered to be close relations. He argues that they do not purposely determine who the "owner" of the meat is or give meat as a gift; they simply "share" food among close relations. Sharing is carried out as a matter of convention among those recognized as "close relations" rather than according to some institution.

What is important in the creation of this convention is for one person to empathize with the person in front of them. When one decides how to behave in relation to the person in front of them in reference to norms and institutions that exist outside of the interaction between the two, one sometimes comes to lose empathy with that person. Convention allows one to fine-tune one's behavior in response to the subtleties of the other's reactions within the bounds of continuous interactions. Concepts such as "family" and "close relations" are of course institutions and people follow the directive "because we are family" or "because they are close relations" in certain situations. Here, however, I would like to point out the significance of the order that is created by the accumulation of conventional acts based on the other party's reaction alone, without any reference to such a directive.

"Societies without government": Institutionalized order

The second type of human society I examine is the pastoralist society of East Africa. In this type of society, institution has a certain meaning and people reduce

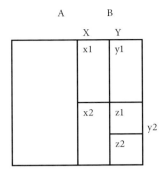

Figure 1.1 The segmentary lineage system of the Nuer

the uncertainty inherent in face-to-face interactions by referring to it. Let us look at the segmentary lineage system as an example. Evans-Pritchard (1969) proposed the following model for the political system of the Nuer, a Nilotic pastoralist people of Sudan.

Nuer society is built on the segmentary lineage system. Suppose a society is divided into Segment A and Segment B, which is divided into X and Y. Further, X is divided into x1 and x2, and Y into y1 and y2, which is divided into z1 and z2 (see Figure 1.1). What would the political attitude of individuals belonging to Segment z1 be?

According to Evans-Pritchard, a conflict between z1 and z2 would not involve any other segments. However, if z1 fights y1, z1 and z2 would unite to form y2. If y1 fights x1, y1 and y2 would unite while x1 and x2 would stand together against them. And if x1 goes to war with A, all sub-segments of B, which include x1, x2, y1 and y2, would unite against A. If A mounts an attack on another non-kin group (e.g., the neighboring Dinka), A and B would unite against them. For Nuer individuals, their political attitude is almost automatically set for life, depending on which section in the segmentary lineage system they were born into. The segmentary lineage system constitutes an external frame of reference that automatically determines the political attitude of the individual, and thus, it is an institution.

The method of describing a society using this kind of segmentary lineage model, i.e., by way of schematic diagrams and legal rules, came to be rejected as fantasy. When three Nuer individuals are observed working together, it is not necessary to explain it through reference to their lineage. The answer can be found by looking at social relationships between individuals, just as urban anthropologists would seek to do (i.e., individual association, preference etc.) (Keesing 1975: 121–131).

While I agree with the importance of micro-level observation as proposed by Keesing, I did observe some examples that fit well into Evans-Pritchard's model when I was studying pastoralist societies in southern Ethiopia. In one example, a young stranger arrived in the village where I was lodging with Guyo (pseudonym), a pastoral Gabra elder. Guyo immediately greeted the young man and asked who he was. When Guyo found out that the man belonged to the same clan and stood in the classificatory position of son, he immediately trusted the man and offered him lodgings for the night. Even though he was meeting the man for the first time, the stranger's "character" was never an issue once their relationship had been identified. A son was a son whether he was a good person or not. As far as Guyo's family was concerned, they were required to welcome the stranger as a son.

Another example can be found in people's attitude toward a young man named Ali (pseudonym), who lived in Guyo's village. Ali was a pleasant man who was clean and hardworking with a good sense of humor, yet he was short-tempered and as a result was often arrested by police and incarcerated. When I visited Guyo's village years later, he was nowhere to be found. I asked his whereabouts and found out that he had been jailed for murder. While the news itself was shocking, I felt a degree of discomfort with the way villagers supported Ali as a matter of course. They thought that it was right "to support a clan member no matter what offense he has committed".

Institution plays a role in significantly diminishing the uncertainties involved in otherwise chaotic human relationships and automatically prescribing actions. In the first example, identifying a relationship with the young visitor enabled Guyo to deal with him without further thought. Even in such a serious case as the latter example, referring to clan enabled clan members to preclude the possibility of not helping him and to orient their actions toward assisting him. While an individual's behavior may be influenced by social association or feelings such as preference, institution sets the course of action automatically and governs behavior when one is faced with a person of insignificance or conversely when one encounters some grave situation.

What is noteworthy here is the fact that the individual is not paying attention to the other person in a face-to-face interaction when they are behaving in an institutional manner. In the first example, age difference might have been a factor, but Guyo paid little attention to the young man's personality or behavior. He was clearly disinterested in him and simply wanted to confirm their relationship in order to treat him appropriately. The young man was also disinterested in Guyo, and once he had secured lodgings for the night, he busied himself in fraternizing with villagers in the same age group. Thus, it is sometimes the case that people neglect to pay attention to the other party in front of them when they follow institutional patterns. This notion applies to the latter example as well. The personality or behavior of the young man who had committed murder was never an issue, and people never discussed whether they approved or disapproved of his actions.

"Society without government": Order by face-to-face negotiation

In the previous section, I described human interaction as if it were strongly regulated by institutions. However, that description is not a sufficient explanation of the ethos of pastoral peoples. East African pastoralists appear to put energy into the negotiative and performative creation of order that is appropriate for the occasion instead of functioning entirely according to institutions.

I once argued in my thesis on the Gabra's inegalitarian system of primogeniture that we should not think that people were conforming to the institution of "primogeniture"; rather, they were practicing primogeniture performatively (Soga 1996). I also argued that clan did not automatically bind or impose obligations on people. For the Gabra, clan constituted a guide for an individual faced with the problem of finding allies, but did not automatically guarantee support (Soga 2002). Itaru Ohta (1986), Koji Kitamura (1996) and Shinsuke Sakumichi (2001), who studied the Turkana pastoralists, also emphasized that pastoralists "negotiated" with the other party in interactions by using an institution as a trump card rather than a set of requirements.

On the other hand, as I mentioned in the previous section, institution does control behavior in some respects. What is the relationship between negotiative or performative order formation and institutional order formation?

First of all, negotiative order formation requires considerable energy. This is particularly evident in the performance of "begging". The level of persistence involved in "begging" in pastoralist societies is extraordinary. Anthropologists are often tormented by the behavior of pastoralists who think nothing of being deceitful when attempting to coax something out of them (Ohta 1986).

Kitamura (1996) observes that the pastoralist Turkana do not judge human behavior (e.g., stealing or lying) as good or bad in accordance with "external" legitimacy criteria, such as ethical value standards, "rules" or "norms". This of course does not mean that the Turkana do not see stealing or lying as bad behavior. The question as to the legitimacy or appropriateness of a certain action is resolved on the level of whether approval can be extracted from the course of communication with the other party. "Begging" is a typical example of this behavior by which pastoralists tenaciously negotiate with others to elicit approval (i.e., to have their demands fulfilled).

Where institutions are formed

I have so far outlined conventional order in primate societies, conventional order in hunting-and-gathering societies and institutional and negotiative order in pastoralist societies. Let us now consider the social conditions for the creation of institution in these three types of society.

"Others" in the society

Others in the society vary according to the state of each society. Human relations in hunter-gatherer societies are comprised of "close relations" such as those involving immediate relatives and spouses, with little room for other categories such as "friends" (Tanno 1991: 55; Tanaka 1971: 123). To hunting-and-gathering peoples, human relations are entirely constituted by kinship relations, including blood relatives and relatives by marriage, and their societies are closed along the lines of these relational categories. On the other hand, pastoralist societies belong to the second type and their social associations extend to institutional organizations such as lineage and clan that reach beyond the family and kin relationships at the core. Lineage and clan are organizational categories that contain people who do not know one another. This allows people to socialize with unknown people from the same lineage or clan.

When it comes to the third type, "society with government", the population size increases exponentially and the opportunity to associate with unknown people expands further. The difference in the breadth of social relationships is quite obvious between the three types of societies. Others in human society thus vary considerably from one society to another.

Despite the fact that there are actually infinite kinds of human "others" constituted according to family, village, lineage, clan, community group, nation, friendship, preference and so on, others who appear in the discourse on institution are always homogeneous. For instance, Masachi Ohsawa (1990) wrote a paper on the basis of skepticism toward rule following discussed by

Wittgenstein and Quine that featured Robinson Crusoe, who washed ashore on an uninhabited island, and an other. While this other plays the important role of adjudicator regarding whether or not Crusoe is following rules, there is no explanation as to whether this person hails from Crusoe's nation, clan or village. In sociological and philosophical thinking, others are simply treated as abstract and homogeneous beings.

Societies are divided by various boundaries and contain domains that reject intrusion by institutions. For example, in Japan we live in a law-bound society that tries to control all aspects of social life by legislation. We expect that everyone is treated equally and equitably before the law and that conflicts are resolved and even prevented by the law. However, even in such a society laws and institutions do not necessarily cover all domains of life homogeneously. For instance, in the early days following the introduction of the long-term care insurance system in Japan in 2000, many people felt uncomfortable about receiving services such as home visits. They had difficulty accepting the intrusion of public services into the private sphere of the home. Let us now consider where conventions and institutions come into existence with a focus on such social boundaries.

Human group size and institution

Robin Dunbar, an evolutionary psychologist, argues that there is a strong correlation between average group size and the average size of the neocortex of the brain. He plotted neocortical volume and average observed group size for thirty-six primate genera and obtained a regression equation on the data (1992). Using the equation, he estimated a mean human group size of around 150 people and named it the Dunbar number. He discovered that the Dunbar number corresponded to the group size commonly found in the organizational units of militaries and hunter-gatherer societies (Dunbar 1993). The group size referred to here correlates with neocortical volume. In other words, this number can be considered to represent the number of people one individual is able to have relationships with (or to recognize). One hundred and fifty is the estimated size of a Neolithic human community as well as the average size of a person's network on modern social media.

Since the birth of modern humans about 200,000 years ago, we have until very recently lived in small groups. Community size in hunter-gatherer societies from past to present has been almost constant in the range of fifteen to fifty, referred to as the "magic numbers" (Lee and Devore 1968). The Bushmen used to live in camps of around fifty people before the government began to promote a permanent settlement policy. The Mbuti Pygmies in the vast forested region of the Democratic Republic of the Congo still live in forest camps containing around sixty people.

Each hunter-gatherer camp would contain fifty to sixty residents at any given time, but as Tanno (1991) reported, its constituent members varied as "close relatives" came and went. The Dunbar number is considered to represent the size of the group of "close relatives", including those who move in and out. Inside this small community of "close relatives", there is no need for institution. In fact, researchers emphasize that there is hardly any level of institution in Bushmen and Pygmy societies.

For example, Jiro Tanaka (1971) reports that Bushmen societies have a very low level of social integration due to the absence of social organizations such as lineage and clan, no division of labor except along gender lines, no hierarchical relationship framework such as status, position or class, no headman, no experts, no judicature and no clearly developed kinship organization. With regard to kinship relations, they recognize paternal and maternal cousins as kin. This is also applicable to relatives by marriage. There are joking relationships and avoidance relationships among relatives, but the distinction is not very rigid and such relationships may change as new marital relations are formed. In Bushmen societies, there is hardly any degree of institution, and if there is, people maneuver it to fit in with reality rather than vice versa.

Similarly, Mitsuo Ichikawa (1982) reports that in Mbuti Pygmy camps no individual holds institutional authority. Although solidarity among men unites each camp, it is only applicable in terms of finding the collective will of the camp and is powerless to solve conflicts or to adjudicate an enforceable decision against others. When a conflict arises between individuals, they can only wait for it to fade over time, otherwise they have no choice but to leave the camp and stay at other camps in order to maintain distance between them.

The evolutionary bases of institution

I have so far stated that in a group that is smaller than the Dunbar number, institution is either nonexistent or if it exists, it is operated to fit reality rather than vice versa. Then, how does institution come into existence? Let us consider the evolutionary bases that give rise to institution.

Ichikawa (1982: 210–211) reports an interesting observation. It concerns a group of men's behavior after they separated two men who had almost come to blows. The other men stood in a public area in the camp and one by one stated their opinions on the conflict, such as "It is foolish to fight over a woman", "They should not say things that hurt one's heart", "Those who start a fight should pay a penalty" and so on. To a certain extent, these speeches have the effect of constraining and controlling the behavior of quarrelling parties. Therefore, Ichikawa states that they are glimpses of "law-bound" behavior. Jiro Tanaka (1978: 126–127) considers that the underlying reason that the Bushmen give things away generously is a fear of incurring the jealousy or resentment of others. With both the Bushmen and the Pygmies, the reaction of others living in the same group can have the effect of controlling individual behavior. "Others" may be the other party in a face-to-face interaction or third parties.

As mentioned earlier, the presence of a third party sometimes influences face-to-face interactions in non-human primate societies as well. As far as this aspect is concerned, there is no marked difference between the societies of the Bushmen and Pygmies and those of non-human primates. While an ability to be concerned about the reaction of the interacting party or to adjust one's behavior out of concern for a third party is an important evolutionary basis for the creation of institution, the ability alone will not give rise to it.

By the same token, institution certainly owes much to the development of language, but the fact that the Pygmies and the Bushmen who have language have few institutions or do not live according to them suggests that having language is not a sufficient condition for the creation of institution. A major clue to the creation of institution must be hidden in the act of connecting with many more people beyond the Dunbar number.

Let us consider the meaning of the Dunbar number by taking incest as an example. Incest is psychologically avoided in smaller groups below the Dunbar number, even though it is not expressly or institutionally forbidden. For instance, Japanese macaque societies are known to avoid incest by a psychological mechanism in the case of mother-son relationships and by a social structural mechanism in the case of father and daughter. While mothers and sons form "intimate" relationships through nurturing, these individuals in specifically proximate relationships avoid sexual behavior with one another (Itani 1987). On the other hand, father-daughter mating is avoided through male emigration to other groups.

It appears that humans are equipped with a similar psychological mechanism to that of Japanese macaques. One example that supports the existence of a psychological incest avoidance mechanism in humans is the kibbutz in Israel.

While boys and girls from different families are raised together at the kibbutz, it is known that the percentage of kibbutz-raised men and women who go on to marry one another is very low (Shepher 1971). In other words, men and women who grew up together from a young age would exclude each other from their sexual relations. This is likely to be due to the psychological incest avoidance mechanism, as there are no institutional barriers to such relationships. In small groups below the Dunbar number, all members know one another and intimate relationships are formed between mothers and sons and fathers and daughters through nurturing from the time the children are babies. There is no need to forbid incest institutionally in such societies.

The institution of a taboo against incest appears when group size becomes considerably larger than the Dunbar number as in the case of clan or lineage. In the case of the pastoralist Gabra, sexual intercourse between men and women who belong to the same clan is forbidden as incest. Nevertheless, I heard of some cases of incest committed by men and women from the same clan at grazing camps. Those who committed incest in these instances did not grow up in the same village. Incest occurs infrequently when men and women from the same clan who grew up and lived separately in remote villages come to stay at a grazing camp together, i.e., when men and women who did not grow up together from the time they were children but who are from the same clan come to live in the same camp. When clan or lineage (itself being an institutional organization) connects people beyond the Dunbar number, it becomes necessary to forbid incest on an institutional level.

Why do institutions come into existence when people connect with one another beyond the Dunbar number? In a group of more than 150 members, the number of people each individual has a relationship with far exceeds their cognitive capacity. When one deals with so many people beyond their capacity to recall each individual, it is difficult to develop conventional face-to-face order with each person. There is perhaps little hope of creating order in this situation unless a transcendent institution is introduced.

The origin of institution

In small groups below the Dunbar number, the facial expression and gaze of the other party in a face-to-face interaction provide major clues in terms of adjusting one's behavior (see Sugiyama in Chapter Sixteen). A face-to-face interaction may also sometimes be controlled or adjusted by the gaze and remark of a specific third party. Conversely, institutions become necessary when people become connected beyond the Dunbar number. Then, is there any phenomenon that can be identified in the stage immediately prior to the formation of an institution?

For any institution to be effective, it needs to be backed by some kind of endorsement. The effectiveness of monarchic societies is supported by a specific figure called the king or queen. Institutional efficacy in African farming societies in some cases is supported by supernatural calamities or sorcery. Be it the concept of king or queen or the idea of sorcery, these notions exist in a place that transcends people's plane of action (see Funabiki in Chapter Fourteen).

On the other hand, as mentioned earlier, pastoralist societies in East Africa show a preference for eliciting agreement through negotiations rather than by reference to an institution. Such negotiations are considered to take place somewhere beyond the Dunbar number. Let us search for some pre-institutional level phenomena in pastoralist societies in considering the formative process of institutions.

East African pastoralist societies have been described as "acephalous societies" by Evans-Pritchard and others. They are built on a segmentary lineage system with no developed unificatory power structure. This is also applicable to Gabra pastoralists, the subject of my study, whose society is divided into five phratries, each of which is divided into eastern and western moieties, each of which is divided into five to ten clans with each clan formed by one to five lineages. Among these segments, clan is important as a unit with regard to exogamy and livestock ownership. People explain that they control their own behavior because they are afraid of drawing criticism from other clan members.

This parallels the conventional order under the influence of a third party that is observed in non-human primate societies, as discussed above. In the case of the clan, which contains about 500 people or more, while institutions such as a taboo against incest become necessary, the conventional order under the influence of a third party, i.e., the fear of clan members, appears to exert some effect in parallel with institutional orders. One question that arises here is how people deal with distant people outside of their own clan.

The Gabra have an institution that is suggestive of the origins of institutionality, called the camel trust system. It is suggestive in this regard because it has the aspect of creating a "fear" of people outside of one's own clan.

Photo 1.1 Milking camels in the morning

The trust system is an institution concerning the exchange of camels (Soga 1998). The Gabra expand their possession of camels not by gifting but by way of a semi-permanent lease system (which I call the "trust" system). The trust system is governed by several rules, including the following.
1. Only nulliparous camels can be "entrusted".
2. The ownership of female offspring of an entrusted camel remains with the original owner, but the rights of possession of male offspring of an entrusted camel belong to the trustee.
3. The trustee can "trust out" the female offspring of an entrusted camel to other Gabra.

When a sub-leased female camel produces offspring, the ownership of female offspring remains with the original owner and the rights of possession of male offspring belong to the trustee of the sub-leased female.

Gabra make a number of camel trust arrangements over their lifetime. As a result, they have trusted out all their camels to others while living off camels that have been entrusted to them by others. Since camels are trusted out on a semi-permanent basis, one's herd of camels often includes the offspring of camels that were entrusted to one's father or grandfather. In some cases people have lost track of the trustees of some of their camels.

Because of this situation, Gabra are afraid of people outside of their own clan. When a camel owner is displeased with the way his trustee deals with him, he may forcibly withdraw his camels from the trust arrangement. There have been some cases in which a traveler was treated badly by someone, and when he later found out that his camels had been entrusted to this person, he forcibly withdrew his camels in retaliation. The news of such forcible withdrawals spreads fast and reminds people to deal with camel owners courteously. The trouble is that people who have inherited entrusted camels from their ancestors do not know the original owners of some of the camels in their possession. It is said that the Gabra treat travelers courteously just in case these strangers happen to be the owners (or their relatives) of some of the camels in their possession.

This is of course the way *they* explain the situation, and it is uncertain as to whether the Gabra actually live in constant fear of anonymous and unknown camel owners. Nevertheless, the fact that they interpret the trust system as a fear creating institution is significant. What the Gabra fear is not the presence of a king or the idea of sorcery, which transcend people's plane of action. They are afraid of third parties (i.e., camel owners) who actually exist on their plane of action. Further, the Gabra make camel owners, who may take their livestock away, increasingly difficult to identify by sub-leasing their camels widely. If they deal with overt figures, they only need to fear those specific people. However, by repeatedly entrusting camels in and out and inheriting them over generations, the Gabra distance specific owners and turn them into unidentified figures. This process creates a generalized fear of others. The Gabra create this fear that in reality controls their behavior.

It is impossible to generalize from this example, because not all pastoralist societies have a special system of livestock exchange such as the Gabra's trust system. However, we can consider that the impetus to create an institution is hidden in the process of keeping violent others at a distance on the plane of action and converting them from specific others to unidentified others. In particular, as the number of relationships increases beyond the Dunbar number, the number of unidentified others increases beyond one's cognitive capacity. It appears that in such a society, the threat of the jealousy or violence of unidentified others will constitute the basis of the creation of institution.

In this chapter, I have considered "conventional order under the influence of a third party" within face-to-face behavior as an evolutionary historical basis for institution. I have also introduced a pre-institutional phenomenon in which the presence of unidentified others far removed on the plane of action controls human behavior as if it were an institution, even though institutions are often considered to exist above the plane of action. What is important here is the biological limit of human cognitive capacity. When people form relationships with those beyond the limits of their cognitive capacity, unidentified others come to control their behavior. I would like to suggest for the time being that this is what we call institution.

2 An Institution Called Death: Towards Its *Arche*

Motomitsu Uchibori

Key ideas

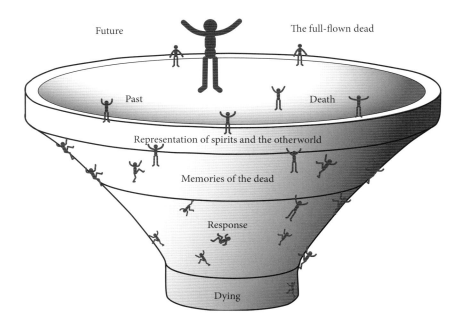

I shall call the above image "the vessel of death". It rises up from "dying" to "death", that is, from immediacy to representation. While it is possible to pass through the vessel from "death" as the past to "death" contained in the future, it is also possible to go from the inside of the vessel back to the beginning. The image represents the possibilities of both circularity and permeability between the inside and the outside and shows humans and other primates climbing up along the course of evolution on the outer surface.

The range of death as an institution

Beginning from before "signification"

Let us see death as an institution. Those who have given any theoretical thought to death that occurs in a particular social or cultural context may take this view for granted. The purpose of this thesis is to critically reconsider this rather common perception from an anthropological perspective.

It is cumbersome to talk about the definition of "institution" in generic terms so as to encompass all possible categories and aspects. Nevertheless, as discussing death as an institution connotes the existence of its "complement" that is not regarded as institutional, I anticipate touching upon the boundaries of institution below, at least implicitly. Such discussion is expected to include what some may call "pre-institution" in relation to death. In venturing to cite death as an exemplar of institution, it could be infused with a strong sense of irony. This is because we tend to regard death as having certain natural foundations that exist outside of our capacity of human reflection, and it does not occur to us to search for any existential basis to deny this assumption in rational terms. The obvious existence of pre-institutionality in relation to death has motivated me to attempt to discover the unique features in imagining the *arche* (beginning, source) from which this institution arises.

Toru Soga argues in Chapter One that "the threat of the jealousy or violence of unidentified others" is the source of the creation of institution. Echoing this argument, I would say that someone who is conventionally referred to as "dead" is the ultimate "unidentified other" whose mode of being is unknown and yet who is almost omnipresent in human society. From this point of view as well, the *arche* of the creation of death and the dead in the human past must be an ideal subject in our attempt to locate institution in the process of human evolution.

At least in the context of lifeforms for which the individual organism is regarded as the basic unit in terms of the sustainment or survival of life, the phenomenon of death *exists* as fundamentally innate to the survival process in a physiological sense. When we shift our focus from the life activity of the individual to the passage of time in a relationship between individuals, we are bound to shift our discussion from the physiological to the ecological level. This ecological level of death can be discussed in terms of various species of organisms. Because we are talking about a relationship between individuals, their perception of the other individual confronting the "self", or the so-called "you/them", is (likely) functioning in some inherent space no matter how rudimentary their cognitive capacity is. It is probably safe to say that the other who confronts the self and responds to the self's action precedes the self as the object of perception. Death at this level is one mode of "somewhat rapid" change in the state of the other individual in front of the self. Death within the temporal and spatial immediacy of the relationship between confronting individuals does not yet deserve to be called an institution.

A "rapid change" in the state of the confronting other may sound too circuitous and loose to use as an expression defining the situation. Still, I have no choice but to use it as I wish to state it with minimal added meaning and believe that this is the correct first step in our discussion of the *arche*. It is, after all, impossible to speak about institution without generating any meaning at all. Yet, it is possible to discuss it as part of the evolutionary basis because there are things that have to be spoken about from the level prior to meaning. In this chapter I attempt to demonstrate that the liminal period in question here possesses substantial spatiality carrying internal multiplicity rather than being a one-dimensional line. My occasional use of loose expressions corresponds to the orientation of our discussion towards capturing this multiplicity as much as possible.

"Death" and "dying"

I shall hereafter use "dying" and "death" as distinct concepts. Simply put, "dying" is a phenomenon ranging from a physiological death to an ecological death whereas "death" is one occurring in a domain that comes into existence only after the introduction of some meaning, thus constituting a higher-level phenomenon, so to speak. Accordingly, what I was talking about above is basically "dying". To summarize my argument in this chapter in advance, death is an institution as "death" and pre-institutional as "dying". This statement taken alone is of course bound to be criticized as oversimplification. My argument below is dialectical for the purpose of avoiding such criticism as well as specifying some desirable conditions.

Other basic concepts required for this argument are "immediacy" and "meaning". More specifically, the fundamental orientation of thinking here is to discuss the relationship between these two concepts. We are dealing with "immediacy" and "meaning" only in relation to the phenomenon of death and its domain and not as abstract concepts. The relationship is not merely oppositional. From a certain perspective, "immediacy" changes its conceptual position within "meaning". In other words, my argument progresses towards "meaning" unidirectionally as far as institution is concerned, but once it reaches the domain of "meaning", "immediacy" can be either incorporated or dismissed within it. "Immediacy" is expected to become the subject of argument distinct from "meaning" when our attention is focused solely on "dying", but it is difficult to gauge the extent to which this can be carried out in a pure form. By using this group of concepts, I should be able to advance my argument without using the concept of "nature" mentioned above, and therefore perhaps also avoid the concept of "culture". (I shall use the terms "immediacy" and "meaning" without emphasis hereafter.)

The matter that is referred to as immediacy is a change in the state of the individual in front of the self, including its process and result. To be exact, however, as the process of "dying" is either an ex-post judgment or an anticipation, there is an infiltration of meaning here. The most concrete manifestation of immediacy is "a dead individual being there" as the result. There is a fundamental gap in the approach to the domain of meaning between one's response to a dead body that appears in front of one and "the dead" that can be spoken of as if "being there" without necessarily appearing. Bridging this gap is the formation of the idea that the corpse before one's eyes is also one of the dead, for example. It is possible to say that this kind of ideation has the action of penetrating through different levels in relation to death. In other words, this incisive effect tends to blur the boundaries between different levels. Generally speaking, the action of the matter of events arising in the domain of ideation, or meaning, regarding death always has the effect of drawing immediacy onto the meaning side through this bridging.

An entity called "the dead" comes to occupy some sort of ontological position as a reappearance/representation of a previously living human. This state of being of the dead spans an infinite length of time after death. This is the crucial difference between the notion of "the dead" and the immediate entity of a dead body in front of one. Dead individuals existing here or there certainly have individual characteristics. Some characteristics are carried over from when they were alive and others are defined by various conditions at the time of their death. However, there are not many general categories (defining attributes) generically applicable to dead bodies as such. On the other hand, a wide variety of modes of being can be conceived in relation to (what is called) the dead, even in a single system of meaning. A dead body here is the dead, and a dead person from a time long ago whose personality traits cannot be remembered is also the dead. It appears that the expanse of the range of modes of the dead between these two extremes—which is a kind of ideation called representation—exemplifies the expanse of death's realm of meaning in a concrete way.

The *arche* of "death" as an institution

Chimpanzee death and the absence of "perception of death"

My discussion above assumes human death. It has often been said that awareness of death is a threshold distinguishing human species from other animal species. E. Morin's (1973) argument is a typical example. Confirmation of this almost clichéd proposition in itself will bring no further benefits. However, analysis can deliver significant outcomes in terms of (re)confirmation and refinement through empirical verification—albeit based on the understanding that empirical verification includes not only indisputable facts but also hypotheses drawing on limited facts.

Awareness of death is an ambiguous expression in itself. Awareness involved in immediacy in terms of time and space, and awareness involved in meaning have different subjects as well as different compositions or expanses. Perception relating to the immediacy of dying can be observed in non-human animals in varying degrees and manners. Records indicate that various species of animals show different attitudes towards the presence of a dead body of a fellow species or group than towards a living individual. While many of these records are based on accurate observations, such observations are often given some interpretation. E. T. Seton's (1994) story surrounding the dead body of a hunted animal is the most widely known to the general public. When literary interpretations are peeled off, the observations themselves illustrate many cognitive behaviors of animals in the face of a "rapid change" in the state of an individual—especially a loss of responsiveness.

Reports of observational studies on great apes, chimpanzees in particular, form the most significant records. While the aforementioned phenomenon is also found in the relationship between these observations and their interpretation, problems arising from the ambiguity of the concept of awareness manifest even more strongly here than in the case of non-apes or non-primate animals. I have the impression that the study of chimpanzees in both the field and the laboratory has progressed significantly over the last three to four decades. Nevertheless, there have been no new observations that differ markedly in quality from Jane Goodall's work (1971) from the 1970s in terms of the response of chimpanzees to dying individuals and dead bodies. The number of observational studies on this subject does not seem to be increasing either. Although this situation appears puzzling, it actually leads us to a certain conclusion. That is to say that chimpanzees' awareness of death is limited to an awareness of the immediate dead body—or a discriminating ability concerning the states of the living and dead bodies present—and that chimpanzees are unlikely to perceive the boundary between the state of living and the state of being dead as the result of temporal transition and discontinuity.[1]

I once stated that an "anthropology of death" is possible but a "primatology of death" is impossible (Uchibori and Yamashita 2006[1986])—with death of course distinct from dying. The above example all but proves that the situation surrounding observational records has not changed significantly, which in itself is disappointing.

Treatment of "death" before *Homo sapiens*

At which branching point or speciation event in a larger evolutionary framework did "death", with "dying" at its core, take on an institutional form? I would venture to further this quixotic inquiry. However, I find very few nodal points that may be relevant to this question when I move my discussion downward from the formation of the genus *Australopithecus* and the genus *Homo* within the tribe Hominina. The only way forward may be to search in the opposite direction to trace lines on the evolution chart from modern humans until the institutionality of the institution of death becomes invisible—even though this is still a search in dim light.

What has been established at this point is that the institution of death is observed in all human populations at the stage where all humans on the earth became modern humans (*Homo sapiens*, "Anatomically Modern Humans (AMH)")—that is, about 32,000 years ago, except perhaps *Homo floresiensis* whose status was still under debate in 2013. The proposition thus expressed does not exclude the possibility that early AMH, say up to 200,000 years ago, did not have this practice, as well as the possibility that non-AMH humans were also instituting death. The focus of our search is naturally located on this point. More specifically, it can be described as the search to discover how death was formed as an institution within many variations that possibly existed between Neanderthals and AMH.

In the early 1970s the remains of Neanderthals found in Shanidar Cave became known as the oldest dead with evidence of ritual treatment. The famous title of "the First Flower People" derives from the presence of flower pollens alongside the human bones in the cave. While it evoked an image that fit comfortably with the modern understanding of "human remains adorned with flowers = the dead", the wide-ranging debate about Neanderthals over the subsequent four decades appeared to oscillate between the denial (destruction) and partial restoration of the "flower people" image in symbolic terms. The debate can be broadly summarized as the estimation of the symbolization capacity of Neanderthals in comparison

Photo 2.1 Male menhirs (1) (Vato lahi)

Photo 2.2 Male menhirs (2) (Vato lahi)

Commemorating the dead near a Zafimaniry village in central Madagascar.

with that of AMH and includes the more specific question of whether the mental faculties and behavioral characteristics of modern humans such as language, art, dress customs and burial are found in Neanderthals.

A number of studies have been conducted on the subject of burial in recent years, particularly since the 1980s. While opposing theories have been proposed, it is reasonable to say that the mainstream view tends to emphasize differences between Neanderthals and AMH. I have no space to elaborate each one of them here, but I shall paraphrase what I consider a middle-ground view as follows: "Neanderthals might have practiced burial of the dead, but they did not practice it in ritual form to the degree that AMH do".[2]

We must be careful when we express such a proposition in the Japanese language, however, as it contains another kind of ambiguity in addition to that contained in the English language (for instance). More specifically, there is a problem concerning differences in the meaning of words such as "burial" and "ceremonial" (or "ritualistic") between different languages. For example, the Japanese word for burial, *maiso*, signifies more than the conventional disposal of the dead body by burying it in the ground because it contains the character "*so*", which signifies behavior involving special dealings with the dead. In the presence of such language bias, it is easy to equate the mere conventionalization of corpse disposal with the emergence of the entity of "the dead".

In any case, it is difficult to determine the absence or presence of ritual treatment with certainty based on the condition of fossil excavation sites, and it becomes a matter of how to interpret the condition of the surrounds. Factors such as what appears to be burial accessories, special markings for corpse placement (e. g., yellow ochre markings), the peculiar configurational working applied to the corpse and so on must be considered. Consequently, the question of burial is actually one of the lifestyle of AMH and the entirety of cognitive processes involved in it rather than an isolated issue. In other words, the question goes back to square one.

In fact, talking about the *arche* of the institution of "death" in conjunction with the emergence of art has almost become commonplace these days, and there seem to be very few objections to the positioning of these two matters in a broad flowering of human symbolization capacities. Nevertheless, if we return to the beginning of our search, it is impossible to determine that the time of the appearance of *Homo sapiens* as AMH matches the time of the blossoming of such symbolization capacities. In the same token it seems equally unreasonable to think that Neanderthals or their contemporary non-AMH humans completely lacked such capacities.[3]

There are strong indications that the technologies and customs of AMH were partially transferred to Neanderthals and others. In a similar vein, we should imagine that the *arche* of "death" was not so much like a Big Bang or a revolution, but more of a gradual fermentation. To look at this from another angle, the great expansion of the domain of "death" to all aspects of human life from social behavior to transcendental imagination is thought to have begun much later than the appearance of AMH.

Functions of "death" as an institution

Reflective amplification of "collectivity"

I must deviate slightly from my initial statement here to touch on the concept of institution. Broadly speaking, there have been two views of this concept that are subtly but clearly different in scope.

1. One sees it as a conventional code of behaviors (i.e., customary behaviors or mores).
2. The other sees it as a socially and/or collectively sanctioned corpus of rules or regulations.

The latter is a commonly used view in human social sciences, but it is not directly applicable to non-human primates. If this narrow view is somewhat loosened (or widened) by the introduction of "convention" and "behavior" as in (1), it becomes possible, to a certain extent, to address it within the framework of the entire Primate order as we can see in other chapters of this volume. This is of course limited to discussions oriented towards conventionality as an existential presupposition rather than towards historically constructed mores.

In this instance, I would like to venture a third view. It may provide a fundamentally different view of institution rather than forming a simple question of scope. I would like to see institution as follows.

3. *An image representing human collectivity that should exist at any level*, or *a social phenomenon that supports and embodies such an image.*

By shifting the centre of gravity away from the conventionalization of behaviors and actions, mores, norms and rules, in the direction of imagination, we will end up farther away from primatology. However, this view can allow us to position institution as an anthropologically basic concept and treat it as something involving a broader area of human life.

To explain a little more, "at any level" signifies the unit of collective existence (actuality of collectivity) at all imaginable levels ranging from a pair of people, small family unit, residential community or kinship group through to regional, national and finally global human societies. I presented the same argument in relation to the "groups" concept within the human evolutionary framework elsewhere (Uchibori 2013). In this chapter, "collectivity" is used as the existential basis for the development of "groups" instead of the concept of "groups" itself, but it can include things that are very similar to groups as real-world situations. Where it is possible or necessary to include non-human beings in collective existence, it is possible to discard the qualifier "human". There are probably only a few situations requiring this in reality, but "objects", "heterogeneous animals", "gods" and so on can be imagined in such circumstances. The extension of institution varies depending on the situation. What becomes a problem at that point, though, is how the intension of institution centering on humans can match the extension. The word "image" refers to a form in which an idea is represented, but the level of representation varies greatly. While it is normally concretized as a result of ideation, it is sometimes concretized in the form of social phenomenon such as people's collective action—or individual action that is suggestive of the presence of collectivity.

Upon seeing "death" as an institution in this sense, I shall consider various forms of representation of its collectivity or, to use a stronger term, "communality", which is an idea in itself, and its social manifestations. There is no need to discuss the emotions of grief and sorrow here. This may sound repetitive, but if we think about the *arche* logically, its sequence entails a succession of transitions as the immediacy of "dying" in individual cases is felt in relation to universality, thought about, dealt with, expressed in behavior and performed as a collective action. In relation to evolution, it seems unlikely that all manifestations in this logical sequence were newly acquired at once and in totality by *Homo sapiens*, as I mentioned in the previous section. In other words, it is more likely that the components of the sequence were realized individually and gradually, then developed in a complex manner at the ultimate stage in its process of realization.

Among the representations of the collectivity of "death" attained in the evolutionary process, the most basic and overt is "the dead". As a result of "the dead" "being there", the scope of human sociality expands greatly. This expansion is temporal as well as spatial. This can be regarded as the core momentum of "the dead as a third term" mentioned by Funabiki in Chapter Fourteen. Temporally, it connects the past to the present and gives certain meanings to the future. Spatially, it not only expands a physical space but also creates spaces of "different" qualities, such as "the otherworld". People who live in the space-time that includes "the dead" come to experience this expanded space-time, which is of course a social space-time, in one way or another. This is *the human world that appears after incorporating "death"*, of which collectivity or communality is made explicit by the dead. The collectivity/communality of human existence creates "death", which in turn reflectively amplifies it. It is possible to say that this reflective amplification of collectivity is the functional core of "death" as an institution.

"The dead" amidst "the living"

A majority of so-called "death" rituals concern the existence of "the dead" within the framework of their relationship with "the living". This corresponds directly to the undeniable centrality of "the dead" in ideation surrounding "death". The rituals constitute a visualization of the institution of "death" and can be divided into two types depending on the orientation of the intent of their organizers and executors from the viewpoint of the existence of "the dead", namely "prospective = forward looking" or "retrospective = backward looking" (Metcalf, 1983). It is possible to say that in many cases this intentionality leaves death-related rituals open to exegetic interpretation by those who conduct them (see Uchibori (1997) for a more detailed discussion).

As "the dead" constitutes "the dead" in relation to "the living", the two orientations above naturally involve both of them. Needless to say, the imagined "different" space involves "the dead" whereas the involvement of "the living" arises in real space. However, to people amidst them—that is, those who make sense of them—these spaces appear as segments that are somehow continuous. In this total space, "the dead" exist side-by-side or concurrently and sometimes have relations with "the living". In this sense, "the dead" is an existence that is capable of interfering in the life of "the living", influencing the society of "the living" and even forming communal society with them. Embracing the workings of social functions is the greatest sufficient condition for something to be an institution. Considering that the living party is aware of a number of such functions, "the dead" must be an institution, or at least partly so in the full sense of the term. From another perspective, stating that "death" is an institution is the same as stating that "the dead" is an institution, simply at a higher level of abstraction.

The extent to which time is expanded into the past and future for the present society by the incorporation of "the dead" as an institution, however, varies considerably among human populations. It may even be appropriate to say that the form and composition of society are determined by this difference. The scope and affiliation rules of certain forms of kinship group are often explicitly and

An Institution Called Death: Toward Its *Arche* 51

sometimes implicitly established on the premise of the existence and positioning of "the dead" in the group. This becomes clearer if we think of relatively small-scale stem-family groups or "houses" (or lineages in some cases). In such groups, the existence of someone connected to the group's past functions (taking the other direction) as if to guarantee its future. The repositioning of "the dead" from just "the dead" to, for instance, "sanctioned ancestors" represents a change in the relationship between "the living" who share the relation to "the dead" in some way (albeit having different relational ties) rather than a change in the mode of existence of "the dead" in a "different" space (if there is such a thing). In this respect, the proposition that present human social relations are functionally defined by "the dead" is not metaphysical rhetoric.

The collectivity/communality made explicit by the dead can sometimes have clearly metaphysical existential value. A typical example of "the dead" positioned at the intersection of metaphysics and functioning sociality is a certain form of "the dead" in modern nation states. This is "the dead" manifested by built monuments; including fighters for independence and revolutions, national heroes, unknown soldiers of wars between nations and so on. It goes without saying that this type of "retrospective" visualization of the past performs present sociopolitical functions. Moreover, its hopes are of course laid upon the future of a collective community comprised of literally unborn members. What we find here is a somewhat ironic aim of rituals that is retrospective in terms of "the dead" and future-oriented regarding "the living". Perhaps because of this irony, "the dead" of this type are placed on a pedestal, so to speak, in polities that emphasize collectivity rather than in a remote "different" space (see Anderson 1983).

The following is one specific example. The idea and practice of "enshrinement of the dead" is found amongst the Iban of Sarawak on the Island of Borneo. As I have reported in detail elsewhere (Uchibori 1984; Uchibori and Yamashita 2006[1986]), a certain kind of the dead, that is those enshrined, are said to remain on elevated locations in this world such as hilltops instead of moving on to "the otherworld". Those who are "enshrined" are typically community leaders and heroes, but some are not socially very prominent. When the living receive messages or requests in their communications with the dead encountered in their dreams, and when certain animals, which are considered to be proof of the authenticity of such communications, are sighted by people, the dead may receive this kind of special treatment.

The development of a wide variety of imaginative narratives in relation to "different" spaces allocated to "the dead" such as heaven, hell and purgatory is a characteristic of human historical times. However, from the broader perspective of all humankind or of the entire history of humanity, it is not strange at all to have nothing like this kind of clear image of the "spirit world" or the "otherworld". As long as there is a place for "the dead", a space for their existence, somewhere, no matter how formless and ambiguous it is, the institution of "death" has achieved sufficient spatial expansion for human collectives. However, the power of religious imagination during historical times has pushed this expansion to the extremes in the form of inverse images of reality. The strength of impacts that the imagining of the inversion of reality has on actual human living depends on the structure and condition of each society formed in human history. Concrete aspects aside, what occurs along with this inverted imagery of the otherworld is a great transformation of "the dead" itself. This great transformation brings to "death" a new heterogeneity that could be called a *second arche* in one sense.

Reversal of "the dead"

"Own death" and collectivity

The new heterogeneous "death" is one's own "death". One's own "death" does not directly relate to "the dead" as the source of "death" itself. If we are to talk about the visible and tangible immediacy of one's own "death", the closest thing would be the immediacy of the "dead body" of the other. Rather than this immediacy, however, it is what might be called a twofold detour mediated through the other as the "dead" that carries a higher degree of involvement in the generation of one's own "death". That is to say one's own "death" is a reflection and an inversion of the category of the entities named "the dead".

Nonetheless, one's own "death" is sometimes discussed as if it were a natural question, because our "dying" as a lifeform and our response surrounding the avoidance of this process and event tend to be regarded as a basis directly connected to the question of "death". Although this kind of biological basis is of course the minimum necessary condition, it is such a long journey from this point to a place from which we are able to comprehend a full-spectrum view of the magnificently constructed structures representing our longings for immortality, during which we pass through anxieties in anticipation of our own "death" in everyday life.

On this topic, basic issues concerning the fundamental differences between "your—second person's—death" and "my—first person's—death" were raised by E. Becker (1989) in his now-classic work. However, his argument about "your death"

An Institution Called Death: Toward Its *Arche*

revolving around psychoanalysis stops at the emotions of loss and grief over the death of someone deeply involved with the subject and in the end converges on the issue of "(my) own death", rather than discussing the death of "the other" in relation to collectivity. On this point, a psychoanalytic argument presented by N. O. Brown (1970) prior to Becker's work is also appealing as it revolves around the contrast between Eros (life) and Thanatos (death) that are competing drives quintessential to human existence, but its orientation is fundamentally the same as that of Becker's argument.

As I have discussed so far, the creation of "death" from "dying" involves fitting a rapid change in the body of the other, its destruction (decay) and the psychological and (inter-)physical response of the living to it, into a single meaning-space, but with the inherent otherness of "death" still running through it. The capacity to recognize a different self in the other is probably shared by humans and chimpanzees. Yet, for the incorporation of the "dying" of the other into a meaning-space that includes one's own dying as part of the generalization of "death", a simple expansion of theory of mind—that is, recognition in the other the working of mental processes similar to but different from those of the self—is utterly insufficient. It is likely that the development of an awareness such as "the self that is projected into the future" becomes a necessary condition for this endeavor. From the perspective oriented to theory of mind, this awareness contains the inverted "theory" of the other within the self, and in this awareness the future "dying" of the self means the "dying" of the other incorporated in the self.

The future is usually filled with anticipated events and one's response to them within the framework of one's survival strategy and tactics. Unlike this future, the future incorporating one's own "death" is paradoxical from the outset. Our longings for immortality do not appear to stem from that sort of human nature. Instead, they seem to be akin to the denial of *the future as a paradox*. There is no doubt that the act of nullifying the future in that sense and producing *the eternal now* is the most overtly irrational and absurd activity in relation to one's own death.

This irrationality has a counterpart in suicide or the killing of oneself, which is another, sometimes gentle and sometimes violent form of irrationality involved in one's own "death". The core motive for an act of suicide is reading the future of the other instead of the self into the situation of the dying of "the self that is projected into the future". This other can be a proximate "you" or the imagined "collectivity at any level" mentioned above. From this viewpoint, saying that non-human animals do not commit suicide is too redundant and obvious an argument. We should rather gainfully talk about the presence or absence of suicide in "primitive societies", which can be empirically proven or disproven.

Tokuji Chiba (1994) presents an argument akin to the assertion that there is no suicide in "primitive" or "uncivilized" societies in the course of his inquiry into "why Japanese commit *seppuku*" (self-disembowelment). Theoretical comparative studies on the subject of suicide in "primitive" societies are certainly few, but P. Bohannan (1960) states in the preface of his edited volume that there are many ethnographic reports of suicide in such societies. Forget about the question of what the imagined "primitive" or "uncivilized" means here, and let's just deal with the cases of suicide as an established institution such as *seppuku*. Even then, I find no firm grounds for Chiba's general assertion about suicide. In considering this, to decipher the act and the subsequent event of suicide, although not in "uncivilized" societies, as described by Nishii in Chapter Seventeen, is not irrelevant to our present discussion.

Both suicide and the craving for immortality are capable of becoming institutions par excellence, i.e., institutions with a strongly normative nature, within those societies defined as historical constructs. The quest for immortality as an institution is situated at a great distance on the scale of the vicissitudes of historical constructs from the innocent image of the otherworld that is undifferentiated in many ways, say being free of heaven or hell. However, even the irrationally segmented otherworld as a covert expression of the human desire for immortality is not completely unrelated to the innocent sort of otherworld. Hazarding a jump in reasoning, my supposition is that the difference is only miniscule between the conditions under which the undifferentiated otherworld of others ("the existing otherworld") is cast off and the highly differentiated otherworld thrust upon the self ("the otherworld to which I am going") is invented, on the one hand, and the conditions that arouse desires for immortality as the denial of all such futures in the otherworld, on the other. Perhaps, may I add, the differentiated otherworld emerges at a specific level of discourses that contain "you" in order to raise the awareness of "I", and paradoxically, suicide can be regarded as a conduct of denial of one's own death that is carried out at the same level. By contrast, the quest for immortality may differ in that it can arise as "I" without addressing "you", certainly beyond that level.

There is no need to discuss the desire for immortality of those who monopolize political power in the mortal world and the various concrete activities taken to fulfill them, as this chapter is focusing on the *arche*. What we should discuss instead is the focalization of the own "death" of people without significant power as a critical concern in those historical constructs. If this is an attempt to find new solutions to the problem rather than constituting a mere downscaled version of the denial of the future and the desire for immortality amongst those in power, it can be considered as the evolution of a new—that is, not "pre-historic"—historical variant of "death" as an institution. Here, it must be possible to imagine one's own "death" together with the "death" of the other so as to form a collective "death", and this possibility must have been the alternate path espoused by historic religions that have created the differentiation of heaven and hell.[4]

In more familiar cases in contemporary Japan, we can explore the depths of one's own "death" in the thinking of those who seek a so-called natural burial. Their seemingly hopeful desire to remove their own "death" from the temporal-spatial expansion of the existing social unit, which is solidified through accumulation of the past dead—i.e., collectivity that manifests in an oppressive or even coercive manner at a certain level—can be regarded as point-symmetrical to the immortality wishes of those in power. However, I am more inclined here to see the fact that it has come to have social significance today as proof of the ongoing self-expansion of "death" as an institution.

The future contained in "death"

On reflection, the fear and stigma of "dying" are emotions, or representational forms of emotions, that manifest with the most prominently unique quality within the institution of "death". As I mentioned earlier, sadness (sorrow, grief) associated with loss is originally an emotion prior to institution and, being an emotion, it derives from immediacy. However, this immediacy does not persist unchanged. The content of its meaning and its carrier transmit and diffuse sometimes simultaneously and sometimes individually. In this action, the domain of "death" propagates the fear and stigma throughout the space or occupies the space entirely. The manner of this propagation is of course not spatially or temporally uniform and even. In the case of rituals in relation to "the dead" occurring over a considerable length of time—in fact, not a particularly long period in some cases—"death" of a collective nature clearly shows its transparent self in the social space, i.e., the concrete social unit, through this action. Various taboos or prohibitive rules are the signifiers of its existence.

When we pick any part of the expanse of human society, it always includes "the dead". In reality, "the dead" that is envisaged to exist is present in diverse phases and situated at points indicating different relationships with the living, in a broad continuum that straddles "dying" and "death", as something which instills fear and stigma in the living or something which bears goodwill or hostility towards the living. In very abstract terms, "the dead" in society carry diverse meanings, including those that are mutually inconsistent. As the invisible other being there—a non-existent existence, or "lost people"—it becomes something that is capable of wielding various influences over the living. Haunting by "the dead" is one concretized example, but there is no need to create such a specific meaning. Without "the dead", the meaning for the living existing as such at this point in time diminishes greatly. To make the "dying" of the self in the future possible, or more precisely, the prospective positioning of one's own being "after death" in the domain of "death" possible, is tantamount to the acceptive recognition that one will join "the dead" in that society. This acceptance occurs unconsciously and in many cases does not require any mental preparedness. If one is able to see society as a community comprised of "the living" and "the dead", one may come to naturally accept that this is the way to guarantee the temporal continuity of society and readily entrust one's own "death" to it.

Thus "the dead" is turned into a social "the dead", so to speak, from an individual "the dead". I would like to reconfirm that both are institutional in their formative logic. The only difference between them is the level of collectivity within institution in the meaning mentioned above—which can be described as a "sanction level" if you like. When "the dead" grow from singular to multiple to a collection, what emerges is the infinite nature of time from the past through to the future—an effect that "the dead" as individuals perhaps cannot produce. Infinite time is of course an illusion and rather similar to the apparition of ghosts, but the meaningfulness of the finiteness of the living time in this world is told in the context of this infinite time. Although the generation of the sense that the living are "indebted to the dead (of the past)" is somewhat understandable, the future in which one becomes "the dead" may also be a debt that the living should owe in the same capacity and therefore may become their responsibility.[5]

Perhaps the future, which "death" necessarily subsumes, has a special meaning. In a society comprised of "the dead" and the living, communication between them promises reciprocal relations, including the acceptance of the meaning, the generation of debts and the acceptance of responsibilities, on the basis of the expectation that it will continue into the future while bearing the weight of the past.

Circular unity of pre-institution and institution: Conclusion

"Death" is an institution, but that is not to say that institution is "death"—although one may be tempted to say so. That human "culture" aims for the denial of death, the concealment of death, or in other words, the mastery and resolution of the death problem, is very much like a second cliché in our discussion on death. I would like to close this chapter with my thoughts on substituting "culture" in the cliché with "institution".

The "death" towards which all of a society's institutions face is something that is constructed as "death" within the institutions, as I have discussed above. The relationship between institution and "death" is an internal logic within institution in this sense. However, it is possible to say that the sustainment of the internal logic in itself constitutes the mastery of individual "dyings" outside of the institution at a fundamental level. If we are to call a collection of the internal logics of the whole institution and its various constructs, in addition to "death", "culture", we will return to the aforementioned cliché.

To consider a society comprised of the living and "the dead" seems to be valid for the purpose of substituting culture with institution in the ordinary use of words. However, perhaps there is no need to even bring up institution if we are to simply envision a collective comprised solely of the dead (the state of "the otherworld"). I have conducted my discussion here in this manner in an attempt to use a single word, be it culture or institution, to describe the concretization of imagination that takes place in something akin to a universal social space beyond confronting and interacting dyads, and that acts potentially in an infinite time that is supposed to continue from before to beyond the immediacy of the present.

With a view to both the immediacy of "dying" and the possibility of a great expansion contained in "death", if a discussion of their continuity and discontinuity leads to one of pre-institution and institution, and not improbably what goes beyond institution, I would like to think that "death" is significant as something that makes this metanarrative possible.

M. de Certeau (1987) speaks of "death" in the final part of his *The Practice of Everyday Life* and calls it, including the act of speaking of it, "the unnamable". He expounds on the ultimate concordance of "dying", "believing" and "speaking" in his turn of phrase. According to de Certeau, the "dying" of "I = self" alone is "the believable" and one's desire to speak to the dead that come before and after "I" within time stems from this *belief*. This statement provides us with many hints as a metanarrative created by speaking of death. Nevertheless, saying and *believing* that death becomes meaningful only when it is received as the death of the "self" is basically a perception of death specific to people within historical constructs, particularly to individuals among modern-contemporary people, and on this point it converges on an even more specific and narrow focus than in Imamura's argument (see note 5).

What I am seeing over the horizon of our discussion in this chapter is perhaps a Moebius strip-like circular unity between continuity and discontinuity rather than a linear progression from pre-institution to institution or iterations between the outside and the inside of institution. This serves as the basis that the act of speaking about any institution, not just death, permits a whole view of institution as such, even though it remains inside of this limit.

All I can do now is to trust that this way of discussing will not turn out to be a useless analogy.

3 Institution and Ritualization

Masakazu Tanaka

Key ideas

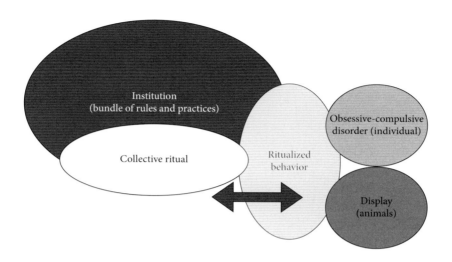

Institution is legitimized by ritualized behavior, which, together with function and meaning, constitutes ritual. It is characterized by formality and repetition and contrasted with display behavior in animals and obsessive-compulsive disorder. Obsessive-compulsive disorder is an individual condition and often antagonizes and opposes institution. Display can be regarded as an excessive act of communication (of the actor's intent) and distinguished from ritualistic behavior in which heightened formality obscures the actor's intent.

Everyday practice and ritual

There is a play entitled *Seirigakuteki shokuji fukei* (Physiological dining scene). It was released in *Chika engeki* (Underground Theater), No. 5 (pp. 100–104), published in the summer of 1972, with the proviso: "For production, please apply to the editor's office. Shuji Terayama, the editor". It is one of three plays featured under the banner "theater in the age of mechanical reproduction" and proposed as a challenge to actors. The other two plays were *Higeki ichimaku Kyojin tai Yakuruto* (Tragedy in one act of a baseball game: The Yomiuri Giants versus the Yakult Swallows) and *Hanzai jiken* (Criminal case). They carry the names of Shuji Terayama and Kaoru Fujiwara as editor and writer respectively, but unlike in the first play, there is no mention of transcribers.

The script of *Seirigakuteki shokuji fukei* is divided into three columns for its three characters. The top column for the wife, the middle for the husband and the bottom column for a guest describe their respective actions in parallel. The columns are combined into a single column for conversations at turns (Figure 3.1).

For example, the wife's part goes as follows.

1. Finish scooping rice into three bowls. "Now, shall we eat?"
2. "Please enjoy."
3. Sip two mouthfuls of soup.

The next column lists the husband's gestures and remarks corresponding to the wife's.

1. Pick up his chopsticks and take a piece of meat onto his plate. "Let's eat".
2. Take a bite off the piece of meat and eat two mouthfuls of rice (chew twenty-five times) … (This is written directly below the wife's action No. 3.)

At a turn, the script goes: Guest 7. "On what?", Husband 8. "On brown rice", Guest 8. "Hmm, this is not too bad at all"… and so on.

This "script" is a detailed description of an everyday dining scene, as suggested by the credit "Transcribers: Yasuyuki Kogure and others". In other words, this is supposed to be an actual dining scene recorded by Mr. Kogure rather than "created" (but of course we cannot preclude the latter possibility as it is Terayama's work). The purpose of this publication is to invite actors to stage (re-enact) it as a play. Terayama seemed to think that the re-enactment of such minutiae of everyday life would be theatrically difficult and impose more physical strain on actors than ever before. Indeed, we may often feel that we must "perform" certain actions in everyday life, but we rarely perform our daily practices or routines such as eating in a conscious manner. I can imagine that the faithful re-enactment of

Physiological dining scene

Time: 8 April1972
Place: In an apartment at Akebono-so, somewhere in Tokyo
Menu: Steamed rice (brown rice cooked in the electric rice cooker), teppanyaki (beef 500g), salad (fried eggs, greens, cucumber, strawberries and sliced lemon), soup (onion, carrot and parsley), pickles (white radish), condiments (sauce and mayonnaise), leftover pre-dinner drink (beer) and tea.

Transcribers: Yasuyuki Kogure and others.

Wife: Age 23, dress designer

1. Finish scooping rice into three bowls. "Now, shall we eat?"

2. "Please enjoy."

3. Sip two mouthfuls of soup.

4. Eat two mouthfuls of rice (chew 12 times).

5. Take two pieces of meat onto her plate and pour sauce over them.

6. Eat one mouthful of meat (chew 42 times

7. "On this, salt and sesame seeds—it's tastier if you sprinkle some salt and sesame seeds."

8. "It's tasty."

Husband: Age 23, journalist

1. Pick up his chopsticks and take a piece of meat onto his plate. "Let's eat."

2. Take a bite off the piece of meat and eat two mouthfuls of rice (chew 25 times)

3. Pour sauce over the remaining piece of meat on his plate.

4. Take a bite off the piece of meat and eat a mouthful of rice.

5. Sip two mouthfuls of soup.

6. Deftly suck in the pieces of onion remaining in his bowl.

7. Sip a mouthful of soup

8. "On brown rice."

Guest: Age 24, public servant at Yokohama City Council. A friend of the husband since high school. A big man weighing over 80kg.

1. "Let's eat." Pick up his chopsticks and take two pieces of meat onto his plate and pour sauce over.

2. Eat a piece of meat in one bite and stuff two mouthfuls of rice into his mouth.

3. Eat cucumber and a green leaf (chew 18 times). (Note: This person almost gulps down everything.)

4. Stuff a piece of meat into his mouth.

5. Wipe his lips with his hand.

6. Stuff three mouthfuls of rice into his mouth (chew 17 times).

7. "On what?"

8. "Hmm, this is not too bad at all."

9. "It is tasty."

Figure 3.1 Chika engeki

detailed practices would be technically difficult. I suspect, however, that what is more significant is a sense of resistance to the re-enactment of daily life itself on the part of actors. Plays that consist of dramatized snapshots of daily life carry no message (meaning) other than the purposes of actions. The act of eating means no more than the fulfillment of a purpose, which is to eat. Where is the meaning in performing such an act? Of course, acting out everyday living can be meaningful if we consider that meaninglessness can be artistic (for example, Warhol's *Sleep*). Nonetheless, if we ignore the artistic potential here, the technical problem and the absence of message make the performance of this play difficult.

What if this script were a description of a certain ritual? If the script describing gestures and speech in detail were regarded as the procedural manual (script) for a ritual, strict acting might still be technically difficult, but psychological resistance might diminish. In other words, the sense of resistance to its minutiae and repetitiveness could disappear if the script was framed as a ritual. Moreover, once we perceived it as a ritual, we would lose the sense of resistance to the absence of clear meanings in each action. Thus it becomes evident that a ritual consists of a set of prescribed meaningless and detailed actions. The purpose of this chapter is to consider these characteristics of rituals in relation to institutions.

I first present an overview of the basic ideas about institution, then consider various ritual theories (ritualization theories, to be more exact) focusing on the normative nature of rituals in order to elucidate the relationship between institution and ritualization. I also touch on their relationships with some behaviors similar to collective ritualization—for example, display behaviors in animals and "individual ritualization" such as obsessive-compulsive disorder. I use the term "collective ritual/ritualization" (or cultural ritual/ritualization) for religious rituals and cultural behaviors such as greeting in order to distinguish them from individual rituals, but I omit the adjectives "collective" or "individual" where it is clear from the context for the sake of simplicity.

What is institution?

Tsutomu Shiobara, a Japanese sociologist, describes institution as follows.

It refers to a system consisting of multiple social norms. In short, it is a complex of norms. Social norms are rules that impose certain constraints and control on social life and regulate people's social behaviors in a concrete manner. Social norms include *conventions*, *mores* and *laws*. A complex of social norms in this sense is called an institution. Take the institution of marriage for example, it includes the conventions of mate selection such as arranged introduction and courting, mores concerning betrothal gift exchange rituals, weddings and receptions, and the law of marriage registration. The institution of marriage exists as a *complex whole* of them. (Shiobara 2012; emphasis added)

Institution is "a complex whole" of "conventions, mores and laws". From an anthropological perspective, it is part of culture. While it contains artificial elements (laws in a narrow sense, for example), the process of and reason for its development are unknown to those who are subjected to it in the sense that it is conventional. When they are asked, they can only repeat such answers as "Since the dawn of time …" or "It has always been done this way …". For this reason, an inquiry into the intention behind the development of any institution is met with an explanation of its outcome, i.e., its purpose or function (teleological approach). Then, what is the purpose of institution?

Institution provides socially approved behavioral rules and therefore functions as a means to satisfy needs safely and efficiently and contributes to the preservation of social order by restricting the confusion. (Shiobara 2012)

Institutions exist for the sake of satisfying psychological needs and preserving social order. In other words, the reason for the formation of institutions was to accomplish these purposes. However, the preservation of social order alone cannot guarantee the survival of institutions nor explain their diversity. Shiobara explains the former as follows.

Where a complex of social norms is, firstly, accepted by a majority of the constituents of society, secondly, safeguarded through the enforcement of sanctions against deviations, and thirdly, internalized in the personality formation of the individuals, it is considered to be "institutionalized". Institutionalization is fundamental to social order and integration.

Institution is "a complex of norms". Accordingly, its survival is made possible by adherence to various rules. What plays an important role here is "institutionaliz-ation", including the acceptance and legitimization of rules and penalties and internalization. It is highly conceivable that people adhere to institutions in fear of penalties. Still, many institutions remain viable because they are legitimized as "the good" and exempt from criticism.

How are they legitimized? Shiobara does not seem to provide an answer to this question. Why are they accepted by many people? I would like to consider this question from the position that it is because institutions are legitimized through "ritualized behavior". Ritualized behavior refers to the formalized and repetitive behavior for ambiguous purposes typically observed at rituals, ceremonies and festivals.

Genealogy of ritualization theory

Japanese dictionaries define rituals as "manners and ceremonies that are observed with formality as social conventions" (*Kojien*, fifth edition: Iwanami Shoten) or "1) the rules of decorum and ceremonies in formats prearranged according to conventions, 2) religious behaviors performed in accordance with certain formality" (*Daijisen*: Shogakukan).

Common elements in these definitions are: 1) conventionality and 2) formality. These are joined by the element of 3) religiosity, although they are separated in *Daijisen*. The first two characteristics can be further divided into 4) repetitiveness, 5) orderliness and 6) traditionalism and retrospection.

The most general definition of ritual is that it represents an action-based aspect of religion more than anything. A ritual is a concept comparable to faith and mythology. However, we would miss the remaining characteristics of rituals if we limited our focus to religious behaviors. Excluding ritualized behaviors in the domain of greeting and diplomacy would be unproductive. Keeping this point in mind, I would like to pursue the discussion of religious rituals in this chapter.

Rational understanding

There are many rituals with clear purposes. Thus, the reasons for their existence are explained by their purposes. Let's take the coronation of a new king as an example. Royal power and coronation are intimately linked. The king would not exist without coronation, and hence royal power would not exist either. The institution of royal power is dependent on and legitimized by coronation (and numerous other factors). Now, was coronation first instituted by a king who needed it most? This might or might not have been the case. It is true that everything could have been explained neatly if it had been created by the king himself. The institution of coronation is thus explained by the purpose (function) of enthronement.

However, rituals and institutions cannot be understood perfectly by their purposes alone. This is because the relationship between the purpose and the effect is hardly explainable in many of the rituals. Rain-making rituals are performed during prolonged droughts. The conscious intention of the participating parties is clear (to call for rain). However, we (at least we in modern times) cannot recognize a clear relationship between the intention/purpose and the means (ritual). For this reason, rituals are often presumed to be a product of ignorance, *or else* many analyses of rituals attempt to discover their hidden purposes and effects, of which the parties are unaware. For example, rain-making may be explained as an attempt to relieve or dispel anxiety in people who are concerned about the impact of a prolonged drought on their future, or an attempt to reinforce solidarity in a community faced with a crisis. These are functionalist analyses that look for hidden reasons outside of the purposes stated by the parties. It is conceivable to think that these functions guarantee the legitimacy of rituals.

However, functionalism cannot explain everything. Why would the slaughter of a black cow induce rain? Why should it be black? If the purpose of the ritual is to relieve anxiety or increase group solidarity, why should the color of the cow matter? This requires a study of the symbolic meaning and the worldview surrounding the color black. Even in that case, we are forced to rely on other systems of explanation (meaning systems) as the parties are unable to offer adequate explanations.

Here is a slightly more specific example. This is the case of a community ritual at a Hindu fishing village in Sri Lanka called Cattiyur where I conducted fieldwork. The village holds an annual festival to celebrate a goddess named Bhadrakali. The festival lasts for ten days and comes to a climax with the sacrifice of a goat on the last day. Bhadrakali is normally feared as a carrier of the plague, but she has another side, which is to protect the village from the plague. As long as the villagers pay respect so as not to anger Bhadrakali, the goddess will keep the village safe.

In the evening of the first day, the villagers perform a ritual to receive the goddess from the sea into a temple. From the third day, a medium possessed by the goddess begins to walk around the village. Houses display *neem (Azadirachta indica)* leaves on the fence to mark the arrival of the goddess. This also serves as a sign that the plague has broken out. Before noon on the tenth day, a large black male goat is led to the front of the temple. This is called the village goat, which is a sacrificial animal offered to Bhadrakali by the Hindu temple management committee on behalf of the village. After this ritual, the goddess returns to the sea, and the brass statue of the goddess enshrined at the temple is paraded around the village at a slow pace to declare the arrival of a new order.

The origin of this festival is said to be an outbreak of the plague at the village in the middle of the nineteenth century. This is said to be the time Bhadrakali took possession of an elderly villager and announced that the village would be saved if the villagers built a temple and worshipped her. The villagers have been worshipping the goddess and conducting the festival since then. The plague is a disaster brought by the goddess and the sick are possessed by the goddess. If worshipped properly, however, the goddess brings peace to the village. The goddess from the sea visiting the village is represented as a febrile illness. The goddess as the plague sweeps over the village for ten days and returns to the sea after the animal sacrifice. In replacement, the goddess normally enshrined at the temple is brought out and tours the village. The villagers regain the expression of joy at the sight of her (Tanaka 1989).

This ritual has two social functions. One is to unite the villagers in the face of a crisis (a visitation of the plague = the goddess). They work together to deal with a negative element. The other is to validate the political and economic structure (power relationship) of the village. What is emphasized here is that this festival serves as an opportunity for the beach seine net-owners and the chairman of the Hindu temple management committee (all belonging to the same fishermen caste) as its sponsors to convert their economic and political powers into religious assets to strengthen their authority.

It is clear from the symbolism of the ritual that the festival is a re-enactment of the visitation of the plague = the goddess. The village is thrown into an extraordinary situation during the festival period, but the festival culminates with the restoration of an order governed by the goddess who brings prosperity to the village.

Thus structural-functionalism attempts to rationalize the irrational cause-and-effect relationship of the ritual with reasons such as social integration and the consolidation of governing orders, while symbolic analysis tries to understand it by exploring the world of meaning. It is possible to say that both legitimize various institutions involved in the village festival—political and economic institutions of the village revolving around the fishermen caste, not to mention religious institutions.

This is not limited to village rituals. The same thing can be said about other rituals such as rites of passage for adulthood. These rituals not only relate to the course of time (passage), but also segregate children into those who are allowed to participate and those who are not. If it involves segregating males (children) from females (children), it serves to legitimize institutions relating to gender. In light of these examples, Bourdieu is highly suggestive in using such expressions as "rites as acts of institution" and "rites of institution". Rituals are indispensable for institutions (Bourdieu 1992).

Nevertheless, these analyses still leave some elements unclear. For instance, why does the medium possessed by the goddess always have to circumambulate the temple three times whenever she steps outside of the temple? This act is not specific to the aforementioned festival and cannot be explained well by either a functionalist or symbolic interpretation. It simply sets off the familiar exchange of "What is the reason?", "That is how we do it here". Are these acts meaningless and unnecessary for rituals? I would like to consider the formality of acts rather than their meaning in the sections below.

Formality of ritualized behavior

Bloch is a social anthropologist who takes an interest in the formalization involved in rituals and draws attention to the fact that various utterances (mantras, songs etc.) are highly formalized (Bloch 1974). According to Bloch, formalized speech is unlike everyday conversation in that it lacks options as well as the ability to describe real events and the freedom to debate or imagine, more than anything. It is almost impossible to have a discussion with others or to criticize someone using formalized speech. Formality alienates the speaker's intention. Formalized speech is intimately related to the formulation of traditional authority, which denies any intent to bring about change and emphasizes repetitions of the past, as they both preclude criticism. Any meeting dominated by formalized speech ceases to be a forum for debate or conversation and becomes a place for the validation of authority. Formats or restricted codes that characterize rituals are considered to be devices to legitimize traditional authority.

It is noteworthy that the formality Bloch is interested in is found in language (prayers and mantras). I wonder if this argument is also applicable to action. The more formalized an action becomes, the less freedom the actor has and the more subordinate the actor becomes to authority. Even (the consciousness of) the actor becomes lost and taken over by another existence. This is a case of the actor being possessed by a god. Again, the pursuit of formality alienates the actor. Bloch's ritual theory has been criticized by Tambiah (1985[1979]) and Ahern (1981) for its overemphasis on the legitimization of power relationships (see Tanaka 2012 for details).

About ritualization

Bell (1992) noticed that ritualized behaviors characterized by formality, among other traits, transform contexts through ritual practices and transform themselves into highly unique practices, although it is impossible to distinguish them completely from everyday behaviors, and considered that this is the essential characteristic of what she calls "ritualization".

> [R]itualization is a way of acting that is designed and orchestrated to distinguish and privilege what is being done in comparison to other, usually more quotidian, activities. As such, ritualization is a matter of various culturally specific strategies for setting some activities off from others, for creating and privileging a qualitative distinction between the "sacred" and the "profane," and for ascribing such distinctions to realities thought to transcend the powers of human actors. (Bell 1992: 74)

Bell appears to emphasize the religious nature of ritual by referring to the "sacred" and "realities thought to transcend the powers of human actors" here, but they are created by the act of ritualization itself and the sacred is not presupposed from the beginning. Unlike some common definitions of ritual as a formalized act for a divine being, Bell argues that the act of ritualization in a sense creates gods. From the perspective of our interest here, it may be appropriate to say that ritualized behavior creates the institution of religion. The institution of religion may be formed by a bundle of various rules, but it comes into existence through the practice of rituals.

Lienard and Boyer (2006) provide a systematic discussion of ritualistic or ritualized behavior. According to their framework, it has the following six characteristics: 1) compulsion, 2) literalism and rigidity, 3) repetition, reiteration and redundancy, 4) goal demotion, 5) order and boundaries and 6) special attention to purification and danger.

1. Compulsion: This refers to the idea that rituals are indispensable for people's lives and does not necessarily indicate a pathological condition. Rituals are performed very frequently, although motives vary widely.
2. Rigidity: It is thought that rituals remain the same over time, regardless of practicality. Lienard and Boyer also use the word "literalism" for this. In addition to acts, ritual equipment and tools must remain the same.
3. Redundancy: Repetition is a type of redundancy. The aforementioned characteristics of ritual, compulsion (repetition) and rigidity (remaining

the same), are also found in acts constituting a ritual. Ritual acts must be compulsively repeated without change. There is no clear motive for repetition, but it is believed to be effective. We do not normally repeat the same act in our daily routine. A succession of individual acts leads to the accomplishment of a purpose. Some acts, such as the act of cleaning our teeth, contain repetitive actions (brushing the same spot a number of times, for example), but this is because a single action is insufficient to achieve the purpose.

4. Goal demotion: The purpose of ritual is unclear. I have pointed out in relation to a rain-making ritual that there is no clear connection between its purpose and its means. However, goal demotion means that there is no connection between the various acts constituting a ritual (ritualized behavior) and the stated purpose of the ritual as a whole, and does not simply indicate that there is no rational connection. The purpose of the rain-making ritual is to induce rain, but the act of circumambulating a dry well three times, which is an essential component of the ritual, cannot be explained by the purpose. This is very different from many of our everyday practices. In everyday practices, all acts are typically connected in a rational manner to form a sequence, at least as far as the actor is concerned.

5. Order and boundaries: There is a predictable order (program) to rituals. The actions of the participants are distinguished from their interactions in daily life by such things as clothing and makeup. Boundaries are established repeatedly so that a ritual space is demarcated. In general, some special space and/or time is created and rituals are performed within those bounds.

6. Special attention: The purity of the participants, venue and materials is considered important in the performance of rituals. They must be purified with water or fire. It is believed that dangers such as attacks by evil spirits increase during rituals.

De-subjectivization

Humphrey and Laidlaw (1994) also attempt to elucidate the characteristics of ritual based on an idea similar to Bell's. They refer to a categorization of ritual made by Atkinson (1992), namely "performer-centered ritual" and "liturgy-centered ritual". This distinction corresponds to rituals revolving around a shaman/priest or charisma/tradition in general terms, or the former can be considered "anti-structural" and the latter "structural" (see Turner (1969) for details). The performer's creativity is important in performer-centered rituals (i.e., whether or not the performer produces the expected effects), while strict adherence to formalities is important in liturgy-centered rituals (i.e., whether or not the ritual is conducted properly according to set procedures). According to Humphrey and Laidlaw, a majority of ritual studies, including that of Atkinson, tend to focus on the former, performer-centered rituals, and neglect to analyze liturgy-centered rituals, especially those that lack a climax or dramatic effects. Liturgy-centered rituals constitute the main type of religious ritual and at the same time share some common ritualistic characteristics (civility, face-saving etc.) with other formalized acts—greeting and conversation, for example. In this sense, analysis of liturgy-centered rituals would be more meaningful in discussing ritual in the context of institution. In doing so, it would be more effective to categorize rituals into ritualized (i.e., acts characterized by repetition and formality) and non-ritualized acts, be they performer-centered or liturgy-centered (Lienard and Boyer 2006).

Humphrey and Laidlaw (1994) analyze the Jain *pūjā* (acts of worship and offering). This ritual is performed in homes and temples, but has no strictly-set format. People perform their acts of worship by following someone's example, be it that of an expert or a fellow member of the public. There are many variations. Nevertheless, people claim that they can tell which acts are genuine acts of worship and which are not. This is because there are conventions by which certain acts are regarded as worship in a regional context. People act in accordance with conventional formats with the intention of performing a certain ritual. Yet these "conventional acts" are neither homogenous nor transparent, even though they follow certain conventions. People's motives are diverse. The intentions and motives referred to here overlap with the meanings of the ritual. Humphrey and Laidlaw have discovered through their observations of the Jains that the performers of acts of worship have various intentions and concluded that ritual in general has no intrinsic intention. What is important in performing a formalized act is its formality rather than its intention (content).

According to Humphrey and Laidlaw (1994), formality means that there is no close relationship between human intention and the meaning of action. For instance, when a man drives a car, the meaning of his driving is closely related to his intention (i.e., enjoying a drive, travelling to a destination, driving away a stolen car etc.). However, this relationship is not important in ritual. A ritualized action exists and is performed even if the intention of its performer is unknown. Yet, the successful performance of the ritual in the end depends on the actor's commitment. Ritual has an actor who performs it, but ritualized action is always external to the actor. There is no room for increasing efficiency or the innovation or improvement of the action from the perspective of means-ends rationality. Ritualization here does not mean that people would blindly perform orderly acts in the context of a ritual. Rather, it means de-subjectivization through subjective action (or in spite of subjective action). People perform a ritual with a firm intention, but they are de-intentionalized through the action. This resonates with Bloch's observation that the formality of songs and mantras eventually leads to de-personalization such as "spirit possession". I shall quote a passage that clearly expresses Humphrey and Laidlaw's argument, albeit a long one.

> So the idea that in ritual you are not the author of your acts is inadequate. While it is true in the sense that your acts are not intentional, they do not just happen to you either. There are two elements to this. The first point is the obvious one that it is you as yourself who actually performs these acts ... The other point is that it is also you, in intending to perform your act as a ritual, who constitutes your action as ritualized and thus make it the case that you are no longer, for a while, author of your acts. You set at one remove, or defer, rather than give up, what one might call the "intentional sovereignty" of the agent. For both these reasons, the fact that ritual acts deflect intentionality does not make them non-actions such as absent-mindedly scratching your chin, or unintentional actions like clumsily knocking something over. In ritual you both are and are not the author of your acts. (Humphrey and Laidlaw 1994: 99)

Ritualization cannot be regarded as mere action. Ritual (ritualization) is an act, but it is not a means-ends rational act with the explicit intention of the actor, as supposed by Weber (1960). It is possible to think that ritualization characterized by excessive formality and repetition divests the actor of their intention and hence denies critique and legitimizes the institution of which the ritual forms part. As I mentioned above, this legitimization becomes possible in three aspects, namely, function, symbolization and formalized action.

As long as an action is explained by the intention of the actor, institution cannot be placed outside of a person. If the action is performed by the individual's intention, it is always susceptible to questioning and denial. Through ritualization that denies intention, institution is always institution produced by us and at the same time exists externally as institution not produced by us. A privileged nature of ritual (formalized action) is evident here. Is it possible to say that ritualization is characteristic of the practices observed across all forms of institutions? In other words, by engaging in ritualized behavior that is consistent with a certain institution, we support the institution partly from internally as actors and partly from externally as non-actors. Unlike legitimization in the aspects of function and meaning, legitimization through ritualization cannot be regarded as active legitimization. Rather, it is legitimization through the omission of critique—maintaining the *status quo*.

Shiobara states in the passage quoted earlier as follows: "Take the institution of marriage for example, it includes the conventions of mate selection such as arranged introduction and courting, the mores concerning betrothal gift exchange rituals, weddings and receptions, and the law of marriage registration. The institution of marriage exists as a *complex whole* of them". Needless to say, typical ritualized behaviors are observable at weddings. Through ritual behaviors, we legitimize the wedding of which they form part and go on to legitimize the institution of marriage of which it forms part. Ritualized behaviors are observable in things other than weddings. Of course, a simple concatenation of legitimization does not happen these days. In many institutions, including marriage, however, it is conceivable that institution is legitimized in the following sequence: ritualized behavior → ritual → institution, or ritualized behavior → institution. Just as the wedding forms part of the institution of marriage, ritual is part of institution and ritualized behavior is part of ritual. Given this perspective, it is possible to think that ritualized behavior as a legitimizing action is *situated both inside and outside of institution*. "Situated outside" means that a ritualized action exists *self-sufficiently* beyond a specific institution. It does not exclusively belong to one institution.

Display behaviors in animals and individual rituals

Finally, I would like to explore the nature of collective ritualized behaviors by comparing collective or cultural ritualization or ritualized behaviors with display behaviors in animals and individual ritualized behaviors that are often regarded as pathological. A symposium entitled *Ritualization of Behaviour in Animals and Man* was convened from 10 to 12 June in 1965. It was the brainchild of biologist Julian Huxley and attended by renowned researchers such as K. Z. Lorenz, R. D. Laing, E. H. Erikson, D. Morris and E. H. Gombrich, as well as anthropologists including E. Leach, M. Fortes and V. Turner (Huxley 1966). Since then, many studies have been undertaken on the subject of ritualized behaviors in humans (including collective ritualized acts and individual ritualized acts) and animals. For example, the aforementioned symposium attendees initiated the formation of a research group whose outcomes were compiled by Hinde (ed.) (1972). The studies cited in this section are only a small part of the many and varied studies that have been published on this subject over the years.

Display behaviors in animals

Display behaviors exhibited by animals are formalized and repetitive behaviors typically observed in acts such as mating and aggression (see Sakurai 2000 among others). They are specialized for communication comprised of signals and exchanges to influence other individuals and their purpose is understood as "to coordinate social life" with other individuals (Sakurai 2000: 43). Display takes many different forms depending on whether it is an approach to conspecific or heterospecific individuals, what signals are used (light, sound, chemical substance, physical contact etc.), what the purpose is (cooperation or deception) and so on. Communicated information also varies greatly.

Display behaviors are characterized by the exaggeration or simplification of action and repetition, and it is evident that there are some similarities in form between them and the ritualized behaviors in humans being considered in this chapter. I mentioned six characteristics of ritualized behavior above: 1) compulsion, 2) rigidity, 3) redundancy, 4) goal demotion, 5) the establishment of order and boundaries and 6) special attention to purification and danger. The first three characteristics are also considered to be applicable to display behavior. The presence of goal demotion can be regarded as one of the characteristics differentiating them. This is because displays appear to have clear goals (even in deceptive behavior, its false purpose is clear).

Huxley argues that display has four purposes: 1) clear transmission of ritualization to conspecific or heterospecific individuals, 2) giving more efficient stimuli to elicit more efficient behavioral patterns from the counterpart, 3) minimizing harm among conspecific individuals and 4) forming sexual and social bonds (Huxley 1966: 250). While he considers that they are applicable to humans in principle, he also refers to the specificity of humans. However, he is looking at rituals in general as defined in this chapter and does not limit his discussion to ritualized behavior (Huxley 1966: 258–9).

Although display is an excessively compulsive and rigid and increasingly redundant type of behavior, its purpose (what the actor wants from the counterpart) is consolidated into one matter, reinforced and realized through the removal of miscellaneous information. Accordingly, display is far removed from goal demotion. It can also be regarded as behavior that produces "institution" itself (whether this expression is appropriate or not is difficult to say), from courting and mating to childbirth. Therefore it is impossible to establish the role of legitimization separately from institution because the behavior itself forms the core of institution. On the other hand, ritualized behavior occupies a peripheral position in institution rather than permeating it. Ritualized behaviors are sometimes not essential for the purpose of ritual or institution; they legitimize institution from a peripheral position.

Obsessive-compulsive disorder

I would like to discuss other individual ritualized behaviors, specifically obsessive-compulsive disorder (OCD). Individual ritualized behaviors can include infants' behaviors (Erikson 1966) and repetitive acts observed at life crises (such as childbirth) (Lienard and Boyer 2006), but they have been excluded from our discussion here.

While Freud (2007[1907]) published a paper on the relationship between OCD and religious rituals as early as 1907, I shall consider Laing's interpretation here (1966). He refers to the following case. A patient repeatedly opens and closes his eyes seven times upon entering Laing's office (closing four times and opening three times). Each action has a meaning. For example, he closes his eyes in order to avoid killing Laing by looking or staring at him. However, he feels that the closing of his eyes may be offensive to Laing. He opens his eyes so as not to offend him, but he may end up killing him. He repeats the opening and closing of his eyes three times each while dealing with this dilemma and finally reaches a resolution at the seventh time. He keeps his eyes closed while consulting Laing. According to Laing, this patient lives in a world in which a single act such as the opening of eyes produces both proper and improper outcomes. He tries to overcome endlessly degenerating situations through formalized repetitive acts. When this behavior was expressed in language, however, the patient returned to a normal way of blinking.

Laing nominates four behavioral characteristics in OCD patients: 1) a high degree of formalization, 2) a limited span of time, 3) strong resistance to change and 4) being cryptic. Laing considers that OCD is a type of communication, but its reciprocal nature is lost and the patient becomes disappointed at the possibility of communicating. Thus he or she suffers excommunication. Laing points out the impossibility of communication in OCD. On this point, he is heralding our discourse on rituals in this chapter. OCD is different from display in animals because of this impossibility. Collective ritual and OCD differ in that a ritualized act is merely part of a collective ritual in the former and various meanings are ascribed to the collective ritual itself. A formalized act in OCD is a ritualized act stripped of its context, so to speak. It resembles a display in animals, but differs from it in the absence of another party.

Humphrey and Laidlaw's conclusion that ritualized behavior in collective ritual is situated midway between an intentional act and lack thereof is also applicable to individual ritual typified by OCD. It suggests disconnection from everyday life. However, collective and individual ritualized behaviors are polar opposite in their relationships with the existing institution. Collective ritualized behavior produces a non-critical attitude toward institution—with legitimization as its consequence—whereas individual ritualized behavior produces maladaptation to institution due to difficulties in daily life—criticism and resistance as its consequence. It may be possible to interpret that ritualized behavior in OCD is situated on the periphery and constitutes a form of resistance to institution. Individual ritualized behavior differs from ritualized behavior in a collective context perhaps because it lacks the frame (semantic domain) defining it as a ritual. It attempts to disconnect from daily life directly in a sense, and consequently disrupts it. It can be regarded as resistance to various institutions that make everyday life what it is through ritualized behaviors.

On this point, a classic study by Lewis (1985[1971]) on spirit possession is informative. Lewis divides possession into the central/institutional type and the peripheral type and points out that the latter is critical toward institutions and functions as a means of rebellion for marginalized people. For example, women who have been oppressed in patriarchal society can temporarily release themselves from exhausting housework by way of spirit possession. This indicates disengagement from everyday life through ritualized behavior. It is of course questionable as to whether disengagement through possession can produce true criticism leading to reform. After all, spirit possession tends to emphasize the male-centered view of women as emotional and physical beings who are easily taken over by evil spirits and ends up reinforcing paternalistic values. However, this individual ritual has some elements of collectivity such as "it is more common among women". It is unclear whether OCD has any element of collectivity—and even if it does, whether it leads to legitimization of the existing institution. Despite these reservations, it is possible to say that there is an antagonistic relationship between individual ritualized behavior and collective ritualized behavior in relation to institution, even though they appear to be similar.

"Hazard-precaution system" and institutionalization

There have been some attempts to systematically explain (often from an evolutionary point of view) characteristic behaviors in collective rituals, animal displays and OCD, but none of them has arrived at a conclusive explanation so far (Eilam et al. 2006). Our discussion in this chapter is comparative rather than focusing on their relationships.

Turner and Erikson summed up the 1965 symposium, but they did not make a conscious effort to draw a clear conclusion. On the other hand, Fiske and others (Dulaney and Fiske 1994; Fiske and Haslam 1997) argue that OCD and collective ritual share the common characteristic of being acts that give meaning to the world. This is problematic in that it views ritual as a system of meanings.

Boyer and Lienard (Boyer and Lienard 2006; Lienard and Boyer 2006) contend that similar cognitive actions are operating in ritualized behaviors in both individual and collective rituals. They postulate that a "hazard-precaution system" exists in the brain in order to avoid dangers to the individual and that not only humans but also many animals have survived by evolving this system. In this case, hazards include the risks of capture, infection, pollution, invasion by others, insult, harm to children and so on. This system exhibits particular responses to such hazards and provides elementary information about precautions. According to Boyer and Lienard, the system causes anxiety, calls attention to particular objects and prompts compulsive behaviors. The hyperactivity of this system leads to OCD. Other individual ritualized behaviors can also be explained by this system. However, they also point out that the relationship between individual ritual and collective ritual is not a simple relationship such as that found in the construction of hazard-precaution systems. They consider that display behavior in animals is distinct from the hazard-precaution system.

Institution as a bundle of practices: In closing

In this chapter I have pointed out the importance of concepts such as ritualization and ritualized behavior by treating institution as an assembly of various practices including speech. Institution is a bundle of rules. Yet, it is perhaps more important to think that institution comes into existence through practicing these rules rather than to think that institution persists because of these rules. This point was also emphasized at study meetings in preparation for the publication of *Groups* (Kawai 2013). My practice-oriented approach to institution in this chapter is different from the more conceptual (semantic) approach adopted in a study by Seiyama (1995, Chapter 9 in particular). One of the reasons for this difference may be that Seiyama does not fully take into account the significance of rituals (ceremonies) (Seiyama 1995: 229–230).

What legitimizes an institution are the rituals that constitute part of it, and in essence the ritualized behaviors that constitute the rituals. The rituals legitimize the institution through their functions, meanings and associated behaviors.

I began with "Physiological dining scene" published in *Chika engeki* and stated that actors would feel uncomfortable acting out a script detailing everyday practices due to the absence of message. Rituals do not have a clear message either. Yet, people do not feel awkward in re-enacting them in a precise manner because rituals (more strictly, ritualized behaviors) are formalized and because we have already accepted that purposelessness is a general characteristic of rituals. It cannot be helped that ritual (ritualized behavior) is boring; let's close our eyes and endure for a short while—thus institution will continue to survive for many years to come.

4 Children, Play, Rules: Places of Expression of Institution

Hitoshige Hayaki

Key ideas

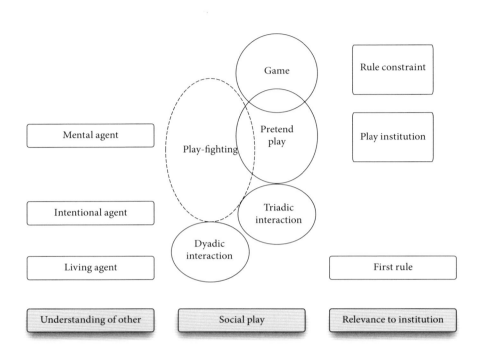

Games that enthrall children are formalized and conventional and have rules as their essence. As we consider the developmental change of social play along with changes in children's understanding of others focusing on the characteristic of rules, we discover that the emergence and disappearance of pretend play occur at interesting junctures. The emergence of pretend play approximately coincides with the time when children begin to understand others as intentional agents and to use language. Pretend play is replaced by games when children begin to understand others as mental agents. Pretend play is about acting out the schemata of expected social relations in a formalized manner and can be regarded as "playing institution".

Rules as the essence of play

Kakurenbo (hide-and-seek), *oni-gokko* (tag), *darumasan-ga-koronda* (statues), *kan-keri* (kick-the-can), dodgeball, *hankachi-otoshi* (drop-the-handkerchief), *hana-ichimonme* (red rover), marbles, tiddlywinks, *menko* (pogs) and *kenpa*[1] (hopscotch)—these are the games we used to play with passion until the sun went down in our childhood, which are now called "traditional games" and are apparently still popular among children. Let's call these play activities with clear rules "games" following psychologist C. Garvey (1980). According to Garvey, the games that enthrall children are institutionalized play activities that are structured by clear rules. Many of them have traditional names, which can precisely communicate the rules to participants. They clearly have a beginning and an end, and players are required to act in a set sequence according to a series of specific procedures in response to various events that happen during each game. Based on this point, games are formal and conventional and their essence lies in their rules.

Some games can be played alone such as early video games[2], but games are basically social play activities involving two or more children as participants. As children who participate in a game need to perform requisite actions either alternately or simultaneously, cooperation is crucial. Games do not work unless the rules are followed, and children therefore willingly adhere to the rules.

These organized forms of play including games tend to emerge when children are aged five or six. This is because the development of certain abilities is a prerequisite for playing games. They include the ability to cooperate and compete continually, to plan and execute a series of purposeful activities and to control oneself and intentionally adhere to restrictions and conventions. Cooperative games such as *kagome-kagome* (poor Mary) tend to be successful among friends of younger ages while competitive win-or-lose games become popular when children reach seven or eight years old (Garvey 1980).

Various institutions in human society exist as bundles of social rules. Where did the social rules underpinning such institutions come from and how did they evolve? I would like to consider how children's play structured by rules is developed, focusing on children and play and comparing this with play in non-human primates in order to explore the origin of institution.

The origin of play with rules

According to ecological psychologist E. S. Reed (2000), the environment human infants live in is not the same as that inhabited by adults—adults select and structure it. Special adults (nurturers) always stay close to infants, and specially selected objects, places and phenomena (toys, games, nursery room, cradle, nursery songs etc.) are arranged for them. Adults engage with infants in a manner different from that with other adults. Infants learn all sorts of things in this socially structured environment.

Reed views infant development in terms of changes of the frame of action. Infants in the earliest growth stage simply gaze at their nurturer, but as they become able to modulate their action in a manner detectable by the other person, a loop of dyadic interactions is established between infant and nurturer. Making the baby smile becomes one of the greatest joys for the nurturer and responding to the nurturer brings a sense of joy to the baby as well. It introduces circularity and internal synchronicity into the dyadic interactions. This is the first interaction frame, which is said to last for the first three months or so after birth.

Infants gradually come to understand their own agency and that of the other while the adults' gestures and rhythmic structure of speech bring about predictability. Thus infants learn to develop anticipation toward external phenomena (especially moving objects) and begin to learn to control their own agency. An interaction frame and a performance frame truly emerge in infants at around three months of age.

The performance frame relates to action toward objects in the environment and is used to selectively explore the affordances of the objects, to develop anticipation regarding the inherent properties of each object and to confirm the anticipation through the infant's own movement. In interactions with the nurturer on the other hand, the outline of the interaction frame is defined as infants learn to exclude the nurturer from their own action framework while switching on interactions through actions such as staring at the face, smiling and vocalizing. Preference for baby talk becomes clear more or less from this stage and "vocal play" increases. Baby talk is a characteristic style of speech directed at infants and features a relatively high-pitched soft voice, short repetitive speech and exaggerated intonation. The face-to-face interaction frame with the nurturer expands to include vocal interactions at around the age of six months and the performance of play activities featuring handclapping, rhythm and rhyming and vocalizing with varying actions, including peek-a-boo, tickling and pat-a-cake[3].

Infants become able to experience interactions within shared contexts while linking their own action phase with that of the nurturer during the period from three to nine months of age.

By around the ninth month, infants acquire an ability to move around on their own and step into a completely new environment-world. As infants move around inside the environment, their environment-world interpenetrates the environment-worlds of their nurturers and other people and the affordances of the environment become shared. Infants acquire an ability to focus on one object or phenomenon together with the nurturer and move on to a dynamic triadic interaction frame including the infant, the nurturer and the object. They begin to share an increasing variety of play and activities with others. M. Tomasello (2006) calls this triadic interaction frame a "joint attentional frame". According to Tomasello, the emergence of a wide variety of triadic interactions in the joint attentional frame indicates the beginning of the infant's understanding that the other is an actor with intentions just like themselves and plays a crucial role in understanding the other's communicative intention, which is a precondition for language development in children.

When we review the process of infant development in this way, we may be able to trace back to the interaction loop based on anticipatability in the dyadic frame, in other words, repetitive and anticipatable behavioral patterns between infants and adults, to locate the origin of play (games) with rules. These interactions undergo gradual expansion and infants respond to approaches from adults with anticipation and expectation. In "peek-a-boo" for example, infants anticipate what will happen after the adult covers their face with two hands, saying "Where is he/she?", and expectantly wait for "Peek-a-boo" to follow. The adult must uncover their face while saying "Peek-a-boo" according to mutually agreed procedures. The baby's joy expressed when the face is uncovered is what delights the adult. It appears that a certain format formulated in dyadic interactions is the first rule shared by the two parties and constitutes the origin of games.

In these interactions, however, adults seem to enjoy seeing the response of infants when they present certain patterns of behavior to them, whereas infants respond with anticipation and expectation to approaches from adults. The ways adults and infants enjoy their interactions are clearly different. Over-interpretation of and overreaction to infants' behavior on the part of adults appear to shape learning in infants. In this sense, perhaps it is the adults who are playing rather than infants (Aso 1998).

Myowa (2009) states that humans have a unique trait of treating the infant as "a being with an independent mind", albeit subconsciously. Adults receive the facial expressions and gestures of infants as if they are appealing with intention and deal with them based on their own interpretations about their mind, such as "You must be hungry" or "Your diaper must be wet". They treat infants as if they have a mature mind even though they do not treat them as physically mature. In these routinely repeated interactions, infants notice the existence of typical rules by which a certain response elicits a certain reaction. They eventually come to anticipate how others will behave toward them and respond with behavior expected by adults.

This type of "officious" (Myowa 2009) over-interpretation by adults is likely to stem from the characteristic cognitive ability of humans to perceive conspecific individuals as actors with intent similar to their own and identify themselves with others, as Tomasello argues, and this extends into the triadic interaction frame. According to Myowa, adults know that infants cannot understand the rules of play as yet, but they give them a role and actively assist them in an attempt to somehow facilitate play. The active "scaffolding" provided by adults in play powerfully guides the development of the infant's mind. If we turn to the infant's part in this, it is possible to say that children are engaging in activities that they are unable to accomplish satisfactorily (Reed 2000). While human children are dragged into the net of highly organized value and meaning systems in human society, they perceive that "something meaningful is going on" in their surroundings well before they begin to understand the individual meaning of a particular situation.

Self-inhibition and formality in play-fighting

The dramatic development of triadic interaction that emerges in human infants is not observed in non-human primates. Young non-human primates come to shift the counterpart in their interaction within the dyadic relationship frame from their mother to other juveniles who are close in age and involve themselves mainly in play-fighting or rough-and-tumble play.

Play-fighting is a social type of play widely observed in all mammals (Fagen 1981; Burghardt 2005). It is common in primates and perhaps forms an archetype of social play for Japanese macaques and chimpanzees. It is of course also widely observed in humans across all cultures.

In recent years, each time I show my university students footage of Japanese macaques and chimpanzees playing and explain that play-fighting such as wrestling and chasing is common in primates and ask them to write comments, I encounter some students who think that "humans do not engage in play like this". Most of them are female students, who appear to have very little idea about play-fighting. A majority of my students in the old days associated the images of primates engaged in play-fighting with their own memories of "rough-and-tumble play with siblings in childhood". I wonder if some Japanese children today grow up with almost no experience of play-fighting because many parents are inhibitive toward rough play and because many children grow up with no siblings in light of the decline in the birth rate.

Play-fighting in human children is observed in many societies, but the incidence and form seems to vary considerably from one society to another (Fry 2005). The incidence of play-fighting is low in hunter-gatherer societies in particular (Gosso et al. 2005) and Kamei (2010), who undertook an exhaustive study of children's play amongst the Baka Pygmies of Cameroon, stresses a lack of competitiveness as a characteristic of Baka children's play. Play-fighting is one of the types of play humans share with non-human primates, but it is probably more common in the case of the former that play-fighting is incorporated into pretend play and games with rules as one element rather than occurring independently. I would like to consider the characteristics of the rules of play-fighting through a comparison of chimpanzees and Japanese macaques.

As you observe immature macaques at a monkey park for a time, you inevitably witness a scene in which they gather, tangle together while hanging from tree branches, wrestle or chase each other in an open space (Photo 4.1). They sometimes use empty cans, sticks or grass at hand in their play. Some visitors think that they are really fighting because juveniles and adolescents play rough and move around aggressively, but they often show their open-mouthed play faces and never make warning calls or squeal as they do in real fighting behavior.

On the other hand, play-fighting among chimpanzees appears to be gentler, but it still involves wrestling and chasing (Photo 4.2). Chimpanzees engaged in grappling show a play face frequently and sometimes make a characteristic play pant when they are pinned down. Unlike in a real fight, in play wrestling they rarely make fast movements. They often chase each other at a near-walking pace, unlike Japanese macaques who run fast. Both the chaser and the chased occasionally slap the ground with their palms or do a somersault as they chase or flee. When two chimpanzees chase one another around the base of a tree, the chaser and the chased sometimes switch roles without realizing it. This is a very unique game in which

Photo 4.1 Juvenile Japanese macaques play-fighting at Funakoshiyama, Hyogo

Photo 4.2 Juvenile chimpanzees play-fighting, showing play faces with their mouths wide open, at Mahale Mountains National Park, Tanzania

they both play the roles of chaser and chased simultaneously. This type of play is also observed among gorillas (Yamagiwa 1993), but not in Japanese macaques.

Observations of Japanese macaques and chimpanzees find many similarities in the process of the progression of play, even though the contents may differ slightly. Firstly, they often exhibit some invitatory behavior at the initiation of play such as shaking a tree branch, glancing at the intended playmate or casually raising a hand. If this invitation fails, play does not start and the resting state continues for a period. If it succeeds, play-chasing, wrestling or some other form of play begins. After playing for a while, both playmates stop moving and enter a restive state. Play is repeated between short rest breaks. Thus play is engaged in repeatedly, with a rest phase in-between, in a chain-like structure (Hayaki 2002).

Play-fighting is of course not the same as a real or pretend fight. Although the parties demonstrate an intention to bite before they are bitten or to pin down before they are pinned down, it is likely that they do not have the faintest idea that what they are doing has anything to do with fighting even on a superficial level. We should rather say that they are engaging in a type of interaction we call play-fighting as they respond to one another's action and behavior synchronously.

In play-fighting, participants cannot necessarily behave at their own discretion and various self-inhibitive devices can instead be observed. One of them is an act called self-handicapping. It refers to the self-inhibitive act on the part of the stronger playmate to adjust the activity level of play downward to suit the weaker playmate, such as deliberately lying under the weaker partner in wrestling or playing the role of the chased in chasing. Self-inhibition in play is observable in other aspects. Invitations to play often fail because parties never force others to participate in play. During wrestling, they are seen to restrain themselves by actually "not biting" after making a "biting" action. Self-inhibition is also present in the phenomenon in which one playmate stops moving when the other stops moving in rough play. Self-inhibition is normally required of individuals in the weaker position in situations where social relations are adjusted by the dominant-subordinate relationship. In play-fighting situations, however, self-inhibition is required of the stronger party equally if not more so than of the weaker.

Self-inhibition on the part of the stronger means that it reduces the intensity of their actions down to the weaker partner's level. This has the effect of increasing the latter's activity by creating a level playing field. Cooperating with each other's action in a responsive manner through this device produces a competitive state in which play may escalate to a rougher level. I believe that the players do enjoy this escalation of play (Hayaki 1985).

Pauses (breaks) that give rise to a chain-like structure of play prevent play-fighting from escalating into a fight. Thanks to these breaks, the players can stop playing at any time when it becomes too intense and reset it to the initial state. This can be considered as a device to prevent the escalation of activity to an uncontrollable level for the weaker party.

These devices of play produce their effects as immature primates learn and develop various forms of self-inhibition in practice as techniques for the enjoyment of play while repeatedly engaging in play-fighting. At the same time, they perhaps develop abilities to cooperate and synchronize with others as well as some techniques to cleverly make others adopt the framework of play. In fact, the chain-like structure is unclear in babies' play as they relate to each other in a fragmented fashion and cannot cooperate responsively, whereas it is clearly observable in juvenile and adolescent play as they skillfully cooperate and respond to the partner's behavior swiftly and appropriately in a smooth flow of play. They clearly improve the way they play as they develop. Playing may in fact serve as training for the improvement of actual fighting skills in intense play-fighting among Japanese macaques, but this kind of skill development is unlikely in chimpanzees' play-fighting in which fast actions are restricted.

It is perhaps fair to say that self-inhibition observable in play-fighting accounts for the essential rules governing the maintenance and continuation of play. Although the players behave according to these rules, they do not necessarily recognize or understand them as mandatory. It is the same with the situation in which fluent speakers of Japanese do not necessarily understand Japanese grammar (grammatical rules). There is no direct penalty for violating the rules of play-fighting, but I am certain that it leads to an undesirable outcome for the players in the form of a forced termination of play. In particular, if a rule violation by the stronger (older) causes the weaker (younger) to scream, it may provoke an intervention by adults and the offender may even be attacked by the mother of the weaker player. The rules in play-fighting are techniques that have been developed through various practices and experiences with many different partners in everyday repetitions and should be referred to as conventions that have been formed through repetitive play (see Chapter Two and Chapter Six) rather than as norms of play.

Finally, I would like to look at differences between chimpanzees and Japanese macaques in play-fighting. The fact that chimpanzees are much larger and physically stronger than Japanese macaques perhaps has something to do with it, but chimpanzees move much more slowly in play-fighting than macaques. Chimpanzees rarely make quick motions and appear to restrict their body actions against their playmate to a considerable degree. Particularly, play with adult participation rarely begins from a grappling-type play-fight; it is often initiated through "finger wrestling" in which the players try to grasp each other's hand. It seems as if they are creating new formats of play by restricting body movements. Moreover, highly formalized forms of play have been created such as circling around the base of a tree, which is presumed to be a variant of play-chasing. The players often transition from a wrestling-type game to this circling game. When one player moves away from the partner and begins to walk with a slight swagger toward a tree, the partner responds as if that was a signal for it to follow a short distance behind at a similar pace. Thus they begin to circle the base of a tree together. Here we can see a relationship that can be called complicit cooperation by which the players share a specific format of interaction and commit themselves to it together. It is also possible to see this game as a triadic interaction between two players and a tree. For chimpanzees, the tree provides conventional affordances such as "climbing up and down" and "making loud noises by hitting". They have discarded these conventional affordances and discovered the novel affordance of "circling around it" in this circling game. Moreover, the new affordance is shared instantly by the two parties. Here I sense the opening of a road to pretend play, which I discuss in the next section.

Rules of pretend play

Cases of what is thought to be imaginative play in apes reared for language acquisition experiments have been reported frequently (Gomez and Martin-Andrade 2005) as well as among chimpanzees in the wild on rare occasions (Hayaki 1985; Wrangham and Peterson 1998; Nakamura 2009). Many of these cases, however, involve solitary play and it is fair to say that "pretend play" in which multiple children socially share an imagined phenomenon is a characteristic play activity of human children.

Garvey (1980) finds rules in pretend play as well. According to her, pretending in pretend play does not mean acting at one's discretion. There is a clear agreement on how each player should behave, what to do and what not to do, i.e., a pre-arranged format and certain rules of play.

The content of pretend play is determined by its scenario and cast. Garvey calls the former a plan of action and the latter assuming identities or roles, and describes their characteristics as follows. A majority of pretend play episodes are based on a limited number of themes. The most common plans involve "treating-healing" as in doctor-and-nurse play and "averting threats" as in chased-by-monsters play. Packing, traveling, shopping, cooking, eating, repairing and telephone conversations are also used. Children have a repertoire of these action-centered play plans and are able to continue playing without discussing what to do next. Individual plans are sometimes combined to form a long series of plans. On the other hand, roles in pretend play include conventional occupations such as firefighter, policeman, bride, doctor and nurse as well as imagined beings who appear in television shows or story books and familial roles such as mother, father, wife, husband, baby, child, brother and sister. Acting in these roles is formulaic but realistic and rather schematic as only prominent events are represented and details are omitted. Behaviors represented in children's acting reflect their understanding of the world around them. The characteristics of the social world and the "expected characteristics" of the manner of interaction between objects, actions and people are the main materials for their pretend play.

K. Nishimura (1989) refers to a case in which real sisters "play sisters" as described by Vygotsky and comments as follows. What is crucial to pretend play are generalized formats extracted and emphasized from what is most authentic and typical among all interpersonal relations and activity situations that participants actually see, hear and experience such as sisterhood, as well as series of certain behavioral patterns typically contained in these relations as rules, representations or symbols of real behaviors rather than imagination or images. The term "play sisters" obviously demands typically elder sister-like and younger sister-like behaviors and excludes deviations from them. Players are not free within this relationship schema. However, the terms of play permit the players to switch roles as they wish. These are the formats and rules of pretend play. Pretend play adopts the schematics of social relations as its formats and offers free play relationships in the exchanges that take place there. It is in this pretending that the behavioral routine that is characteristic of each of the terms extracted in the form of a relationship schema is found to serve as a rule to facilitate play. In other words, acting out a typical relationship schema in a formalized manner is the rule that makes pretend play work.

Players pretend to be someone other than themselves in pretend play. When one "pretends" for some purpose in relation to others, the pretender is aware that their behavior represents someone else and understands that this behavior will cause the other to misunderstand who they are, as in the case of a con artist for example. To think that others have views, beliefs and thoughts that are different from one's own is nothing special for adults, but this is not the case for infants and non-human animals.

According to Tomasello (2006), children's understanding of others follows a process of successive development. Firstly, they begin to understand others as "living actors" or agents during infancy. This way of understanding is also shared by non-human primates. At the age of about one, they begin to understand others as "intentional agents" through their experiences of synchronizing their relationships with objects with other's relationships with objects, or vice versa, and sharing their relationships with objects with others in the triadic interaction (joint attention) frame, which starts in the ninth month or so. This is the uniquely human way of understanding conspecific individuals and encompasses understanding both goal-oriented behavior and the other's attention[4]. At the age of around four, they begin to understand others as "mental agents". This is the understanding of "theory of mind", the ability to understand that others have thoughts and beliefs in addition to the intentions and attention expressed in their behaviors. There is a possibility that these thoughts and beliefs are not expressed in behaviors or that they are even fictitious and different from reality.

In view of this process of the development of children's understanding of others, it becomes apparent that the period during which children become enthralled by pretend play is situated at an interesting juncture. Pretend play emerges when children begin to understand others as intentional agents and to use language. When they begin to understand others as mental agents, institutional games with clear rules emerge and gradually replace pretend play. By the time children reach the upper elementary grades, pretend play all but disappears.

Pretending to be someone else in pretend play looks to adults as if children are constructing fiction. Yet, the understanding of others among children engrossed in pretend play is still immature and children do not necessarily understand the fictitious nature of pretend play. When they understand its fictitiousness fully, pretend play, which used to be so enthralling and appealing, transforms into a "bore" and heads toward extinction.

Play, rules and institution

The rules of a game as in what Garvey calls institutionalized play are slightly different in nature from the social rules and norms underpinning human social institutions. The rules of a game are what make playing it possible. They specifically prescribe "how to play", more than anything, and therefore define what the game is about. Following the rules is an essential behavior solely for the purpose of making the game work (Nishimura 1989). The rules of play are procedural rules for the playing of a game and in this sense they are practical rules generated among the players as well as rules constituting play itself. The rules of play are altered locally to match the circumstances of the players, and such alteration is made for the sake of the continuation of play. There is always the possibility of some players breaking or deviating from the rules, but there is no penalty for such deviation; play simply stops and players can no longer play. The fact that such games composed of clear rules emerge after children have developed sufficient language skills and acquired theory of mind suggests a link between institution and language. It is said that children enter a new stage of development at the age of about five to seven and begin to internalize various rules set by adults and develop an ability to follow the rules in the absence of the adults who have established them, i.e., an ability to control themselves.

S. Kuroda (1999) provides a comprehensive discussion on the evolutionary formation of "institution" focusing on food sharing behavior found in the genus *Pan*. The development of language is generally thought to be a prerequisite for diverse social institutions that are found across human societies (see Chapter One), but Kuroda calls institution not premised on language "natural institution" and seeks to discover preconditions for its formation in non-human primate societies. Even supposing that institutions in human societies require language, if they developed in the process of evolution, then their archetypal form must have existed in societies before the evolution of language.

According to Kuroda, "natural institution" is something that members of a particular social group expect themselves and others to conform to, and the expectations of others must be able to function to regulate the behavior of other individuals without language. This expectation means perceiving analogy between oneself and another actor, which is in other words a psychological process of self-projection on others based on self-awareness, or an expansion of the self. Moreover, the extent of this self-expansion is the "we" and to maintain the "we"-consciousness, deviators are either excluded or made to re-acknowledge the rules. In this case, the rules function as a symbol of group identification. Based on Kuroda's argument, the formation of human groups with "we"-consciousness appears to concur with the emergence of "natural institution".

When we reconsider the rules of play based on the concept of "natural institution" originating from the shared expectations of people toward the self and others, we realize that pretend play involving the formalized acting of social relations schemata is indeed a form of play to "play institution". This is because these social relations schemata that manifest as rules in pretend play are the archetypes of the social worlds people expect, and the roles played in them such as mother, father, wife, husband, baby and siblings are simply plucked out of the institution of family. It is possible to say that children play various social institutions, of which they have glimpses in the social life unfurling around them, as they come to perceive something that such institutions signify within their own range of cognition.

Of course, this does not mean that pretend play creates institutions. The life-world in which children engage in pretend play is already full of the institutions of adult society and children are merely using them as materials for their play. Having played institutions sufficiently through pretend play, children come to accept being constrained by the institution of social rules.

5 The Day Teaching Becomes Institution: An Evolutionary Horizon From Apes to Humans

Hideaki Terashima

Key ideas

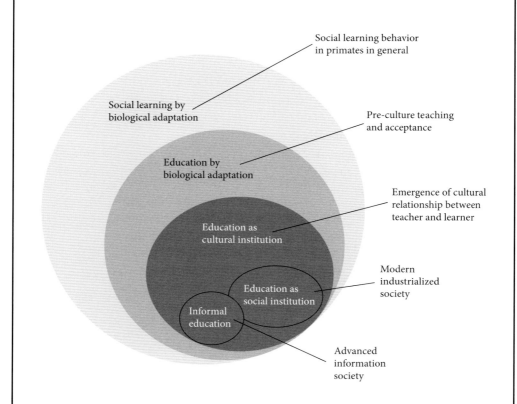

The foundation of learning in humans is social learning, which is also found in animals in general. Innate educational interactions appeared on this basis. When a process to recognize "teacher" and "learner" as statuses emerged, learning as a truly human institution was born. Formal school education catering to modern industrialized society proliferated in the twentieth century, but its limitations have become evident in the advanced information society of the twenty-first century that is searching for forms of education for the next generation. In any case, these are the social adaptations of education and not the educational evolution of society.

Learning and teaching

In this chapter, my aim is to search for the origins of "learning" and "teaching" among everyday human activities from an evolutionary historical perspective and to explore the relationships between them and institution. Both learning and teaching are extremely common behaviors for humans and society is full of all forms of education, including formal and informal education. However, we seldom take notice of their origins or basic functions.

Humans are peculiar animals in that they are born in a very immature biological state and take around fifteen years to reach independence. Children are cared for by parents or guardians during their growth period and it is evident that learning and education undertaken during this prolonged developmental phase make human society very different from those of animals in general. Many distinguished philosophers throughout history have left memorable words about the importance of education. Jean-Jacques Rousseau (1762) asserted in *Emile, or On Education* that "men [are fashioned] by education". Immanuel Kant (1803), who reportedly missed his daily walk one day because he was absorbed in reading *Emile*, stated in *Pedagogy* that "man is the only creature that needs to be educated".

If the acquisition of new behavioral patterns after birth is called learning, it is a widely observed behavior even in phylogenetically primitive animals, not to mention mammals and birds. Sea hares (Aplysiomorpha) are invertebrates with a very simple nervous system that live in shallow water, but they are known to exhibit a certain type of learning behavior. On the other hand, teaching knowledge and skills to other conspecifics is rarely found among animals other than humans. Although learning and teaching are almost always treated together as if they form a behavioral set in contemporary human society, they are clearly different from an evolutionary historical perspective.

In humans, infants begin to learn in response to stimuli from their mothers and other people around them. They become capable of verbal learning from the age of one. Chimpanzees are very human-like animals and also capable of significant learning. Yet, chimpanzees under natural conditions rarely teach things to other individuals (Boesche 1991; Premack and Premack 1994). Humans and chimpanzees diverged from their common ancestor and took separate evolutionary paths about seven million years ago. It is unlikely that teaching behavior existed at the time of the common ancestor. There is little physical evidence left to indicate when humans acquired the knowledge of teaching: was it during the time of ape-men, *Homo erectus, Homo sapiens* or later? As we can see in other animals, most animals can live happily without teaching behavior. Why did education begin to develop as a behavior almost unique to humans? Or did it develop as a by-product of the evolution of human traits? It is no exaggeration to say that the origin of teaching and the reality of its functions are still very much unknown.

Education in contemporary society is perceived as institutional activity practiced in a specific space called "school" for the purpose of cultivating the human resources required by society. Research on education has so far been carried out mainly in the fields of pedagogy, psychology and cognitive sciences. The body of research is enormous. However, a large majority of the studies have been devoted to education in contemporary or post-modernization society, and especially formal education as a national institution. Education is regarded as a forward thinking national policy and no one doubts its importance. While our discussion covers this type of education as well, the main focus of this chapter is on the actual condition of teaching and learning in hunter-gatherer and other societies yet to be swallowed up by the waves of modernization. We of course do not see the life of hunter-gatherer people today as identical to that of prehistoric human populations, but we believe that learning and teaching in societies least affected by the specific context of modernity can inform our search for their earliest forms from an evolutionary perspective.

The forms of learning and teaching we explore in this chapter predate education as a modern social institution. Nevertheless, they are connected at the fundamental level to the existence of institution underpinning human society. This is because various abilities humans have acquired in their evolutionary process are utilized in human learning and teaching and at the same time form the foundations of various other institutions.

The beginning of learning

Learning in chimpanzees and humans

Let us first look at similarities and differences between human and chimpanzee learning. We now know that various behaviors that can be regarded as culture exist even among wild chimpanzees, including the use and production of tools (McGrew 1996; Nishida 1999; Boesch and Boesch 2000). These behaviors are clearly not innate. They are acquired in various ways, including individual trial-and-error learning, imitative learning and learning supported by other individuals.

Photo 5.1 shows ant fishing by chimpanzees in Tanzania. The older sister uses a thin twig to fish out ants from a tree hollow. The younger sister watches her

The Day Teaching Becomes Institution: An Evolutionary Horizon From Apes to Humans

Photo 5.1 A chimpanzee watching an older sister ant fishing

Photo 5.2 An Efe Pygmy daughter watching her mother preparing food

intently. Ant fishing is quite a complex skill and takes time to learn. Ants are a high-quality food source that enhances the fitness of the individual.

Photo 5.2 shows a scene in the daily life of the Efe Pygmies, a hunting-and-gathering people of the African tropical rainforest. The child attentively watches the hands of the mother in the process of cooking small fish. In the case of humans, verbal exchange may occasionally take place between observer and observed, but not often.

As these photos show, both chimpanzees and human children often watch the behaviors of their mothers or their elders with great interest. They sometimes try to imitate these behaviors immediately or after an interval. This constitutes learning through observing the behaviors of other conspecific individuals, which is a type of social learning. It is also called learning by imitation as the learner attempts to copy the behaviors of others. Through this type of learning, children acquire the skills handed down socially as they grow up.

We can see that chimpanzees and humans learn by apparently similar means. Juvenile chimpanzees take about seven years to master the art of ant fishing and between five and nine years to learn nut cracking, and only manage to perfect these skills around the time of maturity (Nishida 1999; Boesch and Boesch 2000). On the other hand, human children quickly learn simple skills such as the one shown in Photo 5.2. However, the mastering of difficult skills such as spear hunting, bow-and-arrow hunting and basket weaving generally happens during adolescence or later. In other words, one's ability to use these skills properly serves as proof of one's "maturity".

Learning is the keystone of cultural transmission. Let us look at the methods of learning in more detail. Social learning in chimpanzees entails a wide variety of methods such as "stimulus enhancement", "observational conditioning" and "goal emulation" (Nishida 1999). In learning by stimulus enhancement, a child with a mother who is ant fishing, for example, pays attention to the mother's handling of the ants' nest and fishing stick and while playing with ants and the stick afterward it happens to catch some by chance. In learning by goal emulation, a child watching its mother who is ant fishing understands the goal of her behavior and learns the relevant skills on its own by trial-and-error afterward. However, learning by this method requires a significant amount of time, as mentioned earlier.

Developmental psychologists consider that chimpanzees are unable to learn skills quickly through observation because they are unable to imitate others' actions very well. Chimpanzees are slow to imitate even seemingly easy actions. They are "goal-oriented" by nature and show little interest in the actions of other individuals (Myowa 2004). On the other hand, humans are particularly adept at imitating action. Babies just twelve to twenty-one days old are found to stick their tongue out or open their mouth by imitating adults' actions (Meltzoff and Moore 1977). Infants between one and two years old may under certain circumstances imitate adults' actions in an exact manner, no matter how inefficient or irrational it may be (Meltzoff 1988).

D. and A. Premack (2003) consider that chimpanzees do not bother imitating actions because they only use simple techniques and are equipped with all of their actions from birth. Meanwhile, humans are required to perform many complex actions and resort to learning by imitating.

On the other hand, imitating is not merely a technical question. According to Tomasello (2006), true imitation in humans involves sharing the others' intentions from their perspective and imitating their actions in entirety. This type of imitative learning is not as efficient as learning by emulation. In that case, why do humans persist with this inefficient imitative learning method? Tomasello (1999: 6, 30) argues that such imitation is "a more social strategy" by which humans become able to "learn not just from the other but through the other". This is associated with metacognition in learning, which I will discuss later.

On the other hand, Tomasello (1999: 33) notes that chimpanzees' "emulation learning and ontogenetic ritualization are precisely the kinds of social learning one would expect of organisms that are very intelligent and quick to learn, but that do not understand others as intentional agents with whom they can align themselves". Cognitive psychologist Richard Byrne (2002) suggests the possibility that the imitation of action in humans has evolved as a mechanism for communication and interaction. However, emulation has not at all disappeared in humans and is in fact frequently used, particularly among adults.

The origin of teaching

There is no doubt that the imitation of action forms an important part of the foundations for human learning ability. However, this does not sufficiently account for considerable differences in learning outcomes between humans and chimpanzees. Why have humans come to be able to perform such a vast array of complex cultural behaviors? And a substantial part of these are accomplished before reaching maturity. On this basis, it is quite natural for us to wonder whether the greatest difference between human learning and chimpanzee learning may lie in the act of "teaching". As humans have a good command of language, they can compulsorily transfer knowledge and technology to the learner through instructions, indications and commands to assist learning. Education has long been considered a human condition as well as a privilege. Is this actually the case? I shall examine this notion using some chimpanzee examples.

Premack and Premack (1994) maintain that chimpanzees in the wild *do not teach* anything to other conspecific individuals. One reason for this is that chimpanzees do not have the "senses of standards or excellence" integral to human education. Another reason is that chimpanzees are not inclined to share their experience and values, whereas humans are. Chimpanzees do not educate others toward ideal goals as humans do. According to Premack and Premack (1994), chimpanzees may appear to teach others something, but they do so for their own benefit rather than the goal of educating others. However, I believe that it is too hasty to draw such a conclusion.

Firstly, the kind of behavior that can be regarded as "teaching" in non-human animals must be clarified. According to an animal behaviorist definition proposed by Caro and Hauser (1992: 153), teaching behavior must satisfy three criteria: 1) the behavior arises only in the presence of a naïve observer (learner), 2) the behavior is costly and devoid of direct rewards for the teacher and 3) the behavior helps the observer (learner) acquire knowledge or learn a skill earlier in life or more rapidly or efficiently than it might otherwise do.

Primatologists C. Boesch and H. Boesch have been studying wild chimpanzees at the Taï National Park in western Côte d'Ivoire for many years. They observed a behavior in which chimpanzees frequently placed walnuts and other nuts on a rock or wooden anvil and cracked them with a rock or wooden hammer to eat. According to their reports (Boesch 1991; Boesch and Boesch 2000), they came across approximately 900 situations in which mothers appeared to support the learning of their children in a total of about seventy hours of nut cracking performed by the mothers. Their means of support can be divided into three types, namely, "stimulation", "facilitation" and "demonstration".

1. Stimulation: In about 300 cases, the mother finished nut cracking and left her hammer and some nuts behind with her child as she went to collect more nuts. The child was then able to try nut cracking with the hammer on its own. The mother exhibited this behavior only when she was with her child, therefore she must have left her tool behind for the purpose of her child's learning. This can be regarded as learning stimulation. In about 100 cases, the mother carried her hammer away and did not leave it with her child.

2. Facilitation: During nut cracking, the mother gave her hammer or nuts to her child when the child asked for them. This is learning facilitation and was observed in around 600 cases.

3. Demonstration: In two cases, the mother corrected the child's placement of nuts on the anvil while the child was trying to crack them, or the mother slowed her nut cracking motion by using her hammer "notably slowly" as if to demonstrate the action to her child. These are considered to be examples of "demonstration" as teaching.

Boesch believes that mother chimpanzees in Taï are interested in the acquisition of nut cracking skills by their children and promote their learning in various ways without regard to concomitant burdens. The mothers appear to have an ability to judge whether their children's actions are better or worse than their own and predict the effect of their own actions on those of their children. Boesch argues that all the functions of teaching are performed in these situations (Boesch 1991; Boesch and Boesch 2000).

Nonetheless, it is difficult to say that learning and teaching in the mother and child chimpanzees in Taï are identical to those practiced by humans. Although leaving the hammer behind seems to motivate learning in children, it cannot be regarded as a mutually agreed behavior. In about half of the 300 stimulation cases, children ignored the hammers left behind by their mothers. The intention of the mother's behavior may be to stimulate learning in her child, but it is not always understood by the child. Similarly in the facilitation cases, it cannot be said with certainty that the mother's intention is to facilitate learning in the child. It is conceivable that the mother simply responded to her child's insistent demand. While the demonstration cases can be recognized as cases of teaching, there were only two cases in about 1,000 observed scenes (Boesch 1991; Boesch and Boesch 2000).

What these examples of learning and teaching in chimpanzees tell us is that while there may not be discontinuity between humans and chimpanzees in terms of learning and teaching, the continuation is neither smooth nor straightforward. In particular, if we consider intentionality of teaching as an important factor (Strauss et al. 2002), then the number of cases of teaching in chimpanzees becomes infinitely small. It is known that, in a number of species other than chimpanzees, individuals teach something beneficial to other conspecifics even when doing so is contrary to their own interests (Caro and Hauser 1992). However, the number of reported cases of this kind is very limited. Although teaching may not be considered as a uniquely human behavior, there is no doubt that it is a highly significant human characteristic as is the production and use of tools. Now the question becomes its origin and development.

Is human teaching innate?

Juko Ando (2011), a behavioral geneticist, argues that education is an adaptation strategy humans acquired evolutionarily for the survival and proliferation of the species and that humans deserve to be called "*Homo educans*". Strauss et al. (2002) state that teaching is a kind of human cognitive development, which emerges at a very early stage (age three to five) despite its complexity, and that it is natural cognition that is learned even if it is not taught.

More recently, developmental psychologists Csibra and Gergely have theorized a mechanism of genetically set teaching behavior in humans based on their studies of interactions between infants and adults and call this knowledge transmission mechanism "natural pedagogy" (Csibra and Gergely 2006, 2009, 2011; Csibra 2007). Natural pedagogy is said to be comprised of the following three steps.

1. Ostension: Teachers emit signals to indicate their intention to teach. Learners receive these signals and prepare themselves to be receptive to the teachings.
2. Reference: Teachers use gesture and gaze to indicate the referent. Learners expect this indication of the referent.
3. Relevance: Teachers give relevant knowledge to learners and learners accept it as relevant.

Natural pedagogy is described as a type of social transmission by special communication, which is an innate characteristic already present in infants as a form of evolutionary adaptation of *Homo sapiens*. What is transmitted by natural pedagogy is abstractable and generalizable knowledge and not transient, specific or episodic knowledge. Experimental results show that if infants are taught multiple contents, they selectively absorb and memorize the part of knowledge that should be generalized (Yoon et al. 2008). It is argued that natural pedagogy does not require advanced cognitive abilities such as language and theory of mind and that it actually emerged before these cognitive abilities in both the phylogenetic history and ontogenesis and formed a foundation that facilitated the development of language and other capacities (Csibra and Gergely 2006).

The argument that "teaching-learning" behaviors are innate adaptational behaviors by which humans acquire uniquely generalized and abstract knowledge and skills can be regarded as Rousseau's or Kant's argument translated to a genetic level. However, natural pedagogy studies have so far concentrated on preverbal infants, and skills and knowledge that are said to be transmitted this way are limited to extremely simple kinds. Human children develop quite high levels of language capability and cognitive ability by the age of three to four. It can be said that comprehensive learning as a cultural being, a truly human trait, starts from that point (Schmidt et al. 2011). While Csibra and Gergely (2011) appear to attribute all human learning to natural pedagogy, they unfortunately fail to shed light on how natural pedagogy in infancy develops thereafter and how it enables learning for subsequent development in relation to cultural learning.

Csibra and Gergely (2006) also try to locate the evolutionary origin of natural pedagogy in the spreading of the production and use of stone and other tools in early humans. Their rationale is that the intended purposes of these tools, especially tools to make tools, are opaque from observations alone and their purposes and applications must be learned from someone else. However, such diversification and sophistication in stone tools occurred from the time of *Homo sapiens* in the upper Paleolithic period during which language and other cognitive abilities clearly improved considerably (Klein and Edgar 2002).

It may be reasonable to think that modern humans are equipped with natural pedagogy-like biological adaptability, but natural pedagogy cannot sufficiently explain the full picture covering the who, whom, what, when, how and why of teaching.

Why don't people teach more?

Aside from its genetic character, the acquisition of the "teaching-learning" interaction must have had the effect of dramatically reinforcing cultural transmission and speeding up cultural evolution in humans. Logical reasoning would predict that such a useful behavior should spread quickly and those populations which failed to adopt this behavioral pattern would become extinct sooner or later. Contrary to this supposition, however, a large number of reports tell us that people have not been teaching so actively across all ages and cultures. It is no exaggeration to say that explicit teaching was rare, especially in pre-modern societies (Lancy et al. 2010). This is the paradox of education.

In the Efe Pygmies depicted in Photo 5.2, adults rarely exhibit teaching behavior in everyday life. It is not that they do not teach at all, but there are very few scenes of explicit teaching. Even for rather complex skills such as basket weaving and mat weaving, skilled people may demonstrate briefly when learners ask them, but they never use a hands-on teaching approach. From the learner's perspective, it is not much more than observational learning. It can be said that in this setting common life skills are transmitted by silent demonstrations and observational learning in everyday life.

The practice of this "education without teaching" or "invisible education" has been observed not only in the hunter-gatherer peoples of African tropical forests but also among those working in towns. Lave and Wenger (1993) revealed the reality of "learning in practice" at apprenticeship-based workplaces in various communities. At apprenticeship-based workplaces, newly employed unskilled workers immediately participate in the practice, albeit on peripheral tasks, rather than receiving full instructions up-front from skilled workers. As they perform actual tasks as members of communities of practice, they acquire various skills and knowledge and develop into fully-fledged craftspeople. Lave and Wenger call this learning process "legitimate peripheral participation". Teaching and learning are built into the field of practice called "workplace" and rarely emerge on the surface.

Paradise and Rogoff (2009) also compared many cases of learning in modern society and traditional communities across the world and concluded that people learn naturally through various forms of participation in the everyday activities of their family and community. If given the chance, children learn through observation, retain relevant knowledge and develop as a result. They sometimes acquire specific knowledge by intently focusing on the object of observation and at other times they spread their attention to all the things in their surrounds to absorb the knowledge slowly oozing out of them.

Anthropologist David Lancy (2010) argues that while "teaching" is synonymous with "parental responsibility" in the Western educated class, this view emerged only in the modern age from a historical perspective and has currency only in very limited regions from a cultural perspective. The majority of parents, both historically and regionally, opt to rely on children's natural curiosity and desire to improve. In fact, the concept of "childhood" did not exist in pre-modern Western society (Ariès 1962). This absence of intervention was due to the view that children could not be educated until they gained some wisdom at a certain age as well as the belief that children would learn naturally when the time was right.

Even when teaching becomes visible, teaching behavior is minimized in most cases. It is quite common in participatory learning that the teacher is not clearly specified. Those who teach in this setting facilitate learning by actively serving as examples while engaging in joint activities with the learners as equals and creating favorable conditions for learning, rather than acting as official teachers who provide explicit instructions and guidance.

In Japan, the "teaching-learning" relationship became common only in the modern age. Psychologist Hiroshi Azuma (1987) calls an education paradigm in which "the teacher provides various activities and encouragement and the learner learns as a result" the "one-to-one model of teaching and learning". While this is a widely accepted model at present, the viability of this paradigm is subject to two conditions: 1) teaching is monopolized by a national institution called the school system, and 2) all learners must be uniform and close to a *tabula rasa* (blank slate). Here, teaching is an act brought about by a special figure called the teacher and the learner is a passive receiver of knowledge and skills.

The fact that the teaching style in modern formal education is not particularly established among many peoples in the world does not mean that they do not teach at all. In refuting the assertion of cultural anthropologists that people rarely "teach", Csibra and Gergely (2011) cite accounts from ethnographic studies written by cultural anthropologists that contain various examples of teaching. Every society certainly needs to teach its own etiquette and norms to children by the time they have reached a certain age. In many cases, however, this is enacted through ritual practices and storytelling rather than the aforementioned "one-to-one model of teaching and learning". When children participate in communal activities or when young people work as apprentices, people demonstrate what to do. People lend a hand when novices experience difficulty. The mode of teaching is the issue here, and this method is not modeled on contemporary formal education.

Teaching and learning in humans are not limited to activities to transmit a certain amount of knowledge or skills to the ignorant. If the learner was a *tabula rasa* and learning would end once the necessary knowledge was injected, then a single-minded transfusion of knowledge might be more effective. This is akin to entering programs or data into a robot. For humans, however, knowledge absorption is merely the tip of a gigantic iceberg called learning.

The importance of independence in learning is often noted, even in the field of modern pedagogy. It is said that people stop thinking for themselves when they are taught. People do not develop when they simply receive teaching in a passive manner. In sports, people do not improve beyond a certain level if they merely follow the training programs given to them. Major growth cannot be expected unless they think for themselves while practicing. Participants must develop a learning attitude involving self-monitoring and reflection. Learning and teaching have breadth and depth that exceed the mere transmission of knowledge and skill. Education is an interactive cognitive activity that takes place between the learner and the teacher and character building happens in such a dynamic. We need to consider education at a level higher than the mere transmission of knowledge and skill. This is learning at the level of metacognition (Sannomiya 2008). At this level, "education without teaching" should no longer be a paradox.

Learning and the teacher's role

The act of teaching is thought to require a person who teaches. It is generally presumed that people cannot learn effectively without a teacher or that people can only learn from a teacher. However, this notion of learning in currency is modeled on modern formal education and not based on any ancient tradition (Inagaki and Hatano 1989). As in the case of Azuma's "one-to-one model" mentioned above, this notion is premised on the perception that the learner is a passive existence devoid of knowledge. It is therefore the teacher's responsibility to transmit as much knowledge as possible to students and control them properly for that purpose. Inagaki and Hatano state that this type of view of and approach to education dampens students' desire for learning and leads to lower levels of autonomy.

Then, what is the role of a teacher and what is a teacher supposed to do? There is a very interesting case cited by philosopher Jacques Rancière (2011) in his *The Ignorant Schoolmaster* involving the experience of Joseph Jacotot, who was invited to teach French literature at a university in Louvain, the Netherlands, in the early nineteenth century. A majority of his students did not speak French, while Jacotot did not know the Flemish they used. In this predicament, Jacotot managed to find the only thing in common—a bilingual edition of *Télémaque*. He had the book delivered to the students and asked them to learn French by themselves with the help of the translation. He did not teach them the basics of the French language at all.

When the students had come to the halfway point, Jacotot had them thoroughly repeat what they had learned and told them to read the second half of the book until they could recite it. He could not have been very hopeful about the outcome of this experiment, but it turned out to be well beyond his expectations. When he asked the students to write what they thought of the novel in French, they did a fine job even though they had almost completely been left to their own devices. Moreover, they wrote sentences as native French writers, not school children, would do.

What did Jacotot as a teacher teach the students? The trio in this curious drama is formed by the student who is eager to learn, the teacher who does not teach anything and a single common thing connecting them in the form of *Télémaque* as a teaching material. This is a very normal educational setting, except the teacher did not actually teach. Because the teacher did not teach anything, his students engaged with the teaching materials on their own and managed to learn the French language at a high level.

Rancière offers the following thoughts on the teacher-student relationship based on the above case. All conscientious teachers wish to impart their knowledge to students and bring them up to their own level of education. They believe that good education involves not only cramming students with knowledge and having them repeat this information, but also explicating by simplifying complex matters. However, believing that teaching is about explication and positioning oneself as an explicator is the primary cause of the stultification of students. It is not that a teacher is required in order to explain something to the students and make them understand because they are ignorant. It is more accurate to say that a teacher needs ignorant students so that they can explicate. Therefore the more conscientious, more learned and more educated the teacher is, the more stultified the students become, because the teacher is so eager to explain and make them understand. Rancière argues that this act stops the flow of reason in the students and destroys their confidence in using it.

Jacotot withdrew his own intelligence and led his students to a challenging place where they were compelled to use their own resources by letting their intelligence grapple directly with that of the book. In doing so, he fulfilled the role of a teacher well. Jacotot taught what he himself did not know by having the students use their own intelligence. According to Rancière, "The master is he who encloses an intelligence in the arbitrary circle from which it can only break out by becoming necessary to itself" (1991: 15). What the teacher should do is believe in the students' potential and allow them to develop their own abilities. As a result, students will learn autonomously what the teacher does not know.

The master-apprentice relationship pointed out by Tatsuru Uchida (2005), a scholar of French literature, has similar connotations. According to Uchida, learners are people who are unsure of what they cannot do or what they do not know. Apprentices believe that the master must know what they do not know, and because of this belief they often learn things that the master has never taught them. Learning emerges when learners presume that there is someone who knows what they do not know and what they want to know. The role of the master here is not to impart the correct answer to the apprentices, but to give them a riddle with no answer. As a result, the apprentices ask themselves what the master is trying to tell them and autonomously search for an answer. When the master and the apprentices have such a relationship, "education without teaching" in effect exceeds "education with teaching".

What is important in learning is the feeling of "I understand". Azuma (1987) describes the sense that one clearly understands something as getting a crystal-clear view of mountains, down to every fold without shadow, on a fine winter's day. This brilliant crystallization of understanding is clearly distinct from the level of understanding that only affords vague verbalization. While gaining a high level of understanding is a difficult thing to do alone, the teacher has an important role to play in nurturing this type of cognitive ability in the learner.

The master would not have to be human if they could effect learning in the apprentice without direct teaching. Nature and wild animals could play the role of master. Hitoshi Anezaki is known as the last Ainu bear hunter and has shot over sixty brown bears in his lifetime. Anezaki says, "I truly consider the bear to be my master" (Anezaki and Katayama 2002). He went to a mountain, found a bear's footprints and tracked it single-mindedly. He walked like the bear, rested like the bear, thought like the bear and behaved like the bear. By doing so, he was able to learn all about mountain walking, bear behavior and hunting. Then he found himself "being no different from wild animals".

The bear simply leaves the marks of its behavior without saying anything, and this presents a riddle to the hunter and drives him to search for an answer. From the moment a will to learn arises in the human, the bear becomes his master. This may sound incredible, but it perhaps becomes more conceivable if we think that the agent in learning is the learner and not the teacher. Where there is a will to learn, a learning environment appears (Azuma 1987). The sense of "learning from nature" is very commonly experienced by people who live in close contact with nature, and their daily activities constitute learning practices. Hunter-gatherer children spend time together and immerse themselves in nature every day as they play, and their activities are filled with all sorts of learning. Blending in with nature and taking nature as their master are the bases of learning for people living with nature.

"Education without teaching" is paradoxical on the surface, but it is perfectly valid at a level above the mere transmission of knowledge and skill, or in other words, in a metacognitive context. If common cognition signifies the acquisition of general information or skills relating to phenomena in the external world, the acquisition of knowledge about cognition and the use of skills relating to cognition means metacognition. The study of metacognition emerged in the 1970s and developed rapidly thereafter. It is becoming clear that metacognition plays a very important part in human learning and holds the key to learning (Sannomiya 2008).

Theory of mind, metacognition and metalearning

While there is a strong connection between learning and metacognition, theory of mind is also closely associated with these concepts. The concept of theory of mind was first introduced by psychologists D. Premack and G. Woodruff (1978) in a paper entitled "Does the chimpanzee have a theory of mind?". This relates to the question as to whether animals can understand that other conspecifics have minds and use this understanding to predict or explain others' behaviors. Since then, theory of mind has been actively studied in the fields of psychology and cognitive sciences as something deeply linked to the cognitive abilities of human infants and autistic children as well as chimpanzees.

We are still far from grasping the whole picture of theory of mind (Suzuki 2002), but its well-known functions include having an ability to handle cognition about one's own and others' cognition and reading others' minds. It allows one to understand the other's behavior or intention based on the other's perception and to adjust one's perception and behavior accordingly. Whether this ability exists in non-human animals such as chimpanzees or is unique to humans has been a topic of debate. However, the view that this is not a clear-cut either/or question is becoming mainstream these days. Although Tomasello, the leading expert in the field, used to consider that the ability of the self to understand the other as a being with intention and psychology was unique to humans, he now acknowledges the presence of such an ability in higher primates such as chimpanzees (Tomasello 2006; Call and Tomasello 2008; Itakura 1999). There may be a degree of continuity in this regard, but it still contains great gaps. If we focus on contemporary humans, it is clear that through the acquisition of language capabilities they have developed a considerably more powerful ability to read the other's mind, to understand the intention behind the other's behavior and to predict the other's behavior. In fact, theory of mind is said to develop sufficiently in infants after the age of four or five.

Theory of mind and metacognition are notably involved in learning. Imitation is the most important element in human learning. Learning does not occur without imitation. While chimpanzees are capable of imitating the goal of the other's action (emulation), the distinctly human form of imitation involves the faithful imitation of bodily action as well as its goal. Kumiko Ikuta (1987) sheds light on the characteristics of the learning process in Japanese traditional performing arts, which is fundamentally different from the Western education process. In Japan, students begin by faithfully imitating the *kata* (form or pattern of movement) shown by the master. In the process of endless repetition of the imitated movements, the students gradually develop an ability to evaluate and scrutinize their own form from the viewpoint of a third party, or "a first-person viewpoint incorporating the master's ethos". After that, they come to comprehend the complex of meanings of the entire world of arts entailing all sorts of elements not limited to the visible and thereby understand the necessity of form practice. At this stage, the imitated forms become their own movements. Learning in traditional performing arts is the process of developing one's own art by acquiring the master's perspective through high fidelity imitation and then subjectifying and internalizing it.

Thus, learning by high fidelity imitation is clearly not a method that values efficiency. As Tomasello (2006) says, it is to learn through the other's feelings, or in other words it is metalearning to develop one's own cognition through the other's cognition. From an analytical perspective, it is a uniquely human way of learning and teaching in which theory of mind and metacognition are fully operating and forms the foundation of "education without teaching".

Institution and education

Institutional facts and constitutive rules

Finally, let us examine in what sense the aforementioned learning and teaching are involved in "institution". As institution clearly forms the foundation of human society, there have been frequent discussions on the forms and functions of various institutions and the interrelationships between them. However, the question of what forms the foundation of institution is seldom addressed properly, and the true identity of institution itself is treated like a black box (Dubreuil 2008). Under these circumstances, philosopher John Searle (1995, 2005) has been actively discussing the fundamentals of institution. To put Searle's definition in very simple terms, an institution is "a system of collectively recognized rights and obligations".

Searle makes a distinction between brute facts that exist irrespective of human intentions and behaviors and social facts that contain collective intentionality, and he treats institutional facts as a subset of the latter. Institutional facts are characterized by status functions. "Status function" is a status and its function is assigned to Y as collective intentionality according to the rule "X counts as Y in context C". Y can be an object, a person, an event or anything else. The point of status function is that it is not an intrinsic function of the person (object, event etc.) to whom a certain status is assigned, rather the person comes to perform the function only by virtue of the assigned status. For example, a US twenty dollar bill is physically a piece of printed paper, but it has the status of a twenty dollar bill and associated rights and obligations that guarantee its currency to the extent that people recognize it as a twenty dollar bill. In the US, one person who is elected to be the national political leader is assigned the status of president and has rights and obligations in relation to the people.

Thus the application of the rule "X counts as Y in context C" creates status functions and institution, which is a set of status functions. The rules of this form are constitutive rules that create structures comprised of new activities and are not regulative rules that regulate already existing activities. Searle (2005) emphasizes that the existence of status functions imposed by constitutive rules is the very thing that differentiates human society from social structures and social behaviors in other animals. The essence of institution is to generate various obligations and rights at the same time as status functions. This equates to the generation of human relationships with new forces. The emergence of institutions has resulted in the possession of great social powers by humans.

Cognitive abilities and social conditions supporting institution

In Searle's view institution as an application of constitutive rules clearly presupposes language. He states that we cannot have institutions without the development of language. In that case, institutions must have emerged after the acquisition of language abilities by early humans. However, language itself is an accumulation of various abilities and could not have emerged overnight. Therefore, in considering the emergence of primordial institutions from an evolutionary historical perspective, it would be necessary to study how cognitive abilities, including language, were involved and what levels they were at. This is likely to be an extremely difficult task. Perhaps it is better to think in the reverse direction, that is, to examine the reality and characteristics of the cognitive abilities of contemporary humans and identify the factors that appear to support what we call institution.

Philosopher of science Benoit Dubreuil (2008) seeks to locate the abilities involved in the design of institutions and assign status functions in the domain-general cognitive skills associated with the development of the brain's executive functions, rather than looking at language itself, while preserving the framework of Searle's institution theory. They include enhanced theory of mind, the development of working memory, the emergence of multiple representations and metarepresentations of the same thing and so on. Theory of mind is intimately linked to "a system of collectively recognized rights and obligations" posited by Searle as the core of institution. A twenty-dollar bill is not just a small piece of paper depicting a portrait, rather it constitutes paper money exchangeable for goods and services because "everyone thinks so". I make such a judgment precisely because "I believe that everyone thinks so". When this belief circuit is broken, a twenty-dollar bill becomes just a piece of paper.

The emergence of status functions according to constitutive rules means that the functions of social phenomena are dependent on their contexts. What makes this possible is a cognitive ability to see one thing in multiple ways, or in other words, an ability to ascribe multiple representations and multiple frames of reference to the same thing (Searle 2005). "Symbolic play" emerges in human infants around eighteen months after birth and this signifies the development of a metarepresentational ability to handle multiple representations and to represent the representations of others (Leslie 1987). Metarepresentation operates in all facets of life, including metaphor and abstraction in language and artistic expression, symbolic elements in rituals and various social attributes of the individual.

By the way, adaptation to the natural environment is said to be a major factor in terms of animal evolution, but it is not the only cause of the evolution of intelligence. While primates have highly developed cognitive abilities, the dynamic of social groups such as troop and herd in primate societies has been a powerful contributor. As Toru Soga described in detail in Chapter One, evolutionary anthropologist Robin Dunbar (1992) notes a proportional relationship between the size of the frontal cortex of the brain and the group size in primates and considers that it stems from a social environmental cause rather than an ecological environmental one. The larger the group size, the more complex the relationships between the individuals in it, and the need for problem solving using cognitive skills arises in various facets of life. As a result, intelligence, which is an important function of the brain, developed rapidly. This type of intelligence is called social intelligence or Machiavellian intelligence, as against technical and other intelligence (Byrne and Whiten 1989).

The development of social intelligence corresponds closely with that of mental abilities such as theory of mind and various representational abilities. Psychologist Nicholas Humphrey (1976) states, "This social intelligence, developed initially to cope with local problems of inter-personal relationships, has in time found expression in the institutional creations of the 'savage mind'—the highly rational structures of kinship, totemism, myth and religion [which] characterise primitive societies (Lévi-Strauss 1962)".

Piecing all these institutional factors together, it is likely that primordial institution in human society came into existence on the back of the evolution of the biological organ the brain, mental abilities created by the brain and the social environment surrounding individuals and groups. It is also conceivable that the evolution of primordial institution occurred incrementally in response to the progression of linguistic evolution. Many of the presently observed institutions finally emerged along with the establishment of language.

Institutional evolution of learning and teaching

As the above conditions for institutional evolution came together, learning and educating behaviors would also have evolved. Various factors involved in the emergence of institution largely overlap with those of learning and education discussed in this chapter. We have already found that mental abilities such as theory of mind, metacognition and metarepresentation in particular form the foundation of learning and teaching unique to humans. Let us consider the relationship between learning, teaching and institution with these conditions in mind. The questions at hand are which parts of learning and teaching are institutional facts as posited by Searle and what can be regarded as collectively intended statuses?

Learning is a general phenomenon that occurs widely throughout the animal world and can be called a brute fact. All animals learn according to their innate abilities and the environment into which they are born and survive as they acquire adaptive behavioral patterns. However, learning as cultural behavior emerges in higher primates in addition to innate abilities. Humans also enhance their life skills through learning as they rely on their innate abilities and adapt to their environment in the early part of their life history. On the other hand, humans have come to manifest the innate "teaching-learning" behavior, which seldom emerges in other animals. This is teaching as natural pedagogy proposed by Csibra and Gergely (2006), or natural cognition as discussed by Strauss et al. (2002). Yet, this involves interactions between teacher and learner as an innate behavioral pattern at this level and cannot be called an intentional and cultural educational behavior.

With subsequent physical and mental development, the "teaching-learning" interaction comes to take place largely intentionally and culturally and is supported by theory of mind and language abilities. Intentional and cultural transmission occur as the involved parties recognize one another as "teacher" and "learner" distinct from the transmission of knowledge and skill in anonymous relationships. In other words, the statuses of teacher and learner appear in the society surrounding the learner. Here, teacher and learner have status functions as defined by Searle. The teacher teaches because they are recognized as such and exercises the associated rights and obligations. The learner learns because they are recognized as such and exercises the associated rights and obligations.

In a society with a formal education system, mechanisms such as school facilities, curriculums and academic assessment form a series of institutions and their substrata and the teacher and the student have been established as statuses. However, the educational relationship as an institution does not have to be confined to formal education at all. As we have seen above, teaching and learning are practiced every day in homes, at workplaces and other locations of various kinds, even though they may not be done explicitly. Nevertheless, educational institutions in formal education and those in general domains are not the same.

Let us look at the master-apprentice relationship in a premodern context. In this setting, the master is recognized as the teacher and the apprentice as the learner and their status functions are clear. Although the relationship appears to be identical to the teacher-student relationship in formal education, there is a substantial difference between them. Formal education was introduced mainly for the purpose of developing human resources in response to the emergence of industrial society during the nineteenth and twentieth centuries (Watabe 2010). If we call this type of formal education "education as social institution" and education in a premodern context "education as cultural institution", control of education in the former rests with schools and teachers and the obligations of the learner are emphasized more than their rights. This revolves around compulsory teaching based on a society-centered view. In "education as cultural institution" on the other hand, the learner takes the initiative in terms of education and people learn voluntarily according to their own needs and interests. In "education as social institution", the status function of the teacher is to transfer knowledge that is deemed necessary for society to ignorant students. The anonymity of the parties in such a relationship does not matter, or may even improve efficiency. On the other hand, the master's function in "education as cultural institution" lies in guiding the apprentices to learn by themselves rather than in transferring certain knowledge. This is so-called "education without teaching" as the apprentices make their own path to learning as they are spontaneously inspired by the master. Both parties recognize one another in a personal relationship and learning matures.

In "education as cultural institution", it is common that the teacher does not exist explicitly. Teaching and learning are quite possible under this condition. According to some experiments, children have the ability to choose the person from whom they learn and to extract what they can learn from the person's behavior on the basis of contexts even when a teacher is not clearly designated (Schmidt et al. 2011; Rakoczy et al. 2010). In a succession of series of day-to-day activities, "teachers" transmit what they are supposed to teach through their behaviors and "learners" absorb it as they see fit. They are not schooled. They learn as they are supposed to learn. As mentioned earlier, where there is a will to learn, a learning environment appears naturally. If we go a step further, learning can be effected with no corporeal "teacher" at all, as in the aforementioned case of learning from animals or nature as the master. Even in this case, however, one needs to recognize oneself as a learner and the master as having the status of teacher.

Searle (2005) asserts that institution is the thing that clearly separates humans from animals. This is because institution brings into society the statuses and functions that do not exist in nature, creates new frameworks and activities for living through the relationships of rights and obligations and thereby injects new power into society. It is social activation at a level above nature. Looking at learning and teaching behaviors from an evolutionary perspective, it is probable that the emergence of the recognition of the "teacher" and "learner" statuses at some stage was the beginning of the ascent from the level of unilateral acceptance of teaching through observational learning and innate abilities to the level of education supported by status functions as a cultural institution. From that point on, humans entered a new dimension in learning and teaching.

Part II
Concrete Phases of the Emergence of Institutions

6 Who is the Alpha Male? The Institutionality of Dominance Rank in Chimpanzee Society

Hitonaru Nishie

Key ideas

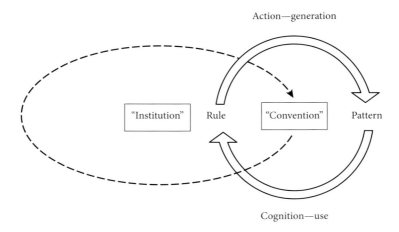

Lifeforms produce a set of actions within a certain range while cognizing and using patterns in the environment. As this cycle is sustained stably and develops into a way of cognizing and acting that has a history, it becomes a "convention". When the "convention" itself becomes a basis for the next choice of action, i.e., when the "convention" is supported and reinforced recursively and self-referentially, the recursive cycle constitutes the *arche* of "institution". The formation of the recursive cycle of "convention" and "institution" is not "artificial" in the sense that it is not designed by someone's "intention" or "reason", nor is it "natural" in the sense that it is not fixed or constrained by completely physical (genetic) conditions; it is "spontaneous" in the sense that it is "the result of human action but not of human design" (Hayek 1967a). Such "convention" and "institution" can generate stable order in the absence of major changes in physical, social and historical conditions as well as "spontaneously" transform in response to changes in the conditions. It is envisaged that the "institution" underpinned by this spontaneous order forms an evolutionary foundation of "institution" in societies of lifeforms including humans.

Tackling an infinite number of unanticipated realities with a finite number of norms; there is room for initiative or intention to sneak in. *Girei ni okeru ba to kozo* (Field and structure of ritual) by Takeo Funabiki (1987)

The goal of this chapter is to provide insights into the evolutionary foundation of "institutions" through an examination of phenomena surrounding "dominance rank" in chimpanzee society in the context of "institutionality". In this analysis, rather than treating "dominance rank" in chimpanzee society as given, I focus on the recursive dynamics of how the phenomenon called "dominance rank" constructs and sustains scenes of interaction, the social meanings it takes on in doing so and conversely by looking at the kinds of interactions involved in constructing and sustaining "dominance rank" relationships. Moreover, in this examination of the evolutionary aspect of "institution", I seek to analyze the specific ways in which the characteristics of the "cosmos of interaction" as an evolutionary foundation of "institutions" shared by humans and chimpanzees manifest in chimpanzee society rather than simply considering "dominance rank" in chimpanzees as a "primordial (embryonic) form of institutions in human society".

"Dominance rank" and the "alpha male" in chimpanzee society

Social relations based on "dominance rank" in animal societies are widely observed in mammals and birds and known to be particularly prominent in non-human primate societies (Hinde 1974). With regard to chimpanzee society as discussed in this chapter, the following phenomena have been identified in relation to "dominance rank": 1) it is particularly prominent among adult males (Nishida 1970); 2) dominance rank among males is not necessarily linear, and it is sometimes unclear which male is more dominant (Hayaki et al. 1989); 3) despite this, the most dominant "alpha male" is clearly identifiable in most cases (Hayaki 1990; Kawanaka 1991); and 4) the formation and maintenance of alliances and associations with other males are important in winning and retaining the highest position (Nishida 1981; de Waal 1982). These phenomena concerning "dominance rank" used to be described as "dominance hierarchy", and there were wide-ranging debates about the connection between them and primate social structure (Itani 1973). However, as primatology subsequently defined itself as an objectivist natural science, the term "dominance hierarchy" gradually fell out of use for such reasons as its "anthropomorphic" association with human social institutions, its incompatibility with scientific verification procedures and the ambiguity of its conceptual definition (its "institutional" connotations in particular). "Dominance rank" phenomena are therefore seldom discussed in an "institutional" context these days (Mizuhara 1986; Kuroda 1999).

The dominance rank of male chimpanzees can be identified from the vocalized interaction called "pant-grunt" as well as the direction of agonistic interaction such as aggression and intimidation. It is said that pant-grunts are uttered by the subordinate toward the dominant, especially when they encounter each other, and the dominance relationship between the two individuals can be identified from the direction of these greetings (Nishida et al. 1999)[1]. It is supposed that the "dominance rank of all males" can be determined by integrating the directions of pant-grunts and agonistic interactions between all pairs and amplifying all dyadic dominant-subordinate relations. However, pant-grunts or agonistic interactions are not performed in some pairs of ambiguous dominance relations, and pant-grunts are not observed in some cases where dominance relations are clear. For these reasons, it is very difficult in practice to treat the meaning and function of pant-grunts that are universally applicable to individual situations as unambiguous identifying factors of "dominance rank" relations (Hayaki 1990; Kawanaka 1991; Sakamaki 2005). The normal pant-grunt is considered to be a typical behavioral pattern involving successive "ahh" calls on exhalation vocalized by a subordinate individual approaching a dominant one. The way this behavior manifests varies widely as the subordinate individual in particular may seem to be very tense or may utter pant-grunts consisting of very short "ah" sounds in a "throwaway" or "cursory" manner as they walk past, depending on circumstances.

Despite some variation in the circumstances or the pairing in which this behavior manifests, however, the existence of the highest-ranked "alpha male" is generally considered to be self-evident because alpha male status can be observed with relative certainty in many chimpanzee societies based on the consistency of the direction of pant-grunts produced by other individuals towards the alpha male and the direction of intimidating or aggressive actions by the alpha male towards other individuals (Kawanaka 1991; Sakamaki 2005).

I, too, accepted the existence of "alpha males" in wild chimpanzee societies as an assumption when I began my observations, and proceeded with my study without questioning it.

My observation was interrupted in December 2003 during my second field study, when Fanana, an adult male in the alpha position at the time, suddenly went missing[2]. In the absence of Fanana, the beta male named Alofu seemed to have ascended to the highest rank in the group. It was difficult to predict (at least for me) what would happen to the relationship between Alofu and Fanana if the latter returned, and this precarious situation in which the alpha male was indeterminable continued for some time.

In the following section, I will discuss the institutional aspects of the manifestation of "dominance rank" in chimpanzee society through an analysis of the course of events in the case of the "disappearance of the alpha male". In doing so, I will pay particular attention to the circumstances under which the aforementioned pant-grunts are produced as well as the purpose of grooming, which is generally regarded as an indicator of mutually affiliative relations.

The circumstances of the disappearance of the alpha male

The disappearance

I conducted my first field study of wild chimpanzees in August 2002. In trying to match the faces and names of the chimpanzees at the start of my observation, I noticed a particularly prominent individual, an adult male named Fanana, the alpha of the group at the time (Photo 6.1). There was always a raucous atmosphere around Fanana as other chimpanzees frequently uttered pant-grunts at him and he would sometimes respond by severely charging them until they ran away screaming. As a novice observer, I found the "tumult" around Fanana somewhat off-putting, while I was confused by his "unreasonableness" when he would charge the subordinates who greeted him with pant-grunts as well as the "thanklessness" he displayed in response to the pant-grunts vocalized loudly by the subordinates who approached him one after another, despite the risk of being charged severely.

When I embarked on my second field study in November 2003 carrying this image of a "particularly prominent" alpha male, Fanana was still behaving in the same way and surrounded by the tumult of pant-grunts and fights. However, Fanana abruptly went missing and remained unseen for a period of time after he was last observed on 26 November. Chimpanzee groups have a typical ranging pattern called "fission-fusion" in which individuals repeatedly form large parties and break up into small subgroups (Itoh 2013; see also Chapters Seven and Eight of this volume). I assumed that Fanana had simply broken away with other individuals temporarily and would return soon. On the contrary, Fanana was not seen in December. Finally in January 2004, Fanana was spotted occasionally with a small number of males, but even from February to early April he was observed

Photo 6.1 Fanana (right) receiving grooming from Kalunde (left), an old male

Photo 6.2 Alofu

much less frequently than other individuals. Even then, he would appear with a small number of individuals and rarely formed a large party. My focal-following observations of Fanana during this period noted Fanana suddenly turning around and running away at high speed in some cases at the sound of pant-hoots (long-distance calls; see Chapter Eight) uttered by a large number of adult males a few hundred meters away. In short, Fanana appeared to be ranging alone or with a small number of individuals to avoid encounters with large parties of individuals (adult males in particular).

The first encounter after disappearance: "Intense" grooming

On 16 April 2004, Fanana was observed to encounter multiple adult males for the first time since his disappearance. He encountered three adult males, Bonobo, Masudi and Alofu (the beta male under Fanana's reign; Photo 6.2) in quick succession and all interacted in a very excited manner. Below is a summary of exchanges at the time focusing on the interactions between adult males.

Case 1: 16 April 2004—Fanana's encounter with multiple adult males (1)
In the morning, I found Fanana alone and began to follow him. He slowly moved southward alone until late in the afternoon while feeding occasionally. When Fanana heard a pant-hoot produced by a single individual some distance away in the late afternoon, he immediately began to move in the direction of the voice at high speed and encountered Bonobo (adult male) first. As soon as they met, Bonobo began to repeatedly engage in charging displays at Fanana and Fanana uttered pant-grunt-like sounds in a state of considerable excitement. Afterwards, Masudi appeared and joined Fanana in exchanging grooming for a prolonged period of time. Fanana gradually began to engage in charging displays at Bonobo in the vicinity and drove him away. Then, Alofu entered the scene, but he screamed and fled to the treetops without any resistance. After chasing Alofu for some time, Fanana exchanged very "intense" grooming with Alofu for a considerable period. Females and young males who subsequently converged from the surrounds uttered pant-grunts to Fanana instead of Alofu. I felt that Fanana had rejoined the group as the "alpha male" mostly successfully, except for a few moments during his encounter with Bonobo, and finished my observation there to return to my camp. When I found Alofu and the group nearby on the following morning, however, Fanana was missing again.

When I observed this encounter between Fanana and multiple males, I felt that Fanana had "successfully returned as the alpha male" for the following reasons.

1. Aside from a few moments during his encounter with Bonobo when he screamed in response to Bonobo's ferocious intimidation, Fanana stood firm and engaged in charging displays at Bonobo and Alofu especially after exchanging grooming with Masudi for a prolonged period.
2. Although Alofu had appeared to be the alpha after Fanana's disappearance, he screamed and fled from Fanana without resistance.
3. Females and young males uttered pant-grunts to Fanana and not Alofu.

This was the first observed case of encounter with multiple adult males since Fanana's disappearance, and Fanana and the other males appeared much more excited than usual. While it was an "extraordinary encounter" outside of the context of the normal male encounter pattern in the course of fission-fusion dynamics in this sense, it appeared that the initial agonistic interaction gradually settled down, pant-grunts were uttered to Fanana and the familiar "usual way of interaction" was restored in the actual exchanges.

Nevertheless, an interaction that "looked different from the usual" caught my attention during observation. This was the "intense grooming" exchanged between Fanana and Alofu that followed the period of commotion sparked by their encounter. Fanana and Alofu sat on a tree branch facing one another and groomed one another's body very intently for a considerable time (about eighteen minutes), while their bodies appeared slightly sweaty with hairs still standing on end perhaps due to the excitement that had preceded. This interaction felt unusually "intense" to me because the sound of their lip-smacking while grooming was audible from my place of observation under the tree and they seemed to be "engrossed in grooming more than necessary" "as if nothing had happened", even though they were still clearly agitated. Although chimpanzees sometimes lip-smack loudly when they are engrossed in grooming, I got the impression that grooming on this occasion was "unnatural", "out of context" and "exaggerated" because this "intense" grooming was immediately preceded by a series of frenzied encounters.

The situation calmed and Fanana appeared to have rejoined the group as the alpha male, but as noted above he had disappeared again by the next day. Fanana continued to range alone most of the time until he was seen encountering other adult males for a second time in late August.

The second encounter: "Excessive" pant-grunts

In the morning of 25 August 2004, I chanced upon Fanana together with Pimu (young male) and his mother, Fatuma, and began following them. Before noon, pant-hoots were heard near a large valley and Fanana ran in the direction of the sound. When I caught up with him, Fanana was sitting on a rock exchanging grooming with Bonobo. Later on, many adult males, including Alofu, and females arrived on the scene and the ensuing fracas lasted until that evening. The course of events is summarized below.

Case 2: 25 August 2004—Fanana's encounter with multiple adult males (2)

As Fanana and Bonobo exchanged grooming, Alofu appeared from the downstream side barking loudly. Bonobo immediately moved away from Fanana and approached Alofu. Alofu and Fanana were screaming at one another in a highly agitated state, but as Alofu gradually advanced, Fanana slowly backed away and fled to the treetops screaming loudly. Young females and young males nearby uttered pant-grunts to Alofu rather than Fanana. Alofu repeatedly approached Fanana, who eventually uttered pant-grunts to him. Females also gathered and made a lot of noise as they watched without getting too close. Then, adult males arrived one after another, including Kalunde, Masudi and Carter. The males, including Alofu, Bonobo and Pimu, repeatedly engaged in ferocious charging displays under the tree on which Fanana was sitting. Fanana did not come down until the evening. While Alofu still had his hair standing on end perhaps due to tension, he no longer screamed as he had done at the time of the initial encounter and he repeatedly tried to approach Fanana slowly on the tree without attacking or intimidating. Fanana continued to keep a distance from Alofu as he uttered pant-grunts and screamed to him frantically. Fanana made several attempts to descend from the tree, but he screamed and retreated every time as the adult males under the tree engaged in charging displays. This exchange was repeated many times. After exchanging grooming with Qanat (young female), Primus and Cadmus (young males) on the tree, Fanana finally exchanged grooming with Alofu. Fanana screamed while grooming and looked very nervous, but grooming with Alofu lasted intermittently for about thirty minutes. After that, Alofu moved up and down the tree and approached Fanana several times, but Fanana would not come down. When Masudi and Primus approached him on the tree, Fanana uttered pant-grunts to them frantically and gripped Primus' foot as he groomed. Then, Alofu approached Fanana on the tree to "lead" him to the other side of the valley. Fanana finally descended from the tree, but he fled at high speed in the opposite direction to the party's movement. Alofu and Masudi chased him, but Fanana disappeared again.

In this case, Fanana's fall from the alpha male position looked definitive to me for the following reasons.

1. Alofu did not utter pant-grunts to Fanana, whereas Fanana did to Alofu.
2. Other individuals uttered pant-grunts to Alofu, not Fanana.
3. Fanana panicked when he was subjected to agonistic interactions (intimidation and aggression) from other adult males and even uttered pant-grunts to Masudi, who was considered a very low-ranked male, and Primus, who was a young male yet to reach adulthood.

More than four months after the previous encounter, the interaction between Fanana and other males looked clearly different from that in Case 1. On the other hand, I noticed that the contents of the actual interactions were in fact very similar, except that they involved different parties (e.g., who uttered pant-grunts to whom). For example, the initial part of the encounters involved two parties approaching each other while screaming in a very agitated manner. This was sometimes followed by pant-grunts (uttered by either party). The scene of encounter was very tumultuous and some individuals produced "exaggerated" pant-grunts that sounded more like screams perhaps due to excitement. Charging displays and attacks happened amid the tumult and escalated the excitement. When the parties began to calm down some time later, one of them approached and initiated grooming. The parties engaged in grooming while they were still tense and agitated from the preceding tumult. When I focus on the common pattern, I can say that this interaction is the "usual way of exchange" observable in the "context of normal encounters" as well as in the "context of extraordinary encounters", but it is simply performed in an escalated, "exaggerated" form (Nishida 1977; Kitamura 2013; Kuroda 2013).

It is certainly possible to interpret this case as the definitive scene of encounter where Fanana lost his alpha male status, but on the other hand some questions remain. For example, "Why does the utterance of pant-grunts constitute an expression of subordination?"; "Why did Fanana have to flee after uttering pant-grunts?"; "Isn't grooming supposed to be a sign of 'reconciliation' or 'intimacy'?" and so on. Propositions such as "the utterer of pant-grunts is the subordinate" and "grooming has the function of maintaining and confirming a mutually affiliative relationship" are rules for behavioral interpretation adopted "arbitrarily" by us the observers primarily for the sake of expediency. There is scope for a reexamination of "social rules" by which chimpanzees perform interactions such as pant-grunts and grooming. I shall explore these questions further based on the above cases from the perspective of "the uncertainty of the situation at the scene of social encounter and the pattern of interaction".

"Excessive" grooming and the pant-grunt

The above two cases occurred when the alpha male encountered other adult males of the same group after his disappearance. There have been several reported cases of alpha males disappearing from wild chimpanzee groups (Nishida 1981; Uehara 1994; Hosaka and Nishida 2002), but the disappearance and reappearance of alpha males does not happen very often. In this sense, the above cases must have constituted "extraordinary encounters" for the chimpanzees. The fact that in both cases both Fanana and other males went into a state of severe agitation and panic upon their encounter indicates that they were "unusual" extraordinary encounters.

An "unusual" extraordinary encounter carries the peculiarity that makes one feel "uncertain about how to behave" because it is "different from what one is used to". In other words, one is unsure of whether the "usual way" of behaving is appropriate or not. It is likely that this "lack of contextual cues" led to a "lack of decision-making cues", which confused the participants and caused agitation and panic.

Nevertheless, the "confusion", "agitation" and "panic" experienced by the participants appeared to subside gradually in the course of ensuing exchanges. How did the chimpanzees overcome this "context of an unusual extraordinary encounter"?

While observing these scenes, I too was quite excited at the "unusual encounter" and felt a certain sense of tension in terms of not being able to predict what would happen next. Contrary to my expectation, however, a review of my records of the above cases has found that the actual interactions chimpanzees were engaged in at those times all consisted of "usual" and "familiar" behaviors. In other words, the "usual" way of exchanges such as pant-grunts, grooming and charging displays were deployed in the context of this extraordinary encounter, albeit in an "exaggerated" and "emphasized" form.

In these extraordinary encounters that appeared to be panic-stricken and chaotic for a period, the situation gradually calmed down as the parties performed respective acts according to the usual ways of exchange. It is conceivable that when chimpanzees were confronted by a "lack of contextual cues" at the scenes of "unusual extraordinary encounter", they tried to add some cues to the unstable social context by following the "usual ways of exchange". By "tentatively trying the usual way" in the face of an uncertain situation in which one encountered the other in an unusual way and felt unsure of what would happen next and how to deal with it, one tried to create a certain order (= pattern) at the scene, used the temporary order as a cue and felt about for connectability between one another's actions.

When one is confronted by a situation where one is unfamiliar and unsure of how to behave, the attempt to create a certain degree of order by "tentatively trying a familiar way and seeing how it works", even though one is confused and panic-stricken, means that the "familiar way" is utilized as an "exploratory action". In other words, the "form" of the action is chosen and employed as "something to try tentatively" in the sense that the action does not "determine" the course of the uncertain situation nor does the "content" of the action itself have any meaning. While "the meaning of performing the action" does not become clear until it is actually performed due to the uncertainty of the situation, one can narrow the "breadth" of the possible course of the situation to a certain extent by "tentatively trying the usual way" and seeing how the other reacts to it. The "breadth of the course of the situation" indicates "the range of choices for mutual actions". As the range of behavioral choices is reduced, decision-making becomes less difficult, and consequently the probability of bringing a certain pattern = order to subsequent situations is likely to be increased.

"Responding to an uncertain situation with a conventional action" is a way to rely on the "form" of the conventional action by momentarily setting aside the "content" it is supposed to have. As long as one is uncertain about the situation, one is unable to choose an "absolutely appropriate action". It is unlikely that the conventional action that is chosen as the "usual way" at that time is selected on the basis of the goal-oriented criteria of suitability for the given situation (i.e., according to the "content" the action is supposed to have) (as the situation is uncertain in the first place); it is rather likely that it has an exploratory and order-creating character to "try to bring a certain order to the situation by presenting the 'form' of the action to the other party". In other words, the chosen conventional action is utilized as a way to explore how the parties respond to one another by relying on the "form" of the "usual way" when they are faced with an uncertain situation, and this consequently produces a certain order between them (i.e., in the uncertain situation)[3].

It is possible to say that a conventional action that is used in a form-dependent manner becomes a "sign-like" action in a general sense because it is separated from its "content" (Kitamura 2008a) as well as a "ritualistic" action in the sense that it is a stylized interaction "performed" for the sake of confirming the parties' membership of the same group, creating a state of stable coexistence and securing the possibility of participating in activities together (Kitamura 2013; see Chapter Eleven). In fact, the aforementioned interactions among chimpanzees exhibit these "signified" and "ritualistic" characteristics in an emphatic form. For instance, the "intense" grooming observed in Case 1 was grooming as a quick and familiar "form" chosen to enable the parties to stay together in the wake of a series of exciting and chaotic activities. By seeing it as "fake" and "acted-out" grooming purely to "make staying together possible" rather than to "realize a close relationship with the other" in an immediate sense, we can comprehend their "excessive" immersion in grooming. In other words, what mattered in this situation was not "the function and meaning (content) of grooming"; "the act of grooming in itself (form)" was used to create a relationship that enabled them to stay together. It is likely that grooming was "acted out" in an "exaggerated" and "excessive" form because it was a "tentative" or "borrowed" action outside of the "usual grooming context" (Kitamura 1986, 2008a)[4]. It is supposed that the "exaggerated" charging displays and pant-grunts observed in the both cases were used to avoid the risk of the excitement of the unforeseen encounter escalating into endless agonistic interactions and to absorb the uncertainty of the context of the encounter into "the usual way of forming a relationship at the scene of encounter" by "acting out" the "form of a usual action" in the context of an extraordinary encounter. Because the action is deployed for the exploratory purpose of "trying the usual way tentatively even though it is uncertain whether it is accepted at this extraordinary encounter", a pant-grunt or a charging display as a form outside of the context of the "usual pant-grunt" or "usual charging display" manifests in a way that emphasizes its "excessiveness" to a greater degree[5].

On the other hand, these kinds of "significations" = "ritualizations" of interactions are likely to be taking place in the "context of usual encounters" as well as the aforementioned "context of extraordinary encounters". I have suggested earlier that interactions such as pant-grunts, charging displays and grooming at the scene of encounter are "usual actions", and for this very reason they were able to generate some order at the unusual encounters outlined above. Even in the context of usual encounters, however, whether the "usual" action one has chosen is appropriate or not cannot be ascertained until after the fact as long as "the other as the ultimate uncertainty" beyond one's control is present, and one cannot act according to a pre-formulated plan in anticipation of a social situation. This would lead to a confusing situation in which one would not know how to behave every time one encountered the other. However, this is not the case in reality perhaps because reliance on the "convention" that "I act as I always act when I encounter someone" narrows the range of choices to a certain extent as each party behaves according to the conventional pattern of the other's action. As a result, a certain degree of order is brought to the course of interaction (i.e., the situation).

A series of arguments on "spontaneous order" published by economist and social philosopher F. A. Hayek as a refinement and expansion of D. Hume's concept of "convention" examines social orders and their normative capacity produced as the result of the use of conventional acts by the actor faced with situational uncertainty (unknowability) (Hayek 1967a, 1967b, 1969, 1973; Morita 2009). In the next section, I further explore the question of order creation through the use of conventional actions in chimpanzee society, especially centering on the relationship between "pant-grunt and dominance rank", by reference to Hayek's argument in an attempt to connect it with one on the evolutionary basis of "institution".

"Dominance rank" as a "spontaneous order"

As I explained at the start of the chapter, it is generally believed that "dominance rank" in chimpanzee society is determined according to the direction of "pant-grunts" (from the subordinate to the dominant) as well as the direction of agonistic interactions such as attacks and intimidation (from the dominant to the subordinate). Conversely, it is sometimes posited that pant-grunts are produced "to confirm the dominant-subordinate relationship between individual chimpanzees" and that agonistic interactions are undertaken "by the dominant individual as a display of its power (dominance)" (Goodall 1986). This means that the relationship between "dominance rank (dominance-subordination)" and "action (pant-grunt/agonistic interaction)" is defined circularly in both cases.

However, Hayaki (1990) suggests that the connection between "dominance rank" and "interaction" is incidental rather than intrinsic (essential). According to Hayaki, greeting behavior such as pant-grunts does not necessarily happen at the time of encounter and its connection with the dominant-subordinate relationship is confined to the social situations that require clarification of such relationships between the parties. If the typical greeting behavior accompanying pant-grunts was used "to confirm the dominance rank", the greeting should be exchanged frequently between individuals unsure of the other's rank. Yet in reality, greeting behavior is seldom observed between such pairs and pant-grunts are uttered to the alpha male whose rank is very evident in the great majority of cases. For this reason, Hayaki is also skeptical about the dominant-subordinate confirmation function of the pant-grunt. With regard to the fact that the subordinate purposely approaches the dominant individual while uttering pant-grunts despite the risk of being attacked, he suggests the existence of something that cannot be measured by dominance-subordination in the sociality behind chimpanzee's greeting behavior, because pant-grunts produced by subordinate individuals are too "conspicuous" even though it is generally believed that the dominant-subordinate relationship is maintained by "self-restraint on the part of the subordinate".

In my opinion, Hayaki's view reflects the reality of chimpanzee society much more accurately than the generally accepted "definition of dominance rank and pant-grunt", but it still leaves questions such as: Why do we the observers believe that we can use "(signified) pant-grunts" to identify "dominance rank", which is essentially unrelated to the action? Why is it that "pant-grunts" appear to bring a certain order (based on the parties' dominance rank relationship) to the subsequent course of exchange in interactions between chimpanzees? And how do chimpanzees recognize and determine if the context of a given encounter "requires the confirmation of the dominant-subordinate relationship", i.e., "if pant-grunts are needed to be chosen as an action for the situation currently underway"? I will consider these points in light of Hayek's institutional theory based on "spontaneous order".

Hayek discusses human action and its ordering as well as the resultant development of law = institution centering around the concept of "spontaneous order". He firstly nominates "classifying" as the most fundamental characteristic of the sensory and cognitive systems in humans and animals in general and premises his argument on the following views:

1. The environment is perceived as an element of a class of phenomena exhibiting a certain pattern.
2. Individual organisms sustain their lives by "learning" through their experience of such patterns.
3. Consequently a perception of the environment inevitably "cannot be an accurate view of the world" because stimuli are selectively perceived through the "frames" of the individual organism's sensory apparatus, or in other words, animals (humans) inevitably have nothing but "ignorance" about the environment.

According to Hayek's basic idea, a biological actor equipped with this type of cognitive system is not a "completely rational" being that gathers accurate information thoroughly from the environment before formulating a plan of action and acting according to that plan. Instead, it enhances the probability of its own survival by treating similar situations within the phylogenetic and ontogenetic constraints as a "class" of situations and generating a regular pattern of action to return the same response to them.

When the actor with "ignorance" tries to ensure its survival in the environment, it must undertake cognition and action assuming a pattern (regularity) composed of highly probable phenomena in the environment because it is incapable of cognizing every piece of information within the environment individually. With regard to lifeforms in general, this phenomenon is called "adaptation" in phylogenetic terms and "learning" in ontogenetic terms. The cognition of patterns in the environment and the generation of patterns of action based on them become even more important in the case of more variable and fluid "social environments". As discussed so far, this is because "the other" plays the role of the ultimate uncertain factor in social events, and the uncertainty of social environments is fundamentally underpinned by the existence of "the other".

Hayek argues that the biological actor faced with this uncertain situation generates a certain order by cognizing and acting according to multilevel "rules" and uses it as a signpost to overcome the uncertain situation. Hayek posits that there are three types of rules.

1. Biological (phylogenetic) rules as the byproduct of the genetically inherited "species learning".
2. Conventional rules as the byproduct of ontogenetic learning.
3. Designed rules constructed intentionally and rational-purposefully.

Three distinctive types of orders are created corresponding to the above types of rules respectively, namely, *physis* (natural order), *cosmos* (spontaneous order) and *taxis* (artificial order). He argues that all lifeforms create natural orders according to their respective phylogenetic rules. He also contends that "positive law" in human society as a manifestation of the *taxis*-creating "designed rules" (thesis) is a derivative of the history of legal institution (or the evolution of rules), whereas "common law" based on "conventional rules" (*nomos*) involved in the creation of "spontaneous order" is more fundamental as a human social institution. In short, Hayek considers that the basis of institutions found in human society lies in the "creation of spontaneous order according to conventional rules".

The "spontaneous order" emphasized by Hayek here is "spontaneous" in the sense that it is a developmental phenomenon which grows through a temporal process; it is not "natural" in the sense that it arises as a result of a biological actor's action and it is not "artificial" in the sense that it is not intentionally designed by a biological actor. The spontaneously grown order becomes a convention when it is shared socially through ontogenetic learning and a social order is gradually formed as the conventional pattern is recognized and applied in the next action. The convention that is a pattern in the social environment that an individual recognizes and assumes in acting is "*a priori*" and "inevitable" for the individual in the sense that it precedes ontogenesis (i.e., it has a history). As the individual acquires the convention through learning and becomes able to act conventionally, the convention whose formation precedes individual experience sinks below the horizon and into the subconscious. This is what M. Polanyi called "tacit knowledge" and is also regarded as particularly important in Hayek's theory of spontaneous order as something corresponding to conventional rules learned by the individual. Thereafter, a circular (recursive) relationship of mutual support arises between (patterns of) the individual's perception/action and social orders (conventions) in the sense that the learning of social orders (conventional rules) enables the individual to produce the same action in similar situations repeatedly (and automatically), while the repetitive (and automatic) production of certain patterns of action by the individual in turn brings certain forms of order to social scenes.

In Hayek's argument, (the *arche* of) "institution" according to spontaneous order points to the emergence of a circular support structure comprised of social orders and the individual's cognition/action (Morita 2009). When an institution develops as this kind of circular (recursive) structure, it is in "a situation in which a majority of members of society 'think the same' about a certain matter that guarantees the cessation of thinking at the individual level, and the actions of the people who have ceased thinking in turn congregate and support this situation" (Morita 2009: 166). In other words, when an "institution" emerges (when it becomes operational), individuals become able to produce a certain order by limiting their range of cognition/action and use it without becoming aware of their own cognition/action according to the "institution" and with other possibilities (options) for cognition/action being invisible. Because "other possibilities (options) for cognition/action" have become invisible, the available pattern of cognition/action becomes "inevitable". Consequently, the "pattern = order" becomes the "rule" that limits and constrains the range of cognition/action as if following it is "necessary", even though it is supposed to only have the "conventional reason" of "everyone always does so". It is likely that lifeforms are able to maintain a stable relationship with the (social/natural) environment for the purpose of survival in this way without cognizing information about the environment fully and accurately or without facing the dilemma of falling into inaction as a negative result of the pursuit of goal-oriented rational actions, as well as by producing a certain order through acting according to "conventions".

It is clear that Hayek's argument above is directly relevant to the question of "order creation through the use of conventional acts" in chimpanzee society that we have been discussing in this chapter. It is reasonable to suppose that the patterns (orders) manifesting in social interactions among chimpanzees as we have seen so far are "spontaneous" in the sense that "they are the result of their actions, but they are not intentionally designed". For example, "forming a relationship with the use of the form of a stylized action (e.g., one party utters pant-grunts to the other)" at the scene of encounter cannot be considered to be an "artificial" rule designed with goal-oriented rationality "for the purpose of avoiding excessive agonistic exchanges", nor can it be thought of as a "natural" rule completely fixed by something akin to a "genetic foundation which prescribes cognition and action to always refer to and confirm dominant-subordinate relationships". "Forming a relationship with the use of the form of a stylized action" becomes possible at the scenes of social encounters in chimpanzee society thanks to the "bottomless reason" of "this is how it has always been done" (i.e., "baseless" in the sense that the basis cannot be found "outside" of the circular support structure of action/cognition and orders), and it has ultimately been supported by the "passive reason ('adaptation' in a weak sense)" that "this is how it has always been done without causing a major problem". Actions supported by this "bottomless reason" have the potential to become "arbitrary" in the sense that "they are not inevitable", and this links to the aforementioned argument that interactions such as pant-grunts, charging displays and grooming are used as kinds of "signs" and "ritualistic acts".

To sum up the above discussion, the way interactions are performed in relation to "dominance rank" in chimpanzee society is a social and historical practice which is supported by their brand of "institution" based on the "convention" of "this is the way it has always been done" which at the same time develops the "institution" based on that "convention". While "their brand of institution" is not supported by the law nor designed by someone and deviations from it are not necessarily subject to sanctions, it is nevertheless an "institution" that spontaneously brings some order to their society by guiding them to create some relational order with others that is *not inappropriate* at each scene of co-presence and to explore and overcome the inevitable uncertainty of the scene of co-presence with the other through cognition and action in accordance with the order. We the human observers, who are not in a position to take a view of "their brand of institution" in its entirety, end up observing the vestiges of "social order" created by the chimpanzees as the occasion arises while being caught up in the same "institution" by adopting the circular support relationship between individual interactions such as pant-grunts and agonistic exchange and "interrelations based on dominant-subordinate relationships".

Toward a theory of the evolution of "institution"

The way to deal with an uncertain situation by creating some order through a combination of an exploration with a conventional action and a response to it can be found widely throughout the animal world as well as in the aforementioned scenes of social interaction in chimpanzees. For example, animals sustain their lives while constantly forming appropriate relationships with the environment. In this relationship building with the environment, there is the basic process of selecting and perceiving what corresponds to their own range of options for action with regard to information about the environment that is too complex in itself. This basic process can be found across all "ecologies" (interrelations with the environment) of lifeforms (see Chapter Twelve) in the sense that it corresponds to the exploration and detection of affordances by them within their living environment (see Chapter Eleven) as well as to their activity to build appropriate niches in the environment.

Moreover, the phenomenon of the use of actions that are "excessively" dependent on "form" at the scenes of interaction has long been known as "ritualization" in animal communication. In general, "ritualization" refers to the evolutionary transformation (and its process) of behaviors without a signaling function into displays, and such behaviors are known to have common characteristics such as exaggeration and repetition, constant intensity, stylization and simplification, and so on (Sakurai 2000). In other words, social institutions in humans and "ritualization" in other animals can be regarded as different phenotypes developed from a common evolutionary foundation in the sense that the use of "form" in interaction as discussed in this chapter is seen not only in human evolution but also across a wide range of phylogenies with "sociality".

The "signified = ritualistic" interactions in chimpanzee society discussed in this chapter typically manifest as "rituals" in human society (see Chapter Three; Chapter Eleven; Funabiki 1985, 1987; Uchibori 1989; Hamamoto 2001), and in this sense it is perhaps possible to say that the institutions found in human society and the forms of "signified = ritualistic" interactions in chimpanzee society share the same evolutionary foundation. This shared evolutionary foundation of "institution" is the "circular relationship between cognition/action and order (convention)" as discussed earlier, and when this relationship arises, lifeforms become able to sustain their lives in a stable manner without an awareness of "institution", to bring a stable order to the situation through the use of the "form" of action, to limit the range of choices for action through reliance on the convention based on the spontaneous order and to overcome the uncertainty of the situation by exploring cues and creating an order for their survival.

Thus, lifeforms constantly generate "institutions" in their worlds and survive as they regenerate the "institutions" while maintaining and producing social exchanges with other conspecifics built upon incessant interactions with their natural environment, generating spontaneous orders and using the generated orders as conventions for the next choice of action. Although "institutions" in chimpanzees are certainly different from human institutions, the difference lies in the resultant "societies" as chimpanzees and humans form groups in different ways, create different orders and organize social interrelations according to different conventions. For this reason, "institution" in chimpanzee society cannot be the evolutionary foundation of institution in human society; their difference should be understood as a difference in their "*a priori* conventions" having certain evolutionary histories deposited in respective societies after diverging from a common foundation and following their long paths of evolution respectively.

Acknowledgement
The idea of reexamining institution theory for this chapter based on Hayek's theory of spontaneous order was given to me by Professor Masahiko Mizutani (Kyoto University). He kindly perused my draft and gave me many useful comments. I would like to take this opportunity to express my deep gratitude for his generosity. Any errors remain the responsibility of the author.

7 Duality of the Mode of Coexistence and Action Selection: Groups and the Emergence of "Institutions" in Chimpanzees

Noriko Itoh

Key ideas

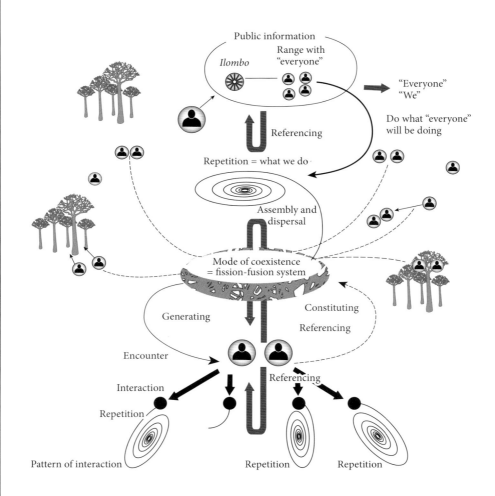

Everything exists in conjunction with the mode of coexistence. Without the mode of coexistence, "what we do", "everyone", "you" and "I" would not exist.

While groups are often taken as an *a priori* concept, *Groups: The Evolution of Human Sociality* (Kawai 2013), which preceded this volume, points out the importance of an aspect of groups that is generated through the concrete interactions of those who live in them. As S. Kuroda states in the final chapter of the book, group in a tangible sense is "the condition of coexistence in a group of living things" that also includes humans (2013b: 325)[1]. He calls it a *social* (social bond) group as distinct from structured *society*. The *social* group is more fundamental in the sense that society cannot exist without it.

This chapter focuses on the *social* group and examines the situation in which wild chimpanzees (*Pan troglodytes*) in Mahale (Tanzania) select their next action at both the group and interaction levels. It is pointed out in a number of chapters in this volume that the conventional response of "everyone does so" plays an important role in action selection at the interaction level. This chapter addresses the meaning of "everyone" in the context of chimpanzees and looks at the convention "what we do" that generates at the group level. While action selection at the interaction level is discussed in detail elsewhere (Chapters One, Four, Six, Eight and Eleven), here I consider why action selection matters to chimpanzees from the perspective of their mode of coexistence. This chapter is an attempt to reframe institution as the mode of coexistence rather than something that is provided to a society from (or existing) outside.

The mode of coexistence: Fission-fusion system[2]

Chimpanzees travel from place to place to feed and rest from the time they arise in the morning to the time they go to bed at night. They sleep at different locations from time to time by making beds with folded leafy branches in the treetops. In the daytime, they may spend time on their own or stay with other(s) for a while, during which other individuals may come and go. After meeting, they do not remain together for long, and the individual they stay with changes constantly. This form of fission-fusion occurs at the individual level rather than between multiple parties. The mode of coexistence in chimpanzees arises through a continuous concatenation of meetings and partings that happen one after another all over the place at the individual level.

When I followed individual chimpanzees targeted for focal following and recorded who they were with and the time they spent together, I found that they normally kept company with four to five individuals (except infants and juveniles) on average, including the target individuals, throughout the year. Of course they also remain alone frequently. The average number of four to five has been found to be the norm at all chimpanzee study sites surveyed so far. These parties of four to five chimpanzees who are in visible contact constantly change their membership composition in an unpredictable fashion, as the target individuals may join different parties or other individuals may come and join their parties.

When observing scenes of such protean fission-fusion phenomenon or individuals in small parties, it is difficult to notice that chimpanzees form groups. Only after compiling the records of their daily meetings do we realize that they only associate with certain members even though they are not always together. The content of their association ranges from explicit social interaction to mere co-presence. This loose group, termed a "unit-group" especially for chimpanzee groups, in Mahale has persisted for almost fifty years at least. In the case of M group in Mahale, the number of members participating in this fission-fusion system now reaches sixty or so, including males and females of various ages. However, they as well as we the observers almost never witness the full extent of this unit-group in reality. The repetition of the chimpanzees' daily fission-fusion constitutes the very mode of their coexistence. In this case, do individual chimpanzees see this invisible group as a single assembly that includes themselves? I will consider this question in the next section.

Everyone does so

Researchers who have studied in Mahale for more than a year can predict when chimpanzees are most observable. The expression "most observable" contains many elements, namely, efficiency of detection, encountering many individuals, encountering them almost daily and so on, but in any case it means we can tell that many members are assembling. On the flip side, it means that there are times when we find very few chimpanzees. It is common for us to find only one or a few individuals, or even none at all, after covering a lot of ground all day. What reinforces our ability to predict when chimpanzees are more or less observable is the availability of a type of fruit locally called "*ilombo*" (*Saba comorensis*).

The issue I am tackling in this section agrees with the researchers' impressions as described above. The mystery in question here is, if individual chimpanzees can live without assembling, why not do this all year round? What enables chimpanzees, who are scattered all over the place, to gather together?

Before exploring these questions, I briefly explain the chimpanzee diet (see Itoh and Nakamura 2015a for details). Chimpanzees feed mainly on fruit and also

Photo 7.1 Ilombo (Saba comorensis, Apocynaceae) fruit

eat almost all parts of plants, including flowers and bark, as well as mammals and birds and at times insects. The types of plant foods known to be eaten by chimpanzees in Mahale reach 224 species and 407 items (Itoh and Nakamura 2015a; Itoh et al. 2015). Different plant species and individual plants have their own seasons and cycles when they produce fruit, flowers and new leaves. Consequently, chimpanzees roam around their habitat according to the phenological dynamics of such plants in search of unevenly distributed food sources as they eat fruit A here, fruit B there and fruit A again somewhere else etc., alone or with a small number of group members.

Photo 7.1 shows the fruit of the aforementioned woody vine, *ilombo*. The chimpanzees of Mahale consume *ilombo* fruit frequently as they ripen to the size of softballs and turn yellow. *Ilombo* fruit remains their staple partly because this species is more widely and densely distributed compared with other plants (Itoh 2002, 2004; Itoh and Nakamura 2015b). Data from 1997 to 2013 show that *ilombo* has a longer fruiting period and small year-to-year variation in high fruiting density and cycle compared to other fruit food species that have annual cycles (Itoh 2004: Itoh and Muramatsu 2015).

As you can see in Figure 7.1, chimpanzees start feeding on *ilombo* fruit intensively in August shortly before the peak of its fruiting season (Itoh 2004; Itoh and Nakamura 2015a). This intensive use continues until *ilombo* fruit becomes unavailable. Such a feeding pattern is unique to *ilombo* fruit. Of course, as they

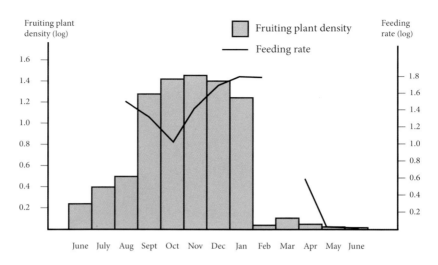

Figure 7.1 Ilombo *fruiting and feeding pattern (1997–1998)*

Note: Feeding data was only available from August. March was omitted due to the small sample size. "Feeding rate" indicates the time spent feeding on *ilombo* fruits to the total time spent feeding on all plant foods.

do not feed exclusively on *ilombo* fruit, they sometimes switch their main food to other foods during the *ilombo* season (e.g., October in Figure 7.1). Nevertheless, it is definitely the most commonly eaten food throughout year irrespective of the year in question (for details see Itoh 2004; Itoh and Nakamura 2015a; Nakamura and Itoh 2015).

Let us look at this from the perspective of chimpanzees' land use pattern. Nakamura et al. (2013) analyzed the land use pattern based on M group's ranging data over sixteen years (see also Nakamura 2015). The analysis reveals that chimpanzees move around most extensively in August, which coincides with the time they begin eating *ilombo* fruit. The increase in their ranging area related to *ilombo* fruit consumption has been known for a long time (Nishida 1968; Itoh and Nakamura 2015a). Combining the above two facts, in August chimpanzees range over a wide area searching for and eating *ilombo* fruit, which are yet to become abundantly available.

Both the feeding pattern and the land use pattern so far may seem to suggest that individual chimpanzees simply search for and eat *ilombo* fruit "efficiently", which grow densely and ubiquitously. One curious point is the fact that they search for and eat *ilombo* fruit as soon as the lianas begin to bear fruit. The collective

Duality of the Mode of Coexistence and Action Selection   147

phenomenon described below triggered by the "sign" of this environmental change is the central subject of this section.

Assembly and dispersal

M group is known to show seasonality in grouping pattern. In one period, almost all unit-group members loosely gather. This pattern continues for several months. As I mentioned in the first section of the chapter, chimpanzees repeatedly form temporal parties within which members are visible to one another in the process of fission-fusion. At the same time, they create a larger, loosely formed party ("nomadic party") through frequent fission-fusion, although the full picture of the nomadic party is never visible. T. Nishida (1990: 26) wrote: "From a bird's eye view, movement of a unit-group may be ameba-like …". The large nomadic party moves in specific directions over the course of a day, while individual members move back and forth freely and meet and part frequently. It certainly could look like a wriggling ameba, which extends and retracts as it travels. Unlike this assembly period, during the dispersal period chimpanzees spread over a large range and hence the frequency of fission-fusion declines. As I mention below, this assembly-dispersal phenomenon that is distinct from fission-fusion at the face-to-face level is a characteristic of M group.

An analysis of data collected over four years has shown that there is a strong positive correlation between this assembly-dispersal phenomenon and fruit availability (Itoh 2004; Itoh and Nishida 2007). Different from other fruit food species, *ilombo* fruit production is stable each year in terms of its fruiting cycle and high density (Itoh 2004; Itoh and Muramatsu 2015). In other words, the assembly-dispersal phenomenon is largely influenced by the fruiting pattern of *ilombo* rather than fruit in general. This assembly period is what I referred to in the beginning as the most observable period, while chimpanzees are very hard to find during the dispersal period. When chimpanzees aggregate in a certain area (assembly period), various individuals can be easily located one after another within short distances, whereas it is difficult to spot scattered chimpanzees (dispersal period).

The positive correlation between the fruiting *ilombo* availability and the degree of assembly can be partially explained by foraging theory, which states that high food abundance makes aggregation possible because of reduced competition for food among individuals. However, this reasoning suggests why it is possible but does not explain why chimpanzees actually aggregate. When they actually feed on *ilombo*, chimpanzees are in temporal parties of four to five members just as they are throughout the rest of the year (Itoh 2004; Itoh and Nishida 2007). Thus, why they form a large nomadic party during a particular season is an intriguing question.

Environmental information and "everyone"

Let us consider what these chimpanzees are doing by piecing together the information at hand: the fruiting characteristics of *ilombo*, the characteristic of *ilombo* fruit feeding and the assembly-dispersal phenomenon.

Firstly, what happens at the start of the *ilombo* feeding season? At first glance, it would seem natural to start consuming *ilombo* fruit when it becomes available. However, intensive feeding on not yet abundant *ilombo* fruit is unlikely to be a simple reaction to an environmental change.

Why they move in a large nomadic party when members do not eat together on the same patch also remains unclear. Another characteristic is that they range over an extensive area at the same time. Theoretically, animals are predicted to travel longer distances where food availability is low relative to group size, or where small food patches are scattered (Wrangham et al. 1993; Chapman et al. 1995). If so, they are traveling a wide range due to aggregation, thus they are behaving in an inefficient way.

Some studies interpret the presence of other individuals at the site of feeding as something more than competition. K. Adachi (2003) regards feeding behavior as ongoing communication that generates social systems. For individuals selecting their next action "in a constantly changing environment", gaining knowledge about "where food is, the quantity of food that is expected to be found there and places to be avoided, through observation of the ranging patterns, feeding behaviors and vocal communication of other individuals" is of practical importance (K. Adachi 2003: 221). Distinct from information based on one's own cognition, which is called private information, such information based on others' cognition is called public information (see K. Adachi 2003).

For the behaviors of other individuals to function as public information, it is essential that they are visible. However, our question here is about the process that generates the phenomenon in which scattered chimpanzees feed on the same food and travel in concert where they cannot see who is eating what, where and when. Moreover, the conditions could be unfavorable in terms of food availability, as mentioned above.

Considering that availability of *ilombo* fruit tends to increase steadily once it enters a fruiting cycle regardless of the year in question, it is conceivable that the "sign" of environmental change in the setting of *ilombo* fruit is so reliable that it can be taken as information that "fruit availability will increase from now on". It is likely to be "predictable" also for the chimpanzees as regular consumers of *ilombo* fruit. This can be classified as private rather than public information in the sense that it is not based on others' cognition. However, this private information cannot be the sole determinant of the actual behavior of individual chimpanzees. The behavior relates to intensive feeding on not yet abundant *ilombo* fruit, traveling an extensive area and the concerted nature of this behavior. What if the above private information is tied to the act of "ranging and eating with everyone"?

Apart from the early fruiting period we have been looking at, the peak of the *ilombo* season certainly meets the conditions that support the formation of a large nomadic party, even though chimpanzees do not need to do so. If the experience of "ranging with everyone during the *ilombo* season" has been repeated and accumulated as "what we do", it may not be far-fetched to think that chimpanzees have come to repeat the behavior that creates this phenomenon triggered by an environmental change in the form of *ilombo* fruit-setting. For example, with regard to recurring events (such as experiments), chimpanzees in captivity behave as if they are "guessing" in advance what they will be doing based on which human attendants have arrived, which equipment or room is used and so on[3]. When the stable yearly *ilombo* fruiting pattern and everyone's similar behavioral pattern in relation to it are repeated, the private information and the "prediction" that other individuals will act the same way may overlap. At this point the information that "*ilombo* has begun to bear fruit" can turn into public information, even though this is perhaps an exceptional case in the sense that other individuals' behaviors are not visible.

I would like to add two points to reinforce the above notion. The formation of a large nomadic party as immense as M group, which continues for several months, has not been observed at other study sites (Itoh and Nishida 2007). In the first place, there have been few reports of such a large nomadic party. This is partially attributable to a lack of abundant *ilombo* or equivalent fruit food. While *ilombo* grows abundantly in the home range of M group, it is not so ubiquitous in the home ranges of neighboring groups whose ranging patterns appear to be different, although they are yet to be ascertained. Accordingly, the public information of M group referred to here is for those who live in their home range. Females who have immigrated from another unit-group to M group follow other chimpanzees for a period of time (Itoh 2013), perhaps because each group has its own public information, of which chimpanzees can "know" only by experiencing it, and without which they cannot live their lives in the group.

"Everyone" does not necessarily have to mean "all". In fact, it is not that all unit-group members assemble in the range of visibility. Some male-female pairs may range away from "everyone", some may have died, others may have been born and yet others may have immigrated from another unit-group or emigrated from M group, hence it is impossible to know "all members" at any given time. Yet, the fact that a large number of chimpanzees who spend time scattered across a large area undertake action selection based on the "prediction" that an invisible "everyone" will do so suggests, in my view, the existence of a *social* group in the image of "everyone" or "we" for them as well as a *social* group created through the concrete action of fission-fusion.

When chimpanzees meet

As we have seen above, M group chimpanzees engage in various kinds of action selection including fission-fusion and assembling or dispersing based on the "prediction" of how "everyone" will behave. Even after numerous observations, there is a gap between the actual behaviors of the chimpanzees and researchers' expectations of them along the lines of "They must have gathered because they wanted to interact with the others" or "They must have a lot of gossip (correction: grooming) to exchange after long separation". Chimpanzees may appear pleased to meet each other and then not do anything together or immediately part company. Their apparent indifference or ambivalence baffles us. This can be rephrased as a lack of direction in terms of action selection at the time of meeting. This lack of direction seems to be rooted in their mode of coexistence that permits both separation and approach.

In this section, I explore why action selection is problematic for chimpanzees by looking at examples of this lack of direction and relating them to their mode of coexistence. These examples entail scenes of encounter. Studies on interaction normally address explicit social interactions that have taken place. However, I would like to proceed here without being overly constrained by the definition of social interaction. Please refer to the "Definitions" text box below for the terms used in the analysis.

Complexity, unpredictability and nonequilibrium of encounter

As explained in other chapters, chimpanzees are known to engage in a wide range of social interactions, including play, grooming, greeting and vocal communication as well as food sharing, peering, fighting and display, in various

> **Definitions**
>
> **Visual contact:** The moment at which another individual enters the field of vision of the target individual (assumed from researcher's view) is regarded as the start of visual contact. Contact is regarded as ended when the individual goes out of sight for longer than one minute.
>
> **Episode:** As long as the membership composition does not change, the party is treated as one episode regardless of whether the target individual is alone or in visual contact with other individuals. A new episode begins as soon as there is a change of membership. It is synonymous with the temporal party mentioned at the beginning of the chapter.
>
> Notes
> 1. As movements of infants and babies are often hard to monitor continuously, only adults and youths are included in the analysis.
> 2. Only completed episodes are included in the analysis.

combinations of individuals from adults to babies (Photo 7.2). Yet, in reality these explicit interactions do not happen frequently as demonstrated in Figure 7.2. Four target chimpanzees had 134 episodes of visual contact with a total of 115 individuals, which consisted of new or repeat contact with seventy-six members.

Various interactions were observed during the 556 minute follow of the four target adult females, including grooming, other types of physical contact, peering, begging, vocalizing and fighting, but the number of these interactions was very small. Opal had more interactions than the others, but they were mostly vocal and the data was generally influenced by the "uproar" that was heard as chimpanzees in the vicinity vocalized frequently[4].

Each episode generally does not last long, although the definition of an episode is purely operational. Episodes tend to last longer in small parties with one to three members. However, it would be overly hasty to assume that episodes last longer because fewer members are involved.

Three of the four longest episodes (eighty–100 minutes) involved the target individuals being alone (or with a baby or infant). The other episode happened during the focal follow of an adult male (Dogura), who joined two other adult males (Hanby and Fanana).

In this case, these three males stayed together for approximately 100 minutes from one to three o'clock in the afternoon. When Dogura was traveling, Hanby joined him first, followed by Fanana one minute later. The three produced a chorus of pant-hoots (long-distance calls), then continued traveling. Nine minutes later, Fanana began to eat the leaves of a shrub along the way while Dogura and Hanby at the front began to climb a tree. Three minutes later, the three chorused again,

Photo 7.2 Various forms of social interaction: Grooming, peering, meat-sharing (from top)

but the two in the tree transitioned to loud vocalizations called "food-grunts" and began to eat fruit.[5] After a one-minute delay, Fanana climbed the same tree and the three ate noisily as they uttered food-grunts. They finished eating in fifteen

Duality of the Mode of Coexistence and Action Selection 153

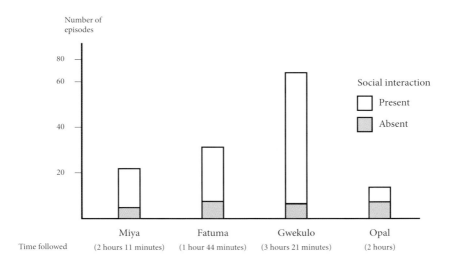

Figure 7.2 Breakdown of episodes per target individual (interacted and did not interact)

Note: Data is from four adult females continually followed for longer than one hour (October 1997).

minutes, traveled for three minutes, and again began feeding in another fruit tree. They made a move again after sixteen minutes during which they chorused twice, and thirteen minutes later they finally settled down and groomed each other. After grooming for forty minutes, the episode ended when Fanana left and Hanby followed him.

The following characteristics can be found in this example. Firstly, multiple activities are undertaken over time, including traveling, feeding and resting at different locations. They also frequently vocalized together. Even for a few members to stay together, they must make a certain degree of "effort" in synchronizing activities—their timing and location—and in this example, also vocalization.

Why does this situation come about? Not only do they engage in explicit social interactions infrequently, they also part ways quickly when they have a "much-awaited" (perhaps only in the eyes of researchers) encounter with another chimpanzee. Figure 7.3 presents data on the duration of visual contact collected from twenty-two adult males and females I followed for one year in 1997–1998. It is evident that a majority of encounters were over in one to two minutes. In the aforementioned case of Dogura, he met Fanana twice and Hanby once during the subsequent three hour follow, but he did not spend more than a minute with

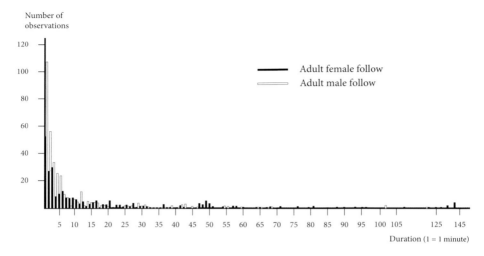

Figure 7.3 Frequency distribution of the length of time the target individual spent with another individual in visual contact

them aside from his first reencounter with Fanana (one hour after the previous encounter), during which they ate fruit and traveled together for thirty-four minutes.

Their successive partings, no matter how many individuals they have visual contact with, inevitably lead to successive encounters with other individuals. While this is the very mode of their coexistence, it also becomes a major disruptive force in the sense that it brings unpredictability and nonequilibrium to the stability of the party membership composition, including the case of being alone and the conduct of explicit social interactions in individual situations.

This disturbed condition occasionally leads to a certain state of equilibrium as the number of members increases. Such situation rarely happens, but when it does, a large number of members come together and the assembly lasts for one to two hours. Although the definition of an episode does not apply to this situation as the membership fluctuates, I would like to examine the situation as it is important for our understanding of what it means for chimpanzees to be at the place of assembly.

The largest aggregation was observed during the focal follow of an adult female, Gwekulo. She remained in the same location, a large fruit tree, for more than two hours. As soon as she reached the tree, other members began to arrive from various directions. Eventually almost all members of the unit-group were assembled. The duration of the actual feeding was not particularly long; Gwekulo ate for about thirty minutes, then lay down clutching a fruit-bearing branch and did not engage with others. Other individuals were acting in a similar fashion around the large fruit tree; they rested, left and returned, moved to two different neighboring fruit tree species to eat, and all casually "hung out" on the spot.

Meat-eating also tends to attract chimpanzees from far and wide from the hunting stage that precedes it (Hosaka 1997). Although many do not participate in hunting itself, they busy themselves by uttering loud vocalizations, watching over the activity and so on. Even when they miss out on the direct sharing of meat pieces, if they search carefully they may be able to find the specks of meat or bone fragments that fell to the ground when the meat was divided up. As in hunting, some chimpanzees simply remain in proximity without attempting to participate in the meat sharing.

In another well-known phenomenon, chimpanzees gather one after another at a place of grooming (Nakamura 2003a). Again, not all individuals fully engage in grooming; some spend time half asleep or groom only intermittently.

Disturbance and problem identification
Chimpanzees' mode of coexistence, fission-fusion, is essentially inconsistent with staying with the same members continuously or all members gathering and staying in one location. Nonetheless, the way "everyone" gathers or attempts to stay together by synchronizing activities and/or vocalization appears to suggest that they do not always "want" to stay apart.

Activity synchronization, which was observed when a small number of members remained together for an extended period of time, was also seen in large gatherings centered on hunting and meat-eating, large and complex food patches and grooming. This implies that on deciding how to relate (including the choice not to relate) when chimpanzees meet others, the key may not only be whether there is room for participation, spatially and behaviorally, but also whether the activity in situ is clear. Chancing upon others and not knowing what they are doing is an uncomfortable situation for humans. If you opened a door inadvertently and found a group of people talking quietly, you would likely be inclined to close the door gently and walk away. Chimpanzees may also be inclined to leave quietly when they come across a scene that is not instantly comprehensible. I use the term "clarity of context" below to describe the clarity of "what to do" in situ.

Another observed tendency was that direct interactions do not occur easily when chimpanzees meet. This will require further analysis, but chimpanzees do not seem to leap straight into approaching or passing others upon encountering them.

Although, as described in the above section, chimpanzees rely on what "everyone" would do without any guarantee of outcome when they encounter others, they do not immediately make an approach and start, for example, grooming. They instead exhibit a degree of hesitation. It is not easy to initiate a direct interaction anytime, anywhere.

While this is likely to be related to the aforementioned clarity of context, at the same time it is a challenging issue for social interaction studies. There have been various studies about patterns and forms of action "after" the initiation of interaction. However, such patterns and forms are irrelevant to the question of "whether to initiate an interaction or not". The answer depends solely on action selections made by the individuals present. In the case of chimpanzees, the everyday source of the identification of the problem of action selection, irrespective of whether interactions are initiated or not, lies in their mode of coexistence, which can be described as disturbance at the scene of encounter. The unpredictability and nonequilibrium of encounters in which one does not know when, where or who in terms of the arrival and departure of others, and one is not directed as to whether to approach or move away upon meeting, increase the complexity of each encounter and this is where action selection is identified as a problem.

Putting these characteristics together, it appears that the clarity of the context of the scene where other members are already participating provides an important foothold on which one can initiate direct or indirect involvement through activity synchronization (e.g., eating). In particular, the frequency of meeting and parting is very high when chimpanzees form large nomadic parties. Considering that one meets with and parts from so many individuals on so many occasions, it would perhaps be impractical to conduct various interactions at each encounter. On the other hand, the seemingly "unnecessary" synchronization of activities such as feeding and traveling appears to be a valuable communication, continuous with direct interaction, for the chimpanzees for the very reason that they are unnecessary.

To recapitulate, individual chimpanzees make a certain kind of "effort" to interact with others directly and indirectly at the unpredictable and individual-specific scenes of encounter. However, their mode of coexistence is not predisposed toward such involvement on a routine basis. Their mode of coexistence, fission-fusion, which equally permits approach and separation, thus serves as a catalyst that compels action selection at the scene of encounter. From another perspective, being compelled to choose which action to take indicates that a problem has been identified.

The jumbled world

The image of institution

The word "institution" probably conjures up images of faceless norms and rules that control the internal workings of large anonymous conglomerates where their entirety is unclear to us, including nations, corporations, universities and so on. It may also be associated with the sanctions that are imposed on breaches of these norms and rules. Or rather, sanctions are considered to be part of the norms and rules. These images suggest that institutions are expected to bring orderliness to conglomerates.

Conversely, these images convey the sense that disorder would prevail without these rules and norms. In order to regulate the potentially dangerous encounters that could happen in a disorderly state, it was considered that human relations needed to be regulated by rules such as dominant-subordinate relationships and rank order. This reverse image has been developed through studies of animal behavior hand-in-hand with human studies (Haraway 2000[1991]).

Similar views are also found in communication studies. In his overview of the discipline, Mizutani (1997) critically points out that many of its works have turned into "books of manners". What is called a "book of manners" here roughly refers to a set of detailed rules, or institutions as systems of (constitutive) rules, found in communication. Here, following such rules is considered to ensure smooth communication.

Social group as a mode of coexistence

The reality of institution is, however, not as regular as one hopes, and is not even consistently positive in nature[6]. What has come to light in the study of the history of modern European institutions is the reality that institutions are a medley of conventions and rules, which were preexisting or created in various ages and places, and that they did not originate from single sources (Omoda 2011). Moreover, these conventions and rules can be trivial or sometimes even born of malicious intent. People are able to live without difficulty even though very few have an intimate or full knowledge of institutions, perhaps because these institutions are built upon conventions that exist on a level where we have no awareness of "why we are doing so" or "that we are doing so".

The same applies to communication. Mizutani (1997) compares the notion of institution as a system of rules with the concept of a form of life as an aggregate of the rules of a language game (Wittgenstein), and points out that unambiguous purposes or goals cannot be set or do not exist in everyday communication. He argues that the communication model "controlled by external ethical or teleological principles" excludes much, if not all, of "mere conversation (chattering)" (Mizutani 1997: 24). This type of communication is "autotelic communication" conducted purely for the enjoyment of communication and with no other purpose unlike, say, communication for the purpose of consensus building at conferences that actually occupies only a very small part of our daily reality. Mizutani states that this type of communication is fundamental to communication in the sense that "debate is impossible where there is no possibility of conversation, but conversation is possible where there is no possibility of debate" (1997: 26).

What is important in Mizutani's argument relevant to the discussion here is that our actual interaction with others is not an externally controlled act of following the rules, even though it appears as if we act according to the rules and as if our social life and communication would fall into disorder without them. This is a phenomenon rather similar to Wittgenstein's "language game" or Austin's "convention" that is more obscure, yet generating from the continual involvement with other people and sometimes creating a new pattern by doing so.

Seen in this light, it is clear that "institutional phenomenon" is contiguous to and almost indistinguishable from "*social* group" as the mode of coexistence. It is impossible to single out and extract something called institution. Yet, there remains a "nebulous feeling" that it is inseparable from the mode of coexistence, but somewhat different from it. I would like to address this point below.

The mode of coexistence and externalization

While implementation is important for the mode of coexistence, it is the possibility of deviation from the institution that is important for the institution. In other words, a *social* group is formed when, and only when, it is implemented and an existing *social* group simply disappears if implementation happens to fail, and it has neither a reason for existence nor a meaning in itself. On the other hand, an institution cannot simply disappear when it is not implemented. Institution is mentioned and has a reason to exist when an institution is not implemented or there is such a possibility. This negation itself is not the focus of discussion in this chapter (but see Chapter Twelve by Adachi). Here I would like to consider the foundations underpinning this negation. The most expedient way is the verbalization of conventions, which are already implemented as the mode of coexistence. The verbalization that takes place here refers to an act of extracting the form of the individual convention of "what we do" that is generated by the mode of coexistence and making it referentiable—the externalization of conventions, so to speak.

Of the externalization based on formalization, the form of interaction used as "what we do" practiced by chimpanzees at the level of social interaction is discussed in other chapters of this volume as well (Chapters Four, Six, Eight and Eleven). This chapter has been exploring the possibility of a different path of generating "what we do" by addressing the form in terms of a phenomenon manifesting in a manner directly connected to the group level.

The section above entitled "Everyone does so" was an attempt to demonstrate that it is not the case that chimpanzees live alone and happen to encounter other individuals who happen to use the same area, but that they do have some image of a "group" in which they are involved, although it is not necessarily identical to a unit-group abstracted and conceptualized by humans (observers). This has been deduced from the possibility that recurring experiences of environmental change and the movements of others overlap and coalesce into the environmental change, "*ilombo* starts to fruit", as public information. If this reasoning is valid, it follows that the conventions of "everyone does so" and "what we do" manifest in a way directly connected to the group phenomenon without relying on face-to-face interactions.

This is linked to the "facelessness" mentioned above in relation to the image of institution. If recurrent experiences of a collective phenomenon alone can establish an action selection option, without being forced by someone or without any need to do so, there are no specific faces attached to that option. "Everyone" for chimpanzees has no identifiable bounds and no visibility; it is backed by their experience of the collective phenomenon of ranging together during the assembly season. These repetitive experiences play an important role in the dispersal season as well. In selecting one's own action, the "prediction" that "everyone" will do so and the "prediction" itself manifest every year as one option.

Chimpanzees do so because they may gain "something good" as a result. However, the key point is that there may be "something good", but it is only realized when everyone acts in a concerted manner. In other words, they can gain "something good" only if they all do it together, just as we gain enjoyment by engaging in conversation (Mizutani 1997).

The fact that it is optional and that "something good" is not something necessary means that its implementation is not guaranteed. In the group phenomenon involving M group members ranging together, they have an option not to do so, i.e., to act separately from everyone else, and in fact such behavior has been observed.

It is perhaps not so strange to identify an autotelic aspect of the phenomenon if we look at it from the standpoint of the phenomenon that generates from one's action selection by relying on the expectation of what everyone else will do where there is no guarantee in the sense that the option not to do so (= to act separately) is available as a normal action. I will touch on this point later in relation to the "problem".

The conversion from a recurring experience into "what we do" can be described as a physicalization of experience. The nonverbal experience of "everyone does so" in chimpanzees overlaps the argument of Omoda (2011: 106) in deciphering Foucault's *Discipline and Punish* (2010[1977]):

> People who are accustomed to disciplinarian authority are trained to increase productivity in every part of their body, and in this sense acquire high skills. At the same time, however, they accept obedience to command and almost subconscious subservience to orders. You may think of soldiers who repeat stylized actions directed by the call of an officer, or students who intently take notes in the classroom, or workers who silently attend an assembly-line.

In terms of the theme of this chapter, the emphasis of Omoda's argument is that we willingly or inadvertently devote ourselves to these tasks. The repeated experience of doing something together promotes a subconscious physical response to similar situations. While not only soldiers, students and workers but also people who patiently stand in line and spectators who react to every move in a sporting event may be doing so for their own purposes, they naturally and willingly launch themselves into the actions that are happening around them. Without the experience of "it is my own action that coexists with others' actions", perhaps a fear of deviation cannot come into being.

We may think that humans are taught "what to do" in words. However, the learning of "what we should do" happens when humans are tamed without realizing it through the repetition, or forced repetition, of the same behavior, as described above. It is impossible to make us act exactly as directed when we are directed only in language. This is obvious if we remember that voluminous and detailed manuals can only frustrate our next action selection. The same is probably true for rituals (Fukushima 2001) as well as the forms of various interactions in animals.

Problem solving

The application of the form of interaction as "what we do" to problem solving in a face-to-face situation is discussed in detail by Nishie (Chapter Six) and Kitamura

(Chapter Eleven). The important key here was the "problem to be solved". Authors successfully extracted how a form of interaction underpinned by a "bottomless reason" (Chapter Six) was referenced as an available option. The success is based on their methodology involving the identification of the problem to be solved in advance. However, the way chimpanzees identify the problem is still veiled. The section entitled "When chimpanzees meet" was an attempt to explore this issue.

It is not easy for chimpanzees to immediately initiate interaction anywhere or at any time, or even to stay in the place where interaction might occur. Although they may choose their next action relying on "what everyone does" that is yet to happen, or use the forms of interactions that can be referenced as "what everyone does", these things do not guarantee the implementation of interactions. Furthermore, encounters happen one after another. These encounters have much scope for freedom of choice, which characterizes their mode of coexistence under which they are able to choose to either approach or leave and not be inclined one way or the other. For individual chimpanzees, a scene of encounter is always one at which they are pressed to make an action selection. Being pressed to select an action means that a "problem" has been identified. In this sense, the "problem" is an ordinary, day-to-day occurrence, and does not need to be something special. This type of "problem" may be too trivial to call a problem that needs to be "solved". This is also the case with the problem that arises in the decision to range with "everyone", as discussed in the early part of the chapter.

On reflection, a majority of the conventions surrounding us are quite trivial. For instance, we greet when we meet acquaintances. This is not an act of serious problem solving, and a failure to greet the other is not fatal for us. Yet, we sometimes agonize over whether or not we should greet, when we should greet, what we should say and so on. A similar situation occurs in operating rooms at the leading edge of modern medicine. It is "believed" that only the bottom two-thirds of the inner surface of a container is clean while the rest of it is "unclean", even though the container is thoroughly sterilized. If a surgical instrument comes into contact with this "unclean" part, it can no longer be used in the operation (Mima 2012). This triviality in itself perhaps creates the cultural diversity of conventions.

However trivial the problem may be, the fact that there is action selection (= problem identification) is important in itself. The trivial problems that occur in the daily lives of chimpanzees stem from fission-fusion as their mode of coexistence. On the other hand, as their mode of coexistence is generated by recurring encounters, it and the emergence of the problem are in a circular relationship where both are built upon each other. As long as recurring encounters continue to generate their mode of coexistence, it indicates that interactions are taking place in those encounters. However, being under their mode of coexistence and how to act at each encounter are different issues for chimpanzees. For example, one can foresee that there will be encounters with others if one plunges into the experience of ranging together with "everyone". When one encounters another, however, one is pressed to choose an action = it is identified as a problem. If looked at from the outside, the simultaneous occurrence of these two phenomena might appear absurd. Nonetheless, the experience of difference between their mode of coexistence (= *social* group) generated by recurring encounters and the individual and concrete encounters generated by their mode of coexistence, upon which one is pressed to make an action selection, can offer us a different perspective about the relationship between institution and group that we normally assume.

The daily experience of the difference between institution and group, despite being in a circular relationship, creates the illusion of being able to externally control the mode of coexistence (= *social* group). When conventions and rules are extracted in the form of language and codified in bundles, this illusion becomes even more realistic. However, an illusion is still an illusion. These institutions quite often become hindrances to problem solving or cause an inability to solve problems at a concrete level of the mode of coexistence. This is why institutions sometimes need to be rewritten according to specific situations. The "nebulous feeling" that institution and the mode of coexistence are indivisible yet not identical perhaps emanates from experiencing difference and/or the illusion of their complete separation when identifying problems anew in individual action selection, even though the problems and the form of problem solving are created by the very mode of coexistence.

Finally, I would like to sum up my argument so far, entailing "everyone", "what we do" and problem identification. The mode of coexistence (= *social* group) and institution are inseparable partly because the former is the underlying support for institution and moreover the content of institution is backed by various conventions in the form of "what we do" that are created by the mode of coexistence. A convention that has become "everyone does so" through repetition is something that is maintained as a result of everyone actually doing so. Inevitability is not particularly important here, and not everyone always has to follow the convention. A convention just manages to exist where the option of "not doing so" always exists at some level.

The above may be rephrased as follows. In an institutional phenomenon, it appears that, facing the object for which an order is to be created, there is something external that acts to maintain the order of the object. However, the object to which an order is to be brought is in fact the actual condition of what we call an order itself and there is no realm exclusively inhabited by institution. Consequently, any attempt to discover the glorious moment of the birth of institution will end up with nothing, as has already been demonstrated in Foucault's pursuit of the history of discipline (2010[1977]).

I initially thought that it would be difficult to discuss institution and the mode of coexistence in the indivisible relationship in languageless animals separately. Yet, the exploration of this indivisible relationship may be important in considering human institutions as well. We know from past history, and are painfully aware especially after 3.11, that the illusion of external control sometimes creates nightmares instead of order or security. Life becomes harder in a world in which institutions have taken on lives of their own.

8 When Keeping One's Ears Open for the Distant Voices of Others: The Process-Oriented Convention in Chimpanzees and Institution

Shunkichi Hanamura

Key ideas

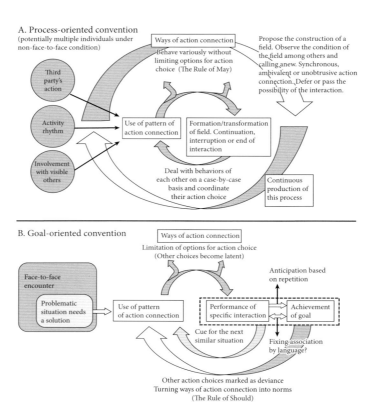

Chimpanzees, who live in a group in which members meet and part repeatedly, sometimes exchange long-distance vocalizations with one another. By using vocal exchange as a "call-response" pattern of action connection, they accomplish a non-face-to-face encounter and create a field that enables them to continue their further interaction with the expectation of being co-present. They behave in diverse ways depending on the situation while coordinating their action choice according to one another's behaviors. Consequently, fields are formed and transformed among various individuals and interactions sometimes continue intermittently or end abruptly. The process-oriented convention (A) that produces the continuation of this process can be regarded as a potential alternative mode of institution as distinct from the goal-oriented convention (B) in humans.

Conventions in the languageless world

In this chapter I examine the "devices" that help individuals in group living make each other's actions understandable when they interact, along with the dynamics of the interactions produced as a result, as an underlying phenomenon of "institution". Institution in this sense supports group living, and through it members coordinate ways of associating with each other. It is generally thought that institutions are unique to humans and underpinned by language. Since language is also an institution, however, the exploration of the possibility of institutions in a languageless world is an important approach in deepening our understanding of institutional phenomena (Kuroda 1999, Chapter Eighteen).

Let us use the term "*encounter*" to describe the state where two animals are both aware that "the other party is aware of my presence". In such a situation, it seems impossible for one to choose a particular action and to expect the other party to do so, because there are theoretically infinite possibilities in terms of choices of action. Yet in reality, according to the context, how to connect one another's actions has been patterned among group-living individuals and by using such "*patterns of action connection*", they can narrow down their choices of action. The patterns of action connection, through repetitive use, are gradually shared and conventionalized, as "what not only oneself but also everyone else uses". It is thought that interactions using such a pattern come to mean the same event to everyone, including those who just see or hear the interaction.

Humans make each other's actions understandable by using various patterns of action connection, mainly in face-to-face conditions. For instance, interactions using the pattern of "bowing to each other" signify a "greeting" in some contexts to people living in Japan. Chimpanzees, without language, also engage in pattern-using interactions such as the "pant-grunt" (see Chapter Six) and "hand-clasped grooming" (see Chapter Eleven) in face-to-face conditions.

These patterns of action connection in humans and chimpanzees do not exist independently of their respective group lives. "When and who chooses which action" using a certain pattern can vary depending on the situation and each individual's position or activity on that occasion. In human greeting for instance, the same pair of individuals sometimes greets each other and sometimes does not; or when one team composed of multiple individuals encounter another such party, two particular individuals from the different teams may greet each other and not the rest. I shall call such ways of coordinating pattern-using action choice "*ways of action connection*" below.

Humans at least reproduce a specific interaction stably by mutually coordinating their action choices through the use of one or more patterns of action connection in a certain way, while having the mutual expectation that "everyone does so in this situation". In the case of "greeting" for example, when two acquaintances meet, they perform an appropriate pattern-using interaction by limiting their action choices as "what we should do in this situation", and by doing so they create a certain order (the *goal*) for the occasion (see Chapter Eleven). In the case of children's "play" (see Chapter Four), participants enjoy the *process* of repeating an interaction using patterns such as "chase-chased" and/or "hide-seek" by mutually expecting the other to use the pattern, but not limiting their action choices (see the final section of this chapter for details). As shown in these two examples, a way of connecting action in a given interaction can perhaps be called a "*convention*" when it is practiced with the mutual assumption that everyone will coordinate their respective action choice in the specific way. In other words, when a pattern of action connection is conventionalized, the way of using the pattern must be conventionalized at the same time, and humans produce various specific interactions stably according to such conventions.

In this chapter, I treat such conventions as the underlying phenomena of institutions and focus on the reality of conventions in wild chimpanzees who do not have language. More specifically, I analyze the ways of action connection via long-distance vocalizations and the dynamics of the resulting interactions in chimpanzees. However, we must keep in mind that chimpanzees and humans have formed different societies after our common ancestor evolved into different species. Moreover, interactions via long-distance vocalizations are practiced in non-face-to-face conditions potentially in the presence of multiple others, as introduced in the next section. Consequently, I explore the commonality (foundation in evolutionary history) between chimpanzee and human conventions as well as the potentiality for chimpanzee institutions as distinct from human institutions, rather than the beginning of pre-language human institutions in chimpanzee societies.

Fission-fusion and long-distance vocalization (pant-hoots)

While chimpanzees form a lasting group ("unit-group") with stable membership, aside from the birth, death and inter-group transferring of individuals, members of the group show a unique grouping pattern called "fission-fusion", that is, they repeatedly meet and part (see Chapter Seven). The focal following of a chimpanzee finds three to four others on average in the range of visibility, but the lineup can change at any time and it is impossible to predict when, where and with whom the target chimpanzee will meet and part company. Chimpanzees who have parted sometimes meet each other again a few hours later, and sometimes do not meet again for several weeks or months.

I have been studying the M group (comprised of approximately sixty members) of Mahale, Tanzania (fieldwork was undertaken for one year from 2005 to 2006 and four months between 2012 and 2014). Since they range in undulating forest with low visibility and their home range is almost thirty square kilometers, it is difficult to find chimpanzees by just roaming around the forest. One thing I can rely on under such conditions is the voices of chimpanzees. In particular, a long-distance vocalization called a pant-hoot can travel one to two kilometers if conditions are right. The pant-hoot is a stylized vocalization lasting five to fifteen seconds and consists of repeated cycles of aspiratory and inspiratory sounds, usually beginning with a low-volume introduction, followed by a progressively louder buildup and reaching a high-volume climax. The pant-hoot is produced in various contexts, such as during or at the start of traveling, during feeding or upon arrival at a feeding tree, while making a bed in a tree at night, upon meeting with other chimpanzees and so on (Goodall 1986). Nevertheless, sonographic analysis found almost no consistent difference in the acoustic features between pant-hoots produced in different contexts (Notman and Rendall 2005), and hence it is not possible to identify the context in which pant-hoots are produced outside of the visible range.

Because of their fission-fusion grouping, chimpanzees who are located by the sound of their pant-hoots constitute only part of the M group members. Moreover, pant-hoots do not ring out constantly from outside of the visible range in the course of observation: on some occasions, many pant-hoots are heard from all over the place within a matter of minutes, and at other times no forms of vocalization are heard for days. Chimpanzees do not always even aggregate within range of hearing each other's pant-hoots. Accordingly, two parties may be far apart beyond the hearing range or may pass close by without even noticing. As such, it is likely that not only human observers but also the target chimpanzees are not able to know where other members are unless they are in visible contact or hear pant-hoots or other vocalizations from them.

While chimpanzees lead this way of group living, they sometimes emit pant-hoots in chorus with other individuals within the visible range, and individuals outside of the visible range sometimes emit pant-hoots in response. These phenomena suggest that some sort of interactions take place via pant-hoots among individuals at some distance from and out of sight of each other. In the next section, I first introduce a conventionalized pattern of pant-hoot exchange used by the M group chimpanzees and discuss the meaning of interactions using the "pattern of action connection".

As I became more familiar with their pant-hoots, I was sometimes able to identify individual chimpanzees by their pant-hoots from outside the visible range, or I could tell the vocalizer's sex and/or age-class from the characteristics of the sound. It has been reported that when a trained chimpanzee in captivity heard recordings of single or two-individual-chorusing pant-hoots emitted by her peers, she choose the correct vocalizer(s) from photographs; thus it is thought that chimpanzees can identify individuals by their pant-hoots (Kojima et al. 2003). In the wild, however, it is likely that they, like me, are unable to identify vocalizers all the time due to factors such as distance and hearing a pant-hoot chorus emitted by multiple individuals or a mixture of other vocalizations[1].

Pattern of pant-hoot exchange

Chimpanzees often do not respond to pant-hoots heard from outside of the visible range. When they do, however, my analysis using data from the focal following of various M group chimpanzees shows that almost ninety percent of pant-hoots emitted by the target individual within one minute of the pant-hoots heard from outside of the visible range were produced within ten seconds from the completion of the incoming pant-hoots (For the results of a preliminary analysis see Hanamura 2010b). In other words, pant-hoot exchanges between distant and invisible chimpanzees mostly occur within ten seconds.

Moreover, vocalizers of the initial pant-hoots are sometimes seen to stay motionless for ten seconds or so after their utterances. Considering that a majority of pant-hoot exchanges occur within ten seconds, this "*silence right after the end of uttering a pant-hoot*" can be interpreted as the vocalizers' behavior to keep their ears open for a "response" from other individuals to their own voice; and it is conceivable that the vocalizers in exhibiting this behavior have uttered the pant-hoot as a "call" to other individuals (Hanamura 2010a, 2010b).

When a pant-hoot is heard from outside the visible range, sometimes chimpanzees not only stop the activities they have been engaged in, such as traveling or feeding, or turn to the direction of the voice, but also continue to stay

Photo 8.1 Zola (adult female) and her daughter Zuhura, turn toward the sound of a pant-hoot from outside the visible range

motionless for ten seconds or so after the end of the voice. This *"silence continuing even after the end of hearing a distant pant-hoot"* can be interpreted as the hearers' behavior to keep their ears open for a "response" from other individuals to the voice; and it is conceivable that the hearers in exhibiting this behavior are listening for the possible pant-hoot exchange between other individuals as a "call" and "response" set (Hanamura 2010a, 2010b).

Although these behaviors of listening for responses after uttering/hearing a pant-hoot, especially those obvious enough to record as "silence", are not observed frequently, they have been confirmed in many individuals. Accordingly, it is believed that the pant-hoot exchange within ten seconds is used as a pattern of action connection that takes on the meaning of "call-response" among M group chimpanzees, including vocalizers and hearers as well as responders. In other words, the uttering of and listening for a pant-hoot using this pattern has been conventionalized at least in M group, and because this pattern has become "something used by not only oneself but also everyone else", it has become possible for the vocalizer to listen for a response from other individuals and for the hearer to listen for a pant-hoot exchange between other individuals.

It is conceivable that chimpanzees accomplish "non-face-to-face encounters" by exchanging pant-hoots using this pattern and make "who is interacting with whom now" understandable to each other, including hearers listening for a pant-hoot exchange between others. As I mentioned in the opening section of this chapter, however, interactions using a "pattern of action connection" need to be analyzed in combination with the ways of coordinating the individual's action choice according to the situation and each individual's position or activity on that occasion. I will examine below the "ways of action connection" in interactions via pant-hoots and the dynamics of the resultant interactions.

Ways of action connection when attempting to interact

Proposing the construction of a field

What is the state of the non-face-to-face encounter? How do chimpanzees accomplish the encounter using the pattern of pant-hoot exchange and continue interacting with invisible others they have not been involved with before that moment? I will introduce a typical way this occurs by referring to Case 1 below.

Case 1 (4 April 2006)
I had moved my observation point several times during the morning to wait for chimpanzee vocalizations, but I heard none. At **13:50**, I found Darwin (adult male) and Christmas (young male) slowly heading west along an observation trail, foraging along the way. At **15:03**, the two reached an intersection with another observation trail running north-south and rested, and eventually resumed traveling and headed south slowly along the observation trail while foraging.

15:56:00 A chorus of pant-hoots (presumably—see Note 1—the voices of one adult male and multiple females) rang out about 500 meters to the east. Darwin and Christmas paused, turning their face/ear to the east and remained motionless.
15:56:10 Several seconds after the end of the vocalization, the pair began running southward while producing a chorus of pant-hoots [Response].
15:56:20 They finished vocalizing, traveled for a short distance, then sat down on the observation trail.
15:56:45 The pair resumed traveling, but repeatedly paused at different times and remained motionless for five seconds or so with their face turned down or forward.

15:57:05 A pant-hoot by one individual (presumably the voice of Pimu, an adult male) rang out from the same place to the east. The pair paused simultaneously and remained motionless.

15:57:10 Just before the voice disappeared, the two began running while producing a chorus of pant-hoots [Response] and headed south at a brisk pace.

15:58:50 They reached an intersection with another observation trail running east-west and headed east without stopping.

15:59:10 The pair sat down on the observation trail.

15:59:45 The pair began running east while producing a chorus of pant-hoots.

15:59:55 After the utterance, the pair paused and remained motionless for ten seconds or so [Silence right after the end of uttering pant-hoots], then resumed traveling east.

16:01:25 The pair reached a hilltop, climbed on a fallen tree and sat down facing east.

16:03:15 The pair got off the fallen tree and resumed traveling, then wandered off the observation trail onto an animal trail, and slowly headed east while foraging.

16:18:00 They reached another observation trail running north-south and sat down.

16:18:25 Soon after Christmas had set off to the north and Darwin had headed south, a pant-hoot chorus rang out somewhere close to the north (the same area as reported at **15:56:00** and **57:05,** but it was to the north as the two had traveled east-southeast). Just before the voices disappeared, Christmas began running northward while producing a pant-hoot [Response], and Darwin returned and began to run after Christmas.

At **16:21,** the pair joined a party feeding in a tree, consisting of Pimu, adult females (Ako, Ikocha, Effie, Totzy and Sally) with their children and young female Jidda. The two visitors fed in the vicinity for about one hour without any explicit interactions aside from pant-grunts uttered by Ikocha to them, and then headed east and parted with the other individuals.

In Case 1 above, Darwin and Christmas did not utter anything nor have visible contact with anyone for at least two hours until a pant-hoot rang out from the east. The vocalizer(s) in the east were therefore presumed to have no way of knowing that the pair was there. As I mentioned above, pant-hoots are produced in various contexts. In some cases, one of which is analyzed in detail below (see section entitled "Deferring or passing the potential for interaction"), pant-hoots seem to be uttered without any expectation of a response. However, like these two chimpanzees (and I as an observer), hearers out of sight of the vocalizer(s) are unable to see them and therefore unable to know clearly in what context the pant-hoot has been produced and whether the vocalizer(s) is expecting a response.

Furthermore, even when the hearers have responded to the vocalizer(s), they are unable to (visually) confirm that the vocalizer(s) has heard their response (i.e., the vocalizer(s) has noticed the presence of the responders).

Under these circumstances, Darwin and Christmas stopped and turned their face/ear to the pant-hoots that suddenly rang out in the east and responded several seconds after the cessation of the sound. After responding to the voice, they sat motionless or paused repeatedly while traveling. When the second pant-hoot rang out from the same location (east), the pair responded quickly, that is, uttered pant-hoots partially overlapping the other party's voice and began running in an excited manner, unlike on the first occasion where there was a short delay between call and response. These behaviors demonstrate that the pair kept their ears open to see if the other party would utter another pant-hoot as a result of their first response and listened to the second pant-hoot from the same location as if it was addressed to them. Therefore, it is possible to say that after responding to the first vocalization, the pair were expecting that "the other party is aware of our presence"—that is, "the other party and we have been encountering".

As suggested by the behavior of waiting for the next vocalization from the other party after responding to the first vocalization, chimpanzees, by responding to the pant-hoots from previously uninvolved other individuals outside of the visible range, accomplish a non-face-to-face encounter with those individuals and create a state that enables them to continue further interaction with the expectation of being co-present from that point (hereafter called a "*field of interaction*" or "*field*"). On this basis, the two chimpanzees' first response and subsequent waiting in Case 1 can be regarded as an attempt to "fabricate", so to speak, such a field, that is, to propose the construction of a field to the other party when it is unclear whether the other party is expecting a response, and to explore the other party's subsequent behavior.

At least in this initial scene of interaction via pant-hoots in Case 1, the interaction continued on the basis of syntonic behaviors on both sides for the construction of a field such that after the pair responded to the first vocalization, one individual in the other party again uttered a pant-hoot and the pair again responded. After the second response, the pair went straight to an observation trail leading in the direction of the voice in the east, traveled east for a short distance and sat down. However, no further voice was heard from the east. The pair shortly afterward produced an initial pant-hoot chorus themselves and listened for responses to the chorus, but there was no response. The pair traveled to a hilltop where voices would be more audible and sat down facing east, but no voice was heard there. They then deviated from an observation trail and resumed foraging while traveling east slowly. About twenty minutes after the first pant-hoot exchange, when another pant-hoot rang out from the same area, Christmas immediately responded and began running and Darwin followed him without responding. The pair (visually) met with the individuals (Pimu and several females) who were presumably part of the party they had exchanged pant-hoots with twice earlier.

As shown in this example, responding to pant-hoots from other individuals outside of the visible range creates the potential for further interaction, but whether or not the interaction actually continues depends on what the other party does next. Importantly, the pair in Case 1 was not making desperate efforts to interact, although they were certainly excited by the two pant-hoot exchanges. Firstly, they took the opportunity afforded by hearing pant-hoots from outside of the visible range to propose constructing a field to the vocalizers; they had not emitted any calls before then. Secondly, when the other party neither responded to their calls nor uttered any vocalizations for some time, the pair resumed foraging as if nothing had happened and did not repeat their calls. Instead, the subsequent third pant-hoot emitted by the other party eventually enabled them to continue the interaction. This series of behaviors taken by the pair demonstrates chimpanzees' basic attitude in dealing with the contingency of the other party's behavior in that they coordinated their action choice according to the action actually chosen by the other party on a case-by-case basis while accepting its contingent nature (responding or uttering another vocalization is a possibility but not a necessity). On the basis of such attitude (see also Hanamura 2010a), the pair in this case seemed to let the course of interaction change depending on what the other party did without bothering about the lack of response or next vocalization while listening or waiting for it.

To sum up, chimpanzees, when attempting to interact with other individuals outside of the visible range, sometimes make an exploratory approach by responding to a vocalization to propose constructing a field, waiting for the next vocalization from the other party and calling themselves if there is no subsequent vocalization, while coordinating their own action choice according to the other party's behaviors each time. Consequently, their interaction can become temporarily frenzied, cease or resume after an intermission depending on what the other party does. It is rather unlikely that there is a prearranged common *goal* for these pant-hoot interactions, such as meeting visually and engaging in some sort of face-to-face interaction or conforming traveling direction through repeated pant-hoot exchanges. In fact, although the two chimpanzees in Case 1 did meet visually with at least some of the individuals who had been presumed to exchange pant-hoots with them, they did not engage in any explicit interactions such as grooming or fighting, aside from receiving a pant-grant, which can be interpreted as a "greeting behavior" (Hayaki 1990). The pair again parted company with the others after feeding with them. In addition, though they were temporarily excited about the repetition of the pant-hoot exchange and might even have enjoyed it, the whole course of interactions in this case was too drawn out to consider that they were enjoying the *process* as "play"; this is a scene of their daily life.

Calling anew while observing the condition of a field among other parties

Case 2 (Hanamura 2010b, revised with additions) shows another way practiced by chimpanzees when attempting to interact with others outside of the visible range. Unlike Case 1, the presence of others at multiple locations outside of the visible range is obvious in this case.

Case 2 (5 April 2006)
While I was waiting to hear chimpanzee vocalizations, I heard three pant-hoots that were not responded to from different locations at around **08:30**. A pant-hoot chorus was heard from another place at **08:35** (one of the voices was presumed to be adult male Alofu's), and I headed toward that location. Although I heard a pant-hoot from another place on the way, I kept going and found Alofu, Kalunde (adult male) and Nkombo (adult female) sitting on an observation trail at **08:51**.

08:54:55 A clamor, consisting of screams and barks but without pant-hoots, by multiple chimpanzees was heard from the eastern mountains where as yet no voice had arisen. The trio turned to the east and immediately headed in that direction along the observation trail.
08:57:30 A pant-hoot chorus from the same location in the east. The trio paused almost simultaneously, each with a hind leg in the air.
08:57:35 Even after the voices from the east disappeared, the trio remained motionless in the same posture [Silence continuing even after the end of hearing distant pant-hoots]. A pant-hoot chorus rang out from a different location (northeast) about five seconds later [Response to a pant-hoot chorus from the east]. As soon as the northeastern voices disappeared, the trio resumed traveling.

Twice at around **08:59**, pant-hoots accompanied by a clamor rang out from the same location on the eastern mountains. The trio paused each time, remained motionless for around ten seconds after the voices disappeared [Silence continuing even after the end of hearing distant pant-hoots] and resumed traveling.

08:59:45 The trio began running while producing a chorus of pant-hoots.
09:00:00 They paused immediately after the vocalization, remained motionless for about ten seconds [Silence right after the end of uttering pant-hoots] and resumed traveling east.
09:03:10 They uttered another pant-hoot chorus and began running.
09:03:20 They finished the vocalization, paused and remained motionless [Silence right after the end of uttering pant-hoots]. Five seconds later, a pant-hoot chorus rang out from the same location on the eastern mountains [Response to the trio's pant-hoot chorus]. They resumed traveling when the voices were about to disappear and broke into a run to the east.

At **09:04**, Nkombo climbed a tree and began feeding while Alofu and Kalunde kept traveling east along the observation trail. Along the way the pair repeatedly paused abruptly and remained motionless for five seconds. A party of three males approached while uttering pant-grunts at **09:06**, but the pair kept traveling without stopping. At **09:08**, the pair reached a T-junction with another observation trail running north-east and sat down facing east. There was a scrubby steep hillside (the eastern mountains) in front of them. The party of three males the pair had passed earlier reappeared at **09:09** and began grooming nearby, but Alofu and Kalunde stayed put until at least **09:11** when I turned back to observe Nkombo.

At the beginning of Case 2, at least part of the pant-hoots I had heard before finding Alofu, Kalunde and Nkombo would have also been heard by the trio, judging by the location (for map see Hanamura 2010b). Therefore, it is likely that the presence of others outside of the visible range had already become obvious to the trio. They began traveling east as soon as they heard a clamor from the eastern mountains. This behavior suggests that the trio became aware of the presence of other individuals in the eastern mountains upon hearing their voices and began to seek involvement with them.

Under these circumstances, when another chorus of pant-hoots rose from the same location on the eastern mountains around three minutes later, the trio paused and exhibited the behavior of "silence continuing even after the end of hearing distant pant-hoots" and heard a response from another party in the northeast. The trio resumed traveling east after hearing the response and when a clamor with pant-hoots rang out from the same location on the eastern mountains twice along the way, they paused and exhibited the "silence" each time to keep their ears open for whether other individuals would respond.

In this way, when pant-hoots by the other party they are seeking involvement with ring out repeatedly, especially when those by another party have also rung out or pant-hoot exchanges between the target party and another party have occurred, chimpanzees sometimes observe (auditory) whether the target party and another party construct a field of interaction through exchanging pant-hoots and/or continue to exchange pant-hoots. In Case 2, after hearing pant-hoots from the party in the east twice, of which the first voice was responded to and the second was not responded to, the trio produced an initial pant-hoot chorus and listened for responses to the chorus. Their call was not responded to, however, and around three minutes after the resumption of their journey eastward, the trio again attempted to call. This time they received a response from the party in the east and began running in that direction in an excited manner as soon as they finished hearing the voice.

To sum up the behaviors of the trio up to the point of receiving a response, they were interested in being involved with the individuals whose presence came to their attention through hearing their utterances from a distance, but instead of responding to the subsequent pant-hoots from the same location, they monitored possible interactions between the target party and another party. They then "called anew" to explore whether the target party would respond to them. As suggested by this series of the trio's behaviors, when chimpanzees attempt to interact through pant-hoots with other individuals outside of the visible range, they understand the potential presence of third parties—peers beyond a dyadic relationship—who may respond to the target party's voice just as they themselves may do. They therefore sometimes make a restrained approach by "calling anew" while monitoring the behaviors of such third parties, and coordinate their own action choice according to the target and third party's behaviors each time.

Accordingly, it is supposed that when three or more parties of individuals attempt to interact through pant-hoots, each party either makes a restrained approach by "calling anew" while monitoring the behaviors of other parties or makes an exploratory approach by responding straight away, just as the pair did in Case 1. In fact, whereas the trio in Case 2 attempted to call after hearing unresponded pant-hoots from the party in the east twice, the party in the east, who had probably constructed a field with another party in the northeast after receiving their response at the beginning of Case 2, responded to the trio's second pant-hoot chorus. Thus the trio came to accomplish a non-face-to-face encounter with the target party in this case. The behaviors of the two males after receiving a response at the end of Case 2 demonstrate, just as the pair in Case 1 did, that these two males were waiting and keeping their ears open for the next vocalization from the other party they had exchanged pant-hoots with. Since there is no preset common *goal* in pant-hoot interactions, regardless of whether they respond to propose the construction of a field or call and receive a response proposing the construction of a field, whether the interaction will continue thereafter and how it will unfold depends on the behaviors of each party.

Diversity of ways of action connection after field construction

While the main focus of my discussion so far has been on the ways of action connection when attempting to form a field with others outside of the visible range through pant-hoots, let's shift our gaze to those after field construction. After the end of Case 2, I returned to observe Nkombo, who was still feeding at the place where she parted company with Alofu and Kalunde, at 09:14. Although pant-hoots from Alofu and Kalunde, who continued to be observed by my research assistant, as well as from other individuals in the east were heard intermittently, Nkombo headed west, the opposite direction to the source of those voices, while foraging. This epilogue (see Hanamura 2010b for details) demonstrates that, even though chimpanzees construct a field with other individuals through exchanging pant-hoots, they sometimes "lose interest" in continuing the interaction according to the rhythm of their activities such as feeding, traveling and resting. In fact, Darwin in Case 1 also did not respond to the last pant-hoot. However, he followed Christmas, who had responded and begun running, as if he was being pulled along. As Darwin's behavior indicates, chimpanzees' action choices in interactions with others outside of the visible range often occur in the context of their involvement with others in the visible range (see Hanamura 2010b for other cases).

Accordingly, when we consider chimpanzees' ways of action connection with invisible others via pant-hoots, there is a need to pay attention to the aspect that they coordinate action choice according to their activity rhythm and involvement with visible others, in addition to the behaviors of invisible others. I analyze fluctuations and changes in their action choices following the construction of a field over a longer time-period below.

Case 3 (12 March 2006)

Target individual: Fatuma (adult female, estimated age forty-three, accompanying daughters, Flavia, seven, and Fimbi, two)

Arrow legend

⟶ Pant-hoot vocalization by target individual

┈┈▶ Pant-hoot vocalization by visible others

⟹ Pant-hoot chorus by target and visible others

◀— Pant-hoot outside the visible range (see Note 1 about identification of vocalizers)

↗ Target's response to pant-hoot outside the visible range (pant-hoot utterance within ten seconds of the end of the preceding incoming pant-hoot)

Events in the visible range	Events outside the visible range
Scene 1	
At **08:30**, Fatuma is found grooming Pimu (her son, adult male). Masudi (adult male) and Orion (young male) are found nearby.	
08:43:05 Fatuma interrupts grooming while looking to the east.	**08:43:05** A pant-hoot uttered by one individual in close proximity to the east (Bonobo, adult male, visually confirmed by research assistant).
08:43:15 Three males and Fatuma produce a pant-hoot chorus [Response] ①.	
08:43:40 Bonobo gallops toward them; Fatuma utters a pant-grunt.	
08:44:15 Four males scamper around while producing a pant-hoot chorus; Fatuma holds Fimbi to her belly and climbs up a tree while looking toward the males.	
08:45:05 Four males depart in all directions dragging tree branches.	**08:45:05** The sound of branches being dragged by the males fades away.
08:51:20 Fatuma stands up on a tree branch and utters a pant-hoot in a way that overlaps the second half of the other party's voice [Response] ②.	**08:51:15** A pant-hoot uttered by one individual in close proximity to the east (Bonobo, who departed a short time ago, visually confirmed by research assistant).
08:53:20 Fatuma, who has come down and begun traveling, utters a pant-hoot in a way that overlaps with the second half of the other party's voice [Response], and slowly heads in the direction of the voice (south) ③.	**08:53:15** A pant-hoot chorus uttered in close proximity to the south (Pimu and Masudi, who departed a short time ago, visually confirmed by research assistant).
08:54:45 Fatuma meets with Pimu and Masudi again, who are in a tree.	
08:55:20 Bonobo reappears.	

08:58:45 Fatuma parts with three males, travels farther south. Flavia remains. Fatuma drinks water from a river about 100 meters away, rests in a tree.

09:06:20 Without turning, Fatuma utters a pant-hoot partially overlapping the other party's voice in a tree [Response], begins feeding ④.

09:06:15 A pant-hoot chorus from the former location where Fatuma stayed with Pimu and others (coming from the north as Fatuma has traveled south) (Pimu and Bonobo, visually confirmed by research assistant who remained with Flavia).

09:07:25 Flavia (and research assistant) appears.

09:15:15 Fatuma finishes feeding, descends from the tree, travels southeast. After traveling about another 100 meters, she rests on an observation trail and begins to groom Fimbi.

09:19:50 Fatuma interrupts grooming while looking to the northwest but immediately resumes grooming ⑤.

09:24:35 Fimbi and Flavia begin playing together.

09:26:10 On the observation trail, Fatuma passes two males who are not Pimu, Masudi, Orion or Bonobo heading northwest at a fast pace.

09:28:15 Fatuma remains motionless sitting on the ground ⑥.

09:19:50 A pant-hoot chorus from the former location (coming from the northwest as Fatuma has traveled southeast) (one of the vocalizers is presumed to be Pimu).

09:28:15 Screams and a pant-hoot from the same location (northwest).

09:30:30 A pant-hoot chorus from the same location (northwest).

09:30:40 Fatuma utters a pant-hoot [Response] without turning and continues resting ⑦.

09:31:10 Fatuma resumes grooming Fimbi.

Scene 2

09:32:45 Fatuma interrupts grooming while turning east and remains motionless even after a voice from the east fades away [Silence continuing even after the end of hearing a distant pant-hoot]; she resumes grooming after listening to a voice from the northwest ⑧.

09:32:45 A pant-hoot chorus from a different location (east). Immediately after it, a pant-hoot chorus from the same location (northwest) (one of the vocalizers is presumed to be Bonobo) [Response to a pant-hoot chorus from the east].

09:34:20 Fatuma turns her face to the northwest, keeps looking in that direction for about five seconds after the end of the vocalization [Silence continuing even after the end of hearing distant pant-hoots], then turns her face back to where it was ⑨.

09:34:20 A pant-hoot chorus from the same location (northwest) (one of the vocalizers is presumed to be Pimu).

09:34:50 Fatuma begins to backtrack the observation trail to the northwest.

09:45:20 Fatuma returns to the location where she parted with Pimu and others but no one is around. She looks around, then heads to the northeast along another observation trail.

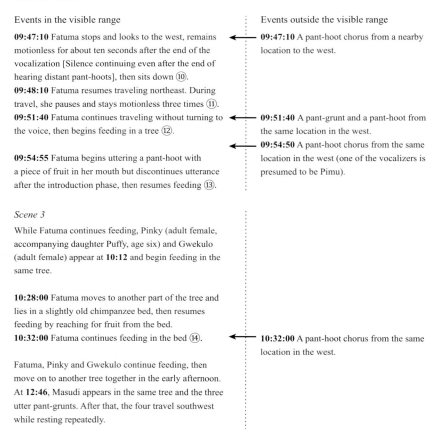

Case 3: Continued

Events in the visible range

09:47:10 Fatuma stops and looks to the west, remains motionless for about ten seconds after the end of the vocalization [Silence continuing even after the end of hearing distant pant-hoots], then sits down ⑩.
09:48:10 Fatuma resumes traveling northeast. During travel, she pauses and stays motionless three times ⑪.
09:51:40 Fatuma continues traveling without turning to the voice, then begins feeding in a tree ⑫.

09:54:55 Fatuma begins uttering a pant-hoot with a piece of fruit in her mouth but discontinues utterance after the introduction phase, then resumes feeding ⑬.

Scene 3
While Fatuma continues feeding, Pinky (adult female, accompanying daughter Puffy, age six) and Gwekulo (adult female) appear at **10:12** and begin feeding in the same tree.

10:28:00 Fatuma moves to another part of the tree and lies in a slightly old chimpanzee bed, then resumes feeding by reaching for fruit from the bed.
10:32:00 Fatuma continues feeding in the bed ⑭.

Fatuma, Pinky and Gwekulo continue feeding, then move on to another tree together in the early afternoon. At **12:46**, Masudi appears in the same tree and the three utter pant-grunts. After that, the four travel southwest while resting repeatedly.

Events outside the visible range

09:47:10 A pant-hoot chorus from a nearby location to the west.

09:51:40 A pant-grunt and a pant-hoot from the same location in the west.
09:54:50 A pant-hoot chorus from the same location in the west (one of the vocalizers is presumed to be Pimu).

10:32:00 A pant-hoot chorus from the same location in the west.

Redundantly protracted interaction and field dissolution

Case 3 shows the events that took place over half a day in the life of Fatuma, an adult female, divided into those that occurred in the visible range and those that occurred outside of the visible range listed in chronological order. For the purpose of analysis, this extended case has been divided into three "scenes" based on changes in the way of action connection with others outside of the visible range.

At the start of Scene 1, Fatuma produced a chorus of pant-hoots together with the males she had been visually encountering, including her son Pimu, in response to a pant-hoot from outside the visible range (①), and met with the male vocalizer (Bonobo). The males (called "Pimu and others" in this section) left and produced pant-hoots from outside the visible range about five and ten minutes after their departure. Fatuma responded by partially overlapping her utterance with theirs like a chorus and traveled toward them while responding, respectively, and then met them again (②③). After that, Fatuma again parted from Pimu and others, drank water from a river and climbed a tree to rest, but when a pant-hoot chorus from Pimu and others was heard about ten minutes after the second parting, she produced an overlapping response without even turning toward the voice (④).

On this occasion (④), Fatuma neither showed behaviors such as turning her face or ear to the direction of the voice before responding, as did the pair in Case 1 when they heard the first pant-hoots, nor exhibitted "silence continuing even after the end of hearing distant pant-hoots" as did the trio in Case 2. She instead responded immediately to the voice as if she took it for granted. In the sense that Fatuma listened to the voice of the other party as if it was addressed to her, it is possible to say that for her a field with Pimu and others had already been constructed through repeated pant-hoot exchanges and visual encounters up to that point. However, Fatuma began feeding after responding and neither ran toward the voice excitedly nor attempted to call herself, unlike the pair in Case 1 after responding for the second time. About ten minutes after that, she traveled farther away from Pimu and others and began grooming with one of her daughters.

Subsequently, when another pant-hoot chorus was heard, presumably coming from Pimu and others again, Fatuma stopped grooming while turning her face to the voice, but she immediately resumed grooming without responding (⑤). While her daughters started playing, Fatuma passed two males traveling in the direction of Pimu and others at a brisk pace. When pant-hoots rang out from the same place soon afterward, she behaved ambivalently by remaining on her haunches without responding (⑥) or by responding without turning (⑦), then resumed grooming with her daughter.

The series of Fatuma's behaviors up to this point (Scene 1) demonstrate that when she heard the voices of Pimu and others she had repeatedly exchanged pant-hoots with, she sometimes responded synchronously while continuing her own activity and involvements with others in the visible range, and sometimes just continued such activity and involvement without responding. Thus Fatuma continued protracted and intermittent interaction with Pimu and others redundantly for around thirty minutes after they remained separate visually and initiated different activities.

In Scene 2, however, a pant-hoot chorus rang out from a different location and Fatuma heard a response to it from the party supposedly of Pimu and others (one identifiable responder was Bonobo, who was with the party in Scene 1) (⑧). This means that Fatuma observed the construction of a field by presumably at least some members of the party with whom she had had ongoing interaction and another party. Under such circumstances, when pant-hoots presumably from Pimu and others rang out again soon after, Fatuma came to exhibit "silence continuing even after the end of hearing distant pant-hoots", that is, she listened for a response from another party, just as the trio in Case 2 did (⑨). In the sense that Fatuma listened to the voice as a vocalization with the possibility of evoking a response from the third party rather than as a call addressed to herself, it is possible to say that the field of interaction with Pimu and others became ambiguous for her.

Although Fatuma did not attempt to call afterward, it does not seem to be the case that she "lost interest" in continuing to interact with Pimu and others because she did return to the place where they had parted company earlier and utterances had continued thereafter. However, Pimu and others were no longer there when Fatuma returned. She looked around and then headed northeast. When a pant-hoot chorus rang out from somewhere close to the west along the way, she exhibited "silence continuing even after the end of hearing distant pant-hoots", then sat down for about one minute (⑩), and after resuming her journey to the northeast, she paused many times (⑪). She did not turn to the west, however. When a pant-hoot with a pant-grunt sounded again from the same location in the west, Fatuma continued traveling without turning to the voices and began feeding (⑫). When a pant-hoot chorus presumably produced by Pimu and others came from the same location in the west during her feeding, she uttered a pant-hoot, but it would not have constituted an audible response because she ceased vocalization after the introduction phase (⑬).

In Scene 3, Fatuma met with another party (Pinky, Puffy and Gwekulo) and continued feeding with these individuals. Although a pant-hoot chorus rose from the same location in the west (⑭), Fatuma just continued feeding and did not travel in the direction of the voice. Thereafter, no pant-hoots were heard and Fatuma and others did not produce them.

As above, the field of interaction that develops beyond the visible range is an ephemeral field that is bound to vanish eventually unless pant-hoot exchanges are repeated. Even if one is "interested" in continuing the interaction, the other party is also traveling constantly and a new (visual/auditory) encounter with a third party can always occur for both the other party and oneself. However, while Fatuma accepted the contingent nature of the behaviors of the other party (they were no longer there when she returned) and the third party (who produced pant-hoots and the other party responded to it), she coordinated her action choice according to what the other and third parties did as well as to her own activity rhythm (drinking water, resting, traveling, feeding, etc.) and her involvements with others within the visible range (grooming her daughter, co-feeding with others, etc.).

In sum, chimpanzees sometimes exert "synchrony" with the other party's action such that when a field has been developed through pant-hoot exchanges, they repeatedly respond to the other party's vocalizations even while continuing their own activities and involvement with visible others. On the other hand, they also have "autonomy" in the sense that their behaviors are not constrained by the other party's action (although it can be the inverted outcome of their "synchrony" with visible others), such as traveling away from the other party without responding to their vocalizations or continuing their own activites and involvement with visible others without even turning toward the voice of the other party. For this reason, they sometimes engage in interaction in an "ambivalent" manner, as Fatuma exhibited when she responded on some occasions but not on others to repeated vocalizations from the other party with whom she had been exchanging pant-hoots (Scene 1). In addition, chimpanzees may not actively seek to continue the interaction with the other party, while leaving the field between them and the other party may become ambiguous depending on the behaviors of the other and third parties, but they may not "lose interest" in the continuation either. They therefore sometimes connect their actions to those of the other party in an "unobtrusive" manner, such as moving in the direction of the place from which they heard vocalizations or remaining in the vicinity while continuing their own activities and involvement with visible others (Scenes 2 and 3). It is possible to say that Fatuma in Case 3 behaved in diverse manners while fluctuating between synchrony and autonomy according to each situation.

Deferring or passing the potential for interaction

In Scene 3 of Case 3, a new visual encounter arose. Finally, through analyzing Case 4 (which followed Case 3), I will confirm that such an encounter can provide an opportunity for non-face-to-face (auditory) encounters with yet another party, but that this does not necessarily entail the continuation of the interaction with the invisible party. I then consider the ways of action connection in such situations.

As I mentioned in the second section of this chapter, pant-hoot utterances are sometimes triggered by interactions among individuals within the visible range. At the beginning of Case 4, some individuals within the visible range initiated a fight

186   Chapter 8

Case 4 (12 March 2006), sequel to Case 3

Sex and age classes of targets and other individuals and arrow legend: see Case 3

Events in the visible range	Events outside the visible range

At **14:02**, Puffy's scream triggers a fight between
Masudi and the pair of Pinky and Gwekulo.
Together with their screams and barks, Fatuma and
Masudi utter a chorus of pant-hoots twice. Although
Fatuma and others have spent their time together
afterward, Pinky (with Puffy) leaves at around **14:30**
and Gwekulo leaves at around **15:30**.

16:18:20 While Fatuma and Masudi feed in a tree,
Gwekulo reappears and climbs up the same tree while
uttering a pant-hoot. Fatuma and Masudi join her in a
chorus of pant-hoots ⑮. The two resume feeding right
after the end of the utterance. Gwekulo begins feeding
shortly after ⑯.

16:18:30 Fatuma turns to the east and immediately   **16:18:30** A pant-hoot by an individual in
resumes feeding ⑱.   the east [Response] (presumed to be
16:19:10 Masudi begins uttering a pant-hoot but   Darwin, adult male) ⑰.
discontinues utterances after the introduction phase.
16:21:15 Masudi descends from the tree and
departs to the west along an observation trail. Fatuma
and Gwekulo stay and continue feeding.
16:22:45 Fatuma looks to the east and resumes feeding   **16:22:45** A pant-hoot by an individual at a
in a second ⑳.   closer location in the east (presumed to be
                                                            Darwin) ⑲.

At **16:27**, Fatuma descends from the tree and
slowly heads east along an observation trail. Gwekulo
follows her after a short delay. At **16:34**, they come to
an intersection with another observation trail running
north-south, rest for a while, then travel south for a short
distance. At **16:39**, Fatuma walks off the trail into the
bush to the east and begins foraging; Gwekulo continues
traveling south and leaves.

and together with their screams and barks Fatuma and Masudi (who appeared alone
when Fatuma and others were foraging in a tree at the end of Case 3) twice produced
a chorus of pant-hoots. Another pant-hoot chorus was produced when Fatuma and
Masudi met Gwekulo again afterward (⑮). At the scene of this reunion, the three
resumed or began feeding immediately after producing the chorus: they did not
exhibit the "silence right after the end of uttering pant-hoots" as the chimpanzees

in Cases 1 and 2 did after attempting to call (⑯). Accordingly, it is likely that the three were not expecting any response to their vocalization.

Nevertheless, a response came from the east (⑰). A pant-hoot that rings out outside the visible range is heard by the hearers as a voice that can be used for "call-response", and the hearers can respond to it at any time, regardless of the context of the vocalization (although the hearers cannot know it clearly), as confirmed in Case 1. By receiving a response, the pant-hoot chorus of the three chimpanzees retrospectively takes on the meaning of a call. In other words, at this scene (⑰), Fatuma unexpectedly received a proposal to form a field with others from outside the visible range with whom she had had no previous involvement, and the potential for further interaction with them arose. However, Fatuma merely glanced in the direction of the voice and continued to feed in the same way as before, as if nothing had happened (⑱). Unlike the trio in Case 2 who repeatedly attempted to call, she did not start running in the direction of the voice after receiving a response. When a pant-hoot was uttered by presumably the same individual from a closer location to the east about four minutes later (⑲), Fatuma again merely turned toward the voice and immediately resumed feeding (⑳).

While I identified these two pant-hoots as vocalizations by Darwin, Fatuma, too, would have been able to identify the vocalizer, since the characteristics of the sound produced by a single vocalizer were clear. Moreover, the second pant-hoot came shortly after the first, which had been produced as a response, from the same direction. In addition to these conditions, given that the two males in Case 2 were able to wait and keep their ears open for the next voice from the other party after receiving a response, Fatuma would have been able to listen to the second pant-hoot as if it was addressed to her party, i.e., a call to her party, from the other party who had made a response (the first pant-hoot). If chimpanzees were not expecting the workings of a field that create the potential for further interaction in this way, the "fabrication" of a field and the subsequent calling after waiting for the next vocalization from the other party practiced by the two males in Case 1 would not make sense.

Yet, Fatuma continued to feed regardless of this working of the field. On the basis of the above discussion on Case 3, this means that Fatuma chose not to synchronize with the actions of the other party she had been exchanging pant-hoots with according to her own rhythm of activity and involvement with visible others.

However, she did turn in the direction of the other party's voice in the east and about five minutes after hearing the second pant-hoot she traveled in that direction, resumed feeding and remained there. Accordingly, following the construction of the field, the potential for further interaction, such as hearing another vocalization or the arrival of the other party, had not vanished. Fatuma's party might again produce pant-hoots. It is therefore possible to say that Fatuma in Case 4 "deferred" the potential for interaction and left the possibility up in the air; she was neither "disinterested" in continuing to interact with the other party with whom her party had exchanged pant-hoots nor actively seeking to continue the interaction. In addition, as the behaviors of Masudi who departed to the west and Gwekulo who headed south show, chimpanzees sometimes behave as if to "pass" the potential for interaction with the other party they have been exchanging pant-hoots with; they do not move in the direction of or stay in the vicinity of the location the other party's voice has been heard from.

Incidentally, approximately twenty minutes after Fatuma moved east and resumed feeding, Darwin, presumed to be the other party she had exchanged pant-hoots with, arrived from the east and they ranged together until shortly before Fatuma went to bed in a tree. Of course, "deferring" does not guarantee that a visual encounter with the other party will happen at a later stage, and "passing" does not preclude a possible chance meeting with the other party later on. What is more important is that "deferring" and "passing" are ways of action connection also available to the individuals who have been attempting to construct a field and to continue interaction, as confirmed by the behavior of Nkombo after Case 2 as well as that of Darwin, who might not have headed in the direction of the last pant-hoot in Case 1 if Christmas had not been with him. Fatuma's behavior of not responding to the other party she had been exchanging pant-hoots with in Case 3 can be seen as "deferring" or "passing".

Process-oriented convention and field transformation

I have analyzed the ways of action connection via pant-hoots and the dynamics of the resultant interactions in the M group chimpanzees above. In this section, I compare these with some of the face-to-face interactions in chimpanzees mentioned in the opening section of this chapter and human conventions and institutions (rules) illustrated as examples below, while summing up the results of the case analysis.

A conventionalized pattern of vocal exchange in chimpanzees' interaction via pant-hoots was identified, and through the use of this pattern, chimpanzees, including those who were listening for exchanges between other chimpanzees, interacted with others as they made each other's actions understandable. As we have seen in the cases presented above, it is possible to say that interactions using this pattern took on the meaning of "call-response" for all individuals in the study group equally.

This pattern of action connection used by chimpanzees in non-face-to-face conditions has characteristics that differ from those of other patterns used in face-to-face conditions. In the latter, encounters happen without the use of any pattern of action connection since encountering chimpanzees are mutually aware through sight that the other party is aware of one's presence (see Chapter Seven). "Pant-grunts" (Chapter Six) and "hand-clasped grooming" (Chapter Eleven) are considered to be "tools" that can be used as a usual way when chimpanzees make an exploratory move in attempting to create some sort of order in an uncertain situation where they do not know how to deal with other(s) they have encountered, and when two chimpanzees aspire to do something at the same time in attempting to bring a certain order to the situation where they cannot just do nothing after encountering, respectively. On the other hand, the exchanging of pant-hoots is a "tool" that can be used in accomplishing a non-face-to-face encounter and creating the potential for further interaction. In other words, it is a "device" to generate an encounter when the actors are invisible to each other rather than to explore or aspire toward a tentative or common *goal* (i.e., order) in an attempt to solve a problem upon encountering. It is an ethnomethod for chimpanzees who are capable of living separately to create a field where they can interact with others outside of the visible range.

For this characteristic, interaction through pant-hoots is hardly subjected to any directional force that would predetermine action choice, such as "who would encounter whom", then "who would do what". Even though a pattern of action connection is used, "who chooses which action and when" is not limited, i.e., there is almost no guideline that this individual should select this action in this situation (e.g., a specific chimpanzee should respond in certain situations and should not in other situations). Consequently, fields simply appear and disappear among various individuals and if discrete scenes are framed and examined, it seems that "anyone can do anything at any time". Yet, their unique ways of action connection did exist and it was not the case that disorder ensued (e.g., having difficulty in action choice or being upset by an incomprehensible event or uncertain situation).

When chimpanzees heard pant-hoots from a party outside of the visible range they had not been previously involved with and wished to interact with, they sometimes made an exploratory approach by responding straight away to "fabricate" a field of interaction, waiting for the party's next vocalization, and if it was not forthcoming, making a call themselves (Case 1). Especially when chimpanzees had been auditorily observing the construction of a field between the other party and a third party, they sometimes made a restrained approach by "calling anew" while monitoring the drift of interaction between the two parties (Case 2). After field construction, they coordinated their action choice without getting upset even when the other party they had exchanged pant-hoots with neither responded to them nor uttered the next vocalization (Case 1). On the other hand, the ways of action connection with invisible others were influenced by chimpanzees' own activity rhythm and involvement with visible others, and accordingly when the other party they had exchanged pant-hoots with emitted vocalization repeatedly, they sometimes connected actions with the other party in an "ambivalent" manner by responding synchronously or not responding autonomously (Case 3). In such a situation, when the other party started exchanging pant-hoots with a third party along the way, they continued to interact in an "unobtrusive" manner without getting upset (Case 3). When chimpanzees unexpectedly received a response to their pant-hoot chorus from invisible others with no ongoing involvement, they continued their own activity and involvement with visible others without getting upset (Case 4). While in such a situation they sometimes "deferred" or "passed" the potential for interaction by not responding to the next voice of the other party they had exchanged pant-hoots with (Case 4), these ways were also practiced by the chimpanzees who were attempting to construct a field and to continue interaction (Cases 1, 2 and 3).

As above, chimpanzees behaved in diverse manners through pant-hoots depending on the situation while dealing with each other's contingent behaviors on a case-by-case basis and coordinating each action choice. It seems that the way in which one makes an exploratory or restrained approach to invisible others and cordinates one's action choice each time according to the other party's reaction is possible under the assumption that "the other party will behave variously, oscillating between behaving synchronously and behaving autonomously without being constrained by any approaches". If they could not expect any synchrony from the other party at all, they would not wait for the next vocalization after responding or listen for a response after making a call. Because they have repeatedly experienced the autonomy of others, they can take for granted the lack of subsequent vocalization or response and spend the subsequent time as if nothing has happened. Furthermore, precisely because they "do not know what the other and third parties will do", they can run excitedly upon receiving a response from the other party or can monitor whether a third party will respond to the other party's voice. Conversely, the assumption that "the other party will deal with one's behavior each time and coordinate their action choice" seems to enable a diverse range of behaviors as follows: responding straight away; behaving ambivalently despite recurring vocalizations from the other party they have exchanged pant-hoots with; and deferring or passing the potential for interaction with the other party. If it were common that when they deferred or passed the opportunity for a potential interaction, the other party would desperately continue making calls or search for them in an upset manner (On very rare occasions chimpanzees become unnerved by a lack of response and make repeated calls while running around in confusion or screaming (Hanamura 2010a)), for example, it would be difficult for them to keep taking the action of deffering or passing.

In sum, it is believed that chimpanzees can deal with the other party's behavior on each occasion and coordinate their action choice because they experientially know that "the other party will behave variously" through pant-hoots and that they can behave variously because they experientially know that "the other party will deal with my behavior on each occasion and coordinate his/her action choice". On this basis, it is possible to treat this set of ways of action connection through pant-hoots as the convention of "everyone does so in associating via pant-hoots" in the sense that all parties mutually assume they do so—that is, "while dealing with the behavior of the other party each time as well as the third party in some cases and coordinating respective action choice, behaving variously depending on the situation as well as respective activity rhythm and involvement with visible others".

In this convention, while chimpanzees know that "doing this will lead to that" (i.e., exchanging pant-hoots generates the potential for further interaction) through the use of the pattern of pant-hoot exchange, they use it with the attitude of "anyone may choose any action at any time", that is, "if that happens, I may do this" (e.g., attempt to continue interacting by waiting for the next voice or making another call) or "I may do that" (e.g., behaving ambivalently when the other party emits vocalizations repeatedly or deferring or passing the potential for interaction). However, choosing the next action depending on what the other party does every time means that each chosen action will influence the next action choice of the other and third parties. Chimpanzees understand the potential influence of their action on others at least when they make an exploratory or restrained approach. Although someone somewhere may be influenced by it and begin moving unbeknown to them, they can understand their unexpected influence through the other's reaction (if it is a response). This is what Adachi (Chapter Twelve) calls a "concatenation of social communication". As a result, fields are formed and transformed among various individuals depending on each other's behaviors, and interaction may warm up temporarily or continue redundantly with interruptions, or the other party may start interacting with a third party along the way or interaction may cease because of a lack of subsequent action. It is envisaged that chimpanzees' convention of action connection through pant-hoots generates the continuation of such processes (see Diagram A on p. 166). For this reason, I hereafter call this chimpanzee convention the "process-oriented convention" in the sense that chimpanzees mutually coordinate their action choice according to one another's behaviors on a case-by-case basis while going with the *process*, i.e., the flow of ongoing interactions and respective changing circumstances, rather than in pursuit of a common *goal*. Of course, it is likely that this process-oriented convention has been physicalized through the repetition of the formation and dissipation of fields among various individuals at a distance and invisible to one another rather than something chimpanzees are aware of.

Incidentally, some pattern-using face-to-face interactions for chimpanzees and humans feel as if "who chooses which action and when" is predetermined, because repetitive performance has made other options for action choice latent or in some cases has caused them to be perceived as deviance. For instance, the aforementioned hand-clasped grooming in chimpanzees is performed by two individuals in mutual anticipation of "doing" this particular interaction prior to the actual action connection in order to achieve the goal of "orderly co-presence" in the situation where they feel compelled to do something, with reference to their past experience and the outcome of engaging in hand-clasped grooming in similar situations (Chapter Eleven). Though very rare, one party's action choice of "not doing" hand-clasped grooming can evoke a negative reaction in the other party (Nakamura 2003b). In this case, it can be said that the chosen action is perceived as deviance, at least by the individual who reacted negatively. "School lessons" in humans begin when one teacher and multiple students greet one another using the pattern of "bowing to one another" or one of the other patterns used for "greeting". While they use various patterns of "turn-taking" such as "question-answer-evaluation" (see Nishizaka 2008), the students refrain from speaking unless they are called on, even when the teacher finishes speaking. Here, in order to achieve the goal of "many students learning from one teacher", all of the participants limit their options of pattern-using action choice according to their roles prior to their actual action connections and also expect the others to do the same. Therefore, any actions deviating from the expected actions, including the students not greeting the teacher, a student speaking before being called on by the teacher and the teacher not evaluating a student's answer, are marked as deviance or acts of failure in the sense that those who have chosen such actions are required to explain the reason themselves or receive warnings or coaching from the others. If the marking of deviation, i.e., turning a way of action connection into norms, is thought to indicate the establishment of an institution, these conventions found in the "school lesson" are already institutions (rules).

It is thought that these "goal-oriented" conventions and institutions (rules) in chimpanzees and humans that utilize the patterns of action connection to limit options for action choice have also been physicalized through repetition (see Diagram B, p. 166). In other words, participants in the given interaction are not always aware of these rules and goals and take them for granted as "what everyone does" (Chapter Eighteen). If we are to view the result in hindsight as the stable production of specific interactions "according to the rule of *should*", we can view the case of chimpanzees' interactions through pant-hoots as the continuous production of the process of the ceaseless formation and transformation of fields "according to the rule of may^2".

In interactions via pant-hoots in chimpanzees, there are also some situations that felt as if their action choices had been preselected before the actual action connection. For example, when pant-hoot exchanges were repeated between the same two parties, chimpanzees repeatedly responded by synchronizing with the other party's voice as if it was a matter of course (Cases 1 and 3). In such scenarios, it is possible to say that action options other than "to respond" had become latent. However, repetitions of pant-hoot exchanges also arise by the force of circumstances and differ from a stably reproducing specific interaction by a goal-oriented convention. For the stable production of a specific identical interaction directed toward a certain goal, it would be necessary for multiple individuals to share a problem that compels them to repeat the specific interaction in order to jointly solve it and a goal that is expected to be achieved by performing the interaction. At the same time, the stabilization may be facilitated by language, which conceptualizes the interaction as "it" and gives them the illusion that it has a fixed association with the goal.

Among face-to-face interactions in chimpanzees and humans, on the other hand, there are many interactions that are produced stably in a manner somewhat similar to that of the process-oriented pant-hoot convention. While a wide variety of patterns of action connection are used in children's "play" in humans and other primates (Chapter Four; Kitamura 1992; Nishie 2010) and "chat", i.e., conversation with no external purpose, such as consensus building and transmission of information, or that with no purpose other than having a conversation itself (Mizutani 1997) in humans, they are autotelic interactions that take advantage of the inherent playfulness (large degree of freedom in terms of action choice) of each pattern. Since the patterns narrow the *range* of action choices, one is able to anticipate the other party's subsequent action or speech to a certain extent. However, rather than limiting action choices with a goal-oriented attitude prior to the actual action connection, fluctuations in action choice are created by the process-oriented attitude. Because of this, a coincidence between anticipation for the other party's action choice and the actual action chosen by the other party causes excitement and a discrepancy between them becomes a resource to produce the next action. In addition, the interruption and resumption of a given interaction as well as mid-course participation and departure are accepted without being marked as deviations. Nevertheless, as we can see in "chasing" that uses the pattern of "chase-chased", for example, "play" is fun because participants repeatedly "perform" the pattern-using interaction while switching roles; hence if one party continuously does "not do" it, the other party would become disappointed and in some cases may recognize the action as a deviation.

In relation to the above, the customs involved in a song-drum-dance ritual of the African hunter-gatherer Baka people called "*be*" (Kimura 2003; Bundo 2010) more closely resembles the process-oriented pant-hoot convention in the sense that "not grooving" in the interaction (one does "not do" the interaction using the pattern) is accepted as a customary option. The performance of "*be*" is initiated by singers and drummers who start performing in order to call others to participate, but those who are called may pass the chance without a sense of obligation and their non-participation does not disappoint the initiators; the performance may begin, but frequent interruptions, intermissions or mid-performance participation and dropping out are commonplace. It is perhaps no accident that this interaction is a non-face-to-face auditory interaction that is performed at midnight when one can know others' behaviors only by listening to voices and sounds.

Just as "play", "chat" and "*be*" in humans can gain or lose momentum on a case-by-case basis according to the process-oriented convention, pant-hoot interactions in chimpanzees can gain and lose momentum in the same way. As Mizutani (1997) points out that various types of purposeful communication originate in autotelic conversations, the process-oriented convention can be regarded as an evolutionary historical foundation for an institutional phenomenon (convention) that is common to humans and chimpanzees and from which a goal-oriented convention may arise.

Of course, unlike human "play", "chat" and "*be*", each of which is conceptualized as a specific interaction and its entire process can be discernible, there is no evidence that leads us to think that in the case of pant-hoot interactions, the chimpanzees are aware of its whole process. The mode of continuously forming and transforming fields through pant-hoots with fission-fusion is the ordinary mode for them[3]. Yet, it is conceivable that the "interest" in one another among the individuals who are capable of living separately has created the pattern of "call-response", although it is uncertain whether this occurred in the long process of evolution or in the history of the M group. Their unique convention using that pattern has been repeatedly producing fields that anyone can propose or defer at any time within the reach of their voices. This enables the individuals who stay apart from and are invisible to one another to attempt to construct a field while monitoring each other's circumstances and to continue interacting depending on each other's action, and at the same time it also enables them to interrupt the interaction according to one another's circumstances or to remain separate without connecting action. As such, if the pant-hoot convention in chimpanzees is considered to be a "device" supporting their group living with repeated meeting and parting and through which they coordinate their way of association with others, it is possible to treat this process-oriented convention as one of the potentialities for institution as distinct from the goal-oriented institutions (rules) in humans.

9 Peace Building in the Wild: Thinking about Institutions from Cases of Conflict and Peace in Sulu

Ikuya Tokoro

Key ideas

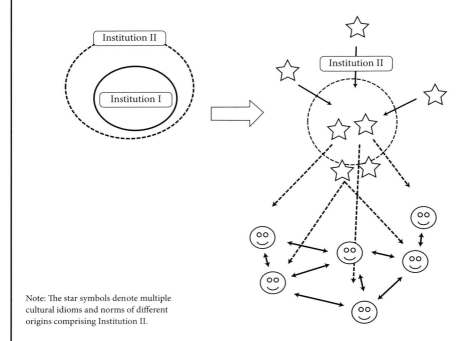

Note: The star symbols denote multiple cultural idioms and norms of different origins comprising Institution II.

Institution I with a relatively distinct outline is subsumed in the less defined Institution II (on the left in the above diagram). When viewed at close range, however, Institution II is comprised of a bricolage of diverse multiple cultural idioms and norms of different origins and histories which are referenced or applied or disapplied depending on the contingency-filled interactions of actors in a given situation.

Toward an institution theory unconstrained by modernist frames

This chapter is my attempt to relativize the narrow concept of "institution" used in so-called everyday usage of language and to reconsider it from a perspective that differs from the generally accepted and/or modernist understanding by analyzing ethnographic examples concerning various types of conflict and conflict resolution from my research field of the Sulu maritime world. To begin with, I briefly explain how this problem came about.

Reflecting on our discussions at meetings of the joint primatology-anthropology Institution Research Project, it is perhaps fair to say that primatologists largely envisioned conditions that existed prior to the formation of institutions in a narrow sense (or as an embryonic stage of the institutional phenomenon) and thus attempted to approach or examine the problem of institution. On the other hand, anthropologists tended to accept the hard fact that various institutions (languages, kinship systems, legal institutions, the state, etc.) were seemingly in existence in human society from the outset and strove to approach the true nature of institution based on that assumption.

However, a careful analysis leads to the suspicion that institutions might actually have existed in humans as an indistinct blend of pre-institutional elements, dysfunctional institutions, "informal institutions", "institutional anomalies" and so on and not as complete orders or closed systems. Furthermore, I argue that the so-called "institution" itself may be multilayered in nature rather than monolithic.

At a more concrete ethnographic level, various modern institutions supposedly exist authoritatively and regulate or control society in the Sulu maritime world in the southern Philippines, at least on paper. Yet, it is possible to point out on the basis of an analysis of the ethnographic data that the high incidence of institutional dysfunction and anomalies suggests failures of formal institutions in a narrow sense as well as the relative predominance of informal institutions and conventions in a broad sense.

This chapter provides descriptions and analysis of how conflicts and disputes are settled locally under the above social conditions based on ethnographic materials, with a particular focus on the process of conflict resolution through symbolic practices such as rituals. For example, I examine specifically how a form of reconciliation ritual of the Sama people in the Sulu Archipelago called *kiparat* displays a certain degree of efficacy as a social device that can convert acts of physical violence to symbolic and manageable violence in order to achieve resolution.

In other words, this is an attempt to define human institution from a broader perspective unconstrained by the modernist notion of institution.

How to approach institution

What is an institution in the first place? While I shall leave the connotations and permeation of the concept of "institution", the subject of this work, to the Introduction by Kawai, I would like to touch on some of the views on institution that are particularly relevant to this chapter here.

According to institutional economist T. Yeager (2001: 11–12), institutions are "the rules of the game in a society. Institutions reduce the uncertainty involved in human interaction by giving us patterns for our behavior"[1]. Yeager's understanding seems to have something in common with the argument of sociologist N. Luhmann in that institutions reduce complexity in the establishment of social order, given the situation of "double contingency" or complex social interaction (Luhmann 1993), but in any case it is relevant as one of the broadest definitions of institution.

I would like to proceed with my analysis from the standpoint that "institutions" are not necessarily limited to codified judicial institutions (statutory law) and the like commonly assumed in modern society and that it is possible to find the existence (however vague) of something institutional wherever there are mechanisms or processes (including conventions or customary frameworks, for example) that reduce uncertainty in human society.

Institution I and Institution II

For the sake of expedience, I shall divide institutions into two levels in this chapter—"Institution I" and "Institution II". The former includes the narrow definition of institutions (with the capital I, so to speak) and the latter includes those in a broad sense.

Institution I includes the so-called "formal institutions" of which typical examples are public or official institutions such as modern states and their dispute resolution systems, including the courts, judiciary, police and statutory law. It is considered that the formation of Institution I is premised on exclusive control over violence in a given society by typically superior public organizations such as the state. This form of institution is reliant upon higher instance organizations (state, police, court, etc.) in society that are formalized, have fixed boundaries and dispense (at least supposedly) formalized sanctions[2].

In contrast to Institution I, I shall call the institutions that manifest in a broad sense "Institution II". More specifically, typical examples of institutions at this level include informal dispute resolution processes through conventions (as opposed to the statutory laws of a state). It can be said that institutions at this level are characterized by a relatively low degree of objectification, reification and codification compared with those termed Institution I. In particular, they are typically institutions under the condition of the nonfunctioning state monopoly of violence.

Institution II (in contrast to Institution I) constellations do not always accompany higher instance organizations that are formalized, have fixed boundaries and dispense formalized sanctions[3].

Regarding the relationship between Institution I and Institution II, I should also add that these categories are idealized types as theoretical constructs purely for the purposes of discussion and it therefore goes without saying that borderline and overlapping cases can be found between the two types in reality. For instance, an institution of a modern nation-state (Institution I) may have an Institution II-like aspect in its actual operation. My main focus in this chapter is to describe and analyze the relationship between Institution I and Institution II based on ethnographic data obtained through my fieldwork.

Case analysis: Conflict and resolution in the Sulu maritime world

The subject of this chapter, the Sulu maritime world, is located in the southernmost part of the Philippines and covers the Sulu Archipelago extending to the border zone between the state of Sabah in East Malaysia and Indonesia and includes the waters surrounding these islands. Demographically, the Tausug and Sama language groups ("Sama Dea" (the land Sama) and "Sama Dilaut" (the sea Sama)) are often said to be the main ethnic groups[4]. This chapter largely revolves around cases involving the sea Sama (hereinafter called "Sama") who live on the island of Sitangkai, the southernmost part of the Sulu Archipelago adjacent to Sabah.

Nowadays, over ninety percent of the population of both the Tausug and Sama groups are Muslim. They have been known as maritime peoples whose livelihoods are traditionally based on maritime trade and fishing, except a small percentage who engage in agriculture. Located on the periphery of the Republic of the Philippines, which is often described as a "weak state", Sulu is in a situation where the order and administrative rule of the central state does not extend in any effective manner to its territory. Even when crimes committed by individuals are set aside, the local area is known for the frequent eruption of all manners of group violence as outlined below.

Conflict and peace in Sama society

As a preliminary step toward analyzing the rituals in relation to conflict resolution in Sama, I will briefly outline the situation surrounding local conflicts and peace. The Sulu Archipelago, including Sitangkai Island, along with the island of Mindanao, were strongly impacted by the so-called "Mindanao conflict", an armed conflict between The Armed Forces of the Philippines and a variety of Muslim secessionist rebel groups inspired by the Muslim secessionist movement that began in the 1970s. The area is still rife with the activities of anti-government forces such as the Moro National Liberation Front (MNLF), the Moro Islamic Liberation Front (MILF) and the Abu Sayyaf Group (ASG). In addition to these, there have been unending streams of killings and assaults in revenge and retaliatory conflicts motivated by personal grudges (*rido*, *magkontra*, *magbalos*) as well as the activities of the private armies of politicians, vigilante groups and various kinds of pirates. The overall security situation is far from being stable in the Sulu maritime world.

In this brutal situation, however, the Sama people on Sitangkai Island (Sama Dilaut) are commonly seen as a "peaceful people" by both themselves and others. In other words, the typical ethnic stereotype among the Sama people on Sitangkai and other islands in the Sulu maritime world is that they are a "peace-loving people", whereas they are often referred to as a "timid people" or a "meek people who don't fight" by other groups.

This contrasts sharply with the stereotype of, for instance, the Tausug-speaking people who claim to be "brave", whereas other groups describe them as "militant", "aggressive" and "cruel". These ethnic stereotypes are not entirely baseless; the actual data on group violence corroborate the assessments to a certain extent. For example, of the twenty-two piracy incidents that happened during my research period in Tawi Tawi province from June 1992 to December 1994 for which I was able to confirm the ethnicity and other details of those involved, perpetrators in sixteen cases (about seventy-two percent) were Tausug while no Sama Dilaut from Sitangkai were involved in any of the cases (Sama Dea from other islands were among the perpetrators in six cases). On the other hand, the Sama of Sitangkai were victims in ten cases. Of the seventeen confirmed cases of retaliatory conflicts involving serious physical violence causing casualties over the same period, seven cases were fights between Sama Dea groups, five cases were among the Tausug, two cases were between the Tausug and the Sama Dea and one case was between the Sama Dea and the Visayans (Christian Filipinos from the Visayan Islands). No Sama from Sitangkai Island was found to be involved in any of the conflicts (see Tokoro 2013 for details).

Considering the above, how is it possible for the Sama to create their reputation as a "peaceful people", an apparently rare exception amid the social environment of the Sulu maritime world plagued by pirates and violent retribution?

In reality, even the society of the "peace-loving" Sama is not exactly a utopian community free of internal conflicts of interest, friction and disputes (e.g., the so-called "noble savages"). This fact is deeply recognized by the Sama themselves, who consider that failure to resolve a conflict invites deep animosity and division that leads to a perilous condition (a "hot" situation, to be discussed later) that poses serious threats and uncertainties to the entire community as well as individuals.

Although the formal institutions of a modern nation-state for security maintenance and justice do exist on paper in the Sulu maritime world, it is clear that they are in a state of dysfunction judging from the prevailing situation in which the authorities have consistently failed to deter or resolve violent incidents of piracy and retaliatory conflicts. In other words, the Sama have found themselves in a situation where the formal institutions or devices of the modern state for conflict resolution are not functioning.

To state the conclusion first, the Sama have been, in reality, dealing with friction and conflict under these circumstances while attempting various informal conflict resolution practices other than state institutions based on all kinds of conventional practices. These informal means of conflict resolution include multiple practices ranging from conflict avoidance by relocation, third-party mediation and self-control by supernatural ideation, to rituals for reconciliation. Before I begin the discussion centering on conflict resolution through symbolic practices such as rituals in particular, I would like to supplement the above overview of conflict and resolution in Sama with more general background information.

Antagonistic relationship

Despite its "peaceful" reputation, Sama society on Sitangkai Island is not free from various forms of friction, dissent and conflict. After living on the island for a certain period, it is not uncommon to encounter scenes of argument or dispute that have broken out for various reasons between Sama people. These disputes sometimes develop into serious situations where curse words or insults are hurled at one another and on relatively rare occasions they can escalate into scuffles or fistfights. When the animosity between parties deepens to the extent that their adversary relationship is recognized by themselves and others, the parties are called "*magbanta*" (enemies) in an antagonistic relationship and their conflict becomes apparent to everyone.

All forms of everyday mutual aid activities are suspended between parties in an antagonistic relationship who are not supposed to talk to one another at all.

Various conventions for conflict resolution

Among the Sama of Sitangkai, the aforementioned antagonistic relationship (*magbanta*) is recognized as a potentially dangerous situation (a "hot" situation in their vernacular) that may have seriously harmful effects on not only the opposing parties and their families but also the entire Sama community. For this reason, conflict resolution is sought via various means according to the Sama's "ancestral ways" or the various conventions that are collectively called "*adat*". They include, among others, conflict resolution by relocation and third-party mediation.

Conflict management by way of relocation is the most temporary of all these measures, typically involving the placing of a physical distance between the antagonistic parties in order to avoid further clashes or escalation of the conflict. However, the act of distancing is often a temporary measure only to prevent exacerbation of the situation and the complete resolution of conflicts themselves tends to require further measures such as conflict resolution rituals, as we shall see later.

Another commonly used means for conflict resolution is third-party mediation. For example, in the case of elopement (*magpole*), which is one of the major causes of conflict among Sama, it is common to attempt mediation by a third party such as an imam from a mosque, *panglima*[5] or shaman. These mediators are called "*fukum*".

Conflict resolution by symbolic practices

In the context of the maintenance and reproduction of social order in Sama society in Sitangkai, the means of conflict resolution via symbolic practices such as rituals and folk beliefs connected to "ancestral ways" occupy a place as important as the other measures. The next section will describe, in particular, a type of trial by ordeal called "*magsapa*" (oath-taking ritual) that is being practiced by modern-day Sama, and a reconciliation ritual called "*magkiparat*", as well as their beliefs surrounding "hot" and "cool" that form the conceptual backdrop, so to speak, behind these rituals.

Conflict resolution by oath-taking ritual

Firstly, I shall describe a ritual called "*magsapa*" (oath-taking ritual). Loosely speaking, *magsapa* is similar to the so-called "trial by ordeal", but more specifically, it is usually performed via the following steps.

For example, conflicts involving stealing can sometimes degenerate into unproductive arguments between parties who endlessly repeat, "Yes, you did"/"No, I didn't". In such cases, a *panglima* (barangay captain) hears claims from both parties to formulate a judgment or to attempt mediation first. If this measure fails to end the dispute, *magsapa* is performed as the next step.

The *magsapa* ritual is often witnessed by a shaman or a *pakil* (a mosque official well versed in religious matters) as well as the *panglima*. At the start of the ritual, the *panglima* brings the Quran and opens the middle page. The two disputing parties (called A and B) take turns placing their right hand on the page while raising their left hand. A and B take the following oaths (let's say that this hypothetical case involves the allegation that B stole gold ornaments from A). A begins by saying "I swear on Thirty Chapters of the Holy Quran. B stole gold from me". B follows with "I swear on Thirty Chapters of the Holy Quran. I did not steal gold from A".

The ritual ends with the above oath-taking. Humans do not take any further action. It is believed that whoever did not tell the truth, either A or B, in front of the Quran will inevitably fall ill in the future. The most common consequence is said to be an unusual illness involving abdominal distension. Falling ill as a result of *magsapa* is expressed as "struck by the oath" (*taluwa sapa*).

Example of *magsapa* on Sitangkai Island

A Sama woman (A) in Sitangkai had successive relationships with a man (B) followed by another man (C). She fell pregnant shortly after she started seeing C, who insisted that he was not the father of the baby and refused to marry her. When the matter became complicated, *magsapa* was performed before an imam. C subsequently became prone to illness.

Magsapa is generally performed at a mosque or in a remote out-of-sight location on the fringe of the island. At a mosque, the ritual is conducted with due considerations so that the news will not spread to the general public outside of the parties to the dispute, their representatives and the *fukum*.

On Sitangkai Island, some people say that performing *magsapa* outside of a mosque may result in punishment by God befalling not only the parties to the dispute but also the entire island, which may be visited by misfortunes such as the withering of palm trees. The notion that the harmful effects of conflicts may extend to not only those directly involved but also their families, relatives and in some cases, unrelated villagers is apparent in the Sama community in general. In particular, there is the latent belief that if neither of the parties to the conflict is met with illness or other misfortunes despite the implementation of *magsapa*, calamities will instead befall innocent bystanders or the entire community.

For instance, a small, uninhabited island adjacent to Sitangkai called Sitangkai Mariki used to have a beautiful palm tree-lined beach, but by the early 1990s all the palm trees were decimated and white sand on the beach was largely lost. Many villagers believe that this disaster was brought on as the consequence of a *magsapa* performed several years earlier.

The belief that misfortunes will befall the entire community or the descendants or relatives of the parties to a conflict if either of the parties escapes them can be found on Simunul Island as well as Sitangkai Island. This belief among Sama is deeply connected to their supernatural ideation surrounding "hotness" and "coolness", as described below.

"Hot" and "cool"

Let us examine their concepts of "hot" and "cool" here. The Sama of Sitangkai generally consider actions in violation of *adat* (traditions and conventions) or "ancestral ways" as "hot" (*apasu*) actions. Accordingly, any violation can spread the danger caused by "hotness" (*pasu*) to people other than the parties involved and potentially the whole community. The opposite of this "hot" state is that of "coolness" (*digin*). Being the very reverse of the "hot" state, the "cool" state is where social order and peace prevail because people live by the "ancestral ways" from the old "ancestral age".

The actions considered to be disrespectful of *adat*, including sexual relationships contravening the incest taboo, lack of faith in various supernatural or spiritual beings such as God, *jinn* (spirit), *sumagat* (spirit of people) and *mbo* (ancestral spirit) and the nonperformance of or nonparticipation in rituals, are regarded as "hot" actions associated with moral culpability (*dusa*).

Besides those who have committed these "hot" actions, the "hotness" is said to ripple through their families, relatives and even the entire village community. The "hotness" is thought to have negative effects on the relationship between nature and humans, bringing on disasters such as pestilence and drought. Disputes, dissension and conflicts within a community are regarded as particularly "hot" incidents that pose a major threat to the community. For example, a prolonged state of "hotness" such as a conflict between relatives or villagers may bring misfortunes, including illnesses, deaths, poor catches of fish and accidents, to unspecified third parties other than the opposing parties.

Peace Building in the Wild

In fact, it is not uncommon among Sama of Sitangkai to hear stories about people who became ill or even died as a result of "hotness" caused by conflicts between relatives, even though they had no direct involvement in them. In the Sama language, being struck down by misfortunes such as illness and death as a result of such "hotness" is expressed as "struck by hotness" (*taluwa pasu*).

The following is one example of people being "struck by hotness".

The case of the death of a baby brought on by the "hotness" of a family conflict

Haji Abdul (pseudonym), a Sama trader in Sitangkai, and his blood sister Burrawang (pseudonym) had been in conflict for over a decade. It started from a petty squabble between the relatives on Haji Abdul's wife's side and his own sister and father. Haji Abdul ended up siding with his wife's relatives and standing against his own father, sister and uncles. Haji Abdul stopped talking to his father and sister and estranged himself from the family. His brother Haji Yunus (pseudonym) did not wish to get involved in this conflict; he maintained his association with both families equally instead of taking sides. The hostile relationship between Haji Abdul and Burrawang (and their respective families) continued for a long time. When they finally reached reconciliation (*maghap*), it was for the following reason.

While this antagonistic relationship was ongoing, Haji Yunus went to work in Sabah, Malaysia, leaving his wife and one-year-old baby in Sitangkai. While he was away, his baby suddenly died of an illness, even though the baby had been healthy and showed no signs of any illness before. This tragedy brought deep grief to Haji Yunus and his wife as well as his relatives, including Haji Abdul and Burrawang. The baby's death was thought to have been a case of being "struck by heat" (*taluwa pasu*). In other words, the baby fell ill and died because of the "hotness" (*pasu*) caused by the antagonistic relationship between siblings Haji Abdul and Burrawang within a blood family. It is believed that conflicts and dissent between Sama of Sitangkai, especially within the immediate family and relatives, are culpable actions in violation of *adat*, and the resultant "hotness" causes illnesses and death among the relatives by way of penance. The situation changed dramatically following the sudden death of the baby. All the related parties to the conflict, including Haji Abdul and Burrawang, gathered to acknowledge and repent that their conflict had brought about the death of an innocent baby. Haji Abdul and Burrawang forgave each other and cried in an embrace. Thus the family and relatives of Haji Abdul were able to reconcile and unite as one (*magdakayu*).

As this case shows, there is the idea that a prolonged state of "hotness" can potentially inflict suffering, including illness and death, on people who are not necessarily involved in the conflict directly. In order to remove this risk, the "hot" state needs to be "cooled" in some way. As one of the "cooling" measures, the "hotness removal" (*nilaanan pasu*) ritual is sometimes performed as required. This ritual is used typically when parties wish to enter into a "hot" marriage that violates *adat*, and the "hotness removal" ritual is performed in exchange for permission to marry.

Among Sama of Sitangkai, a marriage between paternal parallel cousins, for example, is considered to be an inappropriate "hot" marriage from the perspective of *adat*. This is because "blood" (*laha*) is believed to be passed down through the patrilineal line in Sama and that patrilineal parallel cousins (especially first cousins) have the same blood. Accordingly, a marriage between them is seen to have an element of incest (*sumbang*) similar to a marriage between siblings (albeit to a lesser degree). From the viewpoint of *adat*, therefore, paternal parallel cousins are excluded from the list of suitable spousal options. In reality, however, there are a small number of cases in which paternal parallel cousins strongly wish to marry each other (despite opposition from their family and relatives).

In these cases, resolution is sought through a symbolic means by way of performing a "hotness removal" ritual to negate the potential "hotness" of this type of marriage. In the ritual, plates brought by the couple are smashed on the beach or some other location for the removal of the "hotness" surrounding the marriage. Sama use another type of ritual for reconciliation and the resolution of "hot" conflicts, which is called "*magkiparat*".

Magkiparat or reconciliation ritual

The original meaning of *magkiparat* in the Sama language implies "to atone" (*kiparat*) for sins and hotness caused by conflicts. In an ordinary context, it mainly refers to a reconciliation ritual concerning conflicts, antagonistic relationships and disputes. This ritual is performed typically for the purpose of achieving reconciliation between hostile parties as well as healing for stricken persons where a conflict or dispute has persisted in the form of a seriously antagonistic relationship and its "hotness" has caused illnesses or other misfortunes.

More specifically, there are three subcategories of *magkiparat* among the Sama of Sitangkai, namely, *magkiparat mata* (raw *kiparat*), *magkiparat tahak* (cooked *kiparat*) and *magkiparat duwaa* (prayer *kiparat*).

Peace Building in the Wild

Photo 9.1 A reconciliation ritual where previously antagonistic parties ask for forgiveness from one another

Magkiparat mata, in which eggs are used for one of the offerings, is the first-instance ritual for conflict resolution and the removal of "hotness" for healing when someone is struck by illness due to a conflict. This ritual is attended by representatives or family members of the parties to the antagonistic relationship (*magbanta*) and a formal declaration is made in the presence of a mediator (*fukum*) that the hostility has been resolved and the parties have reconciled. The parties to the conflict then ask for forgiveness for their culpability in causing a conflict in breach of *adat* and at the same time pray for the speedy recovery of the sick person stricken by the "hotness". The ritual ends here, and if the patient subsequently makes a recovery, it is deemed that the antagonistic relationship and its "hotness" have been removed and "coolness" has been restored.

In some cases, the patient's condition does not improve at all for months following the performance of the *magkiparat mata* ritual. It is believed that the *magkiparat tahak* (cooked *kiparat*) ritual should be conducted in this situation. Generally, the "cooked *kiparat*" ritual is larger and more costly than the "raw *kiparat*" ritual in its scale and attendance, as villagers who have no direct involvement are also invited. While eggs are used as offerings at the "raw *kirapat*" ritual, cooked chicken meat is always used as offerings at the "cooked *kiparat*" ritual.

The procedures of the ritual and the contents of speeches given can vary greatly depending on the circumstances of the conflict in question. In any case, however, all reconciliation rituals have commonality in that they are attended by the parties to the conflict or hostility, their families, the sick person stricken by "hotness" and the mediators, who declare and witness that the hostility has ended and seek forgiveness for the violation of *adat*.

Ill speech (*ling sangka*) among family and relatives as well as expressions disrespectful of elders are generally regarded as "hot words", the utterance of which often brings misfortunes to the speaker or their family. It is sometimes said that such ill speech amounts to "speaking ill of God" (*ling sangka ma Tuhan*). In particular, ill speech containing statements of severance of kinship ties such as "You are no longer my child" or "You are not my parent" cannot be undone by way of the aforementioned rituals, *magkiparat mata* and *magkiparat tahak*, and therefore the performance of the *magkiparat duwaa* (prayer *kiparat*) ritual is considered necessary.

The *magkiparat duwaa* ritual requires three *ganta* (one *ganta* is equivalent to approximately 1.5 kilograms) of rice, three coconuts, three eggs and sometimes a goat as offerings. The goat is slaughtered by a *pakil*, who cuts its throat while saying a prayer in Arabic, then cooked and offered as an altarage. If the conflict or hostility is more severe, seven *ganta* of rice and seven coconuts are offered, and if the case is even more severe, nine *ganta* of rice and nine coconuts are required. Some say that offerings for this ritual are made in odd numbers because even numbers are associated with a dichotomy between two opposing parties. Thus, it is possible to define the reconciliation rituals as symbolic practices for the resolution of "hot" incidents, especially potentially dangerous situations such as disputes and conflicts, against the backdrop of the concepts of "hotness" and "coolness".

We must take note, however, of the fact that these symbolic practices are not necessarily akin to algorithms that automatically resolve real-life disputes and dissension. Real-life situations are much more complex and conflict is not uncommon in the actual social process, for the reproduction of social order takes place in the context of various twists and turns and the formation of microscopic differences and rifts. I shall examine these conditions based on more specific ethnographic accounts in the next section.

Ethnography of incidents: Elopement, conflict, sickness and death

Incidents surrounding elopement

I have so far outlined how various frameworks of traditional beliefs and ritual practices are involved in the handling of friction, dissent and conflicts in the real

Peace Building in the Wild

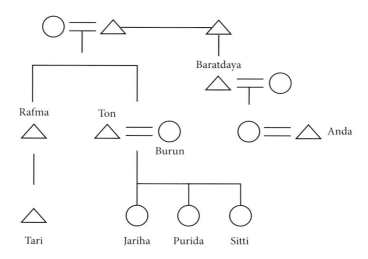

Figure 9.1 Relationships

society of Sama. I have also suggested that these ritual practices can be regarded as something akin to symbolic practices to remove the "hotness" associated with friction or contingency that inevitably arise in Sama's real-life social activities and to restore "coolness" to their society. At the same time, however, they do not always succeed in restoring the integrity of their desirable social order (i.e., sustaining and restoring "coolness") to the extent of their expectations. I shall examine a series of incidents, which I encountered on Sitangkai Island, including a case of elopement, the ongoing antagonistic relationships between relatives surrounding it and the death of a relative that occurred amid a state of tension.

The case of the elopement of Jariha and Tari
The background to the elopement
On October 16, 1992, when I was staying at the home of Rahim, the base for my long-term field research on Sitangkai Island, the following news was brought to us. Jariha, the sister of Sitti, who is related to Rahim, had run off (*magpole*) with a man named Tari the previous night. Jariha's father Ton and Tari's father Rafma are brothers (Ton was older), and therefore Jariha and Tari were paternal parallel first cousins (see Figure 9.1; pseudonyms have been used throughout).

Sama of Sitangkai generally avoid marriage between paternal parallel first cousins as they consider such situations to be "hot" and a form of incestuous relationship. Accordingly, such couples cannot marry unless they resort to unorthodox measures such as elopement.

Tari and Jariha fled to the home of the local barangay captain, one of the *fukum* (mediators) on the island, and announced their intention to elope. The barangay captain notified Tari's and Jariha's respective families of their elopement according to tradition.

The marriage between Jariha and Tari met strong opposition, particularly from Jariha's mother Burun. She adamantly disapproved, not simply because it was a "hot" marriage between first cousins.

Before Tari eloped with Jariha, he had been living at Ton's home as a member of his family. Tari and Jariha eventually fell in love and he formally asked Jariha's parents (Ton and Burun) to approve their marriage, but his request was refused. Jariha's parents took this stance because the marriage would bring shame to the family if people suspected that premarital sex had occurred at Ton's home, as the two had been living in the same house prior to marriage. Another factor was that Tari left Ton's home immediately after the marriage proposal was refused, traveled to Semporna and spoke ill of Ton and his family among his relatives there. His actions reached the ears of Ton and the family and heightened their anger. As Ton's family hardened their stance further, Tari made a plan to run off with Jariha and elope.

The next day, the families of Jariha and Tari met to discuss the problem before the barangay captain as the *fukum*. Although Tari's family approved of the marriage, Jariha's family opposed it. Accordingly, the *fukum* recommended that they postpone the marriage. It was decided that Tari and Jariha would lodge in the barangay captain's home until the problem was solved. In November the couple managed to marry by overriding the objections from Burun and others thanks to mediation by the *fukum*. However, the incident left hard feelings in those who were involved and Burun in particular continued to hold grudges against Tari and his father Rafma. Under these circumstances, Jariha's father and Burun's husband Ton suddenly succumbed to an illness, as described below.

Ton's illness and death
It was the afternoon of January 7, 1993. Ton's first daughter Sitti (Jariha's sister) came to see me at the home of Rahim and said in a panicked manner that Ton was having chest pains. I gave Ton some over-the-counter painkiller tablets and took

his temperature with a thermometer, which was as high as thirty-eight degrees C. Although I momentarily suspected some kind of heart disease, I, not being a doctor, had no way of making an accurate diagnosis. As the doctor at the Sitangkai clinic was away at the time, I called a nurse and midwife, who arrived at around five in the evening. I was able to hear the faint voice of Ton muttering "La ilaha illallah" amid severe pain.

Rahim's brothers and relatives gathered at his house in large numbers. I found it a little odd that at the time Rahim was telling jokes and his female relatives were laughing. While it gave the impression of being "cool" or disrespectful toward the sick, it also looked as if they were trying to prevent the mood from becoming more serious and tense. Amid this atmosphere, Ton's in-law named Anda (pseudonym) let out a grunt sound. When I looked, I saw him groaning with a pained expression on his face as he extended and retracted one arm.

Anda appeared possessed by something and in a trance. In Sama, when someone falls ill, a relative can go into a trance even if that person is not a shaman. Anda was possessed by the *sumagat* (spirit) of the late Baratdaya, Ton's paternal parallel first cousin and renowned shaman leader. Baratdaya was Anda's father-in-law.

The words of Anda in a trance were interpreted to the effect that the spirit of Baratdaya gave Ton an episode of pain to punish him for not helping Anda's shed-building project because he was too preoccupied with the production of his own *lepa* (a type of houseboat).

However, this interpretation was rejected by those present. Next, a man named Mijar, another of Ton's relatives (whose wife is Ton's niece), hung a gold ring from a thread over a white dish filled with water. Mijar kept his arm stationary while another man Buwasu put forward possible causes of Ton's illness. This method of diagnosis by a golden ring (*sinsin*) is called *pangdaan*.

The *pangdaan* began as people looked on. Firstly, Buwasu asked, "Is it because Ton didn't help Anda build his shed?", but the ring hanging from Mijar's hand did not move. Buwasu continued, "Is it because Ton gave priority to building his own *lepa* and put off *tempel* (a type of houseboat) building for the *jinn*?" but the ring did not move. As soon as Buwasu asked, "Is it because the *sumagat* of Tongnon, Ton's father, is angry that he made his daughters unhappy?" (referring to the family discord caused by the elopement of Jariha), the ring began to swing in large circles and this conflict was thus identified as the cause of Ton's illness.

In time, Ton's brother Rafma arrived to see his sick brother. As soon as Ton's wife Burun saw Rafma, she assaulted him. Sitti desperately pulled her away shouting, "Mother! Stop!". Rafma had to forget about seeing his brother, as he was not allowed to enter the house. Burun had attacked him because of her resentment about the elopement incident as well as her belief that Ton's illness had been caused by the "hotness" of the act of elopement.

On the other hand, Rahim's wife, who was present at the time, said, "It won't be resolved unless the brothers (Ton and Rafma and their families) reconcile. Because they haven't reconciled, the spirit of the brothers' late father Tongnon made Ton sick as a punishment for their conflict".

The following day, Ton's wife and relatives visited the graves of Tongnon (Ton's father) and Baratdaya (Ton's paternal parallel first cousin) and performed a ritual to ask for forgiveness (a type of *magpakan sumagat* ritual) by lighting the favorite cigarettes of the deceased, burning incense and sprinkling green scented water. Tongnon was implicated as one of the causes of Ton's illness at the aforementioned séance by the ring, and Baratdaya in the *jinn's* revelation.

At the gravesites, Burun and Ton's mother-in-law Ranka made calls such as "Please make (Ton's) body strong" (*Akosogin baran na.*) and "Please heal his body" (*Pahapin baran na.*). Ton's children and others pulled out weeds from around the gravesites. After that, they visited and paid their respects to the graves of seven relatives in total. They repeated the same calls at each gravesite.

At a later date, the family took Ton to a hospital on Bongao Island for some tests on Rahim's advice. He was hospitalized and underwent an examination, which found terminal lung cancer. Ton died in hospital almost suddenly on January 24, less than one month after he first complained of chest pain.

Incidents and the generation of stories

While the events surrounding Ton's illness and death took place as described above, Ton's illness (and death) was not confined to a physiological or medical event that happened to the body of a particular individual, but it went on to involve other related people and incidents. In more specific terms, Ton's illness incited another's body to resonate with it as demonstrated by Anda's trance state, and evolved while several different versions of the story were generated as it was associated with the contexts of separate incidents such as the elopement in the family and the hostile relationship within the family surrounding this event. Certain versions focused on a particular incident (e.g., a family conflict between Ton and Rafma) out of many possible causes of Ton's illness, identified it as the "cause" and offered that interpretation for circulation. In other versions, other incidents (e.g., the "hot" marriage between Jariha and Tari itself) were associated with the illness and contextualized.

For instance, Ton's wife Burun maintained or even intensified her animosity toward Rafma, his family and Tari after her husband's death and her antagonistic relationship with them continued. This was because Burun believed that her husband's death had been caused by the "hot" marriage between Jariha and Tari, and this interpretation of the incident was also favored by many of her relatives. Her bitterness remained long after Ton's almost sudden death, and Burun held animosity toward Tari, his family and even her eloped daughter Jariha. Villagers speculated that Burun even loathed her other daughter Purida as she had discovered that Purida had secretly helped her younger sister Jariha to run off.

In this case, despite the existence of beliefs surrounding "hotness" and "coolness" (or rather because of them), people were unable to remove the repercussions and "hotness" of the incident to reincorporate it into a stable and desirable (i.e., "cool" according to *adat*) frame of cultural interpretation (story) of social order and unity.

Especially regarding Ton's illness and sudden death, interpretation surrounding the cause itself has diverged into multiple narratives and is yet to be consolidated. In other words, at least three different narratives surrounding Ton's illness and death are still circulating among the parties and their relatives:

1. The *sumagat* of Baratdaya inflicted an illness on Ton as he failed to help Anda with his building project.
2. The *sumagat* of Ton's father caused the illness because Ton and Rafma failed to reconcile and made Jariha unhappy.
3. The elopement and "hot" marriage of Tari and Jariha caused the illness and death.

(2) and (3) in particular treat Ton and Jariha in completely opposite ways in terms of who the culpable party was. In version (2), Ton himself was responsible for the unfortunate incident that befell him and Jariha was seen as a victim. By contrast, version (3) held Jariha responsible for Ton's misfortune because she, along with Tari, caused "hotness" by committing a first-cousin marriage.

When I visited Sitangkai five years after Ton's passing, I discovered the generation of a new version (4) explaining Ton's illness and death. According to this interpretation, "The direct cause of Ton's death was hemorrhaging from severe impact when he fell off the roof and hit his back against his *lepa* three months earlier, but that accident was caused by the *saitan* (bad spirit)".

This type of story-creation through the association of separate incidents provides a glimpse into the generation of multiple narratives (interpretations) branching out one after another. When we take a closer look, we can identify the existence of situations which do not necessarily fit into this schema in which stories about these kinds of shocking events coalesce and evolve to fit into a desirable and stable social order or become a uniform and shared cultural story (interpretive frame) via symbolic practices.

In reality, as we have seen above, conventional institutional devices, including symbolic practices, need to be understood as something that provides actors with multiple cultural idioms (e.g., "hotness", "*sumagat*", etc.) to weave different (and sometimes non-conjugatable) stories from their respective standpoints rather than as algorithms that automatically determine actors' behaviors even at the Institution II level.

From this perspective, it is clear that the processes of reconciliation and peacemaking via rituals and other devices are also built upon complex interactions or dynamic multistep processes rather than planned harmonious automatic ones.

The aforementioned series of incidents visibly demonstrates that even in a so-called traditional society actors are not automaton-like beings who always follow the courses of action prescribed by cultural norms, values and traditions (at the Institution II level), and at the same time suggests that these incidents themselves contain the potential possibility of sometimes producing irreversible and irreparable changes in the society or cultural framework, albeit on a microscopic scale.

Institution as a collection of contingent processes

Let us return to a more abstract level and see what the aforementioned cases are pointing to. Firstly, in the Sulu maritime world in the southern Philippines, various institutions of modernity at the level of what I call Institution I exist, including a modern nation-state and a legislature, that on paper (supposedly) control and constrain the society. Looking at the situation at an ethnographic level in more detail, however, it is no exaggeration to say that those formal institutions in the narrow sense are in effect more or less dysfunctional or anomalous in general, as demonstrated by the prevalence of all sorts of violence and conflict in the local area and the difficulty of enforcing security or resolving dissent through the justice system. We have seen in this chapter that a variety of informal conflict resolution measures, including rituals and other symbolic practices, show a certain degree of effectiveness in terms of filling the void left by the dysfunction and virtual absence of formal institutions.

In other words, it is reasonable to say that what is found in the area is the failure of institutions at the Institution I level and, on the reverse side, the relative foregrounding of informal institutions and conventions in the broad sense, i.e., at the Institution II level. We have seen that Institution II contains various gradations and diversity in terms of conflict management ranging from conflict avoidance by physical relocation, third-party mediation or arbitration to the utilization of rituals and other symbolic practices. While this chapter has provided detailed descriptions of conflict resolution through ritual practices and beliefs surrounding the concepts of "hotness" and "coolness", it is becoming more common among the locals to refer to Islamic law (*sharia*), which is becoming more influential in the area, for the resolution of conflicts concerning marriage and property inheritance. To sum up, it is evident in today's Sama society that "Institution II" exists along with the so-called modern legal institutions in the narrow sense (including state organizations such as the police and the courts), and within Institution II many institutions of different origins exert various actions and interactions on each other, including traditional ritual practices, a variety of beliefs and ideological practices surrounding "hotness" and "coolness" and Islamic codes. Thus, upon closer examination, Institution II is in a state that can be described as an assemblage (discontinuous aggregation, collection) of all kinds of idioms such as practices and ideas of different origins and never forms a monolithic (or coherent) system.

If this understanding is correct, the conclusion of this chapter—that the processes of conflict resolution via Institution II are quite dynamic rather than static—will prove convincing. In other words, Institution II is a collection of multiple cultural practices and ideas of different origins rather than a set of algorithms to restore peace in a planned harmonious manner through the adjustment of actors' behaviors; in the conflict resolution process, multiple actors interact with one another through this bricolage-like assembly. It is understandable that this kind of ad hoc process inevitably has an extremely dynamic nature filled with the contingencies inherent in every incident. It has also been suggested here that, as a result, the existence of Institution II in itself does not necessarily guarantee the reduction of uncertainties associated with interactions such as conflicts and dissent or restore peaceful social order.

For example, despite the existence of the local practices of these rituals, it is true that there are many cases where a conflict becomes protracted with no resolution in sight or an attempt (ritual) for reconciliation fails. It is also possible to point out the fact that conflict handling through reconciliation rituals is generally effective only for "internal" conflicts within the same ethnic group, even in the Sulu maritime world, and not so for conflicts and violence "between" different ethnic groups. Thus, this chapter has confirmed that while informal conflict resolution measures at the Institution II level, especially symbolic practices such as rituals, have a certain degree of effectiveness under the dysfunctional condition of Institution I belonging to modern nation-states, their effectiveness has certain limitations.

These arguments call fresh attention to this (somewhat startling) situation, in which social order in humans is like a tiny island just staying afloat in the vast ocean of disorder in spite of (or because of) the existence of various institutional devices. In other words, it is possible to observe that although human society appears to have institutional orders, which on paper remove the complexities of social orders and interaction *a priori*, the process is in some aspects actually founded on rather tenuous contingencies rather than rock-solid foundations.

Finally, I would like to consider the significance of the aforementioned cases in the context of anthropological research concerning institutions. As is well known, there is a line of argument in the field of cultural (social) anthropology that is critical of structuralism and other paradigms that describe others one encounters in the field as beings driven by socio-cultural devices, that is, automated machine-like mechanisms. In particular, the arguments of Bourdieu (1988) and Ortner (1984) focusing on the "habitus" and practices of actors are widely known.

However, these arguments, especially the concept of habitus, have drawn criticism for relying on a kind of black box-like concept that fails to provide a full explanation as to why it produces practices without recourse to the existing cultural and social rules in a given situation (Tanabe 2010: 197). It is possible to say in this context that the cases referred to here have pointed out the existence of the broad frameworks for what I call "Institution II" and at the same time articulated through concrete ethnographic accounts and analysis the extremely dynamic way they operate at the microscopic level, in the process of conflict resolution for example, as they inevitably involve the contingencies inherent in interactions between actors. On this point, the cases analyzed in this chapter appear to offer a major clue to a more relative view of the commonly accepted notion of institution that tends to treat the existence of strict rules or norms or the higher authorities (typically formal organizations) that guarantee their enforcement as given.

10 Institutionalized Cattle Raiding: Its Formalization and Value Creation Amongst the Pastoral Dodoth

Kaori Kawai

Key ideas

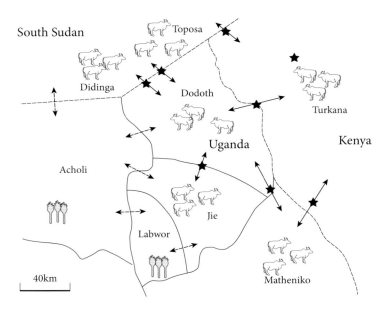

The lines marked with a star at the borders between ethnic groups indicate that their relationship involves engaging (during hostilities) in mutual raiding (livestock rustling) and moving freely across shared borders (in times of peace). Where there is no star, the ethnic groups have neither friendly nor hostile relations with each other. Usually, over time, both sides alternate between hostile and friendly relations. The Dodoth, for example, are repeatedly hostile to and then friendly with the Toposa, Didinga, Turkana, Jie and Matheniko. These ethnic groups are all heavily reliant on cattle (livestock); they are assemblies of raiding peoples who are repeatedly hostile to/friendly with one another; and herds of cattle move to and fro between these ethnic groups. I will refer to this sphere as the supracommunal pastoral value-sharing sphere (pastoral value-sharing sphere).

Raiding and being raided

Raiding, as widely recognized in East African pastoral societies, refers to "raids aimed at the mutual rustling of herds of livestock by neighboring ethnic groups who subsist mainly on their livestock". This state of affairs is the subject of the present chapter, and I examine it from the perspective that this raiding is an "institution". Pastoral peoples who live in the arid and semi-arid areas of East Africa have long been known as "warlike pastoral peoples" because of their raiding response and their "ferocity". In an ethnography full of rich descriptions of the lifestyle and inner psychological world of the Dodoth people, E. M. Thomas, who surveyed the Dodoth of Uganda in the 1960s, bluntly called them "Warrior Herdsmen" (1979). I have been conducting field research on the Dodoth ethnic group since 1996. Various cultural and social phenomena in Thomas' description of the world of the Dodoth have disappeared with the passage of more than half a century. Alternatively, they have achieved a new prominence. The weapons used in raiding have now become small arms such as AK47-type automatic rifles. Not knowing how to deal with the "brutality" of the pastoral peoples, who were acting in a thoroughly extreme manner as a result of the modernization of their weapons, the Ugandan government embarked on a program of disarmament. This initiative commenced amongst the Dodoth in 2002, and after resorting to military force that even included aerial bombing, government troops appear to have had some success in confiscating firearms. However, raiding still continues today (2012) with little sign that it will disappear.

Raiding—*ajore* in Dodoth—consists of hostile mutual acts of violent rustling/ being rustled of the livestock that is indispensible to the livelihoods of pastoral peoples. It is a phenomenon that is directly and profoundly related to their lives and lifestyles. For this reason, raiding has often been the focus of anthropological research on pastoralists in these regions and the subject of various arguments. Many Japanese anthropologists continue to study this area (for example Sagawa 2011; Miyawaki 2006; Fukui 2004b; Kurimoto 1996, 1999). During my field research with the Dodoth, I was aware of the fact that the young men of the settlement where I was staying had embarked on raiding activities on several occasions, that the settlement head's herd of cattle had suffered the most over the course of two raids and that there were also times when practically all of the cattle owned by settlements were lost. Raiding is thus not at all an unusual or infrequent "incident". It is an event that is unpredictable in terms of who will be the victim and when. I see raiding as a social phenomenon that can occur routinely. During fieldwork, I studied ritual acts on a daily basis, such as the various forms of ritual and divination carried out in order to avoid and repel raiding, the installation of fetishes and the smearing of faces and bodies with red and white mud. Much more than raiding itself, it was rather the extremely exaggerated ritual actions of pastoral peoples—who are generally said to have limited ritual practices compared with agricultural peoples—that drew my interest. Participants were the epitome of earnestness itself, carrying out these practices in a deadly serious manner. This indicates the extent to which raiding was a matter-of-fact event for these people.

Raiding was a commonly suffered phenomenon that males would encounter two or three times during their lives, from the time that they first possessed their own animal herds (around thirty to thirty-five years of age). Moreover, losing their entire herd in one go represents the greatest disaster that can befall a Dodoth herdsman. I questioned people about the circumstances of the seemingly daily reports of raiding: "Who suffered the loss and where and when?", "Roughly how many head of animals were in the herd that had been rustled?" and "Which ethnic group had carried out the raiding and what was its scale in terms of the number of participants?" Some of the other questions I would ask the owner of a herd included: "How many times have you been the victim of raiding thus far?" and "How many times, to date, have you set out on raids and how many head of animals have you captured and on these occasions, how many people were injured or killed?"[1]

Whenever raiding became the topic of conversation, I listened carefully. I sometimes also visited previous raiding sites with people who told me about the raids on the spot. People performed on-site detailed re-enactments for me of the exchanges that had occurred there. In the course of these sorts of experiences, I discussed the function of raiding, its generative mechanisms and the reasons for its existence, and I also considered the specific feelings and emotions that raiding arouses (see for example, Kawai 2004, 2006, 2007, 2013).

The format of this chapter is as follows. Firstly, after having outlined the actual state of raiding amongst the Dodoth, I describe the "arrangement" that is evident between the assembly of people who go out raiding together (hereafter, the raiding group) and the assembly of those who will be the targets of the raid (hereafter, the raided group). Next, I use matters such as behavioral tendencies that do not necessarily have murder as their aim and also the absence of revenge or retaliation as the basis for considering the fact that raiding is only ever a scramble to acquire livestock, and is quite separate from wars and conflicts. Then, shifting focus, I concentrate on the nature of the coexistence between the Dodoth and the

Institutionalized Raiding: Its Formalization and Value Creation Amongst the Dodoth

Photo 10.1 A Dodoth girl hugging her little sister

neighboring pastoral peoples. Accordingly, we will see that whilst relationships between ethnic groups exist within "instability", in which they fluctuate between hostility and enmity, they are nonetheless "stable" in the sense that no group carries out massacres and nor do we see the emergence of ruler/ruled relationships. Finally, I examine the following questions: Is it possible to regard the social phenomenon of raiding as an institution in terms of the standard everyday use of the word? Or, should it be understood as what Suehisa Kuroda calls a "natural institution" (Chapter 18, Kuroda 1999)? Alternatively, can it be described as a concept that is closer to a convention in the sense of the mores and customs that are frequently referred to in the chapters of this book? In addition, I would like to rework our understanding of raiding as the embodiment of values, and confirm the characteristic that amongst the Dodoth it is cattle that occupy the pragmatic existence as the central part of human institutions. While continuing to refer to the "institutions" found amongst human and non-human primates that are dealt with in other chapters of this book, I would like to touch on the relationship between the creation of values and the evolution of institutions.

Raiding amongst the Dodoth

Raiding targets and unstable intergroup relationships

The Dodoth peoples of northeastern Uganda form a population of about 90,000 (Statistics Department, Ministry of Finance and Economic Planning 1994) dispersed throughout the highland areas, approximately 1,300–1,700 meters above sea level. To the east, their residence/activity range neighbors that of the Turkana who live in the north-western part of Kenya, at the base of a steep descent of about 1,000 meters from the Great Rift Valley. To the north, Dodothlands—with the Kidepo Valley National Park sandwiched between them—adjoin the Toposa and Didinga of South Sudan. To the south, they border the domestic pastoral ethnic groups of the Jie and Matheniko. Finally, to the west live the agriculturalist Acholi, and—on a plateau, located at an elevation of about 2,000 meters above sea level at the heart of the north-eastern part of Dodothland—the Ik, whose main forms of subsistence are hunting and gathering and collecting honey[2]. The mutual raiding targets for the Dodoth are five ethnic groups, whose main form of subsistence is livestock: the Turkana, Toposa, Didinga, Jie and Matheniko (hereafter, pastoral peoples or ethnic groups). In the case of neighboring groups, it is whether or not they possess herds of livestock that forms the basis of whether mutual raiding/being raided occurs (this refers particularly to herds of cattle). Language group, culture and social background play practically no part in this process. In other words, the Acholi and Ik are not raiding targets because they do not possess cattle[3].

However, it is not necessarily the case that simply being pastoralists will uniformly make an ethnic group the target of raiding. It is the ethnic groups with whom there are unstable relations that are subject to frequent change that fall into this category. That is, fellow adjacent pastoral peoples will at times be in hostile relations where they carry out mutual raids and at other times their relations will be non-hostile and they will not raid one another. What is important here is that these relations are not fixed; they are unstable, as they are liable to reverse at any time, and thus unreliable. It is a case of "yesterday's enemy is today's ally" and "today's ally is tomorrow's enemy". For example, whilst there are no ethnic groups who could be called "longstanding enemies" that the Dodoth have persistently hostile relations with, neither are there any "alliances" or "friendships" with groups who can be trusted not to engage in raiding the Dodoth for an extended period of time. It is not at all peculiar for fellow ethnic groups in hostile relations to become non-hostile, and vice versa; rather, this could be said to be the norm. This could occur over a short period of several weeks, while longer cases could span several years.

If, on the other hand, we shift our focus to the individual level, almost all Dodoth men construct friendly relations beyond their ethnic group, with members of several other ethnic groups. Whilst the numbers have been decreasing recently, there have also been people with in-laws from these other groups. This means that intermarriage has occurred between neighboring pastoral people. During non-hostile relations, people in these sorts of friendships and in-law relations visit each other's settlements and engage in gift giving and livestock exchange, construct animal camps on the same site, embark on grazing day trips together and help each other at watering places and with the provision of water for livestock. They are in intimate relationships akin to friends belonging to the same ethnic group and close in-laws. When, however, relations turn hostile on the level of the ethnic group, they are unable to come and go between each other's lands, and non-hostile relations are suspended. Even so, relations on the individual level continue, and once non-hostile relations are again restored on the level of the ethnic group, inter-ethnic friendships are also revived.

Raiding aims and measures

The aim of raiding among the Dodoth is clearly and unmistakably to "rustle cattle". In the opening paragraph of this chapter, I pointed out that at the time of writing, in 2012, the weapons used in raiding had changed to automatic small arms, and I also touched on the fact that there has been a tendency for more deaths and injuries to occur as a result. However, using guns to kill or injure the other party is not the intention of Dodoth people in itself. Injuries and deaths caused by guns are the result of stray bullets. Events such as stray bullets ricocheting off rocks or stones are accidental (contingent) occurrences, and it is even said that most shots fired are warning shots. Also, since the shepherds of the raided group usually carry guns to the pastures for self-protection and in order to guard their cattle, gun battles between the raiding group and those grazing their herds (the raided group) are a possibility, and this does actually occur at times. However, the most desirable outcome, as far as those in the raiding group are concerned, is that the shepherds of the raided party will abandon their herds and flee once shots are fired.

Guns, which until twenty years ago had cost twelve head of cattle to purchase, can now be purchased with two (as of March 2012). There is no doubt that this present-day influx of cheap weapons has made raiding more extreme and increased the number of deaths and injuries. Meanwhile, since the desire to rustle cattle and the strength of attitudes and value attached to cattle, in particular, have not changed at all, the increasingly extreme nature of raiding and the rising numbers of deaths and injuries may be inevitable consequences. The unwavering aim of an armed raiding party is to rustle cattle. That of the raided party, which guards its pastures with firearms, is self-defense in order to protect against the rustling of their cattle. My research confirms that neither side is at all intent on killing the other in a gun battle.

Raiding "arrangements"

Raiding is not a chaotic act in which one simply violently rustles cattle. Whilst it may not be as organized as modern warfare, we can see that it does contain several "arrangements" along the lines of quasi-agreements. Saying "It happens like this/ it was like this" is a feature of "institutional" phenomena of behavioral practices. Let us now look at two examples.

Raiding does not occur/is not practiced within the same ethnic group

The most fundamental rule of raiding between the Dodoth and the five ethnic pastoral groups mentioned above who engage in mutual raiding is that "raiding targets other ethnic groups". As this rule is powerfully internalized as part of critical consciousness and verbalized, it can be called an "arrangement" that is held as a shared concept. On the one hand, if we look at tangible behavior, these arrangements set out what will happen in particular situations. In other words, "when we want more cattle, we raid other ethnic groups", and raiding is subsequently carried out with everything proceeding in a natural and almost unconscious manner.

These arrangements are thoroughly obeyed and observed, without exception. At least, this is the general belief, and I also think that this is the case. This may be the reason why no punishments for acts of raiding have been instituted. It is generally thought that the function of deviation is "to produce outsiders". If this is the case, then raiding is an act that confirms other ethnic groups as clear outsiders. Thus, the need to construct a raiding target disappears, and consequently punishments do not exist.

This does not mean that cattle can be acquired from anywhere at all. Acquiring herds of cattle from within the ethnic group (here: within the Dodoth) does not constitute something that must not be done, but rather something that is just not done. This is the case whether the herds belong to total strangers or to someone one is angry with or holds a grudge against. This can be seen as the most fundamental arrangement regarding raiding. It also clearly shows that the restrictions on behavior and the acts that are chosen—such as "who becomes (is made)/does not become (is not made) the target of raiding"—shape the boundaries of the ethnic group. This plays a decisive part in the construction of one's identity as being/not being Dodoth.

Ethnic identity is frequently linked to place. However, strict borders and a rigid idea of territory do not exist between the usually nomadic Dodoth and their various neighboring ethnic groups, or amongst these other groups. The expression "Dodothland" does exist, as do actual places that correspond to it. Borders with neighboring ethnic groups also exist (conceptually) in a narrow sense, but these are vague and broad, and frequently very elastic with mutual overlapping. The same is true of territory. During non-hostile relations, neighboring tribes allow and are allowed the mutual use of pastures and watering places. Thus, belonging is not determined by the places and areas where one lives or grazes one's herds, and there is no change of ethnic identity despite grazing and watering herds on the lands of neighboring ethnic groups.

Methods of and limits to recovering raided livestock

When a Dodoth cattle herd is attacked by a raiding group from another ethnic group—whether in the early morning or the middle of the night—an alarm call (a particular high-pitched vocalization) or a whistle resounds conveying the appropriate state of emergency throughout all areas of Dodothland. The males sleeping or relaxing in the settlements or animal camps respond immediately, unconditionally rushing off with their rifles without even having a clear idea of whose settlement has been attacked or the location of the animal camp. The men assemble to form a pursuit party. The raided group chases the raiding group and their own raided herd in an attempt to retrieve their livestock. Meanwhile, the raiding group deploys several squads en route to repel their pursuers as they drive the cattle towards their own lands. Consequently, at this stage, in order to catch up with the raiding group and the cattle, the raided group and its pursuit parties must dodge gunfights with the repel squads. Even if the squads are effective, the raiding group cannot move too far ahead as they must herd the rustled livestock along with them. As a result, in cases where the raiding group has not gone far, it is not uncommon for the pursuit parties to get past the repel squads and catch up with the raiding group and the livestock. They then fight a final battle with the tail end (the rear guard) of the raiding group, and if this group can be overwhelmed, the glory of finally retrieving the herd will have been achieved. The raided group and its pursuit parties can recover their cattle if they catch up with the raiding group—who run intently chasing the rustled cattle before them—and engage them in another battle finally causing the raiders to flee the battlefield in disarray, leaving the cattle behind.

Examples of these types of attempted raids are reasonably frequent. However, inherent in the pursuit and recovery of the herd by the raided group and their pursuit parties is a quasi-agreement that is extremely important when considering the true nature of raiding. This appears to be similar to what Sagawa (2011) reported seeing amongst the Daasanetch pastoralists, who live in the south-western part of Ethiopia, in that should the rustled herd of cattle be herded into the animal enclosure of one of the members of the raiding group, then the game is over at that point. That is, an arrangement is in place that the raided group and its pursuit parties cannot, or will not, pursue beyond this point. The raided group and its pursuit parties accordingly abandon the recovery of their livestock and return to Dodothland. It appears that these events transpire without any acts of harassment or venting of anger such as, for example, destructive or violent acts like setting fire to the other group's settlement or the firing of random gunshots. There are numerous stories of these sorts of failed attempts at recovering rustled herds.

I will give a concrete example that shows the extremely important, practical and symbolic meaning of "animal enclosure" with regard to this arrangement.

Cattle acquired via raiding are distributed amongst the participants, and once they have been placed in their respective animal enclosures they formally become the property of those participants. A Dodoth man, who had lost his herd of cattle during a Turkana raid, went to visit his Turkana friend when relations were once again non-hostile. This friend had not himself taken part in the raid because the target had been an animal camp where his own friend resided (the Dodoth man who was now visiting). However, his unmarried sons had taken part, and the cattle in question had been distributed to them. Since the sons were still young and did not possess their own animal enclosures, they were using their father's. There was, however, no budging from the rule. "Once [cattle] are in a animal enclosure" they are the property of the owner of that enclosure. No matter how much his friend might have told him that the cattle had formerly been his property and appealed for their return, this would, nevertheless, not have constituted a reason for handing them over. In the case of cattle that one acquires or are acquired through raiding, it may generally be best to think in terms of there being no concept of or even process for "returning them to their former owners".

The arrangements discussed above are clearly understood by Dodoth people as "X is like this", and these arrangements are also shared by neighboring ethnic peoples. In addition, there are also societies with set "rules" just like those found in sports such as martial arts. For example, amongst the Hoor (pastoral people who live in the south-western part of Ethiopia) it is said that when attacking an adversary one must always stand facing him; attacks from the rear are not permitted (Miyawaki 2006). In these circumstances, raiding could be said to resemble and be codified as a "cattle rustling battle game" equipped with rules. At this stage, I would like to point out that we can now read a certain kind of "formalization"—what we have just referred to as having become "codified"—into raiding, which is a mutual act between hostile groups. This formalization could be framed as mores, customs and even conventions from the perspective of institution and, depending on the definition, raiding could even be called an "institution". Malinowski goes so far as to say that an "institution" is "a group of people united by common interest" (Bohannan 1960). On the basis of this definition, raiding is a fine institution.

The "killing" mentality and the motives for raiding

These days, when the use of automatic rifles has become commonplace, it is no longer rare for raiding to result in injuries and deaths, but from my perspective the raiders do their best to avoid these outcomes. At the very least, they clearly do not set out with the intent to kill. They absolutely do not engage in activities such as organized training for gun battles. Participants getting their guns ready and picking up their bows as they dance and fool around are invariably taking part in a process that resembles a ritual dance. As these sights are frequently seen in the settlements and grazing pastures, we might wonder whether we are seeing the same behavior at raiding sites because the participants have become so used to this playing around. It is easy to understand that running around carrying a gun is inevitably enjoyable for them, but it is done with no sense of anxiety at all that "someone will be killed" as a result.

The Dodoth have body ornamentations that can only be applied to a person who has killed an enemy—countless small circular scars are cut all the way from the shoulders down the back. This person is thus marked with the reputation of having "killed an enemy". The Dodoth do not, however, attach any particular merit to killing people. This can be confirmed by the fact that one practically never hears epic tales recounting episodes in which an enemy was killed; this is in contrast to stories of successful raiding, tales in which another ethnic group who had come to raid was ambushed and repelled, or episodes of the recapturing and return of herds of cattle that had been rustled temporarily.

The family head of the settlement where I was staying had multiple circular scars spanning his shoulders and back. It was considerably later that I learnt that these were marks indicating murders he had carried out. Without ever having sought confirmation, I was convinced these were simply ornamental or ritual scarification or marks left by medical treatments. When the family head did talk about the scars as signs of the murders he had committed, this was not at all done boastfully but as a disinterested recounting of facts without any attempt at detailed descriptions of the raiding that had occurred on those occasions. As with other East African pastoral peoples, the Dodoth are very self-assertive. When talking about this kind of raiding episode, they may be caught in a somewhat ambivalent situation in terms of just how triumphant, satisfied, happy and cheerful they feel and their sense of the agreeable/disagreeable nature of the murders that occurred during the raiding (the fact that they would have preferred to have avoided them). The Dodoth's social estimation of murder is conspicuously lower than that of pastoral peoples from the south-western part of Ethiopia, who are known for their "ferocity", and those from the southern part of Sudan (currently South Sudan): both of these peoples place a higher value on murder.

Another difference between the Dodoth and the pastoral peoples of South Sudan and Ethiopia is the fact that the targets of offensives launched by the latter are not limited to pastoral peoples, but include a considerable number of attacks on unarmed agricultural peoples. The pastoral peoples in both South Sudan and Ethiopia have also been experiencing extended periods of civil war. It may, therefore, be quite natural for them and the Dodoth to attach different meanings and estimations to "killing someone". However, as colonial documents record that the Bodi of Ethiopia "find killing people easy", their mentality regarding "killing people" may have been intensified as a result of civil war, but then again there may not be any direct relationship. In any case, the Japanese researchers who study the pastoral peoples of this region use the terms "battles" and "wars" (for example, Miyawaki 2006; Sagawa 2011; Kurimoto 1996, 1999), but I have used the words "raiding" and "rustling" in this chapter. English language researchers use "war" and "warfare" (for example, Hutchinson 1996, Simonse 1998). Raiding, which here is the rustling of cattle, is merely one aspect of "battles" and "wars". It is not grudge and cruelty, revenge and retaliation, or indeed aggression and domination that are the central motivations of raiding for the Dodoth. The aim is always only the acquisition of cattle.

The fact that the Dodoth do not engage in violence in retaliation or revenge for murders and raiding by other ethnic groups should be noted as a point of distinction between them and these other groups (Tokoro Chapter 13, 2013). Groups such as Ethiopia's Hoor (Miyawaki 2006), Bodi (Fukui 2004a) and Daasanetch (Sagawa 2011) as well as the Pari of South Sudan (Kurimoto 1996, 1999) all regard killings as matters of individual pride and deal with the murder of group members with revenge and retaliation. Compared with these peoples, Dodoth raiding, as mentioned earlier, is, at most, the act of rustling cattle in which killings *may possibly happen*. To me it appears to have a somewhat idyllic nature that could even be seen as a pastime.

As stated in the opening section, the Dodoth always form raiding parties. This is yet another point of difference between them and the pastoral peoples of south-west Ethiopia and South Sudan. There are, of course, many pastoral peoples amongst the latter, and they frequently form attack groups of large numbers of people and go raiding, but, by the same token, their main reasons for setting out on attacks (killings) are "retaliation", "revenge" and "anger"[4]. On these attacks, just one male sets out, and after killing a man, cuts off his penis and returns with it. I cannot but feel that there are fundamental differences between the Dodoth and the previously referred to image of pastoral peoples depicted in the ethnography in which the colonial administration's official documents stated that the Bodi of Ethiopia "find killing people easy". These are differences in perceptions of the "lives" of other people and also differences in the ontology of "other ethnic groups".

If ambushes and pursuits ultimately occur during raiding or while being raided, these are just. However, killing itself as an independent act—that is, out of context—cannot be called just. It is likely that the Dodoth do not possess either a culture or customs that encourage and praise killings for the purpose of retaliation or revenge.

In the case of the previously mentioned settlement head of the place where I was staying, in spite of the fact that it had been the Turkana who had raided him, he later raided and rustled cattle not from the Turkana but from a separate ethnic group, the Jie; an altogether common occurrence. From the outset, the Dodoth do not aim to "recover" rustled animals from the relevant party—this could be rephrased as "they do not seek to get even". In their consciousness, raiding is not an act of "recovery"; it is always an act of "taking". They simply take cattle without attempting to recover individual cattle from the party that rustled them and without accusing the other party. It is neither a victim's revenge orientation of recovering what has been taken, nor a balance orientation, in which a person takes something back because it belonged to them in the first place. The way to view it is that "raiding is a matter of looting cattle from other pastoral peoples"—it could even be said to be purely an extremely simple, forward-looking orientation for "gaining (acquiring) cattle".

Affirmation of raiding and shared pastoral values

Large numbers of pastoral peoples speaking a variety of languages inhabit the border areas of East and North East Africa formed by Uganda, Kenya, South Sudan and Ethiopia. They hail from arid and semi-arid areas, which are largely "remote regions" far removed from each country's capital city. The Dodoth are among them.

As I have repeatedly reiterated, whilst there is a continuous alternation between mutually hostile and non-hostile relations on a group level between the Dodoth and other ethnic pastoral groups they have contact with, on the individual level, they appear to maintain easy contact through inter-ethnic friendships. It also seems possible to say that mutual raiding relations are carried out in assemblies of these pastoral peoples. The reason we can say this is that it is unimaginable that the targets of raiding would ever be other than the neighboring pastoral peoples.

On this basis, I propose that we regard assemblies of pastoral groups that neighbor one another and maintain a multiplicity of mutually hostile/non-hostile relations as a meta-assembly of pastoral peoples, and I would suggest a new broad term that bundles together and includes multiple ethnicities. This assembly is a type of regional group; a collection of pastoral peoples who live on the same land and use its natural resources (water and grass for their animals). It is not the case, however, that they can graze their animals on and live in any area of their choosing. This is because, for the Dodoth, this collection will always include ethnic groups they are in hostile relations with and, viewed diachronically, it is to be expected that they will have, at times, been enemies with all other ethnic groups. Also, as pointed out previously, we can say that raiding, which is the embodiment of hostile relations, is carried out in these assemblies. People's daily lives are settled geographically in these pastoral assemblies. It is precisely the pastoral peoples who live adjacent to one another and who are partners in raiding and being raided that jointly make up these assemblies of pastoral peoples.

However, the members of these pastoral assemblies—the Dodoth people, for example—should be thought of as not having a conceptual perspective of a higher-order integrated unity (assembly) than these assemblies. When it comes to the voluntary relations between one's own ethnic group and other ethnic groups, the focus of attention is understandably, however, always on whether specific other groups are presently in hostile or non-hostile relations with each other: this is the state of affairs that people understand. Nevertheless, this does not constitute proof of the existence of a concept of a higher-order assembly bundling together multiple ethnic groups including one's own; this sort of concept is practically meaningless in the normal course of life, and is totally unnecessary. And yet it is, nonetheless, daring to consider this sort of assembly that should be thought of as holding the key to understanding people who live under the intricate relations between ethnic groups in this region.

Let us view this from another perspective. Raiding has the clear objective of "rustling cattle". Dodothland, where the Dodoth live, is in the west and neighbors the Turkana of Kenya. The Turkana live in scorching hot vast lands that are more than 1,000 meters lower than Dodothland. Non-hostile relations are not uncommon between the Dodoth and Turkana, and most Dodoth males have Turkana friends. At the height of the dry season in 2002, the two were in hostile relations with each other, and Turkana raiding parties seemed to be attacking Dodoth settlements and animal camps every day and night. At a gathering at this time, in the midst of resounding censure of the Turkana concerning this situation, the settlement head, who was seated at the rear, spoke. He observed, in a manner that could be regarded as meek acceptance of the Turkana raiding of the Dodoth, that "Turkanaland is a scorched land that is far hotter than where we live. Sorghum, maize and other edible plants wither where they stand; they do not have sufficient pasture, water or grass; their animals readily succumb to illness; or they die one after another of malnutrition or dehydration. They needed some animals". He did not, of course, want to give his own cattle to the Turkana, nor was he hoping for a situation in which his own herd of cattle would be rustled by the Turkana.

How, then, are we to interpret his arguments? Was he not simply indicating that the act of raiding, as a general rule, is a just act? And also that this general rule cannot be applied indiscriminately or beyond assemblies of pastoral peoples as gatherings of ethnic groups that engage in mutual raiding and being raided? I think that the settlement head's observation, which understood Turkana raiding in a positive light, is the general argument and value system that is found in the assembly of pastoral peoples that includes the Dodoth. When I thought about it in this way the settlement head's baffling words finally made sense to me. He further added that "Turkanaland is a scorched land with far less rain than we have and a place where the crops in the fields do not grow well. All of the Turkana—not just the young men, but also the settlement head, his wife, the elderly, babies and whole families—live nomadic lives". If assemblies of pastoral peoples lead to some sort of emotional connections between their members, then—because of visiting friends and extending pastoral activities including raiding to wider areas—as in the case of the settlement head mentioned here, each knows the natural environment in which the other lives. To put it another way, among neighboring ethnic groups with loose ties in the form of an assembly of pastoral peoples there is sometimes mutual raiding, they sometimes visit as friends and sometimes graze animals together. It can be said that this is how relations of mutually understanding the other have been constructed. It seems that the unit of the assembly of pastoral peoples could be regarded as an assembly of those who share the common value system that has been acquired in this way—with cattle as the pragmatic existence at its centre. If this is the case, then we should probably change the name of this assembly to something like a "supracommunal pastoral values-sharing sphere". Alternatively, if this is overly complicated, it could be abbreviated to "pastoral values-sharing sphere". As a result of changing its name in this way—that is, as a result of adding the element of "shared pastoral (people's) values"—this concept of an assembly of pastoral peoples is transformed from a closed system comprised of ethnic peoples living geographically adjacent to one another to being open; it becomes an open assembly that also includes pastoral peoples who live on distant lands that are not geographical neighbors. In fact, they know of the existence of large numbers of pastoral peoples who are not their neighbors, and there are those in their midst who have travelled to these unfamiliar lands. For example, the Dodoth do not border the Pokot pastoral people of Kenya, but they are always interested in whether the Pokot are in hostile or non-hostile relations with the Turkana and Matheniko, who are their neighbors.

Raiding as the embodiment of values: Conclusion

As this chapter comes to a conclusion, I would like to make the point once again that we must emphasize the institutional perspective—and, in particular, the viewpoint of the institution in relation to human evolution—in the case of Dodoth raiding. Firstly, let me stress once again the fact that at the heart of the Dodoth's daily life, either consciously or unconsciously, there is the pragmatic existence of cattle. Having confirmed this, the point of the remainder of this section is to make the connection between the value of cattle among the Dodoth and raiding, which embodies this value and bestows further increased value. Then, based on the arguments thus far, and while comparing these to the food sharing associated with two species of chimpanzee (*Pan*), I will attempt to surmise regarding the human evolutionary basis of "the institution of raiding".

As mentioned earlier, Dodoth raiding is by no means a disorderly scramble for livestock. In raiding, several arrangements are shared between various ethnic groups and, either consciously or unconsciously, people act in ways that abide by these. Seeing that this is the case, we cannot deny outright the possibility that raiding is an institution. This can be seen as an institution (or at least the germ of one) because people are obeying some sort of convention or arrangement, just as contests between knights in medieval Europe were decided according to previously agreed methods and just as modern wars constitute planned battles by soldiers deployed in precisely organized armies. Kuroda (1991) gives Jun'ichiro Itani's definition of an institution as, "culture that has a binding force with regard to the actions of individuals", and Dodoth raiding can be seen as sufficiently conforming to this.

With the exception of the rapid introduction of modern weapons, Dodoth raiding has hardly changed either in terms of its economic significance or its socio-cultural value, from around the time of E. M. Thomas' field surveys in the 1960s. It would not be wrong to say that the lives of the modern-day Dodoth are based around "cattle". This was most likely the social characteristic of almost all groups of East African pastoralists that was referred to as a "Cattle Complex" in the past. In addition to cattle, they also keep goats, sheep and donkeys, but these fall far short of cattle in terms of both social value and as objects of attachment. The Dodoth also return home from raiding with rustled goats, sheep, donkeys and camels, but camels are almost certain to be eaten on the return journey, while donkeys are either eaten or soon exchanged for cattle. Since goats and sheep are used either as sacrificial animals or to show hospitality to guests, they are temporarily placed within animal enclosures. The manner in which these four types of animals and cattle are dealt with is completely distinct. When news reaches the settlement that scores or hundreds of cattle have been acquired through raiding, there is wild dancing amongst old and young, male and female, and when, conversely, a man who has 100 head of cattle loses one through illness, he falls into an uncommon despondency. Both these examples express the feelings that people have for cattle and also the strong bonds in the relationship between people and cattle. Where does this partiality towards, or rather this high value placed on, cattle come from?

Now that using automatic rifles is the norm, raiding has become an extreme life and death struggle. The image of the Dodoth, who engage in this avidly and repeatedly, as well as that of neighboring groups, clearly shows which things and objects have value in their lives. Raiding is nothing short of an act that presents and embodies this value by laying their bodies on the line. Livestock, particularly cattle, are indispensible not only in terms of their economic significance in providing daily provisions, but also in a variety of situations ranging from people's daily lives to ritual acts. People also love their cattle deeply. Raiding consists precisely of transforming (rustling) cattle, which are central to Dodoth culture, from "someone else's" property to "my own" property.

In this way, a high value is attached to cattle, and this value is expressed and represented through various daily practices concerning cattle. It is via these practices that further value is added and continually reinforced. But, this is hardly likely to be how things end. What we need to point out here is that cattle are the supreme object of raiding. It was cattle, above all other types of livestock, which both the Dodoth and neighboring groups sought most ardently to acquire through raiding and, at the same time, were constantly exposed to the danger of having their cattle rustled. Because theirs was a targeted existence, people protected their cattle all the more carefully and were prepared for raiding during both the grazing and watering of their cattle, never neglecting their rigorous patrols. Value is added as a result of looking after them in this way, and the value of the cattle keeps increasing. Then raiding occurs.

Ultimately, as a result of raiding, cattle are beings, animals that come and go between ethnic groups. This "moving" adds further value to the cattle. Tomorrow they may well be raided and become another person's property. This sort of being strikes us as precious, and leads us to show it great care. The value (image) independently assigned to cattle on the part of people and the value attached to cattle because they are the targets of raiding influence each other to create even more value. And then, although perhaps unconsciously, raiding is repeated in an attempt to acquire what is valuable. No, the order of things is actually the other way around: it is, in fact, as a result of repeated raiding that value is reproduced, and that higher value is attached and maintained. On this point, raiding resembles, as it were, a confirmed practice of the communal society that I have called a "pastoral value-sharing sphere". This is like the case of goods not creating a market, but rather the market turning things into goods and thus creating their value.

It becomes a bit of a circular argument, but it is not grudges or cruelty, not revenge or retaliation, not aggression or control, and not punishment or reprisal that lies at the core of Dodoth raiding. Their sole aim is the acquisition of

Institutionalized Raiding: Its Formalization and Value Creation Amongst the Dodoth

Photo 10.2 Evening in Dodothland

cattle. They are probably not at all concerned with reasons. It is precisely the fact that cattle became mobile entities as a result of raiding that appears to have been important.

Suehisa Kuroda (1999) argues that food sharing was one key to the evolution of primate societies, which include us humans. Kuroda proposes that—given that aside from humans, sharing food with others, apart from the feeding behavior of mothers to their infants, is only seen in two species of chimpanzees—this food sharing is behavior linked to the thoroughly equal distribution of food seen in human hunter-gatherer societies. When elucidating what it was that changed as a result of this sharing, Kuroda maintains that it is more appropriate to amend the expression, "'what is valuable' is the distribution of food that moves between individuals (from one individual to another)" to "food becomes a 'valuable item' as a result of sharing". He adds that when it becomes possible for food to move between individuals, this leads to food being socialized and to universal value being ascribed to it. "Food" as used here does not refer to any food at all that can be shared, but rather high-value foods, on the basis that they are scarce to begin with, such as meat (chimpanzees) and large fruits (bonobos). The course pursued by these kinds of valuable foods is significant because it applies almost intact to the case of cattle for the Dodoth. To what extent is it possible to recognize similarities between the two? There is, unfortunately, no more space to discuss this, but I will be giving the subject further consideration as part of future research after having collected more detailed data. I would, however, like to suggest that the discussion concerning the value of cattle and raiding is linked in the distant past to the food sharing that is observable in two species of chimpanzees and that it can be considered an issue in terms of the evolution of human sociality.

Part III
Theory for the Evolution of Institutions

11 What Connects and Separates Pre- and Post-Institution

Koji Kitamura

Key ideas

Combinations of two types of processes in collective problem solving: (a) selection of an appropriate relationship building pattern; (b) performance of appropriate relationship building

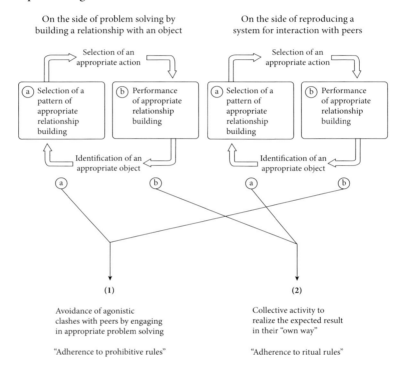

Combination (1) corresponds to a situation in which the parties think that the selected pattern of relationship building for problem solving is appropriate, and avoidance of agonistic clashes with peers becomes the objective for the performance of relationship building. This corresponds to the approach of "adherence to prohibitive rules". Combination (2) corresponds to a situation in which the parties are unsure of selection for problem solving, and their objective is to adopt a relationship building pattern that is selected according to the criterion of their "own way" that can be shared among peers so that they can adjust their individual actions toward the realization of an expected result. This corresponds to the approach of "adherence to ritual rules".

Perceiving and giving "meaning"

The purpose of this chapter is to shed light on what happened during the transition from pre-institutional primate societies to human societies through an exploration of institution from an evolutionary perspective. Accordingly, I examine institutions by looking at pre-institutional primates with particular focus on the things that cannot be called institutions and the kinds of changes that these things have undergone that led to the emergence of institutions. Next, I sum up the viewpoints behind the assumptions in the discussion here and thus clarify the outline of the phenomena in question.

The first assumption underpinning the discussion below is that institutions are devices that people innovate in their attempts to deal with the problems that must be faced in order to survive. According to this view, institutions are created because of the existence of problems that need to be solved. This means that the criterion for action selection provided by an institution at a given time and place is based on the distinction between "appropriate" and "inappropriate", which refers to the anticipated pattern of the relationship configured by the action and the anticipated result of that relationship.

Secondly, an institution is thought to be a device that is needed for a collective approach that people adopt for survival, such as the collective use of resources and collective response to challenges, and not something that has been created for the purpose of problem solving at an individual level. Even in a situation in which a relationship with a "thing" formed by each individual in, for example, the process of using resources or dealing with an issue can be regarded as a problem, what matters is not only the relationship with such "thing" per se but also what is generated by the collective action of people, including what happens to interaction that is created by connections between individual actions in the relationship. Therefore, the criterion for action selection provided by an institution at a given time and place becomes something that is directly reflected in the state of interaction comprised of such actions. In this sense, it must be premised on the distinction between "shared with peers" and "not shared with peers".

It is ordinarily possible even in pre-institutional primate societies that collective action is performed based on action selection premised on the "appropriate/inappropriate" distinction as well as the "shared with peers/not shared with peers" distinction in problem solving at a given time and place. For instance, in Japanese macaque society, comprising groups with stable membership, all members engage in collective action at the start of ranging every morning to generate the outcome of traveling in the same direction together. Similar phenomena can ordinarily occur in human societies. What is evident as a distinction between these phenomena and what is realized by institutions is that the selection in question in the former is left to the force of circumstances at a given time and place, whereas a selection is made in the latter basically on the assumption that the selection process is reproducible. Accordingly, the third characteristic in terms of the criterion for action selection provided by institutions is premised on the distinction between "reproducible" and "not reproducible", of which institutions designate the former.

In forming a relationship with a particular object, what provides a reproducible criterion for action selection is the "meaning" of the object targeted by the action. The meaning of such an object is the identity of that which is appropriate which corresponds to the distinction between being "appropriate" and "inappropriate" as the object of relationship building perceived by reference to the prediction regarding the pattern of relationship formed by the action at the time[1]. This meaning is also thought to be associated with the distinction between what is "shared with peers" and "not shared with peers". In other words, when we think that we are selecting our action based on our understanding of the meaning of the object, then we must be understanding the meaning presently appropriate for action selection, shared with peers and reproducible at all times[2].

On the other hand, the identity, which we regard as the "meaning" of the action that acts on the object and creates some kind of change, is thought to correspond to the distinction between being "appropriate" and "inappropriate" as an act of relationship building given by reference to predicting the result of such process, and at the same time, associated with the distinction between "shared with peers" and "not shared with peers" as well as that between "reproducible" and "not reproducible". In other words, when we think that we are performing an action based on imbuing the action with meaning at the time, we must be trying to perform an action that has an appropriate meaning in relation to the predicted result, and is given a meaning that is shared with peers and reproducible at all times.

Among tentative insights drawn from the above discussion, the following can be pointed out as relevant to the position of exploring institutions from the perspective of pre-institutional primate societies. The phenomena produced by institutions are, firstly, related to the perception of the meaning of an object and the giving of meaning to an action in the process of building a relationship with the object by the action. Secondly, the phenomena are thought to arise when this meaning is provided as something previously defined and not reliant on the circumstances of the time and place in the act of collective problem solving based on the sharing of this meaning.

In the next section, we shall divide typical institutions in human societies into two types: those focusing on the generation and maintenance of social orders such as legal systems and those focusing on the designation of meaning for the perception of reality and actions in relation to living practices and conventions such as cultural systems. Then, we shall consider adherence to "prohibitive rules" for the former and "ritual rules" for the latter as the core of the phenomenon created by each institution. It is thought that adherence to "prohibitive rules" is a phenomenon that corresponds to "adjustment" toward the outcome of interaction with peers, while adherence to "ritual rules" is one corresponding to "selection" toward the formation of patterns of interaction. Upon differentiating the routes to these two destinations, I would like to consider what happened during the transition from pre- to post-institutional societies in concrete terms.

Circular decision making

Circular decisions in building relationships with "things"

Before we begin our discussion on institutions from an evolutionary perspective, let us carry out a preliminary exploration of a theoretical problem concerning the perception of meaning in an object or the giving of meaning to an action in building a relationship with the object by the action, as well as the activity of collective problem solving based on sharing meaning. Firstly, we shall address the problem of "circular decision making" in building a relationship with an object using a meaningful action.

According to the approach used in this chapter, in order to accurately understand the process of building a relationship with something using a meaningful action, the following two procedures need to be differentiated in relation to the process. The first is the selection of a pattern of building an appropriate relationship with an appropriate object based on the distinction between "appropriate object" and "inappropriate object" used when prediction about such a pattern is referenced. The identity of being appropriate for relationship building at the time becomes the meaning of the object, and based on that meaning an appropriate object is identified and an appropriate relationship building pattern is selected. In this case, it is thought that the reproducibility of this relationship building pattern is ensured through a process based on the meaning of the object.

In contrast, the other procedure involves executing the building of an appropriate relationship by an appropriate action on the basis of the distinction between "appropriate action" and "inappropriate action" applied when predictions about the result of the process is referenced. As the identity of being appropriate to realize the expected result becomes the "meaning" of the action, and an appropriate action is envisioned on the basis of the "meaning", then the building of an appropriate relationship is executed through the action; in this case, regularity in the link between cause and effect in chronological order, that is, causality-based predictability is thought to be ensured via relationship building based on the meaning of the action.

These two procedures need to be differentiated solely because they must be seen as processes only made possible by the use of the "meaning". The meaning in question here refers to the identity of the "appropriate object" and that of the "appropriate action", to recapitulate the above exposition. As is blatantly obvious, however, the identity of the "appropriate object" can vary greatly depending on what action is taken to build a relationship with it, and similarly the identity of the "appropriate action" is highly variable depending on the object the action is attempting to build a relationship with. In other words, in building a relationship with an object via an action, it is thought that selection of an "appropriate object" becomes possible only on the basis of the performance of an "appropriate action", and at the same time the performance of an "appropriate action" becomes possible only after an "appropriate object" has been selected. Accordingly, if we are to accurately understand the process of building a relationship with an object through an action based on "meaning", then we need to first distinguish these two processes properly.

Having done so, we need to consider next in concrete terms how these two processes are interconnected. Based on our understanding in this chapter, it is thought that on the assumption that a pattern of appropriate relationship building is selected based on the perception of the meaning of an object, an appropriate action for the expected result is realized through the performance and adjustment of relationship building according to that pattern. At the same time, based on the assumption that an appropriate action for the realization of the expected result is available, the perception of the meaning of an object appropriate for the action and the selection of an appropriate relationship building pattern based on that become possible. In short, these two processes are thought to have a "circular decision making" relationship as depicted above (see Key Ideas Diagram on p. 242). This type of circulative relationship can be expected to exist between two processes such as diagnosis and treatment in dealing with an illness. Normally, it is assumed that appropriate treatment is selected depending on diagnosis and administered accordingly, but on the other hand, diagnosis is only possible in relation to current available treatment methods in the context of traditional symptomatic treatments.

We must take note here that we who live in this post-institutional world seem to have no reservations about deeming the meaning of an object of relationship building and the meaning of the action that builds a relationship as "something pre-determined" in the process of building a relationship with an object by an action. Accordingly, we think that we can realize the expected result by selecting an appropriate action for relationship building based on the "predetermined meaning", and at the same time identify an appropriate object for relationship building based on the "predetermined meaning" and use the action to carry out this process. However, even if we think this is the case, when we come to deal with an unprecedented problem or one with no known solution in real life, we find ourselves in a situation where we simply have to resort to trial and error without reliable criteria for judgment regarding the perception of the meaning of the object or the selection of an action appropriate for problem solving—a situation that is no different from that of the pre-institutional world of animals.

Nevertheless, we are usually unaware of this problem. This is likely because we assume, perhaps due to our susceptibility to simplification, that humans are "completely rational" beings who plan their actions after gathering information from the environment thoroughly and accurately and perform the actions according to that plan. In reality, however, humans and other animals can only have incomplete knowledge about the environment and therefore must not think they are capable of composing an "accurate picture of the world". While it must be obvious to everyone that this assumption is unrealistic, it is a matter of practical importance to keep in mind that we cannot assume the existence of a simple causal relationship in which, for example, "treatment" is determined by "diagnosis", which corresponds to gathering information from the environment.

It is possible to say that the process of building adaptive relationships with the environment engaged in by individual animals assumed by affordance theory[3] is premised on the same "circulative decision making". According to this theory, individuals of a species that secures its survival through adaptation to its ecological niche realize specific values that lead to their survival by selecting an appropriate relationship building pattern based on the detection of affordances provided by an object and performing the act of relationship building while making adjustments in response to the individual attributes of the object in building a relationship with a resource essential for their survival. In other words, all individuals of the species share not only the ability to detect affordances provided by an object in building a relationship with a resource essential for their survival, but also the ability to realize values that lead to their survival through the performance of relationship building based on the detected affordances (Reed 2000).

If it is the case that the process of natural selection has allowed these abilities to be shared by all individuals as genetically based traits, then there lies the "circulative decision making" in which these two abilities can only manifest under the condition of mutual dependency. In other words, for individuals of a particular species to manifest an ability to detect the affordances of resources comprising a niche for the species through natural selection, these individuals must already be equipped with an ability to perform such actions so as to realize particular values that prolong their survival through relationship building based on them. Similarly, for these individuals to manifest an ability to perform such actions so as to realize certain values that prolong their survival, they must already be equipped with an ability to detect affordances that permit the stable reproduction of object selection appropriate for such relationship building.

Humans, as members of a species that ensures its survival through adaptation to its ecological niche, select appropriate relationship building patterns based on the detected affordances of objects and realize certain values that prolong our survival in building relationships with resources essential for our survival. Moreover, we appear to share these abilities with all other members of the human species as genetically based traits. Not only that, humans appear to realize the situation in which they can share both the ability to identify appropriate objects and the ability to perform appropriate actions that have been developed through individual learning with many other members who share the same cultural tradition by using "meaning".

Through learning in the latter process it should be possible for certain values for prolonging survival to be realized through the selection of appropriate relationship building patterns based on the perceived meaning in objects and the performance of relationship building by appropriate actions for the purpose. For this situation to occur, however, the following special steps for problem solving must be available. To begin with, the first clue can be found in trying to realize the expected values through trial and error and developing the ability to occasionally succeed. Then, we need to develop the capacity to have a rough idea of particular combinations of objects and actions that are likely to lead to the realization of the expected values by modifying our actions so that this can be achieved for each category of objects and attempting relationship building by applying the same type of action to different objects. It is conceivable that by doing so, before building such relationships we become able to distinguish the objects that are appropriate for configuring ordered patterns of relationship building from those that are not, as well as the actions that are appropriate for realizing expected results from those that are not.

For instance, when we are in the process of developing the ability to realize a certain value by using a new tool, we need to try to understand the overall picture of its usage by figuring out what we can do by using it in certain ways. In doing so, we develop the ability to identify an appropriate object for forming a reproducible relationship building pattern before building a specific relationship and to select an appropriate action for realizing the expected result before building a specific relationship for the first time. And we become able to realize the expected result when we subsequently perform the actual relationship building by selecting an appropriate object and action from a range of options and adjusting our action according to the individual characteristics of a specific object.

Nevertheless, we have not yet discussed a situation that requires the device of institution. From the perspective of this chapter, the invention of a new tool and the learning of techniques to use it, for example, are still considered to be problem solving in building relationships with "things" performed at the individual level. In the following, we shall consider that institutions are required when not only the results of building relationships with "things" in the environment themselves but also the results of people's collective action, including interactions produced when individuals' actions are interconnected, come into the picture.

Configuration of interaction systems in collective problem solving

At the end of this preliminary discussion concerning theoretical problems, let us consider those posed by the combination of the act of building relationships with "things" by individuals and the configuration of interaction systems corresponding to the interconnection of their respective actions in collective problem solving in relation to the collective use of resources or challenges at hand.

Firstly, the individuals who participate in an interaction system at a particular time are considered to be in basically symmetrical positions as parties to the building of a relationship with a "thing" for survival, and let us call such individuals of the same species "peers" in this chapter. When resource use or problem solving performed by individual peers combine to form something that is more than a simple parallel configuration of individual actions, it is called the collective use of a resource or collective action to deal with a challenge. The substance of "collective" in this case is about forming a stable and reproducible interaction system at the intersection of individuals' acts of problem solving through building a relationship with an object.

Accordingly, in addressing below the collective activities performed by individual peers for survival, we shall differentiate the aspect of problem solving activities through building relationships with objects and the aspect of the reproducing activities of interaction systems as the substance of "collective" and examine their combinations. Furthermore, we shall consider the distinction between the two processes underpinning problem solving by an action, i.e., selecting an appropriate pattern of relationship building by an action and performing and adjusting such to realize an expected result, in the context of the configuration of an interaction system, and examine the possible combinations of these processes. In more concrete terms, we will consider whether the selection of a pattern of appropriate relationship building by an action and the performance of appropriate relationship building to realize an expected result respectively places more emphasis on the aspect of problem solving or the aspect of the reproducing activities of interaction systems (see Key Ideas Diagram on page 242).

Because it is unlikely that either problem solving or the stable reproduction of an interaction system is completely ignored in the process of dealing with a problem through collective action, we can imagine the following two combinations. Firstly, in selecting a pattern of appropriate relationship building focusing on problem solving, the performance and adjustment of such relationship building to realize an expected result is, inevitably, likely to focus on the stable reproduction of an interaction system (otherwise this aspect would be completely ignored). On the other hand, in selecting an appropriate relationship building pattern focusing on the stable reproduction of an interaction system, the performance of such to realize an expected result is likely to focus on the aspect of problem solving (see Key Ideas Diagram on page 242).

The former applies to a situation in which each party believes that their problem solving selection is appropriate and the only challenge that needs to be addressed collectively in performing this pattern of relationship building is to make their interaction with peers non-agonistic. In other words, they focus on the stable reproduction of an interaction system and make adjustments so that their interaction with peers becomes non-agonistic rather than making adjustments to realize an expected result focusing on problem solving.

In contrast, the latter applies to a situation in which each party is unsure about action selection in relation to problem solving, and the challenge they need to address collectively is to find a way to share the same problem solving selection with their peers. At this time, each party regards the problem solving activity as something that has been selected according to the criterion of "our own way", participates in the activity as required sharing the same attitude with their peers and tries to perform and adjust their individual action toward the realization of an expected result in problem solving. In doing so, they come to share a positive assessment of the result with their peers.

These two activities also correspond to the two basic approaches adopted to effect the stable reproduction of an interaction system configured in the collective use of a resource or collective handling of a challenge. The first approach involves an attempt to make interaction with peers non-agonistic and create a state of peaceful coexistence while securing the possibility of developing the interaction system into a more complex one. This corresponds to the approach of "adhering to prohibitive rules" in the post-institution world as we shall discuss later. The second approach involves an attempt to establish a way to flexibly deal with separate issues under a coherent guideline that can be called "our own way" by referring to the problem solving measures used in previous cases credited with eliminating the possibility of disorder through active alteration of the present situation and obtaining a more generalized understanding of correspondence between problem solving measures and their effects. This corresponds to the approach of "adherence to ritual rules" (see Key Ideas Diagram on page 242).

In the following section, I identify the conventionality in relation to the meaning perceived in an object or given to an action that provides clues along the path to the stable reproduction of an interaction system at different stages of evolution toward institutionalization.

Road to institution (1): Route to "prohibitive rules"

Adherence to "prohibitive rules"

"Prohibitive rules" should not be taken simply as something that creates a situation in which the events proscribed by such rules do not occur. For instance, adherence to an incest taboo does not simply create a situation in which sexual intercourse between people in particular relationships is avoided. Lévi-Strauss states that "the content of the prohibition is not exhausted by the fact of the prohibited" and considers that incest taboos are the rules at the foundation of the "institution" of exogamy which creates a social order around "an exchange of women between social groups" (Lévi-Strauss 1969). However, Lévi-Strauss did not give further thought to the interrelationship between incest taboos and exogamy as he viewed them as the same thing. I shall interpret the connotations of prohibitive rules in the form of incest taboos in an extended manner according to the context of this chapter and elucidate the road along which they create an alliance between social groups through the exchange of women.

Based on the assumptions underpinning our discussion here, it is thought that the act of following a prohibitive rule is a phenomenon related to the challenge of avoiding conflict at the level of interaction with peers and creates a condition in which conflict is avoided between the close kinsmen of a particular woman and other men through the prohibition of sexual relationships between kin. As a next step, the possibility of marriage between this woman and a man outside of her kinship group is made available. In other words, the men who are prohibited from having a sexual relationship with this woman acquire the authority to approve the exclusive right to enable a particular man to enter into a sexual union with her and exercise the authority to marry her off. As a result, so-called "marriage" becomes available as a situation that has been approved by all rival men.

The incest taboo also functions to identify and make known those "kinsmen" who are prohibited from having a sexual relationship with a particular woman. A decision made by the "kin" regarding which man should be given the legitimate right to exclusive sexual union with the woman is, to those men who are competing for it, a decision made by a third party who is not their current rival, and therefore is shared by the rival men and treated as a socially legitimate decision. This creates a relationship between the giver and the receiver of a particular woman corresponding to a unique social order concerning the manner of sexual relationships between men and women. It is thought that the very substance of solidarity between social groups through an exchange of women is found here, i.e., in the relationship between the givers who are prohibited from having sexual relations with the woman in question and the receiver who is given the exclusive right to do so (Kitamura 1982, 2003).

In this chapter, we are attempting to understand "prohibitive rules" in relation to an approach to create a state of peaceful coexistence by making interaction with peers non-agonistic while at the same time ensuring the possibility of developing the interaction system into a more complex one. The above discussion corresponds to the standpoint adopted in this chapter. Unlike Lévi-Strauss' idea that this prohibition alone creates the exchange of women between social groups, it is thought that the possibility of the migration of women between groups under social approval and the inter-group solidarity this creates is manifest on the premise of the peaceful coexistence created by the prohibition. This distinction has significant ramifications in terms of our consideration of this question in comparison with pre-human societies. In chimpanzee societies, the "migration of women between groups" is a very normal phenomenon, although the existence of this "prohibitive rule" cannot be assumed, whereas "solidarity between groups" based on this process is completely out of the question. In other words, while a state of peaceful coexistence prevails in chimpanzee societies as if realized through adherence to this "prohibitive rule", a path to a more complex interaction system that is supposed to be provided by this rule does not show any signs of appearing.

Food sharing in the genus *Pan*

We shall now examine an example in which, although the above device—a "prohibitive rule" to ensure the possibility of the emergence of a more complex interaction system—cannot be found, a state of conflict avoidance comes to be realized as if such a rule is being followed.

Although food sharing is a phenomenon widely evident in the animal kingdom if cases of parents feeding their offspring are included, food sharing in the genus *Pan* (chimpanzees and bonobos) can be regarded as a distinct phenomenon in that it is a form of interaction routinely performed among adults (Nishida and Hosaka 2001). This phenomenon is rarely seen in other phylogenetically close monkeys and has a direct link to food sharing and gifting phenomena in human society. Food sharing in the genus *Pan* involves an individual possessing food and another individual requesting it. A state of peaceful coexistence is realized when the latter does not attempt to take it with force and the former does not overreact to the request, and subsequently and occasionally the food is transferred to the one requesting it.

Let us examine the phenomenon of food sharing in the genus *Pan* from the perspective of how it differs from what occurs in other primate societies where food sharing is rare. It is conceivable that food sharing is uncommon in many primate species because when an individual tries to take food that is in the possession or kept by the side of another individual, the latter may respond by consuming it immediately or trying to defend it desperately, and therefore the former needs to be prepared to accept the risk of getting into a serious fight. In such cases, the individual eventually gives up trying to acquire the food. Consequently, in a normal situation food does not change hands once its ownership becomes evident.

In the genus *Pan*, however, when an individual has food and another individual tries to acquire it by making a demand, the former may refuse, but the latter patiently waits for a voluntary response without challenging it, thus creating a condition in which agonistic interaction is at least avoided. At the monkey stage, in a situation where a particular individual has a particular food, the order of coexistence between individuals can only be realized by excluding the possibility that another individual will take and consume it. On the other hand, it is conceivable that the transition to the chimpanzee stage permits the realization of such order upon securing the possibility for an individual to request food from the individual who possesses it.

In the societies of the genus *Pan*, where the individual without food refrains from challenging the individual with food's refusal and waits for a positive response, the owner accepts the structure of reciprocal relationship building to "avoid agonistic interaction with the other party" and responds by refraining from making a fuss. In this way, the condition in which an agonistic clash is avoided is created as something repeatedly reproducible. In other words, it is likely that in the configuration and continuation of an interaction system being created there, each individual action that is built into the system, be it the act of demanding or the act of refusal, takes on the character of being an action intended to create a state of non-agonistic coexistence.

In this situation, just as in humans, it appears that the act of asking for food serves as a demonstration of one's respect for the other's ownership of the food, while the act of refusing the request functions as a demonstration of the understanding that one's ownership of the food is endorsed by the other's approval. If this is the case, it means that each of the parties recognizes the meaning of the food in question as "something owned by an individual who is in possession of it", regardless of their position, and selects their action based on this meaning. When these actions are reciprocally connected, this type of event arises (Kitamura 2008b). By replacing the meaning of "something owned by an individual (i.e., property)" with "something that must not be acquired or consumed without the consent of the owner", an action selected based on the meaning of the "property" is supposed to comply with a rule prohibiting the acquisition and consumption of property without the consent of its owner.

Nevertheless, when we look at food sharing in the genus *Pan* from the perspective of differences from that in human society where the perception of the meaning of food that is "something owned by an individual in possession of it" arises on its own prior to the building of a reciprocal relationship, food sharing in the genus *Pan* cannot be regarded as a phenomenon emerging through the action selection based on it. What is markedly different from food sharing in human society lies in the way the event of food transfer arises. The following description and analysis will focus on this point.

The party asking for food tries to realize the goal of acquiring it through its request while emphasizing building a relationship with a "thing", as in acquiring and consuming the food in the possession of the other party. The former cannot expect the other party to easily relinquish the consumption of the food in response to the request, because the other party intends to consume the food. Accordingly, what the requesting party is doing is creating a stalemate by continuing to request in the face of the other party's refusal. It is likely that by continuing to wait for a voluntary response from the other party, one is encouraging the other to try to build a relationship that can result in the resolution of the stalemate. The other party occasionally makes concessions in an attempt to resolve the stalemate, thus giving rise to the transfer of food.

The rare event of food transfer, therefore, should be regarded as something clearly different from food sharing or gifting in human society. In other words, the other party's range of actions in this situation include not distributing unless requested, the prolonged deferment of distribution and giving a smaller or less palatable portion (Nishida 1973; Kuroda 1999). To highlight the difference between this and food sharing and gifting in human society, food transfer in this case is either a reluctant action in response to a party's persistent request or a passive response in "giving the other party a hand-out" rather than active sharing.

In this case, what is our understanding of the nature of "active giving" in food sharing and gifting in human society? The question "Why do humans perform the act of food sharing or gifting which results in the loss of the 'thing'?" has fascinated many anthropologists and produced various theories to explain this phenomenon. Yet, a universal theory that explains all types of "gifting" phenomena seems a long way off. Let us consider this question in relation to the perception that food in the possession of a particular individual means "something owned by the individual in possession of it". By considering whether this perception gives rise to the difference between "active sharing" in human society and passive food transfer in chimpanzee societies, we shall be examining the possibility of an evolutionary approach to this "gifting" phenomenon.

Based on the assumptions of our discussion here, the perception of the meaning of "something owned by the individual in possession of it" that gives rise to this difference means, to be more precise, the distinction between perceiving a meaning that arises independently of concrete reciprocal relationship building and perceiving a meaning that manifests only within the interaction system at the time. In the case of chimpanzees, the building of a reciprocal relationship through the requesting of a share of food and the owner's refusal is sustained for a period of time by the persistent request by the non-owner, but this relationship building ends when the non-owner gives up and leaves or when the owner concedes and hands over some food. The latter case presents a problem here because if the relationship building ends with the transfer of food, the meaning that the food has been the other party's property until just before that point is thought to vanish as if it had never existed.

In human society, by contrast, the perception of the meaning that something is or isn't someone's property normally arises independently of whether or not any relationship building takes place between the owner and the non-owner of the property. If I willingly give the other party the "thing", which they recognize as my property, it is transferred into the other party's ownership, but the meaning that the "thing" was my property before this time will remain despite this. As a reflection of this, there may be an occasion on which I can expect the other party to show a willingness to give me a share of their property, for example. Nevertheless, there is no reason to think that such an action is guaranteed. It is thought that the substance of "active sharing" lies in the possibility of developing subsequent interaction systems into more complex ones, which is brought about by the act of continuous reference to the meaning that what is given to the other party has been another party's property.

As the above analysis demonstrates, a state of peaceful coexistence is observed in food distribution in the genus *Pan* as if it has been realized by adherence to the prohibitive rule of "someone's property must not be acquired or consumed without the consent of its owner", but nothing is found in this case to guarantee the possibility of a more complex interaction system that is supposed to result from adherence to the rule. In this case, whether or not the event of food transfer will take place in this state of peaceful coexistence will depend on exploratory mutual responses between the parties involved. After these responses, the owner may hand over food in some cases or the relationship building may end when the non-owner gives up and leaves. On another occasion later on, the same non-owner may ask the same owner for a share of food, but this merely constitutes the start of another interaction separate from the previous one.

Accordingly, if we regard food sharing in the genus *Pan* as a phenomenon that occurs in the liminal space between the pre- and post-institution stages on route to "prohibitive rules", we can envisage, as a link between the two stages, a situation in which exploratory mutual responses toward problem solving are ensured between parties through the creation of peaceful coexistence by non-agonistic interaction with peers where there are conflicting interests. From the approach adopted by Nishie in Chapter Six, this is a phenomenon that is understood as the production of a cosmos based on conventional rules which corresponds to what is recognized as the emergence of a "state of adherence to the rules" or an institution. However, this is not our understanding in this chapter, as I shall explain below.

Conversely, what separates these two stages is the meaning, which is perceived in a resource in question and guarantees non-agonistic reciprocal relationship building, that has become perceivable prior to the relationship building at the time, and this only becomes possible after the transition. Action selection based on the perception of the meaning that can be shared by anyone any time is precisely what we call adherence to a "prohibitive rule" here. It is envisaged that adherence to this same rule offers a structure that ensures the possibility of a society developing toward a more complex interaction system as in active food sharing and gifting.

Road to institution (2): Route to "ritual rules"

Adherence to "ritual rules"

"Ritual rules" should not be taken as guidelines for problem solving in the conduct of a ritual. If what they prescribed were mere guidelines, people might not act according to them or even when they did they might or might not succeed in solving their problem. Yet, they are not a device that forces people to deal with the problem in a particular manner. In the sense in some cases that they are thought to be useless for problem solving at the individual level, they do not teach people which natural laws they should follow either. According to the perspective presented in this chapter, by following "ritual rules" people collectively figure out an appropriate relationship building pattern to deal with the problem at hand and by performing this action jointly with peers they attempt to realize a desirable result.

This act of "performing appropriate relationship building by following the rules" differs from the act of receiving a guideline and referring to it, in that one interprets the act instructed by the rule as something one should do as a party, voluntarily selects this act and performs it with the intention of realizing the result it points to. It also differs from a forced act because the person who follows the rule thinks about what they should do and acts accordingly. Moreover, it differs from the act of following natural laws because in this case people think that what they do corresponds to their "own way" of trying to realize an expected result, and they actually perform the act in trying to realize the expected result because they think that is what they should do.

In relation to the last point, a hurdle in performing the option of dealing with an intractable problem collectively with peers using their "own way" is found in selecting a particular problem solving measure out of a range of "problem solving measures at hand" in their repertoire of "own ways" and making it available to share with peers. A device to ensure the clearing of this hurdle is the "ritual rule". However, following a rule does not only ensure the formation of an interaction pattern in collective problem solving; it also ensures that people believe that the creation of an interactive event chosen on that occasion will directly lead to the resolution of a particular issue in question.

In this chapter, we are trying to understand the "ritual rule" as something akin to a path to realize the "restoration of order = resolution of disorder" through the creation of a particular interactive event by ensuring the formation of a pattern of interaction in the collective solving of a problem at hand. Accordingly, it is thought that this rule specifies an appropriate means of resolution in realizing the result of the "formation of a particular order = resolution of a particular disorder that is the problem at hand" using the conventional assumption about the correspondence relationship between the configuration of an interactive event and the result expected to be realized by it. It follows that the generation of the particular specified interactive event is regarded as the resolution of the particular disorder that is the problem in question.

The greatest obstacle to making the phenomenon of problem solving by adherence to "ritual rules" comprehensible to a third party observer lies in "the conventional assumption about the correspondence relationship between the configuration of an interactive event and the result expected to be realized by it". This is because, in the eyes of those who do not think that the problem solving measure specified by the "ritual rule" is selected according to their "own way", this conventional assumption of the correspondence relationship seems to be "completely groundless and arbitrary" (Hamamoto 2001: 13). There is a gap that cannot be filled between the experience of those acting according to their "own way" as the party and the understanding of those making third-party observations. The following is considered to be the mechanism by which those who think they have their "own way" of realizing an expected result and act on it are led to believe that the expected result has been realized by their action.

The following two points are important for the approach to problem solving by adherence to "ritual rules". Firstly, adherence to this form of rule specifies the framework of interaction that must be performed for problem solving, thus ensuring the formation of the pattern of interaction. Secondly, the correspondence relationship between the production of an interactive event by connecting actions and the result expected to be realized by it is given as an established fact prior to the actual connection of actions by people and independently of the context surrounding it.

All parties adjust their actions in a reciprocal manner for the production of an interactive event that directly leads to the expected result in their actual interaction within the framework specified by the rule in question. Consequently, if the targeted interactive event is actually produced on that occasion through the performance and adjustment of their interaction, they will come to believe that the expected result has been realized because of the effectiveness of the presumption of the correspondence relationship between the means and the realization of the expected result. Thus, for people to come to believe that the expected result has been realized by the ritual, it is of critical importance that they are able to share the concrete experience of reciprocally adjusting their actions toward the result.

Rituals are sometimes considered to be hollow and insubstantial because the mere performance of the act prescribed by the ritual rule cannot realize anything. For it to become a "ritual" to realize an expected result, all parties, including the audience, must participate holding the desire to realize the expected result through the performance and be able to share the experience of performing and adjusting their actions on that occasion for the realization of that result.

Hand-clasped grooming in chimpanzees

Let us look at one example in which even though the meaning of being an appropriate measure for problem solving does not seem to be given to the parties' actions prior to the actual interaction, it appears as if adherence to that type of rule makes problem solving possible. Here it appears that, not by their initiative coming from their desire to do so, nor by subordination to the other party because they have to, all parties voluntarily produce an interactive event based on the equal and neutral relationship between peers and it brings about the "generation of a particular order = resolution of a particular disorder that is the problem".

The reciprocal action in question is called "hand-clasped grooming" in chimpanzees, and involves two chimpanzees each raising their right or left hand high and clasping them over their heads while grooming the other's armpit with their free hand. This interaction is characterized by the performance of identical actions as well as the almost simultaneous hand-raising at initiation by both parties. Whereas this pattern of interaction involving the simultaneous performance of the same action to/on one another is typified by "greetings" of various forms in human societies, it is seldom observed in other primate societies except when they simultaneously threaten one another in a fight situation. As an exception, however, some forms of this type of interaction appear in the societies of great apes such as chimpanzees and bonobos somewhat abruptly.

In this chapter, we treat "hand-clasped grooming" in chimpanzees as an interaction similar to greeting in human society. In human greeting, one feels that doing nothing is a problem that requires a solution when one finds oneself in a situation in which one is able to encounter and remain with another. It is envisaged that, when neither party is keen enough to initiate joint activity, even though they think that doing something together would bring about a pleasant situation, greeting is performed in the form of simultaneous presentation of identical acts as "what we should do". A characteristic common to chimpanzee hand-clasped grooming and human greeting seems to be that the highly generalized situation of "production of some order" is formed by the creation of an interactive event by individual parties, and an ordered state of coexistence is brought about as a result.

In contrast, there is a repertoire of stylized interactions called "mounting" in primate societies. Although they differ from human greeting and chimpanzee hand-clasped grooming in many respects, one commonality is that "a state in which the possibility of agonistic interaction is avoided = ordered coexistence" is brought about through the performance of this stylized interaction. I shall describe the characteristics of the phenomenon of hand-clasped grooming below by contrasting it with the interaction of mounting.

The interaction of mounting is observed in situations where one cannot simply avoid contact with another in the face of the danger of an agonistic clash or where one feels that some form of interaction is unavoidable because simple avoidance of contact would be unnatural in the presence of a possibility for transition to intimate contact. When one party engages in a behavior called "presenting" and the other party connects a behavior called "mounting" to it, an interactive event that is almost indistinguishable from mating between a male and a female is created. It is thought that the performance of this pattern of interaction creates a state in which agonistic interaction is at least avoided (Kitamura 2007).

The manner of configuring this interaction system in this case is characterized by reciprocal relationship building, which is initiated by one party and followed by the other, whether they are attempting to avoid an agonistic clash or seeking intimate contact. Here, each party is dealing with the problem of interaction system configuration as a choice at the individual level. It is possible to understand that this event has been created based on the condition of a prior one-to-one relationship between the parties or in an attempt to create a new one-to-one relationship, that is, the reciprocal connection of actions selected by each party for the purpose of the configuration and confirmation of their reciprocal relationship building.

In contrast, hand-clasped grooming in chimpanzees is not the type of relationship building involving one initiating party and one following party, as is clear from its format in which both parties present their actions to one another simultaneously. If we pay attention to this simultaneous presentation of the same action, it is likely that the parties voluntarily choose the "same action" with the meaning of being appropriate for the production of a stylized interactive event. By connecting their actions they collectively produce the interactive event based on an equal and neutral relationship between peers rather than something that is created by respective parties' choices where the parties aspire to configure and confirm their reciprocal relationship building. The production of such an event makes the parties look as if they are collectively solving the problem at hand, that is, "the discomfort of not doing anything together in the presence of the other".

Viewed from the perspective of its difference from human greeting, however, it becomes clear that hand-clasped grooming in chimpanzees is far from an event configured by the performance of the action "what we should do" perceived by the parties in dealing with the problem at hand. What cannot be ignored as a difference is that hand-clasped grooming is basically not the type of interaction that happens between any acquaintances among peers at any time. According to Michio Nakamura, who has been conducting a detailed study of this phenomenon on an ongoing basis, there is a clear tendency in the interaction between a young male and an adult male that "basically neither of those pairs of individuals who do not practice this type of grooming in the first place attempts to invite the other to engage in this" (Nakamura 2003b: 280). Further, among pairs of adult chimpanzees some engage in hand-clasped grooming often while others rarely do (Nakamura, personal correspondence).

The fact that there is a clear difference in the frequency of hand-clasped grooming depending on the combination of individual chimpanzees means that whether the action is going to be performed or not is a choice made by the individuals based on the past one-to-one relationship between them. It follows that this practice shares a characteristic with the interaction of mounting in primates created by an action selected by each party for the configuration and confirmation of relationship building with the other party. In other words, it cannot be regarded as a choice made according to the criterion of being appropriate as a problem solving measure. This is because such a criterion is the same one employed in adhering to a ritual rule and in principle must be applicable to all individuals recognized as legitimate members of the society.

Nonetheless, this does not mean that this places hand-clasped grooming in the same league as mounting in primates. Although chimpanzees do not engage in this action based on the idea that "what we should do" exists as a means to solve the problem at hand, they appear to think prior to relationship building with the other party that some interactive event should be configured in order to realize "ordered coexistence", which is a generalized value that can be shared with anyone, and attempt to realize it on the strength of mutual readiness rather than one party's initiative and the other's submission. In practice, they engage in this interaction only when they think that the other party has the same level of readiness based on the past experience of engaging in hand-clasped grooming with the other party in similar situations. Accordingly, this type of interaction performed between particular parties is likely to be implemented based on the voluntary choice of each party on the grounds of equal readiness and by neither initiation by one party nor submission by the other due to lack of other options.

If we regard hand-clasped grooming in chimpanzees as a phenomenon in the liminal space between the pre- and post-institution stage on route to "ritual rules", a stable and reproducible interaction system is configured there as a connection between the two stages, when both parties voluntarily deal with the problem at hand on the grounds of the same level of readiness to get involved in the realization of a general value that can be shared by all peers. When both parties adjust their actions in a reciprocal manner toward the generation of a particular interactive event, they are able to share the experience surrounding "ordered coexistence" with peers.

Conversely, what separates these two stages is the condition in which the meaning of being appropriate for the realization of the expected result is perceivable at all times in either the actions selected by the parties or the interactive event configured by connecting these actions, both of which become possible only after the transition. Thus, the problem solving measure to actively change the situation and to remove the possibility for disorder is given as something concrete that precedes the subsequent interaction. This offers the following new direction for subsequent societies in order to make collective problem solving more reliable. That is, through finding a more generalized understanding of the correspondence relationship between a problem solving measure and its result as well as the possibility for specialized measures to deal with the individuality of each problem in their attempt to collectively solve various problems, they develop a framework to deal with a more diverse range of issues in a flexible manner based on a coherent guideline that can be called their "own way".

"Adherence to rules" and language acquisition

A distinctive aspect of the analysis in this chapter in its discussion of institution from an evolutionary perspective is its exploration of the collective use of resources and collective problem solving as something common to the pre- and post-institution stages in the category of activities addressed here. It is thought that when individual action connection gives rise to an interactive event in order to solve a problem, the institution is the device that makes it stable and reproducible.

The chapter began the analysis by distinguishing two types of institutions in human societies: one focuses on the generation and maintenance of social orders such as legal systems and the other on designating the meaning of an understanding of reality or actions concerning living practices such as cultural institutions. We treated adherence to "prohibitive rules" for the former and "ritual rules" for the latter as the core of the phenomenon created by each type of institution and examined in a concrete fashion what had happened in the transition from the pre- to the post-institution stage on respective routes.

In the process, we addressed phenomena relating to the perception of "meaning" in an object or the giving of "meaning" to an action in building a relationship with it through the action as a domain that underwent a major change upon the emergence of institutions. It was thought that after the emergence of institutions, their "meaning" was offered as something predetermined and not reliant on the circumstances of each occasion, thus making a collective problem solving measure based on the sharing of the "meaning" reliable and reproducible. In other words, adherence to a "prohibitive rule" enables one to share with the other party the "meaning" of a "thing" that mediates relationship building with peers, and this enables them to ensure their interaction is non-agonistic when configured through the interconnection of actions to build relationships with the "thing" at the time. On the other hand, adherence to "ritual rules" enables peers to solve the problem at hand by configuring an interactive event that has been given the meaning of being appropriate for the realization of an expected result on that occasion based on the sharing of the "meaning" in the action prescribed by such rules.

Finally, I shall point to the path of understanding in relation to the question of language acquisition in terms of why a particular "meaning" has come to be treated as something predetermined independently of the context of the interaction at the time.

On the route to a "prohibitive rule", conventional meaning is perceived in a "thing" that mediates reciprocal relationship building among peers, and this enables the configuration of an interaction system that can realize a state of peaceful coexistence. When the meaning is perceived in a "thing" as something akin to an unshakable fact prior to the occasion of reciprocal relationship building and independently of what is done there, the action selection at the time becomes compliant to the rule. For the meaning to become something akin to an unshakable fact, the "thing" must be replaced with something that can denote the meaning all the time, for example, "language". That is, the "thing" must be named in language and referred to by that name. Naming in language means that through replacement of the "thing" with a name, the meaning of the "thing" becomes perceivable at all times as the signified represented by the name as the signifier. This makes the stable reproduction of an interactive event more reliable and at the same time offers the possibility for a more complex system based on extended conditions.

On the other hand, on the route to a "ritual rule", individuals can share the framework for collective problem solving with peers based on a conventional understanding of the correspondence relationship between the configuration of an interactive event and the result realized by it brought about by making reference to "problem solving measures at hand". However, for the correspondence relationship between the measure and its effect to be given in advance as something akin to an unshakable fact prior to the configuration of an interaction system, the meaning of being appropriate for the realization of an expected result must be available for perception in the actions selected by the parties or the interactive event that arises from the connection of such actions at all times. For this to happen, it is thought that the naming of these actions and interactive event in language to denote their meaning must be implemented. It is thought that doing so can make it possible to develop a system to deal with various problems in a flexible manner under a coherent guideline through the discovery of a more generalized understanding of the problem solving measures and their effects and create the possibility for the segmentalization of individual measures in the collective resolution of a wide range of problems.

12 Living One's Role Under Institution: Ecological Niches and Animal Societies

Kaoru Adachi

Key ideas

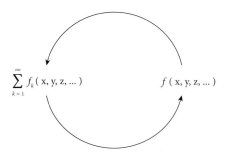

The above terms denote behavior selection by animals according to the environment in a given scene. It is a function for choosing one output appropriate for survival from a number of behavioral options while being influenced by interactions with other individuals or factors such as the context of reciprocal actions with the physical environment. The term on the left enumerates and summates all such behavioral options. Because it is impossible to enumerate all scenes in an observation, the niche and the role are proximate to the left term but not the same. There is a recursive relationship where the bundle of behavioral options enumerated here influences behavior selection in a given scene and a choice in a given scene influences the overall manner of behavior selection. This chapter addresses concrete conditions under which "institution" emerges focusing on this recursive repetition.

Conditions of niches and behavior selection

A "niche" refers to a set of environmental factors that a certain species needs for survival or a form of impact a species has on environmental factors in an ecosystem. "Niche" is also interpreted as the ecological status of an organism and refers to the environmental components that are absolutely imperative for its survival such as habitat and food. While this concept has been developed in the field of ecology in its attempts to understand community structure, in recent years it has been appropriated for use in other fields (e.g., niche market, stem cell niche). The original meaning of the word refers to a hollow recess in a wall used to display ornaments or flowers in western architecture, and in turn refers to an alcove or aperture housing something important.

Participating in a certain social group and continuously engaging in a certain pattern of action can be regarded as a "role" here. "Role" assumes the existence of a group as a whole or interaction with others and cannot emerge in a single individual. At the same time, it can be said that the appropriate positioning of roles within a social group serves the purpose of the group which is to maintain its normal functioning by dealing with problems and challenges. If the continuation of a routine action becomes a rule and its contribution to the formation and maintenance of the group is an important aspect of "institution", then "role" can be regarded as its leading example.

In this chapter, the emergence of institution is discussed in terms of the function of a niche in an ecosystem as an analogy for a role in a social institution. The positioning of a role as part of a group shares similarities with the functioning of a niche in an ecosystem in various aspects. We will look at niches found in an assemblage of heterogeneous individuals called a mixed species association in primates and explain how they form and how they are assessed by observers. While we address the question of niches in the context of relationships between heterogeneous individuals, we advance our discussion on the assumption that the social mechanism by which niches are positioned in an ecosystem is also applicable to behavioral adjustments between individuals of the same species.

Just like roles, we extract niches based on patterned behaviors and also pay attention to the condition of behavior selection (action selection)[1] that occurs there. In doing so, we attempt to consider institution without being caught up in the great disconnect that is believed to exist between humans and other animals.

Roles in mixed species associations

In the tropical rainforests of Côte d'Ivore (Ivory Coast) in West Africa, mixed species associations formed by different species of guenons are frequently observed. Three species—the Diana monkey, Campbell's guenon and lesser spot-nosed guenon—coexist in the Taï National Park and frequently form mixed species associations. Not living in a mixed species association is an unusual situation for them, as all three species rarely live in a monospecific group. Although in many primate species an association is usually a group of conspecifics and rarely includes heterogeneous individuals, forming a group with individuals of other species is the normal condition for the guenons in this region and an assemblage of only conspecifics is a very rare condition.

The three are phylogenetically close species whose niches substantially overlap as they feed on similar foods and live in similar habitats. Ecology predicts that this kind of sympatric habitation of heterospecifics with overlapping resource use produces intense interspecific competition. In particular, many fruits are commonly consumed by the three species. The most frequent consumer of fruit with high proportions of overlapping use is the Diana monkey, which maintains high feeding ratios of fruit regardless of the season. On the other hand, insects and leaves account for high ratios in the overall diets of the Campbell's guenon and the lesser spot-nosed guenon respectively, and the utilization rates increase during periods of decreased fruit availability. In other words, Taï's three species of guenons engage in overlapping consumption of fruit when they are in abundance and shift their feeding niches when fruit is in short supply, in that the Campbell's guenon and the lesser spot-nosed guenon utilize foods other than fruit. Moreover, they avoid potential feeding competition by separating their dietary menus when resources are scarce and even choose to feed on the kinds of fruit that minimize direct competition during the periods of increased demand.

The Diana monkey makes the smallest shift in terms of food utilization while consuming overlapped food resources. The Diana monkey is thought to have an advantage in competition for resources as it has the largest body size among the three species. Diana monkeys act as effective lookouts for both flying predators because they mostly use the high canopy stratum and ambushers such as feline carnivores as they live in large groups and move about actively (Bshary 2001). It is likely that in forming mixed species associations, Campbell's guenons and lesser spot-nosed guenons enjoy the benefits of the Diana monkeys' vigilance against predators at the expense of competition for food. According to cultural

Living One's Role Under Institution: Ecological Niches and Animal Societies

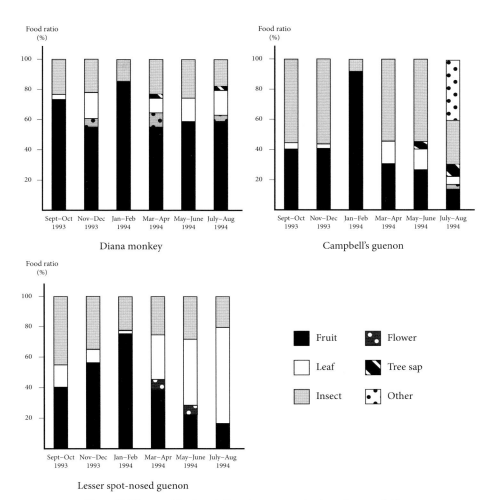

Figure 12.1 Seasonal food variations in guenon mixed species associations

anthropologist Ichiro Majima (1997), the Dan people of Ivory Coast call the Diana monkey "*gao*", which is "the name of the greatest monkey among all the monkeys inhabiting the forests". According to oral tradition, "when a *gao* walks in the forest, all other monkeys follow", indicating the perception that Diana monkeys were the leaders of many types of monkeys as they traversed the forests. It is highly likely that the Diana monkey forms the core of a mixed species association that draws in other species because it fulfills the role of lookout that benefits the others.

In broad terms, the small-sized lesser spot-nosed guenons are folivores, the medium-sized Campbell's guenons are insectivores and the large-sized Diana monkeys are frugivores. It is generally expected that smaller animals feed on insects and fruit while larger animals are more likely to consume leaves (Oates 1986), but the guenons of Taï prove contrary to this expectation. According to W. McGraw (2000), the locomotion and postures of the guenons of Taï closely correspond with the overall lifestyle of each species and do not relate to the body weight. The Diana monkey exhibits postures that are suitable for feeding on actively moving or unevenly distributed foods such as insects and fruit and utilizes the canopy layer often. They frequently travel from one feeding location to another and actively move about. By contrast, the Campbell's guenon and the lesser spot-nosed guenon use the lower strata below the canopy and travel at slower speeds. The lesser spot-nosed guenon often feeds while sitting on a tree branch and exhibits postures suitable for immobile and evenly distributed food, i.e. leaves. The result of the analysis here is consistent with McGraw's finding. Both the Diana monkey and the Campbell's guenon commonly eat fruit and insects, but the former mainly feeds on insects in the upper stratum of the forest, whereas the latter mostly consumes insects in the lower stratum.

Between the different species that comprise mixed species associations, overlapping, separation and fluctuation are observed in various aspects of the lifestyle, including the foods they feed on, the height of feeding trees they use and the locomotion type. It is possible to identify certain tendencies from the way these species change their attributes in coordination with temporal changes in the environment. For example, the Diana monkey is the "frugivore", and fulfills the role of the "leader" of the mixed species association. The Campbell's guenon is the "insectivore" and the lesser spot-nosed guenon is the "folivore", both of which are the "followers" of the Diana monkey in the mixed species association. It is possible to assign these ecological roles on the constituent species in the context of the overall assemblage called a mixed species association.

Niche theory

What is a niche?

Ecologists have recognized the fact that organisms live in a community in which they exert influence on one another and have explored the factors underpinning a stable community structure. "Niche" is the key concept for this endeavor. Using the concept of niche, we can explain what the individuals eat, where they go and how they engage with the environment. The ultimate goal of ecology lies in the elucidation of the functions and processes of the entire ecosystem.

Niche theory was first proposed in ecology in and around the 1920s and reached the peak of its popularity as a research subject in the 1970s and 1980s. Since the turn of the twenty-first century, interest in this concept has comparatively waned.

While niche is a concept employed to explain the relationship between organisms and the environment, there are two broadly classified models based on different modalities. One is called a habitat niche or environmental niche, proposed by J. Grinnell (1917) and others. A niche here means a position in the environment occupied by a certain species. It is a set of minimum resources and habitats required for the organisms' survival. It is a place offered by the environment to organisms and relates to the aforementioned "recess in a wall" in the sense that it is a place in which something fits. Grinnell's definition was later extended by G. Hutchinson (1957), who produced the concept of n-dimensional hypervolume. This theory suggests that a niche is realized in a multi-dimensional space with n axes, including food type, foraging location, rest location, humidity and ambient temperature.

The other model, proposed by C. Elton (1927), is called a role niche or functional niche. Elton considers that organisms play a certain role in the food chain in an ecosystem. "Role" refers to their environmental impact, i.e., what they eat. He took an interest in the interactions between organisms in a given environment and tried to explain the phenomenon in which an entire community of organisms is sustained by multiple species that function together in a balanced manner. Consequently, the environment recedes into the background and organisms become the influential actors. The most important question here is how individual organisms adjust their relationships reciprocally to live together, and the environment is provided as a field in which such adjustment takes place.

Grinnell's definition of niche concerns the environment's effects on organisms, while Elton's emphasizes organisms' effects on the environment. In the environmental niche model, the existence of a niche precedes the activity of organisms and gives rise to the possibility of a "vacant niche", which is currently not used by any organisms (but will be used by some in the future). This view was linked with psychology and later developed into ecological psychology by J. Gibson and others. By contrast, a functional niche arises only when the activity of organisms impacts on the environment, and therefore a niche without the activity of organisms is impossible.

Ecology of equilibrium and non-equilibrium

Niche theory was adopted for the purpose of understanding the structures and dynamics of ecosystems. The goal of community ecology is to measure and analyze the variety and amount of organism species contained in a given ecosystem and to elucidate their dynamics.

In *The Theory of Island Biogeography* (MacArthur and Wilson 1967), R. MacArthur studied fluctuations in the number of species in an insular island ecosystem and this formed the foundation of equilibrium theory in ecology. The point of interest here is the number and composition of species in a given ecological community. In particular, the existence of multiple closely related species in the same environment is treated as a problem that needs to be addressed from the perspective of interspecific competition. According to Gause's law of competitive exclusion (Gause 1936), multiple species cannot coexist in the same niche. Empirical and theoretical studies have been conducted on the niches of various organism communities and interspecific competition using the Lotka-Volterra equations.

Equilibrium theory assumes that shortages of resources utilized by organisms can occur at any time. Two closely related species occupying similar niches compete for common resources and, in an extreme case envisaged by Gause, one species may drive the other out. Cases of interspecific niche overlap are observed in the actual organism communities. Interspecific competition is thought to occur for resources in the overlapping sections of the niches. Limiting similarity theory predicts the degree of similarity between niches at which coexistence of different species becomes impossible. When niche overlap becomes too large, character displacement occurs in the process of evolution and changes the species so that their niches differ. A situation in which sympatric and closely related species are using different resources is called niche separation, which enables them to coexist without competing as each niche is narrowed to avoid overlap. Niche separation is analogous to a phenomenon commonly known as habitat segregation or food segregation. However, niche separation and character displacement are theories for analyzing the present situation on the assumption that the environment and past competition ("ghost of competition past") due to resource shortages remain constant.

Ecological equilibrium theory hypothesizes that interspecific competition caused by shortages of available resources determines the composition of organism species that occupy various niches and in turn the structure of the organism community. On the other hand, non-equilibrium theory argues that there are hardly any circumstances that give rise to equilibrium. It is thought that some of the conditions assumed by equilibrium theory almost never exist in real ecosystems. And it is largely impossible to ascertain resource shortages in reality. Although niche separation and habitat segregation are interpreted as the consequences of competition triggered by resource shortages, it may well be the case that there was no competition, and niche separation occurred as a result of adaptation to different habitats by respective species. Equilibrium theory assumes that the environment remains unchanged, while in reality, all sorts of disturbances happen at significant frequency. They range from large-scale disturbances that destroy entire ecosystems such as volcanic activity, bush fires and flooding, to medium-scale biological factors such as changes in the population or behavior of predators. It is possible that equilibrium theory cannot be validated because "biological communities are always recovering from the last disturbance" (Reice 1994). Non-equilibrium theory considers that what contributes to community formation are such things as predation pressure and contingency rather than niche separation by interspecific competition.

Niche measurement

Most mixed species associations of primates are formed by closely related species in tropical forests (Cords 1987; Terborgh 1983). For this reason, there was a proliferation of ecological studies on the subject of interspecific feeding competition riding on the wave of popularity of equilibrium theory research from the beginning of the 1970s. From the 1980s, increasing numbers of mixed species association studies emphasized the effect of predators at the same time as the emergence of non-equilibrium theory as a critique of equilibrium theory. In order to use niche separation as evidence of competition, it is necessary to compare the sympatric and allopatric situation of the same combination of species and to demonstrate that there is less niche overlap in the former. However, there is little chance of satisfying the assumption that all environmental conditions other than the target species remain equal for allopatric and sympatric habitats in the real world. Alternatively, if there is a resource shortage at the time of niche separation, it can be regarded as evidence that directly supports the existence of competition. According to non-equilibrium theory, it is thought that interspecific competition is not particularly intense in organism associations in the tropics with high species diversity, allowing the different species using the same resources to coexist even if the degree of niche overlap is high. It is difficult to determine whether niche separation is the result of niche shift to avoid potential competition or interspecific difference in preference unrelated to competition.

In mixed species associations of primates, closely related species not only inhabit sympatrically but also engage in various activities such as foraging and ranging synchronously. The level of direct competition is therefore expected to be higher than when they simply utilize the same geographic area. The benefits of forming mixed species associations need to outweigh the costs of competition. On the other hand, the formation of mixed species associations may offer the benefits of foraging for the same foods. As guenons live on a staple diet of fruits, which exhibit a clumped distribution, the guide hypothesis suggesting that they form mixed species associations with species that are well-versed on food locations, or the renewal hypothesis suggesting that they avoid feeding locations that have been exhausted by other species, are considered to be highly relevant. With regard to insects, which constitute another important food resource for guenons, one hypothesis suggests that they feed on insects that have been driven out from foliage by more active species.

Food separation between species in a mixed species association influences the benefits and costs of forming the association. It is thought that a low level of food separation at the time of formation increases the benefits through increased foraging efficiency and therefore the cost of feeding competition becomes relatively small. It is also conceivable that species temporarily gather at the same feeding location simply to utilize the same resources. Food separation in a mixed species association means that these species are eating different foods while forming a mixed species association, and hence the benefits achieved through foraging efficiency are small. The possible reasons for eating different foods include niche shift caused by potential feeding competition and food segregation due to differences in species-specific feeding behavior preferences. In this case, a mixed species association is formed because other benefits such as predator avoidance outweigh the costs of feeding competition. If a mixed species association is not formed where there is significant food overlap, it is possible that the species disperse to feed because of the large feeding competition cost of forming an association.

In order to estimate the level of feeding competition, we need to measure the degree of niche overlap. The primates in mixed species associations mainly feed on fruit and also consume leaves and insects. The types of food they eat and the number of times they feed provide data for overlap measurement. Feeding frequency is measured according to standard ethological methods so that data are comparable between species and geographic areas with minimal bias. The following are some examples of indices used to measure the degree of niche overlap.

Percentage Overlap Index

$$P_{jk} = \left[\sum_{}^{n} (\min p_{ij}, p_{ik}) \right] 100$$

Morishita-Horn Index

$$C_H = \frac{2 \sum P_{ij} P_{ik}}{\sum p^2_{ij} + \sum p^2_{ik}}$$

Notes: P_{ij}, P_{ik}: Proportion of food i is used by species j and k respectively. n: Total number of food types used.

Both indices involve enumerating all feeding activities (type and frequency) and calculating the proportion of the times (n_i) the i_{th} type of food item is eaten of the total observed feeding data N, i.e., the percentage a certain item-use accounts for in the total food use (p_i). This value is treated as an index that represents the degree of niche overlap between two organism species j and k. For the aforementioned mixed species associations of guenons in the Taï National Park, the Percentage Overlap Index has been used.

Finding a gradient by enumerating behaviors

According to the Eltonian interpretation, a niche is defined as "a role or status occupied by a certain species in an organism association". In terms of a mixed species association, it is described as "frugivore" and "folivore". Observers turn the organism behavior of feeding into data and introduce various indices in order to measure niches. They calculate numerical values such as niche overlap, similarity and breadth. The index calculation operation involves pooling and integrating events that have occurred in a certain period of time and generating an output as one attribute. While the Diana monkey feeds on more fruit and less leaves, it is categorized as the "frugivore" as a result of pooling feeding data and comparing the indices with other species.

The niche is a behavioral tendency elicited from a pool of events that have occurred over a certain timeframe. The indices for niche measurements take the form of formulae to enumerate and integrate all resource uses. The "frugivore" tendency is not only derived from the actual observation finding of frequent fruit feeding at various locations, but also refers to the category to which the species will shift as a result of food segregation to avoid competition. Where the Diana monkey and other guenon species in a mixed species association are co-present at the scenes of individual feeding behaviors, a phenomenon has been observed in

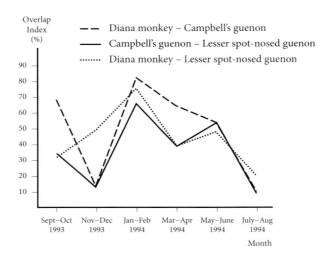

Figure 12.2 Seasonal feeding overlap variations in guenon mixed species associations

which Diana monkeys feed on the common menu first and the heterospecifics feed on leaves or insects in the meantime. There are observed differences in the choice of feeding menu and timing between the Diana monkey with a strong "frugivore" tendency and the other species that feed on other foods as well. It seems as if the niche defines the choice in terms of the feeding behavior of each species. It appears that the niche as an index calculated from a pool of individual feeding behaviors assigns a role to each species such as "frugivore" and "insectivore", and that each species behaves according to its assigned role.

It seems that the temporal integration of behavioral events defines a niche and at the same time the niche defines the behavioral choices of the relevant species as well as the other species that interact with it. In mixed species communities of guenons, an accumulation of fruit-eating behavior forms the niche of frugivore. This role is assumed by the Diana monkey species, which occupies the role and status of frugivore in an ecosystem. A niche is a behavioral tendency derived from an accumulation of discrete data collected, pooled and averaged by observers. The niche as an accumulation of parts is at the same time defined by the role it has within a whole, such as a community and an ecosystem. The whole such as a mixed species association and a tropical rainforest community revolves around the mutually intertwined activities of various organisms in sustaining their functions. In one such mixed species association of guenons, Diana monkeys occupying the frugivore niche engage in feeding behavior with the other folivore and insectivore guenons, sometimes cooperatively and at other times in a complementary fashion. They feed on the same menu at the same time when it is possible to do so, and when it is not possible they dissolve and reform their mixed species association by changing the feeding time, location or menu on an ongoing basis.

A niche comes into existence on the premise of behavior, which is in turn influenced by the niche. There is a reciprocal feedback relationship between the existence of a niche and the choice of behavior by which they influence one another. If behavior is the smallest element of society, its role is intertwined with society as a whole via a niche. The niche can be regarded as a key concept linking part to whole within the duality of feedback.

"Field" enables recursive determination between part and whole

Our attempt to understand the niche as an evolutionary "pre-institution" leading to human institutions may become possible when we pay attention to the recursive relationship between part and whole. This is because an institution is thought to be shared by many members of a human social group as a set of criteria that have some impacts on their action selection within the group. In animal communities, however, whole does not precede part as we can see from the actual observation procedures for niche measurements. A niche or a role does not occur in advance, that is, the desired harmonious whole does not come first. A niche or a role category simply looms out of a whole as an accumulation of discrete behaviors or a pooled tendency at the hand of observers. It is not the case that something is provided as a criterion for individual behavioral choice in advance of behavior. In this sense, there is a crucial difference between many human institutions and the niche phenomenon in other animal communities.

When we think of what serves as a criterion that determines the part of behavioral choice, the phenomenon of the formation of an ecological niche or role may present new conditions through the medium of the concept of "field" (Endo 1992; Funabiki 2013, Chapter Fourteen). In the communities of guenons that form mixed species associations, niche formation would not occur if there was no mixed species association as a "field". Guenons become able to adjust their behaviors reciprocally and accumulate feeding behaviors through the formation of the mixed species association community. Here, the mixed species association functions as a "field". It is possible to say that the role of a niche to connect part to whole is supported by the existence of this "field". Only when there is a "field" called a mixed species association does niche separation and overlap become possible. This type of "field" theory has been repeatedly addressed in the discipline of ecology.

Mayflies and habitat segregation around the Kamo River

A phenomenon in which multiple species whose niches overlap coexist by niche partitioning is generally called habitat segregation. Kinji Imanishi (1949) explains niche separation using his unique theory of habitat segregation from the perspective of the social structure of organisms. According to Imanishi, the environment in which an organism lives and its activities are indivisible, and the environment and the organism/actor as a whole constitute a lifeform. Organisms that share the same lifeform constitute a species, which forms the specia. Different specias have different lifeforms, that is, they live in different fields and carry out different activities, hence habitat segregation is observed there. The occurrence of niche separation between different species is self-evident in Imanishi's argument on the specia. The "guild" formed by closely related species using similar niches is called synusia in Imanishi's theory and gives rise to habitat segregation in the micro-habitat environment to avoid potential interspecific competition.

Imanishi's habitat segregation theory and the notion of a holospecia (whole ecological society) are based on a study of aquatic insects by Tokichi Kani. Kani, born in 1908, was an entomologist who conducted a survey around the Kamo River in Kyoto from 1938 to 1939. He was drafted in 1943 and killed in the war in 1944. The main part of his study was published in *Nippon seibutsu shi* (The Japanese journal of biology) as "Keiryusei konchu no seitai" (Ecology of stream-living insects) (1944), after he had been sent to the front. The rest of the study was published after the war through the efforts of Masaaki Morishita, an ecologist who was Kani's close friend. "Keiryusei konchu no seitai" addressed habitat segregation in the biotope of aquatic insects such as mayflies, caddis flies and stoneflies around the Kamo River. A substantial number of pages are devoted to an effort to understand the river morphology from its beginning. Kani states that "the first task I must carry out is to analyze the stream scientifically" in order to understand the ecology of the insects. Specifically, he did this to find out "what a stream is, what its peculiarities are" in order to identify "the smallest units when a river is broken down into its component parts, or what can be called the river's building blocks". The river as a whole is thoroughly segmentalized and classified based on the two structural types of rapid and pool as well as the bend of the river. The stream habitat becomes differentiated from of various types of watercourses from the upper to lower reaches.

Following the identification of the peculiarities of the stream habitat, micro-habitat differences such as differences in flow rate, stone size and rock stratification are analyzed and the types and life histories of organisms distributed in those micro-habitats are surveyed. By carefully superimposing the distribution of insect fauna upon the systematic analysis of micro-habitats, Kani illuminates the insect species' modes of living.

Kani's method of starting from the identification of habitats is close to the aforementioned niche model that is classified as habitat niche or environmental niche. However, Kani began from the concept of environmental niche and surveyed the uneven population distribution among different species in micro-habitats, and went on to observe the way sympatric heterogeneous species sharing the same micro-space separate their niches to suit their respective life histories and forms according to the environmental gradient. From this he derived the interaction-based synusia in which different species reciprocally adjust their habitat use. The theorization of habitat segregation was made possible by Kani's typology of micro-habitats found around a stream and the detailed observation of the way aquatic insects use these habitats.

The concepts of "lifeform" and "place of living" that are important in considering habitat segregation theory (Adachi 2013; Niwa 1993; Saito 2012) include both elements of what Kani tried to classify and thoroughly understand by observing aquatic insects—the environment and the interactivity between different organism species that takes place in it. The environment cannot exist without the activity of organisms and the activity of organisms cannot occur without the environmental elements the organisms need. The environment and the organic actors are indivisibly linked, and Imanishi used terms such as "lifeform" and "place of living" in trying to express this situation.

Niche construction

There are two currents concerning the concept of niche offering different ideas on the relative positions of the environment and organisms. Niche construction theory, which follows in the wake of the Eltonian view that emphasizes organisms' effects on the environment, is drawing attention as a new evolutionary theory based on the concept of niche. The notion of niche construction has a commonality with Imanishi's concept of lifeform. "Lifeform" describes the integration of organisms and the environment on the premise of the existence of a "field" on which the organisms' activities take place.

Niche construction, proposed by F. J. Odling-Smee, K. Laland and M. W. Feldman (2003) among others, refers to the process by which organisms' activities influence and modify the environment. A modified environment sets the stage for the organisms' evolution. Simple examples include structures constructed by organisms such as nests, spider's webs, beaver dams and anthills. When organisms inhabiting environment A create a burrow, environment A changes into environment A'. This new environment A' exerts evolutionary selection pressures on the organisms. This view is attracting interest as an argument that incorporates the effects of organisms on the environment and treats evolution as a bidirectional phenomenon, as against earlier evolution theories that focus on one-way selective pressures from the environment on organisms. Environment A' that has been brought about by niche construction provides not only new selective pressures on the individuals that created the burrow but also a new evolutionary environment for other species and their offspring, which also use environment A'.

The idea of organisms' influences on the environment is within the bounds of common sense in classical biology and ecology and not a new view proposed by niche construction theory. In fact, many of the cases discussed in terms of niche construction are illustrated by R. Dawkins (1987) in *The Extended Phenotype*. The dam-building beaver is a symbolic animal that is cited in both niche construction theory and *The Extended Phenotype*. According to Dawkins, when a beaver blocks a water stream and floods an area, the bounds of the enlarged pool indicate the reaches of the beaver's genes, and the enlarged and extended phenotypes of particular genes relevant to its dam construction behavior include the dam in its entirety. Because a beaver that builds a larger dam can better protect itself from predators and increase its survival potential, this beaver is more fit in the evolutionary process. The distinction between niche construction and Dawkins' theory depends on whether the extended dam is considered to be a new environment A' or the extended phenotypes.

Niche construction is also used in arguments about the evolution of human cultures and cognition. Already at the stage of gene-culture coevolution theory derived from behavioral ecology, the spread of dairy husbandry and the evolution of lactose tolerance genes were theorized. Niche construction has many overlaps with gene-culture coevolution theory and hence there is a move to use it to explain various aspects of human cultural behaviors in addition to lactose tolerance genes. A primary example is a study by economists, including S. Bowles and H. Gintis (2011) on the cultural selection of a series of reciprocal altruistic behaviors.

The center of action

The center of action is a concept that appears in *The Pattern of Animal Communities* published by C. Elton in 1966. According to A. Endo (1992), "various interactions between organisms converge to form interspersed 'fields', each of which contains interrelated dynamic 'processes', which build up entire organism communities into a complex structure". When plants flower, a wide variety of organisms gather in search of nectar and pollen. There is nothing that can be regarded as "order" here because of a lack of reproductive or predator-prey relationships among the gathering organisms, and Elton likened this state to "crowds". Using the analogy that the organism world as a whole is constituted by these "crowds", which are scattered across the environment and interact with one another, he attempted to provide a comprehensive explanation of the complexity of the community structure as a whole based on the interaction of micro-fields in *The Pattern of Animal Communities*.

Endo shaped his ecology around the center of action concept after Elton. He studied the nest of a spider-eating wasp species called *Episyron arrogans* as an example of the center of action and observed the action relationships between spiders in the area as prey, flies parasitic to the wasps and ants and digger wasps that obstruct nesting by the wasps. The phenomenon occurring around the center of action exists in a state of flux as a loose assemblage with no clear regularity, which Endo describes as "ephemeral". Such centers of action are ubiquitous in the natural world, for example decaying bodies (attracting many predators and decomposers), feces, fallen trees, puddles of water, nests and spider webs; even individual living organisms can be regarded as such.

Endo insists on starting with small communities. There is no other way to describe a complex community structure than to record every episode of the activities of various organisms that occur around the center of action on which a structure of interrelations between the centers of action is founded. The center of action proposed by Elton and Endo is a "field" where the actions of organisms accumulate with loose regularity, similar to what is represented by the concepts of niche construction and extended phenotypes. It is also the concept of "place of living", which was classified by Kani and expressed as lifeform by Imanishi, viewed from a different angle.

What happens in the "field"

The notions of niche construction and the center of action identify that the scene of niche formation is the "field" where interactions between the activities of organisms occur. The idea of cultural evolution based on niche construction predicts that the existence of social "fields" called groups function as constructed niches in which various brands of uniquely human sociality such as reciprocal altruism will arise almost automatically (Sterelney 2003). Feeding and breeding are two essential behaviors underpinning the survival of organisms. By forming "fields" called mixed species associations, guenons use these fields to carry out the feeding behaviors essential for their survival as they reciprocally adjust their relationships with other conspecifics and heterospecifics. It is possible to say that individuals communicate about their niches at the scenes of individual feeding behaviors. In a constructed niche habitat of a mixed species association, the feeding niche serves as a behavioral guideline and at the same time is the result of a feeding behavior.

Looking at this concept of "field" from another perspective, a "field" represents a place where interactions between individual organism inhabitants interconnect constantly. The activity of organisms is the very thing that differentiates the "field" from a simple physical environment. The "field" exists as long as the behaviors of the organisms inhabiting the space continue to interact with the inorganic environment and the behaviors of other conspecifics and heterospecifics. In addition to direct or face-to-face interactions, the indirect influences of what is not there cannot be ignored. Not being in the field, that is, being absent, is one of the important behavior selection criteria for those living there (Funabiki 2013; Uchibori 2013).

In the mixed species association phenomenon, for instance, when one species is acting away from its partner species and they are typically together constantly, the absence of the important partner appears to be a concern that always affects behavior selection. Diana monkeys and olive colobus monkeys form mixed species associations almost all the time, but they spend short periods apart on rare occasions. One example is when the active Diana monkeys begin ranging while olive colobus monkeys are still resting in inconspicuous spots under the trees. I as an observer follow Diana monkeys, leaving olive colobus monkeys behind in the field and subsequently become somewhat concerned by my awareness of their absence. I cannot peek inside the minds of the languageless monkeys to find out what they are thinking, but their behavior is almost always the same; Diana monkeys and olive colobus monkeys restore their mixed species association immediately. Their behavior seems straightforward and without hesitation in some cases. The advance party of Diana monkeys stop ranging or feeding as if they have just realized that they left something behind and double back toward the olive colobus monkeys. On the other hand, the olive colobus monkeys wake up and realize they have been left behind and travel straight toward the noisy group of Diana monkeys much faster than their normal ranging speed.

The "field" is a place where the behaviors of the organisms, including absence, exert reciprocal influences on an ongoing basis and this makes niche formation possible. In the aforementioned phenomena such as food niche separation and overlap in guenons, individual behavior selection, which influences the niche, is strongly affected by the behaviors of the partner species in the mixed species association. Important elements include not only the direct reciprocal influencing while they are co-present as partners (e.g., Campbell's guenons feed on insects when Diana monkeys are feeding on fruit in order to avoid competition), but also the effect of the absence of the partners on behavior selection when the mixed species association is dissolved. For example, Campbell's guenons dissolve their mixed species association with Diana monkeys (albeit rarely) to feed on fruits in the absence of Diana monkeys or when they choose to stop feeding in favor of resting or traveling. Behavior selection in the absence of partners does not mean that they can choose their behavior freely to suit their own convenience unaffected by the partners' behavior; it is the very absence that restricts the range of behavior choices. In the phenomenon observed in the mixed species association, the organisms inhabiting the same "field" exert influences on one another's behavior selection whether directly or indirectly and whether in co-presence or in absence.

Considering institution from the concept of niche

Niche as a concatenation of interactions

Organisms living in their roles interact with the environment continuously. The environment here includes not only physical and inorganic matter but also other conspecifics and heterospecifics. While influencing one another, the guenons in a mixed species association sometimes eat fruit, sometimes insects and sometimes nothing. The role of "frugivore" assigned to the Diana monkey is an accumulation of its repetitive choice to engage in fruit eating behavior. Repetitive behavior selection in itself signifies the living of an organism and at the same time indicates the existence of the "field" in which the action takes place. As behavior selection occurs in the "field", it inevitably connects the interactions that take place between the various organisms that share the "field". These interactions can be direct or indirect. Those missing from the field may continue to affect the behavior of those present as absentees in some cases. An institution may be something that arises in repeated behavior selection that is indivisibly connected to the "field". Repetitions of constant interactions do not form a simple accumulation; they show the feasibilities of each interaction, and the series of interactions will continue through the medium of the "field" (which means living itself). Something institutional becomes apparent here.

It is said that language is necessary for human institutions. Institutions in human society are characterized by not only conventions and mores that are observed as concatenations of patterns of action but also bundles of the "must do …" rules shared by many members of society through language. The "must do …" rules contain the value judgment that doing so is a "good" thing and give rise to an institution as an accumulation of appropriate behaviors through the process of the recognition, acquisition and internalization of individual rules. The institution thus attained is utilized for the purpose of conducting interactions efficiently in resolving the various problems and challenges facing a social group. The concatenation of "good deeds" and the series of behaviors appropriate for a given situation only produce conventions, but when they come to be shared by the whole group through learning and internalizing, they are elevated to institutions. For the rules containing the value of "must do …" to be shared within a group, its members are required to have sufficient cognitive ability to learn and internalize them. This is why only humans and some apes are considered to have this ability and the social features that can be called institutions. This view of institution has its origins in a sociological paradigm that treats shared value and consensus formation as the preconditions for the formation of human societies. Because those who have agreed on criteria for evaluating what is "good" can refer to the shared rules that exist externally, social communication becomes possible and human societies can be formed. The bundle of rules for the smooth conduct of interactions becomes an institution.

On the other hand, social systems theorists represented by N. Luhmann (1993) find a prerequisite for the emergence of human societies in a concatenation of assumption-less and baseless trust relationships rather than value sharing. Where value sharing is not achieved and there is no bundle of rules to rely on, humans can launch into communication with others without any basis and continue to concatenate their interactions. The only thing needed for the formation of societies is the continuation of interactions rather than a set of shared norms. As long as one selects one's own behavior on the understanding that the other's next behavior selection depends on the result of the behavior selection one makes now, then social communication will concatenate. A phenomenon in which one modifies one's own behavior allowing for the possibility that the other's behavior will be changed as a result can be considered very close to what happens in a "field" such as a mixed species association and a center of action. The behavior of Diana monkeys eating fruit in a feeding tree connects with that of Campbell's guenons eating insects nearby to avoid competition, and the Diana monkeys which see the Campbell's guenons feeding on insects nearby choose to eat fruit instead of insects to avoid direct competition. Through the accumulation of these phenomena, Diana monkeys acquire the niche of "frugivore" and Campbell's guenons the niche of "insectivore".

Animals live by selecting behaviors continuously appropriate for the occasion most of the time. Because failing to do so raises the probability of non-survival, continuing to behave in an appropriate manner is almost synonymous with living. It is conceivable that even a behavior that is genetically fixed rather than selected consciously or intentionally will lead to the emergence of a process similar to communication in human social systems as long as it is capable of igniting a concatenation of interactions. The premise on which a concatenation of interactions is made possible is the life "field" where organisms reciprocally connect interactions in their various assigned roles. The substance of an institution may be found in the formation of a concatenation of interactions in such a field rather than in a set of internalized and shared norms.

Absence and omission in everyday life

By understanding institution in this way, we are able to see its evolution from a fresh perspective. The institutional mechanism based on the value criterion of "must do …" has always been beset by the problem of rule violation or deviation from institution. If we regard an institution as a bundle of rules, we need to come up with new mechanisms such as sanction and penalty in order to deal with rule violation. Consequently, an attempt to explore the origin of institution in many cases results in speculation regarding the origin of sanction or penalty. By contrast, if we consider the series of interactions to be the only prerequisite for institution, we can contain apparent deviation within the scope of institution. Deviation in this case can be regarded as a "rare occurrence" as against an accumulation of behaviors. As long as values such as "must do …" or "good" or "appropriate" are not imputed to what "we always do", then a "rare occurrence" is neither "good" nor "bad". Because the only prerequisite is the connecting of interactions and not value sharing, a "rare occurrence" is contained as part of institution as long as its action connects with others. Rare occurrences do occur infrequently.

In both humans and other animals, a concatenation of routine interactions that are repeated daily has an element of convention that is delineated as a stationary behavior pattern. Where institution is considered to be a set of socially shared value criteria developed from a concatenation of repeatedly accumulated interactions in conjunction with language and representational ability through high levels of cognitive and learning capabilities, such a view of evolution sometimes fails to understand the absence and omission that occur in repetitive daily activities. The modes of behavior regulation that influence behavior selection such as the occurrence of an unusual event, or feeling scared or uncomfortable or lonely for no reason in the absence of "someone", all deserve to be included in institution.

Phenomena such as mixed species associations, habitat segregation in aquatic insects, niche construction and the center of action emanate the clear sense that repetition in itself is life. In them, heterospecific and conspecific organisms live their conventional roles in a concatenation of constantly repeated everyday interactions while casually including absence and deviation. When we see institution in the context of such repetition, we may be able to understand for the first time the place of the very peculiar conditions of human institutions in the wide world of non-human organisms.

13 Proofs in Mathematics and the Performance of Institutions: A Study of Evolution Starting from Kepler's Equation

Naoki Kasuga

Key ideas

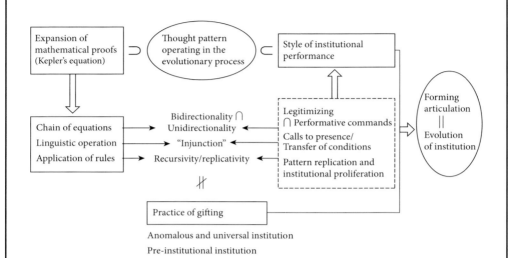

Thought patterns that have continued to operate in the process of human evolution may also be at work in the development of mathematical proofs based on common ground for thinking. From this viewpoint, I firstly examine the thought patterns that are deployed to produce a proof using Kepler's equation as an example. Then, I consider the possibility that these patterns are operating in a similar manner in the evolution of institutions. This is also an attempt to extract a style of thinking that is appropriate for the performance of institutions. At the end of our analysis of a certain pattern, "gifting" comes to the fore as an anomalous yet universal institution.

How do mathematical proofs relate to the evolution of institutions? The answer to this question is as follows. Evolution is a difficult subject to verify no matter how it is treated. Since this is the case, what if we resort to analogical reasoning by associating obviously unrelated subjects rather than attempting to piece together seemingly related fragments? If mathematics has its roots in the universal mode of human cognition, it may be possible to elicit some characteristics in common with the thinking operating in the evolutionary process of institutions. Although sociologists have used mathematical analogies in the past, in most cases they were simplified and distorted. Instead, I shall attempt to associate the mathematical mode of thought with that of anthropology, which is my area of expertise, in an analogical fashion.

You may be concerned that this will make cumbersome reading. The sections that follow contain a proof of a non-linear equation—I believe I have chosen the simplest possible equation that is consistent with the present discussion—as well as mathematical jargon in some places. However, those who are averse to mathematics need not worry about the details; following the general outline should suffice. I can promise one thing: based on my personal experience of grappling with mathematicians' unaccommodating discussions, I will try to be as helpful as I can.

Firstly, I establish the methodology used in this chapter. The aim is to use the chosen mathematical proof as a clue to derive the historical evolutionary theme of human institutions analogically. Anthropologists have often turned to analogy since it was introduced in *The Gender of the Gift* by Marilyn Strathern (1988). The horizon for comparison to elicit similarities between two things that differ in composition and background has been thus constructed (see Jensen 2011). Ethnographies employing the approach of building knowledge collaterally on the part of the researchers as well as on that of the locals are appearing in various forms today (Riles 2000, 2011; Maurer 2006; Miyazaki 2010).

The approach attempted in this chapter is a new type of lateral transfer from one kind of analytical knowledge to another. This transfer can rebut the criticism leveled at ethnography in terms of the way the laterality proposed by the analyst is guaranteed. The methodology in this chapter can be characterized as "unidirectional laterality", which ensures the quality of analysis on the security of the mathematical proof. However, as this analysis of human institutions is required to descend—or ascend—to a level where it can establish connections with mathematics, the level of abstraction in the argument inevitably increases. Since this chapter will only describe the evolution of one institution and not discuss the birth or extinction of institution or the formation of a fractal structure, it may give readers the impression of being overly abstract.

I am sorry to say that I have intentionally created part of this abstractness. In contrast with anthropology that is fixated on actors and agency, this chapter is devoted to pattern extraction and expansion after the fashion of mathematics. Although anthropology claims to place importance on individual concrete phenomena, it has continually been producing "true/false" judgments internally with an eye toward theorizing. On the other hand, mathematics has parted with the true/false question in the concrete realm and become specialized in the adequate extraction and expansion of patterns. I intend to explore the extent to which a lateral line can be drawn between mathematics and anthropology. This method gains more power where cultural relativism concerning mathematics is overwhelmed by cross-cultural arguments (Greiffenhagen and Sharrock 2006). This chapter elicits those elements that pertain to patterns and compose human institutions, including "intention", "interpretation", "injunction" and "legitimization".

The chapter contains three sections. First, a mathematical proof of Kepler's equation is expanded as a specific example. Second, based on this example various elements that yield and advance this proof are extracted. Finally, the proof of the equation and the performance of institutions are connected analogically via these elements, their differences are illuminated and the pattern of institutional evolution is proposed.

Expanding the proof of Kepler's equation

Kepler's equation
The following equation called Kepler's equation is used as the concrete example in this chapter.

$$M = u - e \sin u$$

Let me explain this here in simple terms. Kepler's equation proposes the orbits of the six planets circulating around the Sun and is assembled with a so-called trigonometric function called sine and three variables involved. Of the variables M, u and e, e is the easiest to understand. It represents the eccentricity of the elliptic orbit of a planet which can be defined by

$$e = \frac{\sqrt{a^2 - b^2}}{a}$$

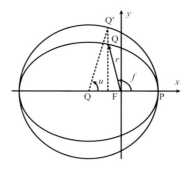

Figure 13.1 True anomaly f and eccentric anomaly u in an elliptical orbit[1]

where a is the length of the major axis and b the length of the minor axis. M is called the "mean anomaly". The location where a planet comes closest to the Sun, which is one of the foci of the ellipse, is called a perihelion point. M is an angle expressing the distance the planet has moved from the perihelion point to another point in time. It is defined as an angular distance of the planet's movement during the period from t_0 at the perihelion point to t and is expressed as

$$M = \frac{2\pi(t-t_0)}{T}$$

where T is the time required for the planet to complete one orbit.

The variable u is a little cumbersome. It is called the "eccentric anomaly" and refers to the angle shown in Figure 13.1. Firstly, a circle is drawn around an ellipse using the length of the semi-major axis, and the planet on its elliptic orbit is shifted perpendicular to the circumference of the circle. The angle u is formed by a line drawn from this imaginary planet's position to the imaginary center of the circle and the semi-major axis of the ellipse. Why is this value important?

It seems that the planetary movement could be formulated in the form of the polar coordinate (r, f) with the Sun being the focus of the ellipse as the base point (see Figure 13.1). However, actually solving r and f analytically is unexpectedly difficult. Moreover, it would have been impossible for Kepler, who lived before the birth of modern calculus. When f is substituted with u as a new parameter, the following can be obtained relatively easily.

$$r = a(1 - e \cos u) \qquad \tan\frac{f}{2} = \sqrt{\frac{1+e}{1-e}} \tan\frac{u}{2}$$

If the length of the major axis a and the eccentricity of the ellipse e are known, only the value of u is needed to find r and f. Kepler's equation provides a solution to u. Kepler[2] proposes with confidence that where e and M are given, u can be presented as $M = u - e \sin u$.

Unfortunately, it is not possible to solve this equation analytically. Nevertheless, it is possible to calculate the value of u by using the values of e and M (solving numerically, so to speak). Just as analytical solutions have been proposed by Lagrange, Bessel and Kapteyn, among others, in the form of infinite series, numerical solutions since Newton inch toward the correct answer iteratively.

Although the equation itself is tricky, proving it is not difficult. A proof provided by Kepler himself can be found on *Wikipedia*[3]. Kepler proposed the law of equal areas prior to the equation. The proof of this law is more difficult, and it had to wait until Newton's *Principia* (the proof that substitutes the ellipse with the circle is in wide circulation today). A proof of Kepler's equation can be derived easily with elementary knowledge of geometry if the equal area law is utilized accurately.

The proof in the example below is not Kepler's. While the equal area law is utilized, it is a straightforward and orthodox proof based on algebraic calculation and primitive analysis. This procedure has been chosen because it manifests salient features of mathematical proofs and offers a way of connecting the argument to the evolution of institutions. I have constructed the framework of this proof under the guidance of mathematician Hiroyuki Hirayama, but any deficiencies here are my own.

If readers find it difficult, please examine the steps without going into detail to get to the argument that follows.

Proof of Kepler's equation

An infinitesimal area $d\omega$ formed by a planet, whose distance to the Sun is r, in an infinitesimal period of time dt has an almost triangular shape. That is

$$d\omega = \frac{1}{2} r(r+dr) \quad \sin f \fallingdotseq \frac{1}{2} r(r+dr) df = \frac{1}{2} r^2 df + \frac{1}{2} rdrdf \fallingdotseq \frac{1}{2} r^2 df$$

On the other hand, according to the equal area law

$$\frac{d\omega}{dt} = C$$

Rewrite this with the elliptical area and the planetary period T

$$C = \frac{\pi ab}{T} \quad \left[\because CT = \int_0^T \frac{d\omega}{dt}\, dt = \pi ab \right]$$

Proofs in Mathematics and the Performance of Institutions

Therefore

$$\frac{\pi ab}{T} = C = \frac{d\omega}{dt} = \frac{1}{2}\,r^2\,\frac{df}{dt} = \frac{1}{2}\,r^2\,\frac{df}{du}\,\frac{du}{dt}\,.$$

Acquiring the Cartesian coordinates relative to the Sun, x, y and r have the following relationships.

$$x = r\cos f = a\,(\cos u - e) \qquad\qquad ①$$

$$y = r\sin f = b\sin u \qquad\qquad ②$$

$$r^2 = x^2 + y^2 \qquad\qquad ③$$

From ②

$$= \sin^{-1}\frac{y}{r}$$

from ①

$$\frac{dx}{du} = -a\sin u = -\frac{a}{b}\,y \qquad\qquad ①'$$

and

$$\frac{dy}{du} = b\cos u = b\left(\frac{a\,(\cos u - e)}{a} + e\right) = b\left(\frac{x}{a} + e\right) = \frac{b}{a}\,(x + ae) \qquad\qquad ②'$$

so

$$\frac{df}{du} = \frac{d}{du}\sin^{-1}\frac{y}{r} = \frac{1}{\sqrt{1 - \left(\frac{y}{r}\right)^2}}\,\frac{d}{du}\left(\frac{y}{r}\right) = \frac{1}{\sqrt{1 - \left(\frac{y}{r}\right)^2}}\,\frac{1}{r^2}\left(r\,\frac{dy}{du} - y\,\frac{dr}{du}\right)$$

$$= \frac{1}{r\sqrt{r^2 - y^2}}\left(r\,\frac{dy}{du} - y\,\frac{d}{du}\sqrt{x^2 + y^2}\right) = \frac{1}{r\sqrt{r^2 - y^2}}\left(r\,\frac{dy}{du} - y\,\frac{2x\,\frac{dx}{du} + 2y\,\frac{dy}{du}}{2\sqrt{x^2 + y^2}}\right)$$

$$= \frac{1}{r^2\sqrt{r^2 - y^2}}\left(r^2 - xy\,\frac{dx}{du} - y^2\,\frac{dy}{du}\right)$$

$$= \frac{1}{r^2\sqrt{r^2 - y^2}}\left(x^2\,\frac{dy}{du} + y^2\,\frac{dy}{du} - xy\,\frac{dx}{du} - y^2\,\frac{dy}{du}\right) = \frac{1}{r^2\sqrt{r^2 - y^2}}\left(x^2\,\frac{dy}{du} - xy\,\frac{dx}{du}\right)$$

$$= \frac{x}{r^2\sqrt{r^2 - v^2}}\left(x\,\frac{dy}{du} - y\,\frac{dx}{du}\right)$$

Substitute ①' and ②'

$$= \frac{x}{r^2\sqrt{r^2 - y^2}}\left\{xb\left(\frac{x}{a} + e\right) - y\left(-\frac{ay}{b}\right)\right\}$$

From ③, $\dfrac{1}{r^2}$ is derived in front of the braces, and the set in the braces expands

as follows.

$$\frac{b^2x^2 + eab^2x + a^2y^2}{ab} = \frac{b^2a^2(\cos u - e)^2 + eab^2(\cos u - e) + a^2b^2\sin^2 u}{ab}$$

$$= ab\,\{(\cos u - e)^2 + e(\cos u - e) + \sin^2 u\}$$

$$= ab\,\{\cos^2 u - 2e\cos u + e^2 + e\cos u - e^2 + \sin^2 u\}$$

$$= ab(1 - e\cos u)$$

Therefore

$$\frac{df}{du} = \frac{ab}{r^2}\,(1 - e\cos u)$$

Return to the first equation and expand

$$\frac{\pi ab}{T} = \frac{1}{2}\,r^2\,\frac{df}{du}\frac{du}{dt} = \frac{r^2}{2}\frac{ab}{r^2}\,(1 - e\cos u)\,\frac{du}{dt}$$

Multiply the left and right sides by $\dfrac{2}{ab}$

$$\frac{2\pi}{T} = (1 - e\cos u)\,\frac{du}{dt}$$

Integrate both sides from $t_0 \to t$

$$\frac{2\pi}{T}(t_0 - t) = \int_{t_0}^{t}(1 - e\cos u)\,\frac{du}{dt}\,dt = \int_{0}^{u}(1 - e\cos u)\,du = u - e\sin u$$

$$\therefore \quad M = u - e\sin u \quad \text{(QED)}$$

This proof has adopted the strategy of rewriting relevant coefficients and variables to u in order to derive Kepler's equation. Moreover, as the equation connotes the equal area law, t (time interval and time point) and T (orbital period with a temporal element) are incorporated in the proof. A quite elaborate tactic has to be employed in order to incorporate time by algebraic and analytical treatments rather than through utilizing the equal area geometrically as Kepler did in his proof. At the beginning of the proof, time is

incorporated into $\dfrac{df}{du}$, the rates of change for f and u, and disappears for a

while. The fraction $\dfrac{df}{du}$ is expanded according to the Cartesian coordinate, then

substitutions ①′ and ②′ are made. When x and y in ① and ② are substituted with

u ("the inside of the braces"), it can be connected with the equality sign to $\dfrac{\pi ab}{T}$ obtained by the supplementation of $\dfrac{du}{dt}$ at the beginning. Kepler's equation is obtained after t is cleared by integration.

Let us analyze the above proof in the next section.

Considering the elements supporting the proof

The nature of the equals sign as a logical "bridge"

The first thing that draws our attention is the statement that "An infinitesimal area $d\omega$ … has an almost triangular shape", which is immediately followed by "that is" and an expanded equation with two "≈" signs. Is it acceptable to have a series of "almost" and "≈" signs in mathematics requiring precision? The conclusion is that it is acceptable, although it makes the equation look clunky. For the time being, we glance through the proof in its entirety, aside from the beginning, and readily notice that chains of equals signs or "=" are repeated with simple words in-between. I must explain the relationship between "≈" in the beginning and "=" in the remainder.

The "≈" sign is related to the "=" sign and they are almost equivalent in the sense that they somewhat fall short of equality. Loosely speaking, "≈" is a member of the equals sign family. In strict terms, "≈" here represents the proposition of a margin of allowable error and indicates that it will eventually be usable in the proof after appearing within a mathematically allowable range. (The logic of "infinitesimal squared equals zero" has underpinned modern mathematics, but we need to discuss "limit" for more exact reasoning.) Accordingly, "≈" appearing in the beginning is intended to converge with "=" and exists to demonstrate through the subsequent expansion of the concatenated equals signs that it is equivalent to the equals sign. In other words, the above proof holds, based on the expansion from one equals sign to another.

So what is the equals sign "="? Equations are often linked using symbols such as "⇒" and "⇔". In the present proof, the derivation of ①′ from ① for example, can be expressed as below.

$$x = r\cos f = a(\cos u - e) \Rightarrow \frac{dx}{du} = -a\sin u = -\frac{a}{b}y$$

The symbol "⇒" is used where equation ①′ is true if equation ① is true. When the opposite is also true, "⇔" is used. These symbols are important elements of symbolic mathematical logic, which represent the relationship between proposition P and proposition Q exactly. Trying to express "=" with similar exactitude will end up producing an awfully complex group of symbols[4]. The equals sign grossly lacks logical exactitude.

Returning to equation ③, it requires you to follow the logic from left to right.
$$x = r \cos f = a \ (\cos u - e)$$
In other words, the x-coordinate can be represented as $r \cos f$ with the Sun as the origin. Then, expressing $r \cos f$ with an angle u on the imaginary circle produces $a \ (\cos u - e)$, factoring in a deviation in the minus direction ae. In this way, equations require you to read them from left to right. For example, what has been inserted into "$\alpha = \beta = \gamma$" is the ordinary linguistic expression "α is β. β is γ". Mathematical equations are made containing rigorous logic, but because they still retain the characteristics of everyday expressions, e.g., "A is B", it is difficult to express equations as a whole with logical exactitude.

Nonetheless, there is a clear line between equations and everyday language. It may be acceptable in everyday usage to express "She is an angel" as "She = Angel", but this makes no sense in mathematics. In short, the equals sign is only usable in numerical calculation (and in this sense "≈" joins the "=" group). In the present proof, the chains of equals signs are formed to guarantee accurate calculation for either real numbers (1, 2, π etc.), algebraic numbers (x, y, e, a, b,

T etc.) or functions ($\frac{df}{dt}$, sin, $\int_0^u$ etc.). Mathematical proofs are built on the

"aesthetic principle" of minimizing the number of equations. Mathematicians and readers are sometimes forced to spend a whole day trying to understand one part of the concatenation, and this is possible only when they accept the assumption that expansions are definitely computable.

Let us confirm the following. A proof is comprised of equation chains, each of which represents the convention that exact calculation of the left side will lead to the right side. A vestige of everyday language found in mathematical equations and the basis of calculation will be discussed in a more detailed fashion in the final section below.

While equations are basically supposed to be read from left to right, the process of calculation is graspable when read in the opposite direction as well.

An equation chain, and two different equations, can also be worked backwards and sometimes tracking a difficult equation backwards provides a clue and makes for easier solving. In this sense, an equation is a bridge that one can cross from either side.

Asymmetry of proof logic

If a proof can be worked backwards from the end to the beginning, a successful proof must be expandable again in the opposite direction. When I attempt this with the present proof, I realize that the reversal is inevitably rather awkward. Stumbling over everyday language and quasi-everyday language from time to time, the proof is reconstructed in reverse order. This point is illustrated below as plainly as possible, using the ∴ and ∵ signs.

Proof: a = f

In order: Firstly, a = b = c. Here, c = d = e = q and f = g = p = q. c = f, ∴ **a = f**.

In reverse order: Firstly, f = c, q = p = g = f and q = e = d = c. Here c = b = a, ∴ **a = f**.

A proper proof must be equally workable from end to beginning.

Nevertheless, the asymmetry of the two procedures is obvious. Besides the reversal of and , for example, the reverse of c = d = e = q can be composed only when the special rule to permit "calculation from right to left" is provided. Here is a concrete example based on the present proof.

$$\frac{1}{r^2\sqrt{r^2-y^2}}\left(r\,\frac{dy}{du} - y\,\frac{d}{du}\sqrt{x^2+y^2}\right) = \frac{1}{\sqrt{1-\left(\frac{y}{r}\right)^2}}\,\frac{1}{r^2}\left(r\,\frac{dy}{du} - y\,\frac{dr}{du}\right)$$

$$= \frac{1}{\sqrt{1-\left(\frac{y}{r}\right)^2}}\,\frac{d}{du}\left(\frac{y}{r}\right) = \frac{d}{du}\sin^{-1}\frac{y}{r}$$

Equational proof is certainly the art of building a bridge that can be crossed from either end equally, but the act of building a bridge in itself is realized by a strong intention—"To get a = f!". The equals signs and (quasi-) everyday language comprising the proof have the imprint of this intention, which creates those differences between the two directions[5].

Asymmetry between the regular and reverse directions hides an order. The priority of the intention to "get a = f", or the proposition, exists as given, and demands a proof. As everyone knows, in mathematics, great numbers of theorems and rules—many of which have often been expressed in equations—form various groups in rank order while new theorems and rules are born day after day. There is the burning desire to work out successful proofs, to build them into the given constituent elements and to discover more theorems and laws. The bidirectionality of the logic guaranteeing a proof is realized in an asymmetrical form because of the intention to accomplish the proof.

Bridge-building for a proof depends greatly on interpretation by the actor performing the proof at both the conscious and subconscious levels. The theorems and formulae deployed in the proof bear relevance to the way both the everyday language part and the equals signs are read. A single equation accepts a wide variety of images, from so-called pure mathematics to applied physics and engineering. For instance, a certain differential equation may prompt mathematicians to find a proof for the existence of a solution, whereas it may lead physicists to look toward stratified variations or infinite connections. Even within the same field, the meanings of functions, parameters and boundary conditions can be interpreted variously. One day, you may suddenly find an association between a familiar equation and one that is supposedly unrelated (for instance, Omiya (2008) describes a stimulating episode similar to this in relation to the KdV equation for nonlinear waves). It may not be as dramatic as this, but a successful proof using a combination of common interpretations can reveal a new image for a given proposition. I believe that the proof in this chapter can make some contribution to the task. What demonstrates the role of interpretation most succinctly is following an equation in the reverse direction, i.e., the possibility of calculating from right to left.

In summary, the bidirectional bridge is built through an act of interpretation and produces asymmetry in terms of the mode of passage and the irreversibility of bridge crossing.

Proofs and laws of form

As we further analyze the manifestation of intentionality and the act of interpreting in mathematical proofs, we notice the role of specific linguistic operation. When we follow the present proof from beginning to end, we can find a common characteristic in most of the everyday expressions attending it:

"Rewrite this with ..."

"Acquiring the Cartesian coordinates relative to the Sun,"

"Substitute ..."

"Return to the first equation and expand"
"Multiply the left and the right sides by ..."
"Integrate both sides ..."

These commands are all about the direction of the procedure. This linguistic operation to call for a new existence by way of invitation is "injunction" according to Spencer-Brown, which constitutes a primitive form of mathematical communication (1969: 77).

Spencer-Brown argues in *Laws of Form* (1969) that "injunction" not only entices something to presence, names it and transforms it into another condition, it also quietly plays the role of deriving a proof. "Such statements are implicit in, or follow from, or are permitted by, the cannons or standing orders hitherto convened or called to presence" (Spencer-Brown 1969: 80). Language with these powers cannot be fully grasped by analyzing descriptive language such as that of Wittgenstein. The argument in *Laws of Form* follows that the basic structural language in mathematics takes this particular injunctive form rather than being descriptive, and that this is probably applicable to more areas of natural science than expected.

I shall discuss Spencer-Brown's masterpiece again in the final section below.

Recursive order formation

There will be a lot of mathematical jargon in this section. I ask math-averse readers to skim through until we get to the next section where we will discuss evolution.

Bidirectionality and asymmetry incidental to a proof are both the foundations and vestiges of the process of discovery, or evolution so to speak, in mathematics. Just as in the case of organisms, there is no such thing as a final destination. Just as the present stage of an organism's evolution is an interim result waiting for the next selection process, the present state of mathematics exists on numerous presumptive and arbitrary assumptions. Where it differs from biological evolution is in the transformation of the presumptive and the arbitrary into the determinate and the inevitable achieved through the proof within the bounds of a universe of conventions[6].

In the conventional universe, various groups of axioms, definitions, theorems and also rules interrelate while establishing their ranks, and the determinate state, the presumptive state and the determinate state requiring a comprehensive review due to its increasing arbitrariness are constantly in progress (e.g., the definition of "infinity" and related theorems and formulae in terms of the present proof). Mathematics is a big tautology as Wittgenstein points out in the sense that it follows the precisely and strictly prearranged rules and methods to establish only the rules and methods inevitably derived thereof. However, if we ask why it is constantly followed by presumptions and arbitrariness and demands a proof and promotes evolution, the answer is that new propositions continue to be born in response to some stimuli from outside of mathematics such as intuition, experience and confrontations with new facts.

Accordingly, the evolution of mathematics can be expressed as the continuous process of following the prearranged rules and methods to produce more rules and methods in an outward direction. The manner in which an existing logic is used to construct a logic that fits the existing logic is recursive. Some of the recursivity is manifest in the present proof. The attempt to prove that Kepler's equation $M = u - e \sin u$ is a determinate rule is premised on the elliptic planetary orbit with the Sun as one center (Kepler's first law), and accepts geometric rules concerning the ellipse. By quickly obtaining

$$\frac{\pi ab}{T} = C = \frac{d\omega}{dt} = \frac{1}{2} r^2 \frac{df}{dt}$$

using the law of equal areas relating to the planetary orbit (Kepler's second law for which Newton provided a proof), $\frac{df}{du}$ that is crucial for the proof is derived

successfully so that all these are available for deployment at the final stage. Numerous conventions are used in the notation of Cartesian coordinates, four arithmetic operations and the calculation of trigonometric functions, derivatives and integrands. Especially in derivative calculation, not only the differential quotient and the derivative of the square root are used as formulae, but also the

rules concerning trigonometric function are fully employed. In expanding $\frac{df}{du}$,

the mutual transformation of the derivatives of sine and cosine and the sum of the squares of the two are combined with notations ①, ② and ③ to clear x and y one after another, and the rewriting to u is largely completed.

Thus, Kepler's equation becomes a rule incorporating rules. When we look at the incorporated rules, we find that each of them has a proof, which in turn contains many rules. Rules proliferate recursively and become convolved in a replicating fashion. Through the creation of orders recursively and replicatively, mathematics realizes self-organization and accomplishes evolution.

Associating proofs in mathematics and the performance of institutions

The basic pattern of institution incorporating "bidirectionality ∩ unidirectionality"

Having extracted such things as the bidirectionality demanded by a proof, asymmetry demanding a proof, intentionality and interpretation, the linguistic operation of "injunction" and recursive and replicative rules to advance a proof at the end, let us find a point of argument that relates to institutions and evolution. This will be the task of discovering the analogies between mathematical proofs and institutions and at the same time finding the differences between them. As I mentioned at the start of this chapter, a comparison between everyday language and the language of mathematics plays a major role.

Firstly, let us compare institutional performance to a mathematical proof. As we have been analyzing a proof for Kepler's equation, we will develop the analogy while continuing to focus on the equational proof. The institution to be performed has some reason for the existence attached to it, which is an assumed quality. If this point is replaced with legitimization, a slightly turgid yet clear word, this comparison to the proof of the equation becomes rather simple.

Let us analyze institutional performance from the perspective of "injunction" and ascertain those parts that have been consciously omitted from the analysis of the mathematical proof. As in the case of the equation, injunction is incidental to institution and elicits something to presence, names it and transforms it into another condition. For example, ceremonial messages, quotations from reliable texts, suitable interpretative explanations, traditions, memories and records assume this role and guide toward the establishment of legitimacy. However, "injunction" cannot be effected without objects such as ceremonial implements and regalia, and the utilization of such objects by humans. Also in the proof of Kepler's equation, "injunction" has changed in conjunction with the development of telescopes and other measuring devices as well as computing equipment, transforming the contents and influences of the proof. I have refrained from mentioning them in this chapter and will also limit references to objects and the standards of practice to the extent necessary in respect to institutions.

In a proof of an equation, bidirectionality must be constructed around a chain of equals signs. It is not easy to find an equals sign in the process of institution except in one example that I will introduce later. Nevertheless, as I can find a similar operational procedure, I shall present it and call it the "proto equality operator". In the proto equality operator, "She is an angel" in everyday language can be expressed as "She = Angel", unlike the equals sign in mathematics.

The meaning of the proto equality operator can range from metaphor to similarity, analogy and categorization and there is no guarantee that it will settle on one meaning either. While the use of the mathematical equality operator is limited to calculation, the proto equality operator deals with a wide range of subjects. However, this role is performable because its logic is more exact in comparison with that of the mathematical equality operator. To use an accurate symbol, "$\Rightarrow$" is more appropriate than "=" for the proto equality operator. In fact, it does not matter whether "She is an angel" is written as "She = Angel" or "She $\Rightarrow$ Angel". People know that this expression is not meant to be read in the reverse direction (!), while they do not bother to think that it represents the relationship between proposition P about She and proposition Q about Angel. Yet, it is written as "She $\Rightarrow$ Angel" because it indicates a simile-like implication and also permits interpretation that covers all from metaphor, similarity and even categorization—her joining the ranks of angels.

As the mathematical equals sign permits reading in the reverse direction, the way to confirm the procedure in both directions will be paved also for "$\Rightarrow$". Assuming that "injunction" provides institutions with a character to be performed, concatenating the proto equality operators will create bidirectionality to legitimize its unidirectionality in a way. Here is a specific example. The closest to a proof of an equation is the legitimization of regulations that have been codified by jurisprudence. They can be traced back to their origins deductively and also permit tracking in the opposite direction. In this case, the proto equality operator functions as similarity or categorization, and "$a \Rightarrow b$, $b \Rightarrow c \therefore a \Rightarrow c$" can expand to "$a \Rightarrow c \because c \Leftarrow b$, $b \Leftarrow a$".

Bidirectionality can be ensured not only deductively but also inductively. Let us insert the proto equality operator "$a \Rightarrow c$" in the example straight into a basic pattern of induction. It follows that "To the nth case '$a \Rightarrow c$'. Therefore apply '$a \Rightarrow c$' to the $n + 1^{st}$ case. Then '$a \Rightarrow c$'". When reversed, legitimacy can be traced in the direction of "The $n + 1^{st}$ case is '$a \Rightarrow c$'. This also applies to the nth case. Then…" When this procedure is abbreviated, "$a \Rightarrow c$" is generalized as what Hume calls a "convention" and becomes a legitimate injunction in itself.

We can see from the above that unidirectionality prompting performance and bidirectionality enabling tracing to the origin are incorporated as the basic style of institution. They can be described as asymmetry and symmetry. Institutions come to realization by taking a "bidirectionality ∩ unidirectionality" or "symmetry ∩ asymmetry" format. It is a pattern that continues to interpose within action and idea without belonging to either level.

Recursive replication of the institutional pattern

Let us proceed with the analysis of institutional format. The format creates a flow between the past, present and future while remaining in a nontemporal phase. The command to perform an institution and the establishment of its legitimacy cannot exist concurrently, just as the driving power and its evidence or origination and its vestige cannot. For people who live institutions, it becomes possible to grasp them as such when they are projected onto the flow between the past, present and future. One of the effects such projection has on people may be that the interpretation of institutions feels like a discovery of something that has existed from the beginning, and the performance of institutions is accepted as the realization of a planned thing.

Maintaining the institutional format in a nontemporal phase can be confirmed by Victor Turner's argument in anthropology. Even in the state of "anti-structure" in which everyday institutions lose their significance, institutions such as rituals, festivals and martial laws will appear and maintain the "symmetry ∩ asymmetry" format. The overturning and extinguishing of status in the anti-structure can take effect because they are commands and legitimized at the same time. Even when it is uncertain how the anti-structure will be resolved, as in the case of a revolution, the institutional format will continue to exist—even if it may be localized. Other terms are simply written into it.

Regardless of historical facts or causal threads, institutions never relinquish the basic "symmetry ∩ asymmetry" pattern. Using the proof of a mathematical equation as an analogy, let us examine how the same pattern is derived from this basic pattern. The proof uses the existing rules and methods to create new rules and methods to fit them. Then, the performance of an institution is expected to also reproduce the basic "symmetry ∩ asymmetry" pattern recursively and replicatively and incorporates concrete rules and methods into this pattern for proliferation. Just as "[W]e do not fully understand a theorem until we are able to contain it in a more general theorem" (Spencer-Brown 1969: 95), the proliferation of institutions encourages us to understand institutions in a broader context. The recursive reproduction of the pattern must give newly formed institutions somewhat familiar characteristics.

Our argument has already reached the stage of institutional evolution. It is not erroneous to replace the comparison between the evolution of organisms and the evolution of mathematics, discussed above, with that between Darwinian evolution and self-organization (see Davies 2008: 342–355). It is also possible to name the finding that evolution and homeostasis in life forms create a fractal structure as a mediator between them (e.g., Damasio 2005). I have limited my discussion on external elements to one necessary sentence in my explanation on mathematical evolution, but it needs a separate subsection below in relation to institutional evolution.

Toward a blueprint of institutional performance

Just as the mathematical proof creates a group of functions by concatenating equals signs, a complex of proto equality operators defines the relationships between various elements and puts them in order in terms of institutional performance. The proto equality operator compares a concrete thing to something else for similarity, then builds it into a generalized and universal category. Institutions are performed by the successful big leaps from the individual to the general and the concrete to the abstract.

Calculation, which appeared in our analysis of mathematical equations, re-enters the discussion here. Calculation derives from the act of counting numbers. Spencer-Brown had the insight to recognize that the act of reckoning formed the foundation of reasoning and that nearly all mathematical proofs use the human ability to compute (1969: 93). However, is the bidirectionality of the equals sign incidental to the act of counting, as Spencer-Brown argues? Counting derives from pointing. It is perhaps natural to think that when the act of pointing "this and that" and "these and those" (eventually) has metaphorical and similarity connotations such as "deeming" and "almost equal", it acquires bidirectionality and unidirectionality at once in the form of proto equality operators. In other words, we should deduce that counting and the equals sign inherit the bidirectionality of proto equality operators as the successors of the pre-existing pointing action.

Counting may be the origin of mathematics, but natural numbers pose an unsolvable problem to mathematics. As Gödel's theorem shows, any axiomatic systems containing natural numbers give rise to propositions about numbers that cannot be proved by the axioms. Counting remains as a domain outside of mathematics. It is difficult to draw an analogy between Gödel's theorem and institutions. The proto equality operators underpinning the success of big leaps are endowed with so many capabilities that far exceed those of mathematics. In this regard, pattern replication and institutional proliferation must progress under fewer constraints than in mathematics.

Then, why does it not sound all that convincing? The rules and methods of calculation contained in mathematical proofs are not required for institutional performance, but it is expected that accurate and specific relationships between various elements are discovered and presented. In terms of mathematical equations, it is the task of deriving one variable's relationship with other variables using other equations as concisely as possible, which constitutes "solving the equation". As I mentioned in the example of Kepler's equation earlier, the solution can be derived analytically or presented numerically.

As Kepler's equation suggests, the world of mathematics is overflowing with unsolved equations. An equation that has proofs but for which a solution has not been found can be likened to an institution that has legitimacy but whose concrete performative forms are indeterminable. Let me remind you that in this chapter the performance command and its legitimization extracted from a proof are already guaranteed as conditions for institutional performance. Besides them, as the state of not being able to present a concrete and accurate blueprint of performance must occur frequently with institutions, I shall attempt to add this to the list of analogies.

How does mathematics deal with an unsolved equation? Firstly, some methods or rules are deployed to derive an approximate solution. Alternatively, other methods and rules are employed to clarify the nature of the solution (e.g., whether or not it exists, the convergence and stability of the solution, its scope and form, etc.). In either case, the methods and rules are often the same as those convolved in proofs in their characteristics, and in some cases the steps are indicated by proofs. Or conversely, the search for a solution can sometimes lead to new theorems or equations.

It is not difficult to find institutional phenomena that are comparable to this way of dealing with this situation. However, as institutional evolution means the successive proposing of equations, it is unlikely that unsolved equations would be chosen preferentially. Pattern replication and institutional proliferation must be subject to the following constraints. Firstly, proofs are feasible, or in other words, they are suited to being solved. Secondly, they are amenable to solution and the concrete relationships between elements are easily identifiable. However, the latter condition cannot be satisfied unless precise relationships are presentable at all times, and therefore they require additional proofs. The process in which these two constraints are met recursively and replicatively through the existing rules and methods is the evolution of institutions. Considering that the intermingling of the two by which proofs help find solutions or the nature of solutions indicate the direction of proofs, only one constraint needs to be met in some cases.

Gifting as the institution connecting other institutions

Now as we come to address the evolution of institutions, we encounter one group of institutions that continues to exist unapologetically even though they do not satisfy the above conditions. They are performative commands that demand a solution rather than a proof; yet it is not easy to find a solution. Moreover, they are better suited to representation by the equals sign, whose usage is limited to calculation, than the more flexible proto equality operators. This group of institutions is deeply involved in counting and pointing.

In any case, here is one example. The following basic equation can be proposed utilizing the recursivity and iterativeness that institutions share with mathematics.

$$x = f(x)$$

Express this as a recurrence relation.

$$x_{n+1} = f(x_n)$$

Add function A and function B to x as variables.

$$x(A, B)_{n+1} = f(x(A, B)_n)$$

One concrete example represented by this primitive equation is the exchanging of gifts between A and B. The independent variables A and B form a relationship $x(A, B)_{n+1}$, and the relationship is dependent on the previous relationship $x(A, B)_n$. This recursive function experiences tremendous change in numerical value in response to the slightest change in initial conditions and internal coefficients. This equation is indeterminate and unpredictable.

So, why is it that this institution, which is not amenable to a solution or a proof, can not only persist but also manage continual connection with a diverse range of institutions in various societies? Anywhere in the world people who happen to sit side-by-side form a relationship through some form of gifting, be it the passing around of tobacco among indigenous peoples of North America or table wines at cafes in southern France. They bring different bundles of rules and methods together and connect them with the institution of the gift. As postulated by numerous anthropologists, gifting appears across the world as a universal human institution.

Of course, gifting is given interpretations for the purpose of legitimization and sometimes inspires a conviction for an optimum solution. In any case, however, it often does not have enough stability or persist long enough to establish bidirectionality. To use a rather exaggerated expression, gifting is the embodiment of an intention toward recursivity and replication. To use a restrained expression, the characteristic of intentional agency is more marked in gifting than in other institutions. Gifting directs the performer to point at (in their mind) and count (silently) people and things and to decide how to utilize and replicate rules and methods recursively on each occasion in a place a certain distance away from interpretations in everyday language or "injunctions" in special terminology. It does so to the extent that it becomes suitable for representation by the equals sign as a recursive function. By compelling the performer as a nested function—a function having another function as a variable—to change its internal coefficients or initial conditions, or by replacing a solution with another function to transform it into a new form of nested function, it constantly generates "I", who is the performer.

Let us summarize the condition of the gift, which is an anomalistic yet universal institution that articulates with other institutions, from the viewpoint of the pattern. While other institutions maintain articulation with gifting, there is no need to trace back the origin of the "bidirectionality ∩ unidirectionality" or "symmetry ∩ asymmetry" format to the gift itself. In other words, each institution follows the format and shares rules and methods with the institutions around it to proliferate new internal rules and methods and convolve inwardly. To rephrase it slightly, the evolution of institutions is a process by which other institutions use the autonomous format to organize themselves through the institution of gifting and repeatedly reproduce the pattern to produce multiple institutions, which form a group of institutions proliferating and sharing rules and methods. (As I mentioned earlier, I shall refrain from discussing the birth and demise of institutions or the formation of fractal structures here.)

Looking from the performer's standpoint, institutions that have acquired autonomy are required to have an ability to use metaphor, similarity and categorization appropriately as the situation demands, because they prepare support for the performance by using the proto equality operators rather than the equals sign regardless of the level of demand. The number of options for the performers in legitimizing their own actions retrospectively increases exponentially. Depending on the situation, they become aware that they are in charge of coefficient adjustment, condition setting and solution substitution, and come to have a keen awareness of taking charge of institutions as the embodiments, successors or reincarnations of something, or even as "once-only I". However, coefficients, initial conditions and functions are mere metaphors. They would not feel that being denoted by the equals sign would be appropriate. A typical example is the performers of an institution called commodities exchange where we find a group of experts in mathematics as the defenders of their self-awareness.

I have so far described the evolution of institutions focusing on their autonomy from gifting without touching on the evolution of the institution of gifting itself. For this reason, I have not embarked on the analysis of the situation in which gifting hinders the performance of other institutions while playing the role of coordinator for them. This may sound like a mundane task, but it is an important one. Just as the internal evolution of mathematics has developed into the present form with the help of external elements, it is likely that the evolution of institutions can trace its origins to the anomalous and universal institution of gifting in large part. I must discuss this subject separately at some time in the future.

14 Basic Components of Institution: Understanding Institution According to Triangular and Tetrahedral Models

Takeo Funabiki

Key ideas

An institution emerges under the tetrahedral model of the tripartite relationship in meaning space

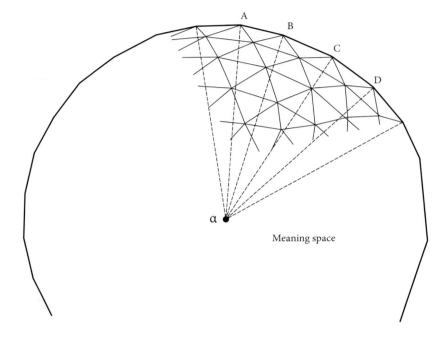

If the ability of third term p to guarantee and mediate a bipartite relationship rests solely in the intrinsic quality of its being, the triangle formed by its participation will not completely guarantee the continuity of the human relationship. However, if p becomes signified as α and there is a meaning space that augmentatively reproduces interpretations that constantly reinforce the sign, then the assembly of tetrahedrons having the sign α at the apex can overcome insufficient unambiguity and memory degradation. This forms an institution.

In my earlier thesis (hereinafter referred to as the first thesis) entitled "human groups at the zero-level" (Funabiki 2013), I began the discussion on the premise that human beings are able to have relations of mutual understanding with others they meet and face (Funabiki 2013: 294). I called the infinite expanse of this position that contains the possibilities of such relations a "field", and an individual position in which such a relationship arises a "scene", which is created from the field. I argued that in this position, it is always possible for a person to enter a face-to-face relationship with another through a shared sensibility regarding inherent language and gestures (Funabiki 2013: 295). However, in order for the person to initiate a relationship with a distant person far behind the other party, the person must move around the other party and thus shift their position. In other words, I stated that the hypothetical individual could only increase the number of face-to-face relationships in a radial manner to the limits of their individual capacity for understanding (Funabiki 2013: 297).

The purpose of the first thesis was to explore how human groups created by the intrinsic non-verbal and verbal abilities to relate to other human beings as the thus assumed cultural beings fall into a situation in which they cannot even "create a situation". In other words, what kind of situation would bring human groups down to their zero-level (Funabiki 2013: 297)?

I shall attempt to examine the opposite situation in this chapter (hereinafter referred to as the second thesis). The purpose of this thesis is to consider the remaining question in the first thesis, that is, how have the human groups we presently live in gone beyond biological group composition, both qualitatively and quantitatively, and come to possess an incomparably larger scale and complexity? At the same time, the aim is to find an answer to the question of human "institution" in an evolutionary sense (Funabiki 2013: 304).

Tripartite relationship

Because so much has already been said about the formation of human institutions, any attempt to discuss institution theoretically through referring to the existing arguments tends to end up sounding like an annotated study. Even though Rousseau (1978), Girard (1971) and Imamura (1982), to whom we refer in this thesis, are very unique and original thinkers, when we try to begin our discussion with their theories, we cannot avoid being dragged into the history of political philosophical theories and find ourselves writing an annotated study concerned with the details of their principles. In order to prevent this situation, I begin with an attempt to construct a simple, theoretical model, as I did in the first thesis.

We began with the premise that humans are able to form one-to-one relationships (see Figure 14.1 below). Theoretically, we are able to form an unlimited number of one-to-one relationships. However, the number of these relationships one person can have simultaneously is physically limited. Yet, the physical limitation can theoretically be removed if one can diachronically accumulate such relationships. However, one relationship becomes overshadowed by a newly created relationship due to the limits of human memory. Although in theory the number of one-to-one relationships can increase infinitely with the passage of time, relationships will deteriorate over time due to the limitations of memory.

What happens if a third being comes between the first party (first being) and the other party (second being) (Figure 14.2(a))? When the first party (A) forms another relationship (R2) separately from the existing relationship (R1), the presence of the third being (p) who mediates the relationship between the first party (A) and the second party (B) can open up the possibility for A to maintain R2 without degrading R1. In other words, the third being synchronically takes over A's physical limits and diachronically guarantees the durability of A's memory.

Before we go on to illustrate this point, I would like to clarify that the third being is not necessarily human. Whether the third being is a person or an object, it does not affect the argument here. However, bringing this point into question would needlessly complicate the discussion, and therefore I shall limit myself to stating that even a person as the third being exists as an objectified figure.

Let's view the third being as a person. A person (P) as the third being to the first party (A) and the second party (B) is able to guarantee the actuality of the relationship to A and B. Firstly, in the case where A and B share the same perception of their relationship (R1), P takes over A's physical limitations (memory durability) as a reinforcement in light of A's limits. On the other hand, where A and B have different perceptions about their relationship (Figure 14.2(b)), P performs a more decisive function. P's decision to agree with either of the two differing views, A's or B's, will lead to the formation of a majority of two to one. This can also be regarded as taking over the synchronic physical limits of A (and B). However, if we look deeper than the shouldering of limitations, we can see that P actually performs the function of prompting an understanding of a higher order between A and B. For example, when A and B disagree on favors and debts surrounding some past event or performance of some promised future act, P plays the role of adjusting the relationship between A and B. At this stage, we may get an inkling that when

Figure 14.1 One-to-one human relationship

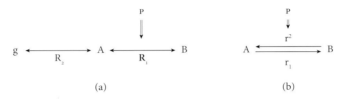

Figure 14.2 One-to-one relationship and mediation by a third party (p)

the adjustment shifts from prompting toward coercion, the situation approaches an institution.

Let us leave it as an inkling for further discussion and consider the case in which this third being is a thing (p). This kind of tripartite relationship takes over the physical limitation and prevents temporal degradation just as did the aforementioned kind, but it has a special property, i.e., a thing is slow to disappear or change relative to a human being in the real world. Its presence prompts agreement and adjusts disagreement.

Be it a human or a thing, the performance of such a function by the third object is further strengthened if such a situation has occurred in the past repeatedly. Past experience in adjustment is not an issue theoretically, but the fact that A and B have experienced adjustment in the past ensures the effectiveness of p's performance in reality.

Here we once again encounter the problem of circular reasoning into which any attempt to trace back to the embryonic point is prone to fail, as I pointed out at the beginning of the first thesis. When we formulate a hypothesis, we use a reality that is a corollary of the hypothesis as an assumption. In this case, we attempt to support the hypothesis about p's adjustment function with the assumption that such adjustment already exists. Nevertheless, we shall continue to use occasional cross-invocation despite the difference in levels between assuming the source (pre-existence of adjustment) and discovering the source by tracing back the stream of reality (demonstration in the second thesis), assuming that its appropriateness will be determined in terms of whether this thesis is meaningful or not in the end.

While this third being p can be human or a thing—and we will eventually discuss it as something that is not human or a thing—let us treat it as human (C) for the time being in order to move our discussion forward and confirm its interchangeability with a thing later on. So, what is the difference between the bipartite relationship and the tripartite relationship?

The bipartite relationship model in Figure 14.1(b) is comprised of four components—A, B, r1 and r2. In this relationship, it is thought that the first party A can perceive how the self in the relationship (A) will behave, understand the state (e.g., intention and intensity) of the relationship that A is engaged in as the actor with B (r1) and have an ability to change it. On the other hand, A cannot perceive, understand or change B and r2 in the way that A perceives the self (A) and the relationship they are engaged in (r1). In other words, A cannot control them. Of the four components, two are controllable and the other two are uncontrollable for both A and B.

A third party is added to this bipartite relationship in Figure 14.3. Unlike Figure 14.2(b), in which p exists as a mediator to a bipartite relationship, a tripartite relationship is formed here because C exists as a party. This relationship has nine components—A, B, C, r1, r2, r3, r4, r5 and r6. Among the nine components, three components, A, r1 and r3 are now within A's control and the remaining six components are outside of A's control if we follow the same line of thinking. When a relationship expands from bipartite to tripartite, it turns into a different relationship for those involved. In other words, it is raised to a level at which it becomes difficult to exert control both qualitatively and quantitatively. It is difficult, but it is an unavoidable type of difficulty. In a bipartite relationship (Figure 14.1), person A can stop the relationship itself by withdrawing from the relationship—discontinue the intention to have the relationship or bring its intensity down to zero—(B's unilateral desire to have a relationship with A is not regarded as the existence of a relationship), whereas a different situation will arise in a tripartite relationship (Figure 14.3). Even if A withdraws from the relationship,

1. the personal relationship between B and C will continue,
2. C (which is P in Figure 14.2(a)) can guarantee to B the existence of a relationship between B and A even though it was discontinued by A's withdrawal, and
3. similarly, B (as P in Figure 14.2(a)) can guarantee to C the existence of a relationship between C and A even though it was discontinued by A's withdrawal.

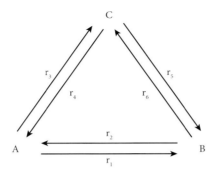

Figure 14.3 Tripartite relationship

Thus, despite A's withdrawal from the tripartite relationship between "A, B and C", the bipartite relationships between "A and B" and "A and C" continue as they are, while the tripartite relationship between "A, B and C" can also continue as a relationship.

A tripartite relationship is in a sense uncontrollable for A because it not only involves many uncontrollable components, but it is also difficult to withdraw from the relationship in a true sense once A enters it. It is clear that what is happening here is a situation that is seemingly paradoxical but empirically normal in real society in which an actor (A, for example) is unable to escape from a relationship precisely because the relationship contains some unknowable and unchangeable components. We can also see that when this relationship expands to a quadripartite relationship, the number of components in A's control is four whereas the number of components outside of A's control increases to twelve. The quadripartite relationship is an even more uncontrollable relationship, or a scene. It is of course easy to imagine using simple arithmetic what happens when there are five or six parties involved.

When we actually try to find this imaginary model in the stream of reality mentioned earlier, we can immediately discern its difficulty as a situation or scene that is encountered and experienced by people every day. In other words, this is what is called society (or *seken* (social circle) may be more appropriate in Japan), which fundamentally cannot be controlled by individual actors. However, we shall advance our discussion on the assumption that institution arises, or is bound to arise, when people attempt to find a possibility of overcoming this uncontrollability.

The third term that does not become the third party

If we turn our discussion back a little, the emergence of a relationship with four, five or six parties can be explained by the model in Figure 14.4 in which a succession of new people appear and form a link to a tripartite relationship one after another. In other words, D, E, F and G join the relationship each as P to A and B. However, this does not occur in the same way that B formed a new relationship with A. Because A already has a relationship with B and C when D forms a relationship with A, this means that D will automatically have a relationship with B and C by forming a relationship with A. At this time, if D has the option of refusing a relationship with B and C while having a relationship with A, then the phrase "D automatically has a relationship with B and C" should instead be "D is drawn into a relationship with B and C". However, even if D is having no relationship with B or C, theoretically D is socially inescapably impregnated in togetherness with B and C as well and there is a potential relationship there, as I explained in my discussion on solitariness and singularity in the first thesis (Funabiki 2013: 300–301). I called it "solitariness" in the first thesis. If D truly becomes singular and has no relationship with B or C, this means D is isolated from society as a singular person who has departed from solitariness and come infinitely close to quitting humanity. This is a matter concerning human groups at the zero-level, which was the subject of the first thesis and therefore not addressed here in the second thesis.

Now, let us consider a situation in which a relationship continues to expand, as illustrated in Figure 14.4. The expansion of this relationship is considered to be theoretically limitless. This was called the "field" in the first thesis. As mentioned in the first thesis, however, A may expand this relationship to the limits of their capacity but empirically, one can only relate to a small number of people at once, say five or six or a dozen or so at most (Funabiki 2013: 295). However, the number is not an issue here. Whether it is four or twenty, having a relationship with two or more others in a radial fashion will eventually reach its limit. Metaphorically, the problem is that in order to confront and form relations with a person horizontally aligned and hidden behind another currently on the scene, one must move away from the person in the existing relation and shift one's position to the distant other by "maneuvering around" that person (Funabiki 2013: 295). Yet, if A maneuvers around B to form a relationship with q, then B becomes the person horizontally aligned and hidden behind another currently on the scene to A, as illustrated in Figure 14.1b in the first thesis (Funabiki 2013: 296). In other words, the relationship does not increase quantitatively other than through the formation of an infinite

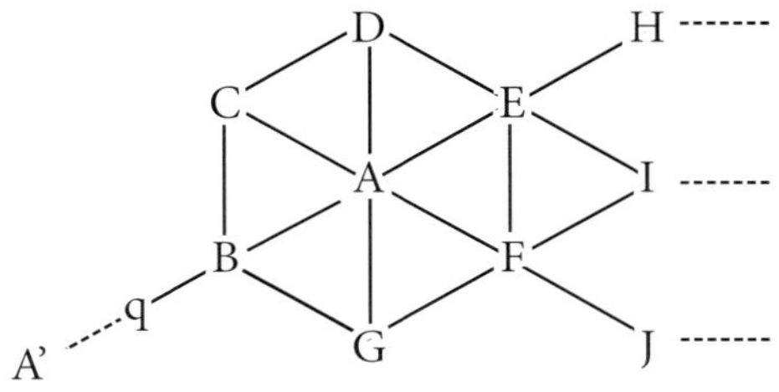

Basic Components of Institution

Figure 14.4 Expansion of a one-to-one relationship

number of bipartite relationships with radially aligned persons. Conversely, because the number can easily reach the limit, it is impossible to find an answer to the evolutionary question of how the human groups we presently live in have gone beyond biological group composition, both qualitatively and quantitatively, and come to possess an incomparably larger scale and complexity.

Now we shall invoke the idea of Buckminster Fuller (1992), a designer and thinker, that triangles form tetrahedrons and give rise to structures in the physical world (Universe, in his words). He describes that "The triangle is the only flex-cornered polygon that holds its shape; ergo, it alone accounts for all structural shaping in the Universe. Triangles do not, however, exist independently of systems" (Fuller 1992: 47). He goes on to say that the triangles, although they seem to be independent, are part of a tetrahedral system that always has four apexes and a height. This fact was already widely known without the help of Fuller's idea. Nevertheless, we can find clues for social modeling in the spherical polygonal structure he built as an architect. In other words, it is a model for the way, or institution, by which A can have a relationship with q without maneuvering around anyone.

The diagrams from Figures 14.1 to 14.4 illustrate the mechanism of expansion by the addition of a third party to a bipartite relationship while guaranteeing that relationship. In this way of expansion, however, when A is regarded as the principal party, A's relationship to H, I, J and so on is a concatenated relationship as shown in Figure 14.4, and hence A is unable to be involved in its overall expansion on a synchronous or continuous basis. This means that in spite of being equipped with a shared sensibility regarding language and gestures, mankind is in a state of only being able to experience the expanse in the form of a field, just as are other species

Photo 14.1 Exchanging a woman for pigs at a wedding in the Mbotgote society where the author conducted a field study

as groups of living beings. But the inferred state is not how we were in the past or how we are now in reality. Where did this modeling go wrong? It appears to have happened somewhere between Figure 14.2(b) and Figure 14.3. As the path of development is direct from Figure 14.1 to 14.2 and from Figure 14.3 to 14.4 without ramifications leading to an error, we shall examine the process of transition from Figure 14.2(b) to 14.3 for the cause of this error.

We hypothesized that in Figure 14.2, the third being (P) appears and forms a tripartite relationship with A and B while guaranteeing their bipartite relationship. What if P remains simply as a being (p) to guarantee the bipartite relationship between A and B and does not become the third party (C) as shown in Figure 14.3?

As I mentioned earlier, if it was a thing, for example, it would guarantee the bipartite relationship without becoming a party or an actor in the form of a third party. A thing could be, for example, a shared tool or resource. If a third party appears in the form of a human, then the person would form a tripartite relationship with A and B as a new party (C) while sharing p. However, be it a tool or a resource, if p as a thing guarantees a human relationship that is expanding in quantity and quality from bipartite to tripartite, quadripartite and so on, then it is unlikely to continue to fulfill the guarantee function amid the expanding relationship as long as it is merely a thing. This is because A and others need to reconcile the meaning and value of the thing continuously in order to maintain the relationship group which is the concatenation of the relationships controllable by Party A and those of others which are uncontrollable (by A) with the help of the guarantee function of the thing as a third party. For this to happen, the thing itself must be something that can be interpreted unambiguously. The closest thing to this in human history must be gold. It certainly evokes scarcity, versatility and a powerful impression in relation to such attributes. However, the quality of gold as a mineral does not always guarantee that it is seen as gold socially. I shall explain the lack of absoluteness below.

Now, what happens if we assume that the being which does not become a third party, which remains a third term or p in relation to the self, is a person and not a thing. As we are already familiar with logical progression in this section, we may as well expedite this discussion. In other words, we may assume a person who does not become a third party. For example, it may be "father". Father is used here because the father-child relationship, even in the very beginning of human groups—which means assuming pre-institutional times—was asymmetrical with a disparity in terms of social dynamic levels[1].

The father of A and B is likely to remain a third term which is different from a third party in a relationship. In this case, the father is likely to keep performing the guarantee function as p to each child even when other siblings (regardless of sex) enter the relationship as C, D and so on. However, the group formed by the father and his children will easily reach the limit of the number of children and perhaps not be able to go beyond biological group composition, both qualitatively and quantitatively, and come to possess an incomparably larger scale and complexity. How about we consider the dead instead of the father? That the person is dead satisfies the requirement to remain as a third term without becoming a third party to a bipartite relationship. However, it is difficult to imagine that the dead in general are adequately capable of fulfilling the guarantee function to the living in an actual scene. The fact that it is easy to ignore them accounts for a large part of their inadequacy.

Would the father as the dead as p retain the expected level of guarantee function on an actual scene (after death) while satisfying the requirement to remain a third term as the dead? Is it possible that the father can sustain a certain level of guarantee function in a father-children group while resisting memory degradation after death? Even so, of course, we are again faced with the question of how the scale and complexity of this biological group composition can go beyond the standards that are seen among other species. Nevertheless, it is not impossible to assume that not only children but also the children's children can be subject to a similar guarantee function of the father as the dead. This can increase the scale and complexity to another level, although it remains at a simple level. If the relationship group is expanded further to include the children's grandchildren, the scale and complexity may increase, but the degradation of memory, which is already identified as a problem, will gradually reduce the guarantee function.[2]

It has become clear in the process of this simple reasoning that, whether a thing is gold, human, the dead, the father or the father as the dead, if the ability to remain a third term is inherent in its being as a third term itself—in other words, as long as its quality is the only thing that matters in basic understanding—then it does not guarantee the continuity of the relationship permanently because of insufficient unambiguity and memory degradation. Gold is gold only if it is recognized as gold. We cannot assume that gold is unerringly and unambiguously recognized as gold by anyone, anytime, for just being a mineral called gold. On the other hand, "social institution" is not something whose existence is limited to certain times or scenes.

Let us return to our statement that maneuvering to initiate a relationship with a "distant" person far behind the other is possible once "height" to mediate relations is introduced into the field (Funabiki 2013: 297). From there, we headed downward to the zero-level in the first thesis, whereas we shall head upward this time in order to explore institutions.

As long as p is a person or a thing, be it a father or gold, in Figure 14.2(a), the relationship will only grow into a human group with an expanse in Figure 14.3. However, if p is a person or a thing but also exists on a "sign" level as father or gold, then they have the potential to overcome insufficient unambiguity and memory degradation. This is because a sign has perfect unambiguity and it is also resistant to degradation as it renews itself infinitely as long as humans repeat it.

The unambiguity of signs should not require a lengthy explanation. Because the sign "father" is not a complex of multiple individual components as an actual "specific father" is, it has the ability to be a father to any person. In other words, a specific father suffers from ambiguity on a level where it varies depending on the

Basic Components of Institution

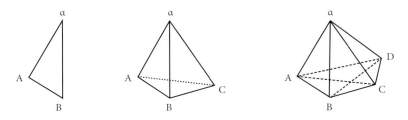

Figure 14.5 Tripartite relationship and tetrahedral model

perception and memory of the individual, whereas the signified father can exist unambiguously. Similarly, a memory of a specific father may fade every time it is recalled, whereas the signified father can be newly reaffirmed as long as it is the signified "father". The same can be said about gold. Figuratively speaking, gold of very high purity still contains more impurities than signified gold as long as it is gold as a thing. It is perhaps better to say that a thing called gold becomes "gold" as a sign when gold is operating as p, that is, as signified gold, except when it is used as a metal thing. This explanation runs the risk of overlapping an argument deduced from the source (quality of gold) with one that traces back to the source, as gold already exists as "gold" as a sign. However, we shall again leave this question to be judged in the context of the overall discussion and move on.

Tetrahedral model

We are more likely to be able to avoid confusion resulting from a qualitative difference between the actual states of father and gold if we move our argument forward here. Figure 14.5(a) shows a situation in which p, a third term to A and B, becomes α as a signified person or thing. In order for this α as a signified being to remain a third term when C enters the bipartite relationship between A and B, C does not need to behave as the third term p; C can form a relationship with A, with α being a third term as shown in Figure 14.5(b). C can not only receive the benefit of guarantee by p, but also escape the aforementioned problem that the relationship not only involves many (six) uncontrollable components. It is also difficult to withdraw from the relationship once A enters it. The uncontrollability, in a sense, is inherent in the tripartite relationship between A, B and C. In this case, three bipartite relationships between A and B, A and C and B and C manifest as a tetrahedron guaranteed by α. As shown more clearly in Figure 14.5(c), when D joins this relationship group, the group manifests as a synthesis of four partially overlapping tetrahedrons consisting of six bipartite relationships between D and A, D and B, D and C, A and C, A and B and B and C, with α being the third term, with minimal uncontrollability in this sense, rather than the even more uncontrollable quadripartite relationship that was previously predicted.

The further participation of E, F, G and so on creates a completely different situation from that illustrated in Figure 14.3 where the human field expands as an increasingly uncontrollable concatenation in which individuals are unable to be involved in its overall expansion on a synchronous or continuous basis. We propose to treat this as the "structure", which was suggested in the first thesis, and to consider that what is produced by this structure is the institution.

Let us backtrack a little here and re-examine why an institution in the form of this structure is able to be involved in the overall expansion synchronously and continuously. It is because in this model all people consider their relationships with others as bipartite relationships and therefore p, which guarantees such relationships, never appears as a third party that increases their uncontrollability.

Now, if there was a third party in this structure, who would it be?

This signifies every other entity that is not the third entity (third term), the self or the other party in a bipartite relationship. In other words, the third party is an entity that can potentially form a bipartite relationship with the self. To rephrase, it is currently not the second party but it has the potential to become one. We think that this is the very entity that ought to be called "other". Let us restrict ourselves to this advance notice for the upcoming third thesis and examine other issues and flaws in the argument we have presented so far.

From any perspective, the idea that p becomes the sign α can be regarded as a leap in logic. The leap manifests as inadequacy found in the explanation that it is unambiguous because it is a sign and that it escapes memory degradation and renews itself every time it is used because it is a sign, if this explanation is taken at face value. I have already stated that if the ability to remain a third term is inherent in its being as a third term itself, in other words, as long as its quality is the only thing that matters in basic understanding, then it does not guarantee the continuity of the relationship permanently because of "insufficient unambiguity" and "memory degradation". Why is α able to guarantee it? It is not only because p becomes the sign α but also because this sign α is the sign α with a "symbolic effect" as a result of it being repeatedly interpreted as α in meaning space.

Again, it is possible to point out the issue of circular reasoning here, in addition to the model's hypothesis, similar to that which we have previously mentioned in relation to p, which is our attempt to support the hypothesis about p's adjustment function with the assumption that such adjustment already exists. One such example is our treatment of α as a sign, which was the father in the preceding argument. Unless it appears as an institution named father or a sign in meaning space, it is impossible for the relationship group illustrated in Figure 14.5(c) onward to go beyond biological group composition, both qualitatively and quantitatively, and come to possess an incomparably larger scale and complexity and at the same time for A in Figure 14.4, for instance, to be involved in its overall expansion on a synchronous or continuous basis. Suppose the children kill the father in order to prevent the father from easily reverting from a sign to a real entity and becoming a party to a tripartite or larger relationship, increasing the uncontrollability of the relationship. In this case, turning the dead father into a "sign" will increase its stability, but the sign will be weak and diminish in its guarantee function. What is needed in order to protect against this is a kind of semantic space in which interpretations that constantly reinforce father as a sign are reproduced augmentatively, i.e., a meaning space in which father is used as a symbol. This is the institution (see the Key Ideas Diagram on p. 310). The basic components of this institution are the triangular relationship with p as well as the tetrahedron where p has become α.

In order to increase the validity of this argument, I shall attempt to compare it with the tripartite relationship theory proposed earlier and to apply the model to specific examples. However, I consider it more appropriate to close this discussion on institutions for the time being and resume our examination in the third thesis, as this is a question about third parties who are potential "second parties"—i.e., others as mentioned earlier—as well as a discussion about institutions.

Part IV
The Expansion of Institution Theory

15 The Ontology of Feeling: The Evolutionary Basis of "Natural Institutions" in Inuit Extended Family Groups

Keiichi Omura

Key ideas

The anatomy of "natural institution"

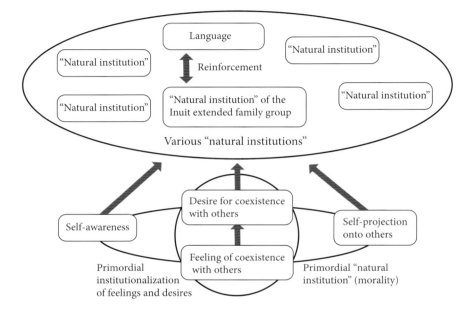

This diagram represents a conceptual dissection of the "natural institution" of extended family group rules continuously produced by the subsistence system of the Inuit and gives us a glimpse into the anatomy of natural institutions as follows. First of all, feelings and desires surrounding coexistence with others are primordially institutionalized in the process of self-awareness and self-projection and a primordial "natural institution" which forms the foundation of all "natural institutions" emerges in the form of "morality". This primordial "natural institution" of morality prescribes "having positive feelings about coexistence with others and desiring to be with others", and thus social groups come to be produced through the continuous maintenance of this rule. This rule and the sustainable social groups are continuously formed in the cyclic process of recursive and reciprocal production. Upon the foundation of this primordial "natural institution" of morality, various "natural institutions" are continuously produced, including the "natural institution" of Inuit extended family group rules and the "natural institution" of language.

"Languageless institution" theory as a starting point

The incipient "natural institution" among human ancestors, for example, was a situation in which people who would not share food with others would receive a disapproving look and those who did not wish to share would have to eat out of view of others. In this case, it is probably reasonable to say that the expectations of others have the effect of controlling individual behavior and give rise to the rule that food must be shared. Therefore, it appears that institutions can arise in the absence of what we consider to be a complete language. (Kuroda 1999: 287–288)

Archaic things would undergo countless transformations more than once (infinitely, in theory) in the course of history. These transformations could be vastly different from their previous formations (discontinuity). Conceptually, however, a certain level of continuity can be found between archaic and present things thanks to transformational preservation. Without it, there would be no knowledge of the past. Abstract knowledge is not mere recognition of fact; it goes beyond that. Abstract understanding of social structures of the past is the very thing that is called comprehension of the past. Marx repeatedly argued about this. His statement about "human anatomy" ("Human anatomy contains a key to the anatomy of the ape" ("Introduction" to *Outlines of the Critique of Political Economy*)) was to publicize the specificity of the abstract understanding of historical phenomena. (Imamura 2005: 182–183)

What is the evolutionary basis of institutions in human society? References are made throughout this volume to a hypothesis proffered by Suehisa Kuroda (1999) as a starting point in terms of considering this question. Kuroda reviewed a discourse on institutions presented by Junichiro Itani (1987), emerging from the tradition of Japanese primatology conceived by Kinji Imanishi, in an effort to solve the mystery of the evolution of human society. He hypothesized that language would not be essential for the formation of institutions as long as self-awareness and the projection of the self onto others were developed, and based on the results of his field studies argued that the evolutionary basis of institutions could be found in the social behaviors of chimpanzees (genus *Pan*).

Kuroda points out that "natural institutions", which precede language-based institutions such as legal systems, are found widely in human society and defines such phenomena as "rules of sustainable social groups" (1999: 288). He argues that if a sustainable social group exists and its members share "the expectation that the self and other members conform to a certain matter" as the norm, then a "natural institution" arises, even if the matter and deviation from it are not clearly articulated in language. As long as conformity to a certain matter becomes the norm and members expect and require one another to conform as if "everyone is supposed to do so", then rules that are "matters to which all members of a certain group expect the self and others to conform" (Kuroda 1999: 288) come to be generated and maintained without the medium of language.

In the case of food sharing, for instance, this practice has been institutionalized as a "natural institution" even when the food sharing rule is not articulated in language. This occurs if there is a situation in which those who deviate from the rule are subjected to negative reactions from others such as discouragement, antipathy and hostility and are compelled to avoid the eyes of others when they keep food to themselves. This suggests that food-sharing behavior has become the norm in the sense that people expect and require each other to conform as a matter of course.

The important point here is that in order for this kind of "natural institution" to arise even in the absence of language, there has to be a situation in which people not only become aware of restrictions on their behavior such as "food must be shared and not monopolized", but also expect and require others with the same awareness to comply with such restrictions. Accordingly, for a "natural institution" to arise, in addition to 1) the self-awareness of restrictions on one's action, 2) one needs to project one's own state onto others and to think that others must also be complying with such restrictions. In short, according to Kuroda, conditions for the emergence of "natural institutions" include 1) self-awareness, and 2) projection of oneself onto others based on this self-awareness, rather than language itself.

As Kuroda himself argues, the pros and cons of his "languageless institution" hypothesis ought to be verified on the basis of primate field studies. Direct verification is difficult in the fields of sociology and cultural anthropology as they only have access to institutions among modern humankind for which the existence of language is presupposed. Nevertheless, as Imamura says in the second quote at the start of this chapter, it is perhaps permissible to indirectly verify Kuroda's "languageless institution" theory by analyzing modern human institutions and discover some of the social structures of past primates (common ancestors of modern humans and troglodytes) that are considered to have been preserved in different forms in modern human institutions. Borrowing Marx's words quoted by Imamura, this involves using the anatomy of human social institutions in order to understand the anatomy of primate institutions in our exploration of the evolutionary basis of institutions in human society.

The aim of this chapter is to explore the evolutionary basis of institutions in human society by verifying Kuroda's "languageless institution" theory indirectly through dissection of the extended family group rules generated and maintained by the subsistence system of the Inuit, the indigenous people of Arctic Canada. Firstly, I demonstrate that the extended family group rules generated and maintained by the Inuit subsistence system are in fact the "natural institutions" hypothesized by Kuroda based on the research results in Arctic anthropology. Then, I test Kuroda's "languageless institutions" indirectly through identifying the logical minimum necessary conditions for the emergence of such "natural institutions" based on ethnographic records on the Inuit. Finally, I discuss some guiding principles provided by the conditions for the development of the Inuit's extended family group rules as "natural institutions" in our exploration of the evolutionary basis of human society.

Extended family group rules of the Inuit

Arctic anthropologists have pointed out that the existence of a social-cultural-economic system called subsistence is commonly observed among the Inuit and Yu'pik peoples who are distributed widely from the Arctic zone of easternmost Siberia through North America to Greenland[1] (e.g., Bodenhorn 1989; Fienup-Riordan 1983; Kishigami 2007; Nuttall 1992; Stewart 1991, 1992, 1995; Wenzel 1991). The subsistence system generates and maintains the relationships between the Inuit and wild animals as well as those among the Inuit and is governed by their worldview conceptualized as an ideal world order to be realized (Omura 2011, 2012, 2013). Under this system, the extended family group, which is the basic unit of Inuit sociality, is generated and maintained through the distribution and consumption of resources acquired through the relationships between the Inuit and wild animals.

As we shall see below, the rules of the extended family group generated and maintained by this subsistence system correspond to Kuroda's definition of "natural institutions". The extended family group is a social group called "*ilagiimariktut*" (true *ilagiit*) and forms the basis of daily social life in Inuit society. Among "*ilagiit*" (kindred), that is "related people who may go away but come back and then share food, help each other, and stay together" (Balikci 1989: 112), this extended family group is defined as "people who live together and have close partnerships in economic and other activities, in other words, people who form a concrete social group" and refers to "ego's parents, siblings, wife and children, grandchildren, uncles, aunts, grandparents and cousins" (Kishigami and Stewart 1994: 421). Firstly, I shall describe how the extended family group rules as "natural institutions" are generated and maintained by the subsistence system.

The mechanism by which the subsistence system of the Inuit continuously produces the extended family group rules can be represented by the following cyclic system model (Omura 2009, 2011, 2012, 2013).

Firstly, the Inuit enter into a "food giver-receiver" relationship with an individual wild animal using their subsistence skills such as hunting, fishing, trapping and gathering. Sharing food and other life resources acquired as the product of such a relationship engenders social relations of mutual trust and equality among the Inuit and leads to the formation of extended family groups. Such trust relationships resulting from sharing generate cooperation within the extended family group and subsistence skills are shared through such cooperation. The accumulation and concentration of subsistence skills through skill-sharing leads to the efficient reproduction of "food giver-receiver" relationships with new individual wild animals. Through this cycle of subsistence processes, Inuit-wild animal relations intertwine with Inuit-Inuit relations as they develop, and the "Inuit" (humans) who are "those to trust and cooperate with" and "wild animals" as "food givers" come to be differentiated in the minds of the Inuit.

What is important with this subsistence system is that the Inuit's food sharing practices have become the rule: however, persons of Inuit society do not occupy a superior position to command or compel other Inuit or wild animals because of the worldview that underpins this system. The Inuit worldview aims to maintain the relationship between the Inuit and wildlife that is realized in their subsistence activities according to the following reciprocal relationship. In their worldview, wild animals are believed to have "spirits" (*tagniq*), which persist after their bodies perish. At the same time, the sharing and consumption of meat among the Inuit is held to be an essential condition for the rebirth of the spirits of wild animals in new bodies. This means that the spirits of wild animals voluntarily offer their bodies to the Inuit for sharing and consumption so that they can be reborn in new bodies. From the Inuit point of view, this means that the resources for survival are given, and it is wild animals that secure the Inuit's survival. Thus, what is aimed for in the Inuit worldview is a reciprocal relationship by which wildlife help the Inuit to survive by offering their bodies as food and the Inuit in turn assist wildlife to be reborn in new bodies by eating and sharing the contributed wildlife.

The Ontology of Feeling

Photo 15.1 An Inuit extended family group

Photo 15.2 Inuit food sharing

Because of this guiding principle, the Inuit as "food receivers" are subordinate to wild animals and must always share food with each other and consume it completely. The food sharing practice is thus turned into a rule. If the Inuit fail to share the food contribution of animals, the wild animals' spirits will not be able to be reborn and therefore will stop giving themselves to the Inuit as food. Importantly, what is ingenious here is that the food-sharing rule is set by wildlife, not the Inuit. This is why, among the Inuit, trust relationships are realized in which everyone shares food according to the same rule without anyone ordering them to do so.

Another notable feature is that the rule is about food sharing rather than giving. This consequently forbids the Inuit from creating the dominant-dependent relationship between "giver and receiver" inherent in food giving. No one holds the dominant status of food "giver" or incurs the burden of being a "receiver". This relationship operates in Inuit extended family groups within which there is a relationship of mutual trust involving the expectation and requirement that food will be shared and the mutual reliance on the willingness of others to meet these conditions; however, no one commands or compels others to share food. By letting wild animals impose food-sharing rules on the Inuit, the Inuit have negated any "dominant-dependent" relationships and attained one of trust and equality within their extended family groups.

As a result, the Inuit are forbidden from resorting to acts of coercion or dominance toward not only members of their own extended family groups but also wild animals. This also stops them from domesticating wild animals. If the Inuit domesticate wild animals, the food sharing rule can no longer be taken as imposed on them by wild animals—the reverse would be the case, and the Inuit domesticating wild animals would be dictating the other Inuit. The "dominant-dependent" relationship that was once removed would return to Inuit relations through the subsistence cycle. For a relationship of equality and trust to arise within an extended family group, wild animals must be in a dominant position to every member of the group. Consequently, the Inuit are compelled to engage in subsistence activities such as hunting, fishing, trapping and gathering in which they, as the dependent in a weak position, use techniques to entice animals, as they are unable to adopt any methods that involve the control and management of wild animals such as pastoralism (Omura 2012, 2013).

As mentioned above, the important point here is that this subsistence system as a whole operates to engender a relationship of trust and equality within the extended family group. To simply enforce the sharing rule, Inuit would not need to go to the trouble of including wild animals in the system in the position of imposer; someone in the extended family group could take on the role of imposing the rule. The view that all of the people are subordinate to wildlife is precisely a device to generate a trust relationship in which everyone willingly meets other's expectations and requirements while preventing the emergence of a person or persons in a dominant position who coerce or command sharing. Thus, the subsistence system of the Inuit, through its cyclic operation, forbids coercion or authoritative behavior and continuously reproduces the rule of mutual trust by which people voluntarily meet each other's expectations and requirements. At the same time, based on the presumed rule of trust, the continuous reproduction of the sharing rule generates and maintains the extended family group. In other words, the Inuit subsistence system has become a device to produce a "natural institution" of the "continuous social group rule" described by Kuroda.

Is it possible, then, for the extended family group rules continuously reproduced by this subsistence system to come into effect in the absence of language? Next I consider this question by dissecting these rules with reference to ethnographic records on the Inuit.

Conditions of "natural institution"

As discussed so far, in the Inuit subsistence system, the trust rule is continuously produced through its cyclic operation, and on that condition the food-sharing rule is continuously produced, thus an extended family group is generated and maintained. What is important here is that, among the two rules continuously produced by this system, the first "trust rule" functions as a precondition for the second "sharing rule" and therefore precludes the possibility of coercion or dictation in the continuous production of the sharing rule. Coercion or authoritative behavior would breach the trust rule of meeting mutual expectations and requirements without such compulsion. Accordingly, for these two rules to be produced continuously and consistently as "natural institutions", a situation must arise in which everyone voluntarily conforms to the sharing rule by choice without being commanded or coerced to do so by others.

The method adopted into the subsistence system in order to realize this situation was to represent wildlife as the entity that ordered extended family groups to share food in their worldview, conceptualized as an ideal world order. Under this subsistence system, by locating wild animals outside of the extended family group, wild animals are in charge of the sharing rule, and the sharing rule is continuously produced without coercion or prescription inside the extended family group. At the same time, the cyclic operation of the system continuously produces the trust rule that entails voluntary participation in meeting mutual expectations and requirements in addition to the sharing rule. In other words, this subsistence system utilizes linguistic imagination in an ingenious manner in order to produce the trust rule and the sharing rule continuously and consistently.

Accordingly, the question of whether the "natural institution" encompassing the sharing and trust rules is possible without language is equivalent to that of whether the two rules can be continuously produced in the absence of the subsistence system that is effected by the ingenious use of the linguistic representation of wild animals as an external authority. The subsistence system becomes operable only after the incorporation of the worldview represented by language. Would these two rules be continuously and congruously produced without the device of the subsistence system?

What we need to clarify first in discussing this question is that the use of language is restricted to begin with, because under the "natural institution" of extended family group rules, giving orders or coercing from a dominant authoritative position is forbidden by the trust rule. This of course does not mean that language use is impermissible. It should be permissible in situations where rules are produced indirectly as a result, as in the case of the aforementioned worldview. However, if forbidden behavior and desired behavior are expressed in words directly, the expression becomes a virtual order. As Ingold (2000) points out, trusting the other person involves mutual respect for each other's autonomy, while mutually relying on each other's autonomous intention; verbally presenting a rule to others or requesting trust from others is akin to declaring your mistrust of them. In a trust relationship, people are required to sense what needs to be done and voluntarily do it for one another without the medium of words.

In fact, there is a tendency in Inuit society to avoid prescribing rules directly in words. This is clearly shown by the difficulties often faced by Arctic anthropologists (e.g., Briggs 1968; Honigman and Honigman 1965; Willmott 1960). When the Inuit are asked by researchers to confirm rules that have been observed during surveys, they tend to evade answering the question. For instance, after discovering that mothers-in-law and sons-in-law tended to avoid uttering each other's name, Briggs (1968: 45) attempted to confirm the fact with the Inuit by asking "Which people avoid each other's names?". She was unable to get a straight answer from them, and responses were as follows: "Anybody who had a mind to." "Whose name does a person avoid?" "Anybody's" "What about mothers-in-law and sons-in-law?" "Sometimes. If they want to. If they feel affectionate (*nakli*)" (Briggs 1968: 45).

In Inuit society, whether it is one's own action or that of another, people say that it is a voluntary action performed autonomously and never admit that they are following social rules. When an adult violates a rule, others use disapproval to implicitly point out the occurrence of some kind of violation, but they never express in words what specific action is the subject of their censure; instead, people are required to have "reason" (*ihuma-*) to realize their own deviant behavior (Briggs 1968). It is held that even children will come to understand adherence to dos and don'ts as they grow up and develop sufficient reason. Thus, rules are rarely articulated directly in words. How, then, are rules and violations communicated in Inuit society?

Allusion to violation is achieved through subtle actions such as glancing away and leaving the scene. Of course, there are times when violations committed by children, not yet possessing sufficient reason, are directly criticized and corrected. However, people never criticize adults for their violations face-to-face; they merely indicate the inappropriateness of their actions by silently moving away from the offender or departing the scene (Briggs 1968, 1970). The most salient example of this is the fact that the strongest form of sanction in Inuit society is a severance of relationships. An individual who has committed an inappropriate action is received silently without greetings. Others continue to respond politely to the individual's proposals and requests, but they stop making proposals and requests to this individual (Briggs 1968, 1970). Others refrain from actively reaching out to the individual, effectively leaving them in social isolation. One who has committed an inappropriate action must use their reason to realize this situation and self-correct their deviant behavior.

It is clear from the Inuit way of interacting that it is possible to generate the two rules of extended family groups and maintain them continuously as "natural institutions" without the use of language. As practiced in Inuit society, one can communicate the inappropriateness of another's action by distancing oneself from the offender without articulating it in words. Just as Kuroda (1999) points out, where appropriate actions are accepted and inappropriate actions are indicated by negative reactions such as discouragement, antipathy and hostility, people become aware of the actions that are considered appropriate or inappropriate as well as the restrictions imposed to elicit appropriate behavior. At the same time, if they project themselves on others, they become aware that other Inuit are also aware of the same restrictions even though they are not verbally expressed. Consequently, people come to have awareness of mutual expectations and requirements for their own and other's appropriate behavior in a concatenation of interactions without the medium of language.

Accordingly, it is possible to say that "natural institutions" can certainly arise in the absence of language so long as one is aware of restrictions on their own actions and projects this awareness onto others in interactions. One element that requires our attention, however, is that even if the awareness of restrictions on one's own actions and the projection of this onto others arise and conformity to such restrictions becomes the norm, the norm will have no binding force nor be continuously produced unless one aspires to be with others.

Even when one is aware that their deviant action would be met with discouragement, antipathy or hostility from others, they would still elect to take such action if indifferent toward such consequences. Kuroda (1999) is correct in arguing that awareness of one's and other's conformity to a certain rule and confirmation of this situation in actual interactions will foster camaraderie between them and alienate violators. In this sense, camaraderie arises through adherence to the same rule. However, if one does not wish to be together with others, then one will not seek camaraderie. In this situation, there is no necessity for this person to adhere to the same rule and the rule has no binding force over them.

As Kuroda (1999) points out, it is certainly possible to say that "natural institution" has arisen in principle even when a rule is not actually adhered to so long as there is awareness of the expectation of adherence by oneself and others and the actions that would be regarded as violations. Nonetheless, because the "natural institution" here is a set of "rules of a sustainable social group", unless such rules are actually adhered to and lead to the development of sustainable camaraderie, the sustainable social group cannot arise in the first place and the rules cannot develop into a "natural institution". Especially in the case of the food sharing rule, continuous adherence to this rule directly leads to the maintenance of the extended family group. In other words, for this rule to develop into a "natural institution", adherence must be sustained to a degree sufficient to ensure the viability of the extended family group. To this end, belonging to the extended family group must be desired by Inuit individuals so that alienation from it is regarded as serious, even though it is not an explicit sanction.

In fact, it is widely known (Briggs 1968, 1970, 1998) that Inuit infants are thoroughly coddled from birth to talking-age and inculcated with strong levels of attachment, almost to the point of fixation, to members of their extended family group. From birth, infants are given love and attention by thirty or so members of their extended family group, being cuddled, kissed, encouraged to mimic movements and voices and so on by different relatives constantly, except when they are asleep. Basically, food and everything else children want are given to them, as long as items are not dangerous. A now-deceased famous sculptor once told me that she took up carving because she wanted to buy sweets for children. Stories of this kind are common. Children who have been raised this way retain strong attachments to their extended family group, particularly their parents and grandparents.

Frequent cases of severe homesickness among the Inuit clearly indicate the strength of these attachments (Briggs 1968, 1970, 1998). Until about a decade ago, the hamlet of Kugaaruk, to which I am a frequent visitor, had only a handful of Inuit high school graduates because young people had to go to a distant city in the south to receive secondary education as there was no high school in the hamlet. The Inuit commonly mentioned homesickness as the reason for their lack of attendance. The adolescents went away to attend high school, but many returned home before graduating because they felt lonely. When I visited Kugaaruk, many Inuit residents I bumped into on the street or in the supermarket asked me, "Are you homesick?", even though it was only my second or third day in the hamlet. When I told them that I was not homesick, they often looked surprised or puzzled. They told me that they were mystified at the fact that I was not homesick despite being so far from Japan.

Such strong attachments to one's extended family group also manifest in the inverse form as the "fear" of rejection and alienation from the people around one. There are two ways to express "fear" in the Inuit language. One is expressed with the use of the root *ikhi-* to mean a fear of dangerous animals, bad spirits and dangers in general. The other is expressed using the root *ilira-* to signify a fear of rejection of one's needs and requests or being denounced and isolated (Briggs 1968, 1970). For example, "*nulijara ikhinakturaaRuq*" (My wife is very scary) would be taken as a funny comment made by a henpecked husband, whereas "*nulijara iliranakturaaRuq*" (I am very afraid of my wife) would be taken as a serious comment pointing to the disastrous state of the couple's relationship. It is said that for the Inuit, the former is a minor fear felt by children and the latter is a serious fear held by adults (Briggs 1968, 1970). For the Inuit, there is nothing more frightening than rejection by and isolation from others. For this reason, outsiders such as myself are often greeted with assuring words such as "Don't be afraid of asking us. We are kind people. We never reject" (Briggs 1968, 1970).

Accordingly, it is possible to conclude that, for the two rules of Inuit extended family groups to be generated and maintained, the following conditions are necessary.

1. Awareness of restrictions on one's own actions.
2. Self-projection on other Inuit.
3. Desire to be with other Inuit.

What is significant here is that language is not a prerequisite for any of these conditions. (1) and (2) can develop in interactions without language, as Kuroda

(1999) points out, and it goes without saying that language is not necessary for (3) to arise. Conversely, as Kuroda argues in Chapter Eighteen, these three conditions are preconditions for the emergence of language, which is also a "natural institution" in itself. If one does not aspire to be with other Inuit, one is unlikely to attempt to communicate via language or coexist through a connection in words to start with. As Tomasello (2006) explains, (2) self-projection on others based on (1) self-awareness is a condition for the genesis of language and forms a preparatory stage for language acquisition, as in the process of language learning by infants.

Nevertheless, this does not mean that language plays no role in the "natural institution" of the extended family group rules. Even if language is not a precondition for "natural institution", it plays an important role in continuously sustaining the institution by reinforcing its conditions. Firstly, expressing the two rules in words, although this is rarely done in Inuit society, can help people have a clearer awareness of these rules. Secondly, in the subsistence system built around the worldview expressed in language, the two rules are necessitated and reinforced reciprocally in the closed cycle where each acts as a precondition for the other, unless one steps out of the logic of this worldview. Thirdly, as shown in the following examples, children are teased verbally in a temporarily constructed fictitious situation once they begin speaking so that attachments to others underpinning the desire for coexistence as well as self-awareness and self-projection on others are reinforced in them.

A visitor—usually, but not necessarily, a woman—who is sitting beside mother and baby on the sleeping platform holds out her arms to the baby, or lifts the edge of her parka invitingly, as if preparing to carry him, and says, in a soft, tender, persuasive voice: "Will you come home with me? I love you. Shall I adopt you? You'll sleep beside me, and we'll cuddle together on the sleeping platform. Just us two. Would you like to sleep beside me? Let's cuddle together. Come, shall I adopt you?'

The baby's response, almost always, is to retreat, with a frightened face, and sometimes with cries of frightened, angry protest, to his mother.

Mother may hold out the baby again toward the visitor, as if, herself, receptive to the idea of his adoption.

Visitor: repeats offer, invitingly, assuring the baby that she loves him.

Baby: retreats, in fear, to mother.

Mother: laughs and cuddles baby.

(Briggs 1979: 31–32)

This play in which an adult teases a child by suggesting adoption and elicits laughter from those present is staged frequently. Especially when I'm visiting, this game is played in the living room of my lodging house many times a day in which a child is teased by comments such as "Do you want to be adopted by Uncle Keichi and go to Japan? You will be able to speak Japanese and become an interpreter". It is not unusual for me to participate in the play by saying "I'm going to adopt you". All children subjected to this teasing become scared and cry as they cling to their parents or grandparents, and all family members present have a good laugh. This kind of teasing appears to not only bring children's usually unconscious attachments to their parents and relatives to the fore, but also has the effect of deepening their attachments by forcing them to notice the potential danger of separation from their beloved parents and relatives.

Some of the verbal teasing games are played with the sharing rule as a direct theme, as in the following example.

A mother and her three-year-old daughter are visiting in a tent where there are a number of other people. The three-year-old's sister, aged four, is outside, playing with other children.

Mother: hands a candy to three-year-old daughter and says in exaggeratedly happy-excited-secret-persuasive voice: "Eat it quickly and don't tell your sister, because it's the last one!"

Three-year-old: breaks the candy into two pieces, eats one and takes the other outdoors to her sister.

Mother: says to the audience, with a pleased (and perhaps amused) smile: "She never keeps things for herself; she always shares."

(Afterward, the daughter was not praised by her mother, but she was praised by her relatives who saw or heard about her behavior.)

(Briggs 1979: 27–28)

Such elaborate and malicious scenes of teasing are uncommon, but posing a dilemma to children regarding sharing happens frequently and routinely. It can be said that this type of play that generates a dilemma in the minds of children not only makes them aware of a restriction on non-sharing by deliberately tempting them to keep all for themselves, but also encourages them to understand that others adhere to the restriction even though they do have the same desire to keep all for themselves. This must have the effect of reinforcing their self-projection onto others as well as raising their awareness that others are watching them all the time.

Accordingly, it is possible to conclude that language, which is a "natural institution" in itself, is founded on the three minimum necessary conditions for the "natural institution" of the extended family group rules noted above. At the same time, it reinforces and maintains not only the "natural institution" of the extended family group rules, but also itself by reinforcing these conditions. As Kitamura points out in Chapter Eleven, language provides support and stability to the sustainability of the existing "natural institution" in various ways: by labeling the known restrictions on one's actions, by reinforcing the three conditions for the existing institution in fictitious situations (as in the case of the Inuit teasing children) and by increasing the binding force of such restrictions through representation of the existing rule in the context of a closed cycle of necessity (as in the case of the Inuit subsistence system). A "natural institution" can probably arise without language, but it is likely that language functions as a "natural institution" that is crucial for the stable continuation of the "natural institution".

Primordial "natural institution"

Based on the anatomy of the "natural institution" of the extended family group rules of the Inuit, we are informed of the following about the evolutionary basis of human institutions.

Firstly, we have found that a desire to coexist with others is essential for the emergence of a "natural institution". Even if self-awareness and self-projection on others develop and people begin to expect and require each other to adhere to a certain rule, the expectation and requirement will be ignored if people do not desire to be with others in the first place. Moreover, the desire for coexistence intertwines with the other two conditions—self-awareness and self-projection—in a process of mutual reinforcement. Unless self-awareness highlights the distinction between self and other and gives rise to the awareness that both live autonomously in reciprocal relationships, there is no chance for the desire for coexistence to arise. At the same time, one's self-awareness is reinforced through contrast with others while one desires to be with others and continues to coexist with them. Then, unless one desires to be with others, why would they bother to project themselves on others in an attempt to understand their intentions or expectations? In projecting oneself onto others, moreover, one's desire for coexistence with others is likely to be reinforced. Thus the minimum necessary factor behind the emergence of a "natural institution" is the dynamic between self-awareness and other-awareness that arises and is reinforced around the desire for coexistence with others.

At the same time, the anatomy of the Inuit extended family group rules has informed us that the desire for coexistence with others, the essential condition for a "natural institution", is not universally shared by all humans. Intense attachments to the extended family group and a fear of isolation held by the Inuit are stably maintained only after many years of relentless inculcation through various interactive measures during infancy. Of course, the desire for coexistence with others may be rooted in the biological characteristic of human beings who sometimes experience positive emotions when they are with others. However, if the desire for coexistence was a biologically inherent nature of the human species, there should be no need to give infants special training; everyone would voluntarily try to be with others. Rather, we sometimes feel lonely when we are alone, but we sometimes become annoyed when we are with others; this ambivalence toward coexistence may be the universal human condition.

This means that for a "natural institution" to arise in human society, there is a need for the exercising of some ingenuity for the purpose of generating a situation in which coexistence with others is continuously desired. This is the third item we have been informed about by the anatomy of the Inuit extended family group rules. Ingenuity in the case of the Inuit extended family group is expressed in the form of the technique to inculcate infants with attachments to its members through thoroughly pampering. What is significant in this technique is the clever use of the process of the development of self-awareness and self-projection in infants. As a result, the state of having positive feelings toward coexistence and wanting to coexist with others becomes institutionalized as a primordial "natural institution" that supports the "natural institution" of extended family group rules by the following mechanism.

According to Damasio (2003, 2010), who has introduced a distinction[2] between "emotion", which is an unconscious physiological reaction, and "feeling", which is a perceived emotion, having positive emotions such as comfort and pleasure or negative emotions such as discomfort and dislike toward the state of being in a certain environment is merely the physiological reaction of one's body to the state and is not necessarily cognized. While such an emotion becomes a feeling when it is cognized through one's growing self-awareness, one's physiological reaction is not cognized in isolation; it can only be cognized as it is embedded in the environment that forms the context for the emotion, as Damasio points out[3]. When an emotion enters one's awareness as a feeling, the change in the environmental state outside of one's body that triggered that emotion is always and necessarily perceived as well.

Then, if the state of being with others as a whole is confined to one that induces only positive emotions, feelings toward the state of being with others as a whole are anchored to positivity (inseparable pairing of positive emotions and the state that triggered such emotions), whether individual feelings perceived in individual states or individual interactions in the process of being with others are positive or negative. The technique used by the Inuit to motivate infants to be with members of their extended family group ingeniously takes advantage of this process of emotions being perceived as feelings. Even if negative emotions triggered by individual states while being with others—for example, when one's action is hindered—are perceived as negative feelings, only positive emotions are induced in the final state—for example, one is ultimately given what one wants—and infants will come to perceive the state of being with others as a state in which they always experience positive feelings.

Moreover, as this process is inextricably linked to that of the development of self-awareness in infants, they begin to perceive only positive feelings in the state of being with others from the moment they begin to develop self-awareness. In other words, having positive feelings about being with others becomes naturalized as normal. If this is projected on others, having positive feelings about being with others will also become naturalized as normal for everyone. In this moment, infants become aware that both self and others expect each other to have positive feelings about being with others; that everyone has positive feelings about being with others becomes a rule in the minds of infants.

Thus, infants are likely to be motivated to seek coexistence with others if they want to experience positive feelings because they know that they are supposed to get positive feelings from it as a rule. If they project this onto others, they come to expect that others, too, have positive feelings about coexistence and are motivated by such feelings to wish to be with others. And infants are likely to require others to have the desire to be with others because the coexistence they want cannot happen in the first place if others reject it due to a lack of desire to be with others. The moment this is projected onto others, infants become aware that both self and others expect and require each other to desire coexistence; wishing to be with others becomes a rule in the minds of infants.

However, even if having positive feelings about coexistence is turned into a rule through the above process, and then desiring coexistence becomes a rule, the continuous maintenance of these rules does not necessarily occur automatically.

No matter how strong the rule of feeling positive about coexistence is, it cannot remove one's awareness of negative feelings about individual interactions that take place in the process of coexistence, such as feeling annoyed when others hinder one's actions. These negative feelings may trigger in some people the negative feeling that coexistence with others is annoying. As discussed earlier, the fact that we need to be given motivation to be with others indicates that the human species does not necessarily desire to coexist with others as part of their biological nature. Even if wanting to be with others has turned into a rule, the desire for coexistence may be dismissed as a result of competition with other desires, such as the desire to exclude others for one's own purposes and the desire to be alone.

These conflicts and uncertainties surrounding coexistence with others play a significant role in institutionalizing the feelings and desire for coexistence as a "natural institution". When the presence of these conflicts and uncertainties in oneself and others enters one's awareness through the processes of self-awareness and self-projection, one becomes aware that both self and others may reject other's company in some cases because they do not necessarily want coexistence. Upon becoming aware of this possibility, one begins to self-regulate one's own actions if one wishes to be with others so that both parties will not have negative feelings about coexistence nor become motivated by these negative feelings to reject coexistence. This constitutes one's attempt to avoid any situations in which one acts in a way that leads others to have negative feelings and reject coexistence. Thus, the rules to have positive feelings toward coexistence and the desire to coexist with others come to be reproduced continuously, and the resultant actual coexistence gives rise to a sustainable social group while these rules are realized as those of the sustainable social group which is the "natural institution".

Accordingly, it is possible to say that the technique used by the Inuit to motivate their infants to coexist with others is a device to institutionalize positive feelings about coexistence and a desire to coexist as the "natural institution". In addition, it is clear that the "natural institution" surrounding coexistence with others functions as a primordial "natural institution" that generates and continuously supports that of the extended family group rules. From this primordial "natural institution" through the processes of self-awareness and self-projection, the "natural institution" of the extended family group of the Inuit is derived as follows.

If a person cannot eat something they want to eat and others eat this thing in their presence, that person ought to perceive having negative feelings about this situation. If that person anticipates encountering the opposite situation to this, i.e., a situation in which they have food while others do not, the person has the option of ignoring others and eating it alone in the absence of the "natural institution" about coexistence with others. Where this "natural institution" exists, the person tries to avoid the situation of eating food alone in front of others because the person is compelled to prevent what they perceive as negative feelings from arising in others so that others do not begin to feel negative about coexistence. To do so, that person must either eat it in secret, share it with others or give away all they have to others. Since the person wants to eat it, too, the first two are the only available options. In this way, the situation to which Kuroda referred in the opening quote of this chapter emerges and the sharing rule becomes institutionalized.

In another situation, a person is forced to do something they do not want to do and becomes aware of negative feelings about the situation. When the person anticipates the opposite situation in which they force others to do what they do not want to do, the person can probably proceed to do so despite strong resistance from others if this "natural institution" does not exist. In the presence of this "natural institution", however, the person tries to refrain from the act of coercion about which they feel negative because they do not want others to feel negative about coexistence. Rather, the person has no choice but to expect that others will conform to the same "natural institution", and that others are willing to do what the person wants and avoid doing what the person does not want because they do not want them to dislike being with others. As a result, people come to convey their own desires indirectly through circuitous statements, facial expressions or actions, and wait for others to voluntarily carry things out rather than directly dictating or forcing others to do so. Thus, the rule of mutual trust becomes institutionalized.

It is important to note that the "natural institution" of rules surrounding coexistence with others is the primordial "natural institution" that underlies not only the "natural institution" of the extended family group rules of the Inuit but also all "natural institutions". Whatever rule a person follows, if their expectation that others must follow the same rule is betrayed, the person inevitably has negative feelings about the betrayal. When the person anticipates that they will be tempted to break the rule due to some desire, they probably will not hesitate to break the rule and betray the expectations of others if this "natural institution" did not exist. Where this "natural institution" exists, however, the person tries to avoid breaking the rules and betraying others' expectations in order to prevent others from feeling negative about coexistence. This is why the "natural institution" surrounding coexistence with others is the primordial "natural institution" that underpins all such institutions. This is the last thing that the anatomy of the "natural institution" of the Inuit extended family group rules tells us.

The ontology of feelings

The technique used by the Inuit to generate a primordial "natural institution" that supports all "natural institutions" through the abovementioned process of institutionalizing the feelings and desire for coexistence with others is perhaps universally observed among the human species, although it may rarely be practiced as relentlessly as in the case of the Inuit. Human infants are biologically incapable of fending for themselves and depend entirely on others, e.g.., the mother, for their survival during infancy. Therefore, coexistence with others which human infants experience during infancy when they develop self-awareness and self-projection must always be perceived in terms of positive feelings, even though they may perceive negative feelings in the process of coexistence. This is because the minimum necessary condition for survival is always met in the end and feelings toward the state of being with others as a whole are anchored to positivity. Otherwise infants are unable to survive. These biological conditions must be utilized to motivate infants to be with others by various human groups, as in the case of the Inuit. In other words, the feelings and desires for coexistence with others are institutionalized into a primordial "natural institution" that forms the foundation of all "natural institutions".

If this hypothesis is correct, it means that there is no realm beyond good and evil for mankind from an ontogenetic perspective. The moment individual humans come into the world, they are destined to grow up and become socialized in their action spaces in which the state of "having positive feelings about coexistence with others and having a desire to coexist with others motivated by such feelings" has been institutionalized as the primordial good. In this sense, this primordial "natural institution" can be called "morality". It is considered that the primordial "natural institution" of morality is founded on the ontogenetic nature of the human species, that is, human beings who are absolutely helpless individuals during infancy and have no choice but to depend on some others, and at the same time provides the foundations for various "natural institutions" that develop in individual social groups, including the "natural institutions" of the Inuit extended family group and languages.

Accordingly, it is possible to conclude that the primordial institutionalization of the feelings and desire for coexistence with others that takes place in the form of the "natural institution" of morality is the node between the universal nature of the human species and the diversity of institutions among human societies. In this sense, the "natural institution" of morality may be considered as the evolutionary basis of institutions in human societies that connects human phylogeny and ontogeny. This conclusion is of course only one hypothesis derived from the anatomy of the "natural institution" of the Inuit extended family group rules. How do the feelings and desires surrounding coexistence with others that have been primordially institutionalized as morality in various human social groups create the feeling world in each society while becoming institutionalized further within the "natural institutions" of individual societies? Through the empirical study of this ontological process of the institutionalization of feelings, this hypothesis should be verified. What is required of the anthropology of feelings that delves into the subtlety of various feeling lives of human beings is to undertake ontological analysis of feelings to provide biologically universal and socio-culturally relative explanations of the process of the institutionalization of human feeling lives based on empirical evidence.

16 The Institution of "Feeling": On "Feeling Inside" and "Institutionalized Envy"

Yuko Sugiyama

Key ideas

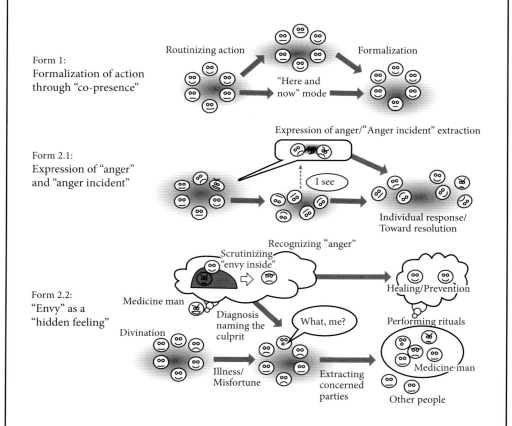

In this chapter, I shall discuss group size expansion and the institution of "feeling" in order to address institutions as an evolutionary foundation for human sociality. There are two forms of processes by which "feeling" is institutionalized. One form is institutionalization at a place of co-presence in which the formalization of action causes disengagement from the "here and now". The other form involves the presumption that "feelings" exist "inside" the individual that separates emotions from the "here and now" field on which emotional experiences arise and demands that a single experience should be dealt with at two different levels. The institution of "feeling" functions not only to deal with conflicts within a group but also to provide resources for the creation of new groups.

Feeling as the basis of common cognition

The history of human evolution corresponds to that of expanding varieties of human lifestyles and group sizes. It is characterized by the fact that modern nations have developed while maintaining all forms of livelihood, including hunting-and-gathering, fishing, pastoralism, shifting cultivation and settled cultivation as well as the fact that group size varies widely from a band of a few dozen people to a nation of billions. Masaki Nishida (1986) points out that sedentism was a major threshold in the process of group size expansion. This was due to the fact that human living was organized in small groups with a high level of mobility, which alleviated conflicts and strained relationships between group members. Sedentism required a means other than migration to avoid conflicts. As Koji Kitamura (2013) argues, "… such activities that are aimed specifically at the formation of a "group" bonded together by affiliative relationships are necessary".

With the expansion and coexistence of wide varieties of lifestyles and group sizes in mind, I shall examine "feelings" in this chapter as part of my discussion on "institutions" as a human evolutionary foundation. In particular, I focus on "emotions" in the face of strained relationships and "feelings" involved in conflict resolution and avoidance. I use the case of the Bemba, an African people living on shifting cultivation, to examine the function of the institution of feeling in group-size expansion.

There has been much discussion about institutions involving agrarian societies and "feelings" in relation to the social function of envy and witchcraft. While the inseparability of institutionalization and norm formation has been discussed by Kazuo Seiyama (1995), a number of ethnographic descriptions in preceding studies in the field of anthropology have demonstrated that anger and envy are deeply involved in the formation and maintenance of norms. In his discussion on the leveling mechanism among the Tongwe, a shifting cultivation people in southern Tanzania, Makoto Kakeya (1983) points out that any behavior contrary to their basic tendencies toward minimal effort and food sharing arouses feelings such as "envy" in people and suggests the involvement of witchcraft. He also stated that a fear of witchcraft caused by feelings such as "envy" underpins their leveling mechanism centering on food sharing. He describes this mechanism as "institutionalized envy" after the fashion of Foster (1972). Kakeya shows that the institutionalization of the feeling of "envy" can provide a way to ease tensions within a group and maintain unity without causing critical fissures. There is a major difference between this social phenomenon and the "sharing" described by Tadashi Tanno (1991) and Kaoru Imamura (2010) in relation to the hunting-and-gathering Aka and San peoples. Tanno reports that sharing is practiced by the Aka "because that is the nature of their relationships" and is not preceded by a "distribution" rule or a fear of envy. Imamura also points out that "sharing" is the very nature of life for the San (see also Terashima 2007). As portrayed by Kazuyoshi Sugawara (1993) and Imamura (2010), the San do envy others, but the fact that envy does not give rise to the sharing rule is a key factor in our discussion of the institution of "feeling" here.

There is a widespread perception among researchers that in agrarian societies envy is one of the sources of social conflict and sorcery is its manifestation. In early studies of agrarian societies in Tanzania and Zambia (Gluckman 1955; Richards 1950; Turner 1972[1957], 1966 among others), the supposition that the feeling of "envy" is held in people's minds is treated as if it is a universal phenomenon. On reflection, however, it appears to be an emotion that arises in the moment rather than something that is present on the "inside" all the time. According to Sugawara (2002), "It should not be supposed that a feeling is an actual state inside an individual; it is a meaning that flows out of the very attitude of a being who enters action space". Thus, feeling is inseparable from the field of co-presence with others and the reciprocal dealings engaged in. In this chapter, the view that such an emotion can be removed from its context and the presumption that a "feeling" is present on the "inside" of every person shall be treated as "institutional", preliminary to "institutionalized envy".

Emotion ("feeling" in Sugawara's writing) is not exclusively human. As shown by numerous studies in other fields, including psychology and cognitive science, some view emotion as a genetic program. Masanao Toda (2007[1992]) calls emotion the human urge system, which is an adaptation program for survival in the natural environment. An emotion is an experience that emerges within one's positionality and its immediacy (here and now) in the process of one's interactions with others.

In this chapter, "emotion" refers to one's experience that arises in the "here and now" (Terashima 2013) in one's dealings with others, while "feeling" refers to an emotional experience that is made somewhat conscious by reference to socialized categories[1].

Where emotions give rise to feelings such as "anger", they are conveyed to those present through "expressional body language" (Sugawara 2002), including face, posture and tone of voice, and heighten tension in that situation. It is often observed that other people who happen to be there are involved in relieving the tension and calming the situation down before it escalates to a serious conflict. Parties to the conflict conduct negotiation with the involvement of others. However, as group size increases, some means develop to reduce this burden through some kind of institutionalization. What is instituted is a means to avoid conflicts almost automatically, rather than relying on negotiations between parties in each situation, that is, a device for disengagement from the "here and now". When I use the word "device" in this chapter, I envisage a kind of mechanism that absorbs the emotional experiences of individuals as more general "feelings" and presents them to people as social, while relying on their ability to sense and resonate with the emotions of others—an ability that is also found in non-human primates such as gorillas and chimpanzees. I am inclined to position this device as something infinitely institutional. It is something that involves people other than the parties concerned, something that forms the basis of the common cognition that others will align with the self. It does not exist by itself; it forms a system together with other institutional things through mutual support. It arises in practice, but at the same time it orients the actions of individuals beyond the "here and now".

I shall examine the case of the Bemba, inhabiting the savanna woodlands of southern Africa, who are famous for their elaborate shifting cultivation system called *chitemene*. The Bemba presume "feelings" to be "internal emotions". Not only "anger" and "envy", but also all emotional experiences such as joy and sadness are included in what I refer to as "feelings" here. However, my observations have found two distinct modes among villagers' emotional experiences. I firstly address the modes of emotional arousal at daily gatherings, and then consider the state of the institution of "feeling" in relation to "anger" and "envy".

Spaces of co-presence in Bemba villages

The Bemba live in the savanna woodland of the Northern Province of Zambia and subsist mainly on shifting cultivation. By the seventeenth century, they had established a powerful matrilineal chiefdom, well before British colonization in the twentieth century. The political system of the chiefdom was preserved, functioning as a part of the colonial administration. It remained after Zambia's independence in 1964 and continues to exist today. The Bemba live in small residential groups called villages (*umushi*, in Bemba language), containing ten to seventy households and organized around matrilineal kin at the core. People maintain a relatively high level of mobility and village sites tend to shift every ten years or so. The lifespan of villages is relatively short as they break up, disappear and reform as new villages in cycles of thirty to fifty years.

For the Bemba, living in the same village means sharing the same space-time. As I mentioned elsewhere, the outline of the Bemba village is drawn by overlapping a series of non-structured "gatherings" formed by the very experience of "being together" in the same space, and another type of "gathering" that creates the experience itself through a more structured process (Sugiyama 2013). The institutionalization of "feelings" is indivisibly linked to these two modes of gatherings.

It is thought to be quite natural for the villagers to be with others constantly, and they go outside to spend time with others as much as possible. They walk around their village many times a day to meet and talk with others. If they haven't seen someone for a few days for some reason, they visit the person's home claiming "I haven't seen you today". The Bemba say that only sorcerers and the very sick prefer to stay at home alone. They have formalized this behavior to create as much space of co-presence as possible and eventually to confirm their mutual affiliations.

Male and female adult villagers gather separately most of the time. Women gather in the front yards of their houses and spend time doing whatever pleases them such as processing food, napping under a tree, looking after children or combing each other's hair. Men bring their chairs and sit in a gazebo or under the eaves, smoking tobacco or sharpening axes. They chatter away continuously while doing so. The topic can be whatever they are seeing at the scene, any events of the day or general gossip. Yet, there is no need for everyone present to join in the discussion or to silently listen to a speaker. They are free to begin a new thread. At this type of gathering, simultaneous speech is frequently observed and people quickly jump from one topic to another.

What is important here is the activity of being and talking with each other itself, and the contents of the talk and the behavior of participants are largely irrelevant to the overall purpose. As people can "naturally sense" (*kuishibikwa*) others' moods at the time, they never try to probe the "inside". Unlike the Inuit who use the exchange of words, as portrayed by Keiichi Omura (2008), the Bemba accept that acting in accordance with the formality of being and talking with people displays the state of "*sansamuka*", which I shall explain next.

Before I became accustomed to the Bemba practice of being and chatting with people, I was repeatedly told by villagers, *Sansamukeni!* (a polite imperative form

The Institution of "Feeling": On "Feeling Inside" and "Institutionalized Envy" 355

Photo 16.1 Married women share snuff while discussing arrangements for a ritual

of the verb *sansamuka*, meaning to be comfortable and happy). "It is not good to sit alone silently. Your friends are here. If you keep sitting alone in silence like that, the wind (*umwela*) builds up in your body and spoils your heart".

What they call the "wind" is also the "voice". It is created from a gathering of the voices of the people present and passes through their bodies every time they speak. The wind thus born and which moves in and out of people's bodies is a good thing, as those who are present feel a sense of joy and keep the village in good condition (*ubusaka*). Conversely, if one remains alone in silence the wind builds up in the body and causes a "lump-in-the-throat (*chikonko pamukoshi*) sickness". They believe that this sickness will lead to an inability to eat and eventual death unless it is treated properly.

These examples suggest that the normal condition for Bemba villagers is the *sansamuka* of the gathered people and an absence of anger and hostility. In other words, what makes non-structured gatherings of "co-presence" possible is mutual feelings of rapport. There is no need to verbalize this feeling; it is considered sufficient to be there and chat with others. The feelings of mutual affinity, pleasure and joy arise from exchanges between those present, waft through the air and are shared without really surfacing to their consciousnesses. It should be noted that all they need in the situation is to just act as above rather than to verbally confirm the sharing of these feelings.

Whereas the appearance of these emotions is inseparable from the situation, sadness (a literal translation is "pain in the heart") is said to develop in the heart of the individual and tend to stagnate there. Borrowing one woman's phrase, "sadness makes people hang their heads, blocking the pathway of the wind". As sadness becomes "solid" if one remains silent, one is encouraged to utter the words "I feel sad" before the situation becomes helpless. It is thought that the sadness can be "shared (*kuakana*) (with others)" if it is verbalized.

Unlike these day-to-day gatherings of close relations, more formal gatherings such as village meetings or ceremonies attended by men require participants to verbalize their "joy" using specific phrases. The most conventional phrase is "I am delighted/have a great joy" (*Ndine nsansa sana*). It is considered that the fact that people are gathering in the normal state of being without anger and hostility, and the declaration of this fact, are politically important.

Whether it is at an everyday gathering or a formal ceremonial gathering, it is believed that emotions related to "anger" and "displeasure" need to be expressed in words. Unlike affinity and joy, the requirement for the verbalization of anger and displeasure places these emotions in a somewhat unnatural position. This leads to the institution of "feeling", which separates and extracts emotions related to anger and displeasure from the situation and exposes them to the eyes of others.

Expressed "anger" and extracted "anger incident"

Close-range expressions of anger

Among various "feelings", emotions linked to "anger" and "displeasure" are thought to be "not sensed unless they are uttered". In particular, "anger" is said to be something that must be verbalized in front of others in a social situation. It is of course unlikely that others really fail to "sense" the anger in an individual. Anyone present would be able to detect from the expression or tone of voice that someone is feeling "anger" or "displeasure" and to perceive a tense atmosphere at the scene. However, villagers act as if the fact that the person is angry does not exist until the person verbalizes that anger and expresses it to the other party in a highly stylized manner.

To express "anger" in a social situation, if the angry person is female, she stands with her feet shoulder-width apart with one hand on her hip, swings the other hand high, points at the concerned party and shouts, "Hey you, I'm angry at you". She then lets her words flow freely in explaining the behaviors of the other party that caused her anger, punctuating her speech with swearwords. If the angry person is male, he generally makes light fists with his elbows slightly bent and proceeds to make a speech in a similar manner.

The party named in the expression of anger responds either by trying to make an excuse for their behavior, smoothing things over or by immediately taking a similar stance to return fire. In either case, villagers in proximity to the parties join in as soon as they hear the initial expression of "anger". They begin loudly telling what they have heard or seen or their views on the conflict based on those facts. The situation plunges into confusion as some endorse a particular party's claim, some try to mediate and others enjoy the show, and eventually things settle down. Those who do not wish to participate depart with an attitude of indifference.

What is peculiar here is the fact that once a party expresses "anger", those present leap to their feet as if it were their own business, but until anger is expressed they pretend as if they were unaware of the tension in the air. Even when they are aware of the conflict, they are not allowed to say "That person is angry" on behalf of the aggrieved party. All they can do is watch the situation nervously. On some occasions, the other villagers present may tell jokes or talk about unrelated topics with the parties concerned in order to relieve the tension, but they never allude to the presence of "anger". This is because "anger" is thought to arise inside the body of an individual and "the party's anger" is considered inseparable from the individual. An unspoken anger is represented as if it were the property of the individual. On the other hand, once verbalized anger can be treated as a visible thing and others at the scene can make their own decision in terms of how to handle it.

Distant expressions of anger

In addition to the expression of anger in proximity, there is a way to express it at a distance called "announcement" (*Mbila*). This pattern, which resembles what Daiji Kimura (1991, 2003) calls "addressee-unspecified loud speech", is usually characterized by the anonymity of the offending party even though the speaker has a particular person in mind. As villagers finish their evening meals and relax around an open fire in the gazebo of their homes into the night, some harboring "anger" begin their "announcement". Just as in the case of expressions of "anger" in proximity, an "anger incident" is explained in the form of "announcement". Below is one case I observed in 1988.

"Announcement" by an elderly man Mr. A in 1988

A: I went to the field to dig up cassavas this morning. To dig up cassavas. I went to dig up cassavas. And I found! I found. One, two, three footprints. One, two, three footprints. Three footprints in all. I followed the footprints and my, my cassavas were gone. My cassavas, my cassavas were gone. My, my cassavas the size of this arm, cassavas the size of my arm were taken from my field. My cassavas were stolen from my field. I am angry.

As this loud "announcement" rang out through the village, villagers in their respective gazebos whispered, "That is Mr. A!", "What is he saying?", and listened carefully.

A (continues): Cassavas the size of my arm were dug up and taken. Cassavas were stolen. The person who took my cassavas, I saw your footprints, your footprints. The person who took my cassavas, you will know my wrath.

Mr. A repeated the entire announcement several times. After listening to him, villagers gossiped about the cassava "thief" and the persistently shouting Mr. A for a while and then continued to talk about something else as if nothing had happened. This type of "announcement" would usually be over in a few minutes, but Mr. A in the above example continued for more than fifteen minutes. When his words became inappropriate, hinting at a curse, elder woman B intervened by making the following announcement addressed to Mr. A from the gazebo of her house.

B: Mr. A, Mr. A.

A: Is it Grandma B? Grandma B, what is it?

B: You say your cassavas were stolen? Cassavas from your field?

A: Yes, cassavas were stolen from my field. (As he was about to continue, B cut in.)

B: We have all heard your announcement. We listened and knew what had happened. We all know what happened. Respectable adults do not make long announcements. (Because) we all heard and understood what had happened. A couple of cassavas are not worth your losing respectability (i.e., it is embarrassing for a respectable adult like you to make a great fuss about a couple of stolen cassavas for such a long time).

A: Oh, oh, I shall shut up. I shut up. My cassavas were stolen. But I shut up now.

Mr. A did not address his announcement to a particular person, and this was the case on all other occasions. However, as the concerned party and other villagers in the know understand what the announcement is about, they immediately begin to gossip about it. Those who know something do not normally respond directly to the "announcement". Instead they visit the aggrieved party at a later date feigning some excuse and indirectly ask for reconciliation. The aggrieved party immediately understands the visitor's intention and usually accepts it without explicitly saying so by acting as if nothing has happened between them.

There are occasions on which someone hears an "announcement" that may be implicitly addressed to them and objects to its claim. The person in question usually shouts back on the spot, announcing "I did it but you have misunderstood". Sometimes other villagers add their opinions and after the exchanging of multiple "announcements", the situation eventually calms down. No resolutions are proposed here. What is important is that each person expresses their thoughts in public through the "announcement". On rare occasions where concurrent announcements continue for a prolonged time, a respected elder woman or the village chief intervenes by way of "announcement" in a timely manner and tries to smooth things over, as in the aforementioned example. Again, the concerned parties are seen around the village working toward reconciliation on the days following the "announcement".

As this example shows, the "announcement" method is used to let people nearby know what is happening rather than to confront the offending party. It is worth noting that "anger" here is spoken as a consequence of the anger-inducing "incident" rather than an expression of the emotion itself. Through the expression of anger in the form of an "announcement", the "anger incident" ceases to be a closed problem between the parties and becomes an issue that offers others in the community the chance to intervene and resolve the conflict socially.

Extracted "anger" and "anger incident"

"Anger" no longer remains inside the individual once it is expressed in words. Those who are present or hear the words are able to treat the story presented as an "anger incident" as if it were a tangible object. When "anger" is thus expressed and extracted as an "anger incident" accompanying the context in which it arose, the parties involved are identified and cut out from everyday space-time. Moreover, by expressing "anger" in words, people holding "anger" inside can draw it out into a social space and commit the handling of it to other villagers. In other words, to express one's anger before villagers who are not directly involved is to invite them to become involved in order to resolve the situation.

Before I learnt "how to show anger" at a Bemba village, one elder woman lectured me as follows.

> Anger cannot be understood unless expressed in words. Why do you always leave without saying anything? Anger will build up in your stomach if you keep doing that. Where will you let it out? When you are angered, you must express anger to the other person. Other people will hear it. They will know that anger is there. Your friends will grab it with their own hands (meaning they will deal with it in their own ways).

According to this woman, once "anger" is expressed in public, it is as good as resolved because those around you will help resolve it. She stresses the importance of letting others get involved.

Thus, although an emotion related to "anger" held by an individual is immediately detected by those who are present, it is treated as "non-existent" until the party expresses it in a specific manner. As soon as it is expressed in words, however, the involvement of other people determines how it is going to be dealt with. Other villagers generally take stances that are expected of their respective positions and statuses. As the patterns of response are limited by the relationships between the parties and individual villagers to a certain extent, the way people respond to the expressed "anger incident" ("anger" story) tends to highlight subgroups who share similar views and positions.

This subgrouping reflects social relations based on kinship or closeness in daily life and represents an institutional practice in itself. However, individuals have the discretion to choose who they align themselves with from the available options.

The recognition of "emotion inside" as socialized feeling through verbal expression gives rise to the existence of unspoken "hidden emotions inside". The aforementioned elder woman commented further.

> If you do not say that you are angry, anger will accumulate in your stomach. Who listens to the pent-up anger? Nobody. You must not talk to yourself when angry. Anger

will spill out and turn into something evil [witchcraft]. That is why you must speak out loud with your hand here [at the hip] in front of people. Say I am angry at you.

As I said earlier, expressing anger at a social situation is a declaration of one's intention to resolve the situation and taken as an invitation for others to participate in the search for resolution.

On the other hand, unspoken anger that is buried in the closed context between parties is believed to be at risk of turning into witchcraft (*buloshi*). When anger is clearly detected by others present but goes without being expressed verbally, people feel a disturbing atmosphere, but all they can do is exit with a vague sense of uneasiness as there is nothing they can do about it. If such incidents accumulate, the level of anxiety escalates. It creates a fear almost akin to the conviction that a future calamity has been prophesized. This will increase tension among people and create a menacing atmosphere in which people begin to suspect witchcraft has been used every time they encounter minor trouble.

"Envy" as a "hidden feeling"

Revelation of trouble by the presumption of "envy"

As reported in many ethnographic accounts, the Bemba view a spate of illnesses or disasters as the result of someone's envy or anger (Richards 1950; Kakeya 1987; Sugiyama 2004). In Bemba villages, both unspoken "anger" and "envy" are thought to trigger an act of witchcraft. As mentioned above, anger-related emotions become the "feeling" of anger through self-awareness and verbal expression, which is exposed to the eyes of the public as a story embedded in a situation for which a path for resolution can be found. "Envy", however, differs from "anger" in character. According to villagers, "anger" wells up in the moment (and is hence inseparable from the situation), whereas "envy" is thought to "reside in the heart" (*kuikala mu mutima*) of the person from the outset. It is possible to say that envy is presumed to be a "feeling" that always exists inside every person. Therefore it is theoretically possible that any Bemba villager can be the originator of misfortunes triggered by "envy".

Unlike "anger", "envy" is never declared by the party because it is equivalent to declaring that one has used witchcraft to bring misfortunes and calamities to others. Envy is revealed through divination by a medicine man or channeling ancestral spirits rather than through the person's admission (who is thought to harbor envy). What is significant here is that the presence of "envy" is exposed by others with special skills and not by the person holding such an emotion. The person's "inside", that is, the kind of emotion and the object of the emotion that the person has, comes under the scrutiny of others. Healing rituals performed in the process include those to soothe such feelings inside the person (*kunasha*), in addition to healing any symptoms.

Besides divination performed for etiological diagnosis after the occurrence of problems such as illnesses and calamities, there are other methods to bring the presence of unspoken "envy" to the surface before it causes a serious problem. The most substantial among them is the "ritual to please ancestral spirits" practiced in conjunction with the thanksgiving festival for the ancestral spirits of the village held after the annual harvesting of finger millet crops. At this ritual, a dozen or so spirit mediums gather at the house of the village chief and invite ancestral spirits to possess their bodies. Villagers sing and dance with these spirits in the bodies of the mediums and listen to their words. All sorts of "envy" and suppressed seeds of trouble hidden inside the village are revealed through the mouths of the mediums spoken as the words of the ancestral spirits.

Another opportunity for ancestral spirits to speak through a medium's mouth is the "*ngulu*" (mediums') gathering that is held irregularly for entertainment purposes where hidden "envy" is at times revealed. However, the word "envy" is carefully avoided and replaced with the word "trouble" at that time. The use of the word "envy" is limited to very serious occasions where a charge of sorcery is brought against someone in a public forum.

Once hidden "envy" or a seed of trouble is revealed during these rituals or gatherings, a countermeasure is promptly taken. The person named or insinuated by an ancestral spirit or their close friend or relative comes forward, places a small amount of cash or white beads in front of the spirit (the medium in reality), and chants as follows while beating the ground with a leafy twig: "Although I have no idea if I've done anything wrong, I must have done something wrong if you (ancestral spirit) say so. I apologize. I apologize. Our trouble has been expelled". After that, the chief who presides over the ritual declares that "the trouble has been cleared away". The villager and the ancestral spirit concerned share a drink and dance to a song before the ritual winds down.

In net-hunting involving the entire village, the success or failure of a hunt itself or the sex of their prey is said to be a message from their ancestral spirit. If there is a diviner among the hunting party, he performs divination between hunts to reveal hidden "envy" or conflicts "that have aroused the displeasure of the ancestral spirit". If present the named villager, or their close kin if absent, steps forward before folded hunting nets and chants while beating the nets with a twig: "I have

The Institution of "Feeling": On "Feeling Inside" and "Institutionalized Envy"

Photo 16.2 Male villagers on their way to a net-hunting location

no idea but I apologize if you say I'm at fault. I apologize. I apologize. Please clear the trouble away". If the presence of trouble has been revealed but no one has been named, the owner of the nets apologizes while beating them with a twig. In either case, the leader of the hunting party then chants while beating the nets with a twig: "The trouble is already as cool and clean as water. Please give us prey". They then depart for the next location to set up their nets.

The trouble revealed at the scene of net-hunting becomes a ready topic for discussion among villagers at dinner-time. Especially when the villagers involved are not named, people speculate as to their identities with enthusiasm. Even those who are suspected to be involved participate in such discussion and state their views publically.

The assumption that every villager has envy inside them means that the expression of various seeds of discord can happen anywhere and involve any of the villagers. Because even a seemingly generous and gentle person harbors envy inside just as everyone else does, trouble can be triggered by envy regardless of the individual's personality or intention. The presumption of envy provides a formula for the perception and expression of "relationship problems" that is applicable to anyone, anytime.

When an envy-related issue is revealed, people make an effort to resolve the problem through medicines or rituals before it manifests as an intractable illness or disaster. What is notable here is that it is experts such as medicine men or spiritual mediums who have the ability to bring envy-related trouble to the surface and into a social forum. Therefore envy has to be brought to the public eye as a problem and dealt with by experts with special skills regardless of the will of the person who harbors it.

At the same time, this identifies a causal link among a particular cluster of incidents and separates it from other incidents. In this context, minor illnesses, injuries and misfortunes can be "expressions" of "envy" and "signs" of uncontrollable witchcraft. People ask medicine men and mediums to manipulate the circuit by which envy invokes sorcery in an attempt to deal with the trouble before a major calamity befalls them. In other words, a misfortune experienced by people in the "here and now" needs to be dealt with in two phases: 1) it is a problem that requires some sort of resolution in itself, and 2) it is a problem that needs to be dealt with as an "expression" of past envy or a "sign" of a future case of witchcraft. In relation to an illness or misfortune currently experienced by villagers, the presence of "envy" experienced by others in the past and "emotions inside" are scrutinized, and the presence of the supernatural forces that invoke an act of witchcraft from envy and a transcendental third party possessing these forces such as gods and spirits are presupposed. It is possible to say that the presupposition of the linkage between "envy" as a feeling preexisting inside a person and supernatural forces creates a separate world existing in another phase at the same time, with the illness or misfortune experienced by people in the "here and now". This forms the foundation of "institutionalized envy".

Witchcraft as an indication of "closeness of kinship"

The "story of a case of witchcraft" that focuses on the "preexisting emotion inside" called "envy" and links it to an existing illness or calamity identifies the "origin" of the misfortune. It also entails selecting specific matters among countless problems in daily village life and identifying the "parties" involved. As it is considered that the "closer" the social distance between people, the stronger the harbored envy and resentment as well as the interacting supernatural forces are, it is usually socially close people who surface as the parties to a "case of witchcraft".

As I mentioned elsewhere, serious "witchcraft cases" at Bemba villages often occur at times of generational change (Sugiyama 2004). In many cases, the village chief and others belonging to the older generation are accused of sorcery, leading to the fission and demise of the village. However, when the divided village is to be reformed or a new village is to be founded, the incoming village chief must learn proper ways to deal with ancestral spirits from the previous chief or someone else in order to gain spiritual forces to protect his villagers from sorcerers. At this time, people resume relations with the previous generation they had been in conflict with, and update the "witchcraft case" that precipitated the disintegration of the previous chief's village.

I now discuss the case of N village that I was told about in an interview. The original version of the story about a "case of witchcraft" began with the "unspoken anger" held by the daughter of the previous chief and his "envy" toward a nephew, which were associated with a villager's serious illness and resulted in an accusation of witchcraft against the chief. An updated story told by the nephew and others several years later began with the "envy" felt by the wife of the seriously ill villager and referred to its connection with a series of misfortunes that continued after the dissolution of the village. Also included was a reference to an unexplained skin disease suffered by the nephew (the chief of the new village) after the expulsion of the former chief and a hint at the influence of the former chief's "anger".

At Bemba villages, it was said that if anger remained unspoken between kin in certain close relationships such as maternal uncle and nephew or paternal aunt and niece, such anger would interact with the forces of ancestral spirits to bring misfortune to the object of anger, even when witchcraft is invoked unintentionally. In other words, the updated "witchcraft case" contained an implicit acknowledgement of error in condemning the previous chief and a recognition of the closeness of the relationship between the previous chief and the new chief to the extent that the former's "unspoken anger" strongly affected the latter, his nephew.

This form of reworking a "witchcraft case" that is intended to show the closeness of a relationship can be observed in other cases. Figure 16.1 shows the relationships that appear in a "witchcraft case" told by a male retiree who returned to his village after working as a salaried employee in the capital for many years.

Informant C resigned from his job after earning a salary in the capital for many years and returned to his village with his family as a candidate for the next

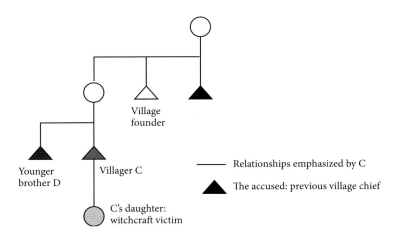

Figure 16.1 A man (Villager C) retelling the story of a witchcraft case

village chief. C's daughter suffered from a mental illness, which he attributed to witchcraft invoked by the previous chief when he and his family last lived in the village. According to the story he told people, the previous chief resented his young and bright nephew (C) who was supposed to be the next chief and brought harm to his daughter as a result.

In this story, the reference to the "case of witchcraft" caused by the previous chief that befell C's daughter actually emphasizes the "close" relationship between the previous chief and C. Moreover, this "witchcraft case" was told with the clarification that "younger brother D was not subjected to the witchcraft of the previous chief", as if C was lamenting his ill fortune in comparison with his younger brother D. One reason for this storyline was his need to show and assure other villagers that he had a legitimate reason to be part of the village after two decades of absence. It also served his political purpose to put a check on D, his rival candidate for village chief, and to emphasize that he was the legitimate successor based on his abilities and status.

As illustrated by these examples, the "witchcraft case" and the "envy" held by others that is considered to have triggered it are told in a place separated from the party's emotional experience and in some cases combined with another context in order to show "closeness" between characters in the story.

In this way, the Bemba have made it possible to extract emotions related to "anger" and to separate particular people and contexts as "anger incidents" from personal experience by assuming the presence of "feelings inside". Further, it is possible to say that by assuming that everyone harbors "envy" and using a device to turn the "feeling" of "envy" into a social affair through divination, they have constructed an institution to manipulate social relationships in a phase separated from the party's experience.

"Feeling inside" and the maneuverability of social relationships

I have discussed so far that by presupposing the presence of feelings "inside", emotions verging on anger in particular are treated as something that must be expressed in words and brought to a social forum as a "feeling". At the same time, the "expression of anger" gives rise to the existence of "unspoken hidden anger". It extracts the "anger" from its field of origin as a single "feeling" so that it can continue to exist away from that field.

The Bemba are not the only people who extract "anger" from the field in which it has arisen and bring it to a kind of social field. The agriculturalist Taita of Kenya practice a ritual to "cast out anger" (Harris 2007), and the pastoralist Turkana also bring out "anger" and reframe an "anger incident" in a certain context.

According to Shinsuke Sakumichi (2004), "anger" experienced by the Turkana is an emotion that arises when violation occurs between an individual and closely-related others in terms of the "cooperation principle" stipulating that "people must cooperate with each other". It is also an emotion that is constructed in the social process of divination and healing, which people perform in the face of crises such as illnesses or calamities in order to identify their cause. What is happening here is institutionalization in which a particular emotional experience is extracted and incorporated into a meaning system linked with other incidents such as illnesses and calamities. Coupled with the implication that the "anger" of others is the cause of illness and calamity, this system promotes behavior that conforms to a kind of norm to take care "not to anger others" in day-to-day affairs (Sakumichi 2004).

It would be safe to say that the Bemba's "unspoken hidden anger" corresponds to the above. I should note that the Turkana also consider that "bad words stay in the stomach", and hence anger opens the doors connecting the past, present and future beyond the "here and now". It can be said that one aspect of the institutionalized feeling is that the extraction of past emotional experiences of anger and the linking of the angry party with concerned parties function as a way to "deal with" illnesses and calamities as well as offer the opportunity to repair their relationships.

To the Bemba, an expression of anger has another function. Extracting anger from the original context through the expression of anger constitutes a declaration that "There is a (social) problem". The presentation of the story as an "anger incident" enables them to identify the "parties" who must get involved and deal with the problem from those present and allow others to intervene and negotiate a resolution. However, this is merely problem solving *after* the fact. It does not open the possibility of maneuvering in advance in order to prevent such an incident from occurring. To prevent an "anger incident" from occurring, people have no option other than to take care "not to anger others", as the Turkana people do.

The way the Bemba take action in advance against undesirable incidents is to assume the presence of "envy" inside every person. By presuming that there is a "feeling inside" or "envy inside", they reinterpret a face-to-face conflict between two parties as something malleable through the intervention of others in dealing with the "feeling inside" or "envy inside" rather than as a voluntary resolution by negotiations between the parties. The situation can be controlled by others through preventative measures against "envy inside" that leads to illnesses or calamities as well as management and manipulation of the circuit by which envy motivates sorcery and develops into witchcraft.

The presupposition that "envy" leads to witchcraft shifts a calamity in the "here and now" to a separate phase as an expression of envy or a sign of witchcraft. In terms of adjustment to a social relationship between two parties, it is best to deal with a "cause" by stopping "envy" from surfacing rather than via direct negotiations between the parties. As "envy" exists inside every person, the countermeasure against it is applicable to the entire population. By presuming that envy is swirling inside all villagers, they redefine their mutual "relationship" as something that can be controlled in advance through some legitimate means, whereas parties in a relationship are normally supposed to adjust their behavior according to the situation.

The Bemba institution of "feeling" creates the possibility of viewing reality from a different perspective by shifting a phenomenon experienced by people in the "here and now" to another world. It reminds people that the individual's emotional experience always has another phase attached to it. It also lays the groundwork for accepting the existence of experts and authorities who have the ability to control "envy" in that phase.

Another aspect of the institution of feeling can be seen in the function of creating the starting point for cohesion. When people wish to establish a new village and live together, they deliberately try to talk about a previous "case of witchcraft" or the "anger incident" triggered by the revelation of witchcraft. However, they do not tell the original story. As they believe that the strong forces of "envy" manifest as witchcraft between genealogically close relatives and close friends, they retell the story making small modifications to the past "envy story" or "anger incident". In doing so, they measure up their kinship relations and social distances and confirm that they are fellow members of a community tied in "a relationship close enough to have experienced witchcraft in the past" and wish to live together once again.

Two forms of "here and now" disengagement

As we have seen so far, the institutionalization of feeling in the Bemba is comprised of distinct aspects related to everyday gatherings, the expression of "anger" and "internal envy". This institutionalization process has two forms.

One form is preceded by "action" at the place of co-presence, or "being with each other", which occurs prominently at everyday non-structured gatherings. What is seen here is a form of institutionalization—separation from the "here and now" through the formalization of behaviors. The other party's action of trying to be together as much as possible is recognized as an intention to maintain a non-hostile, affiliative relationship with the other party and orients both parties' behavior toward affiliation. The repetition of the action formalizes it as a routine, and the formality in turn determines the next action.

Feelings arising here include pleasure and affinity that are incidental to the affiliative form of actions, jointly generated by those present and shared almost subconsciously. They exist as joy embedded in the act of being together in itself, as in the case of the Inuit discussed by Omura (2008). Omura also reports in Chapter Fifteen that the desire for co-presence is reinforced by the dynamics between self-awareness and other-awareness and at the same time stably maintained by "inculcation" through various interactions including the disciplining of children.

This form of feeling is effective in creating deep bonds among members based on reciprocal empathy. However, it is only possible in small groups where members maintain face-to-face relationships. To form larger groups, institutionalization using a different principle needs to be introduced.

This leads us to the other form of institutionalization process—a more institution-like process by which various emotions are presupposed as "inside" the individual separated from the "here and now" field in which experience is created rather than viewing them as inseparable from it. The Bemba are able to separate "feelings" from the context in which an "incident" arises by assuming that various emotions are feelings "inside" them. The assumption that "feelings" as emotions are "inside" can be regarded as an "institution" that requires people to deal with one experience at two different levels. This institution contains two assumptions: an expression of "anger" and the presence of envy inside every person.

In the expression of "anger", the involved party's emotions are sensed by those present and the emotional experience is shared, then an "anger incident" is expressed in the party's own words so that an "anger story" is extracted as if it were a thing. The extracted emotional experience is dealt with as a thing called the story of social "feeling" to which others are able to link their respective stories in order to share the "anger story". As a result, once "anger" is expressed in public, the problem tends to be resolved as villagers other than the parties attempt to deal with the "anger" in their own ways. One does not have to be truly "angry". What is important here is to make one's anger part of social experience by vocally expressing it.

On the other hand, "internal envy" is a "feeling" that is invisible to ordinary villagers, who are unable to identify it, although they may sense it. With the presumption that "envy" is commonly present "inside" every person, this "feeling" is equipped with an institutional device to enable it to be treated as a thing separate from the emotions of the individual as well as to manipulate the social relationships incidental to it. It is also linked to a mechanism to create a narrative about the state of the world by which envy is separated from the meaning of the field on which it arose and readily combined with a totally distinct context such as an illness or calamity.

Only experts with particular divination skills can identify the time and place of the "origin of a calamity" and whose "envy" is involved in it. People can talk about a "case of witchcraft" only on the basis of the results of divination. The need to manipulate "envy" in a phase separated from the "here and now" and the circuitry for its manifestation, together with the acceptance of the existence of experts and authorities with the ability to do so, open up a path to institutionalization for the purpose of further integration.

Viewed in this light, it can be said that the institution of feeling not only deals with conflicts within groups but also generates resources for the creation of new groups through the formation of the new cohesiveness it facilitates.

17 Was the Old Woman's Death a Suicide? A Discussion on the Basis of Institutions

Ryoko Nishii

Key ideas

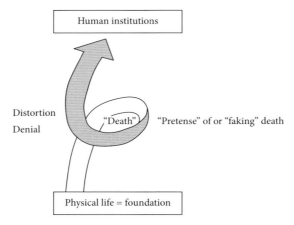

You may consider the basis of human institutions as a "pretense" or denial of specifically human life (or death) in the context of relations with others, or rituals characterized by purposelessness. Both these approaches attribute the emergence of human institutions to the distortion or denial of physical existence, or life, which is essentially the primary element of human institutions. This explanation is relevant only to human beings who are intrinsically contradictory creatures, and solving this paradox paves the way for understanding our sociality.

Various approaches toward death and institutions

I was told that the old woman had committed suicide, but as I conducted my own investigation in the village, the cause of death became increasingly questionable.

In Chapter Two, Motomitsu Uchibori explores the boundary between institutional and pre-institutional environments by examining "death" in the context of institution. In his discussion, he looks at "death" itself as an institution, as distinct from the process of physically "dying". The suicide that I discuss in this chapter is also a "death" per se. In this chapter, however, I take a different approach and look at the development of institutions by drawing on the dichotomy of "death" and the "pretense of death", a notion put forward by Hitoshi Imamura (2007).

Imamura sees suicide as a behavior that establishes the uniqueness of human beings in regards to other animals. "Being a human is an act of self-denial itself. Humans become specifically human beings only after 'killing' our animality, which is essentially what makes us physically alive" (Imamura 2007: 160). He points out, therefore, that our existence as living beings is intrinsically contradictory.

> On the one hand, in order for humans to develop from direct external awareness to (or generate) self-consciousness, we must provide evidence that we are able to commit suicide; however, on the other hand, for humans to continue living in this world as self-conscious beings, we must not die. Humans should die to be humans; yet at the same time, we cannot die, and we should not die. (Imamura 2007: 212)

Imamura uses this paradox to elucidate the relationship between death and institutions.

The interactions with some of the villagers over the "suicide" of the old woman addressed in this chapter are perfect examples of Imamura's paradox—the relationship between the idea that "humans should die to be humans" and "humans cannot die, and humans should not die". As such, I believe that, by uncovering the impacts her death had on the villagers—their concerns and commonality of experience—I will be able to identify the basis of institutions, and in turn, the basis of human cohesion.

The death of an old woman

When I was conducting fieldwork in 2011[1], Na Chua, my hostess every time I visit the village, said to me "Yai[2] Chit killed herself". Why did she commit suicide? The question lingered in my mind for a long time even after returning to Japan. She lived on the same land as her daughter though in a separate house. She had lost her much-adored youngest son, but it was unlikely to have been the direct cause of her suicide since he had passed away over a decade ago. This is why I decided to investigate the reasons behind her suicide and include it in the research objectives of my 2012 fieldwork.

I first provide a brief personal background of Yai Chit and then try to piece together the facts surrounding her death from the villagers' narratives. My aim is to identify, from such narratives, the key talking points that emerged in response to the old woman's death in this rural village in Southern Thailand.

The life of Yai Chit

I remember Yai Chit as a strong and hearty woman, who always stood straight and tall. Na Chua agrees.

> She had a straight back. Her back was as straight as a ruler. She was healthy. She sometimes complained of some aches or pain in her legs, but those were minor issues. She had strong bones. Her body (*tua*) was straight. She was in a much better condition than me.

Na Chua has difficulty walking because of her hunched back and bad knees.

Yai Chit lived alone in a house built just behind her daughter's. She cooked a single serving of rice every day on a charcoal fire. She did not use liquefied petroleum gas, which was now available in just about every home. Her daughter Win had converted to Islam to follow her husband, but the religious difference was not the likely reason behind their separate residences, because Win is not committed to either Islam or Buddhism in terms of her lifestyle. She has been living on her own since her divorce several years ago, and neither does she offer prayer nor visit mosques. Yai Chit was eighty-six years old at the time of her death.

Yai Chit married a police officer from Samut Songkhram in Central Thailand, and they had five children. Her husband was employed as a motor vehicle registrar in Satun City, but left his job over an incident, supposedly involving some form of corruption. After his resignation, the couple moved to Yai Chit's hometown village where she earned their living by selling *khnom cin* (thin noodles served with spicy coconut milk-based sauce, usually consumed as a light meal or snack). Her husband helped her run their store.

Yai Chit had been beautiful in her youth. She had enjoyed dressing up since she was a child. The story goes that even at primary school she would throw a tantrum if she did not like the clothes she was made to wear. Her husband was a very jealous man. When he went on police duty, he would lock her inside the house to keep her away from the eyes of other men. He was afraid that other men would make advances to her. Na Chua has a photo of Yai Chit. Dressed in a skirt, while village women usually wear Thai style waistcloths, she looks beautiful even though the picture was taken after she had had five children. Her husband continued to be insecure, even after they became old and moved to the village. He got jealous every time she went out on the street selling *khnom cin*. He kept all the revenue and did not allow Yai Chit to spend money. She would have been beaten almost to death if she had done anything without his permission. Having said that, he did help her make *khnom cin*. He skillfully sliced noodles and kept the store clean. He was also a good cook. However, he had an anxious disposition, and village life must have been difficult for him. People say he was always drinking alcohol.

He died about thirty-five years ago as a result of hemorrhage after gashing his leg open with an ax while chopping wood. There was no hospital nearby at that time and the only transportation out of the village was by boat. They had to travel over half a day to get to the town of Trang. It was too late by the time they arrived at the hospital.

When her youngest son Iat got married and moved to Rayong in Central Thailand to help his wife's family's transportation business, Yai Chit followed him to look after their child. However, Yai Chit ended up returning to the village after Iat passed away in an accident while driving a dump truck. Since then, Yai Chit had settled permanently in the village. It may be worth mentioning that this is when she apparently stopped speaking the Southern Thai dialect spoken in the village and started speaking with the Central Thai intonation. Although being from Southern Thailand, Yai Chit somehow spoke Central Thai until she died.

The "suicide"
Discovery of the body
Let me trace Yai Chit's movements on the day of her death, based on the villagers' statements.

That day, Yai Chit left her home in the morning. She sneaked out of the house to avoid being noticed by her daughter Win, who was in her own house next door at the time.

Win was watching TV and did not notice that Yai Chit was missing until the afternoon. Win recalls as follows:

> I went to look for her because it was lunch-time and she was not home. She would often go wandering about. I was thinking she had gone wandering about again and she would be back before very long. But I went to look for her because it was past lunch-time. Oldies like to collect bottles. They collect plastic bottles and sell them.

Their village is located on a coastline and all sorts of things get washed up on the shore. Old people walk along the shore and collect cans and bottles, earning them a small amount of pocket money.

At around four in the afternoon, Win told Yai Chit's three grandchildren (Bat, Rai and Chat) to look for her. The three spread out and searched for their grandmother. It was Bat who found her. He describes the situation as follows.

> My mother (Win) came to get me at about four in the evening after my grandmother had been missing for a day. We three went off in different directions to look for her. I found her. I called Rai [and told him] to carry her. We were joined by Chat and carried her home together.
>
> I was scooping out water from a boat in the river [when my mother came to get me]. Rai came and asked me to look for our grandmother. He told me that she had gone missing and that she was on foot. I found her footprints. There was a set of footprints at the back of the house. The footprints seemed to have been made with bare feet. These must have been hers. She must have gone in that direction. I was right. I found her lying on the ground. She was lying face down. She was wearing clothes, but not a wrap skirt (*phathung*). She was wearing a "pampers" (referring to an adult diaper). I shouted, "Rai, Chat, I found her. We will take her home. Help me carry her". She was dead. She was not breathing. Rai and Chat carried her home.

When she was discovered, the tide was low and the water had ebbed away. Yai Chit must have entered the water at high tide and died. Her wrap skirt had probably come off and been swept away while her body was floating around, exposing the diaper. The following is Bat's account of the situation:

> Her body was still flexible. It had not yet become stiff. The sun was blazing down on the body. She died at around twelve during a high tide. We went to look for her after the tide had gone out.

Bat recalls that she was wearing a whitish shirt. They did find the wrap skirt later, but they were too overwhelmed to look for it at the time and instead carried the body straight to his mother's place.

When the body was found, Uda and her fellow Muslim women who lived in the neighborhood were collecting Chinese water spinach (*phak bun*) just behind Yai Chit's next-door neighbor's house and saw Rai and his siblings carrying Yai Chit. Uda says it was around five o'clock.

> Yai Chit died around noon, but she was not found until later. She disappeared around noon, but it was after the tide had ebbed [that she was found]. Chat, Rai and Bat went to look for her. She was lying flat. It was low tide. She collapsed in a dizzy spell and died (*pen lom tai*).

Uda repeatedly said, "She was in the water. She collapsed in a dizzy spell".

Many people gathered at Win's house when the body was brought home. The body was cleaned and dressed in new clothes and subsequently taken to the temple in the cave of Khao Thanan (Thanan Rock) in the village.

Funeral

Yai Chit was a Buddhist. Therefore, her funeral was held in the temple in Khao Thanan. Yai Chit's daughter Win did not cite the difference in religion as the reason for holding the funeral at the temple rather than at her home; she said it was simply because her house was too small. A Buddhist funeral could last from three days to as long as two weeks in some cases. The longer the event, the greater the burden placed on family members of the deceased, because they have to engage monks to recite scripture and also provide meals for them and villagers who attend the rituals each day. Having said that, the longer the funeral, the more condolence money[3], which can offset costs incurred and might even turn some profit.[4] Yai Chit's funeral was a small service, held over the shortest possible timeframe of three days.

The fact that Win was a Muslim may have, I suspect, despite her claims, influenced the decision to hold the funeral at the temple, even though she was not necessarily devout. Uda and other Muslim women who lived in the neighborhood participated in food preparation behind the temple, but never entered the temple during the funeral. Win, who was the host of the funeral, did sit inside the temple for scripture reading, but without joining her palms together in the Buddhist custom. Bat is Win's son, hence a Muslim, whereas Rai and Chat are the children of Win's older brother and are Buddhists.

The following is Uda's explanation:

> The funeral was held at the temple of Rock (Khao Thanan). We helped by preparing food, but we cannot pray there. We know Win so we helped her prepare food. Her husband is a Muslim. Our children also helped her because we are all family. But we do not get involved in what goes on inside [the temple]. We try to do what we can outside.

Some villagers recall that Na Li, a Buddhist and a distant relative of Yai Chit, said that Yai Chit "finally obtained her desire" because she always said she wanted to die. When Na Li arrived at the temple, Yai Chit's body had been cleaned and dressed. A crowd of villagers had gone to the site where Yai Chit died. Uda says they did so out of curiosity.

Meanwhile, Na Chua, who was a close friend of Yai Chit, did not attend her funeral. Na Chua says she had told Yai Chit the following when she was alive:

> "I would not come [to your funeral] if you, aunt Chit, kill yourself". And when she died, I kept my word and did not go to her funeral. Truth be told, I could not go. My back was hurting. People say if you get a backache when a person dies, that means you should not go. It is not good for it. A funeral will make the pain worse. That is what many people say.

Na Chua did not attend the funeral herself, but sent some money for condolence.

Narratives on the time and place of death

The time of death: The Tenth Month Festival

Many years earlier a monk had predicted that Yai Chit would die during the Tenth Month Festival. A Buddhist woman called Myao told me this at the funeral. The Tenth Month Festival is the most important festival in the year for Buddhists in Southern Thailand. The celebration occurs twice a year, on the first and fifteenth day of October in the Thai lunar calendar (September in the solar calendar), with the second celebration being larger in scale. On these occasions, villagers prepare a variety of snacks to take to the temple. Yai Chit died on the day before the first day of the festival, when Buddhist families were busy preparing snacks. Her body was brought into the temple on the day before the festival for the funeral. A significant number of Buddhists gathered at the temple to attend the funeral and also to participate in the festival. The following is Win's account of the events at the temple:

She died in the evening. We all gathered at the temple to make merit[5] the next morning. We celebrated the Tenth Month Festival and then continued the funeral. Then, we carried out the coffin [after three days]. And that was it.

Yai Chit's funeral reminded villagers of another death that had occurred a decade ago, which also involved the Tenth Month Festival. This was the death of Chai, who was killed by the husband of the women with whom he had an adulterous relationship.

The following is Win's account of the incident:

It was exactly like when Chai died. Chuap (Chai's wife) was shredding coconuts to make *tom* (a sweet made from banana and glutinous rice). She was waiting for Chai, who was unusually late coming home. It turned out he was dead.

Na Chua's younger sister's granddaughter Khae, who was with Win when I interviewed her, elaborated further:

I was at [Na Chua's] home [at the time of Chai's death]. I went [to the beach] to do my business or something and saw a dead person lying on the ground. He was lying face down. His throat had been slit.

After hearing that, Win said, "Her death is very similar to Chai's death".

The place of death: History of suicide at the site
The place where Yai Chit died was also reminiscent of another death. A suicide by hanging had taken place at the back of the house where Yai Chit's body was found. I was told it is a place people tend to avoid, except when, very occasionally, some walk past it to set up fish or crab traps.

Uda says that people stay away from the area because it is the site of a violent death.

Jep's child died after hanging himself there. He died around the same time as when my grandmother died. It was almost a decade ago. His body was covered with maggots because it went undiscovered for several days. It was Win who found the body. She found him when she went to do her business. Jep's son was found on higher ground. Yai Chit died in the river. People have been kept away from the area, otherwise they would be haunted by the spirit of violent death (*phi taihon*). I only saw her body as it was carried in the village, too.

I wanted to go to the site where Yai Chit died, but Win seemed hesitant. The site was covered in thick, almost impenetrable bush. Intimidated by a wild dog with a puppy barking and growling at me, I eventually gave up the attempt.

An old woman's death reminded the villagers of other deaths that had occurred in the village, linked by time and place.

Was the old woman's death a suicide?

Upon hearing that Yai Chit had committed suicide, my initial plan was to investigate the cause. However, as I interviewed villagers, it became clear that the focus of the work needed to be on verifying the credibility of the alleged fact that the death was a suicide itself, rather than trying to determine the cause of the suicide. To explain the reasons behind this, I will examine narratives from the following two perspectives: 1) that Yai Chit's death was a suicide, and 2) that it was not.

Yai Chit's death as suicide

After arriving in the village, I first asked Na Chua, who was close to Yai Chit, about the reason for her death. Na Chua's mother is Yai Chit's cousin, and she is therefore a distant relative. Yai Chit often visited her to have a chat, travelling a kilometer or so on foot. Her explanation was more or less in line with my expectation, which was that Yai Chit had died of despair, as her daughter Win was not willing to look after her. She had absolutely no doubt that her death was suicide. The following is an extract of a conversation I had with Na Chua and her sister's grandchild Pla:

> **Ryoko**: Did Yai Chit voluntarily enter the water?
> **Na Chua**: She did. She did that to die. She walked into the water and drowned herself. She entered the river on purpose.
> **Ryoko**: Why?
> **Na Chua**: I do not know. She must have been angry with her children and grandchildren. She did not want to be here [in this world] (*mai yak yu*). Life was a hassle for her. Her children did not look after her well. She was alone.
> **Pla**: They did not look after her well despite living close by. She was disappointed. They did not even cook for her.

Other villagers told me the same story. "Frankly speaking, she wanted to die. She always wanted to die. She barely did anything all day". "She wanted to die. Na Li also said so. Na Li said that it must have been a wish come true (*som cai*) when she was finally able to die. That is what she wanted".

One villager who lived close to Yai Chit even went as far as to comment that "some people say that Win caused her to die", but continued in a lowered voice, "though you should not tell this to anyone". According to this person, Yai Chit had made two previous suicide attempts.

On the first attempt, she took pills and almost died but recovered at the hospital. On the second attempt, she tried to hang herself at home, but was found by her grandchild. On the third attempt, she entered the water and finally died.

This information, that Yai Chit attempted suicide three times, was new even to Na Chua.

Yai Chit's death as an accident

After talking to Na Chua, I visited Phen, an elementary school teacher, to confirm what she had heard to be the reason behind Yai Chit's suicide. Teacher Phen's response was completely unexpected. She suggested that Yai Chit's death was not suicide, but simply an accident that occurred to a wandering aged person. Teacher Phen lives with her husband's mother who was ninety years old.

> She is just like my mother-in-law. She talks in her room as if someone is talking to her. "You are here already. Give me a few minutes. I will get ready now. So is it today that we are leaving?" Like this. Perhaps she thinks someone came to ask her to go somewhere with them. Perhaps. I do not know for sure, but I assume so (*sannitthan*). I would imagine so.
>
> People say it was a suicide, but I will tell you my theory. I have been living with my mother-in-law, who is ninety years old. She does not want to bathe or go out of her room to eat. She sometimes speaks in bed as if someone has come to talk to her. That back door, I have to lock it when she is alone. She tried to go down the ladder into the river the other day [Phen's house is situated by the river]. If we had not found her, she would have fallen into the river. She does things like this. We were caught off guard. That's why Kim [Phen's husband] started to lock that door. When we found her, she was already half way down the ladder. Kim ran to get her. It seemed as if she was being guided by someone. I assume Yai Chit was in a similar state as her. My mother-in-law has been like this since last year. She says that she is getting ready to leave. She says she is leaving soon, to her real home over on the other side. I asked her who she would

be with on the other side and she said she would be with her husband, meaning Kim's father [He died several decades ago]. I assume Yai Chit was just like my mother-in-law. People might say it was a suicide, but look at the similarities. They do not want to live (*mai yak yu lae*). They want to die, but dying is not easy. This is what old people are like (*nisai khon kae*) … Old people are all very similar. It may look like a suicide, but perhaps she was guided by someone. Perhaps someone asked her to be together, and told her that now was the time to leave. They only have fuzzy memories.

Yai Chit was commonly regarded as being "half-conscious" or "delirious" among those who were not very close to her. "She was old. Old people have a short memory and often fall down. She must have stumbled [into the water] in a daze". This was actually a perception shared by most of the villagers.

As a matter of fact, Yai Chit's relatives who were directly involved in the matter have also come to the view that it was not a suicide, but an unintended death that occurred while she was wandering around.

The following is a quote from Yai Chit's daughter Win:

She fell down and became bed-ridden for a few months. She was unable to walk that time. She hit her head and got a big bruise on her forehead. She became confused. Then, she left home and walked into the water and died.

She was staying here (at Win's house) until she was able to move. She went back to her own house after she became able to walk. She could not stay with me. Whenever she tried to leave her house, I scolded her and did not let her. She might fall again somewhere. But she started to sneak out. She sneaked out to go to T village. She would sneak out wherever she wanted to go. Then, that day, she disappeared. When we found her, she was lying face down in the river. She was dead.

She was not happy that I did not allow her to go out. Sometimes she went to Chi Rai's place. Chi Rai, a Buddhist woman who lived in the neighborhood, sometimes brought her home on her motorbike. Other times, she walked in the other direction to go to Na Chua's or Na Li's place. She was all over the place. She walked everywhere. I could not keep track of what she was doing or who's place she was going to visit. She wandered around everywhere. These days, I see Yai Chu (an old woman who lives in the neighborhood) wandering around. She reminds me of my mother. I tried to stop my mother, but she did not listen. I could not walk far because I have bad knees. Whenever she went wandering around, someone had to bring her home on a bike. Sometimes it is Ko Pu, sometimes Ko Thet (her nephew) or sometimes Chira (Ko Thet's wife). Like this, she always went to her children or grandchildren.

Rai, who is Win's son and hence Yai Chit's grandson, who carried Yai Chit's body home with Bat, claims that she collapsed from dizziness. It is evident from his comment "She was old. If someone had seen her collapse, she could have been okay [saved]", that he, too, does not think it was suicide.

Her wandering behavior was well known among those close to her. At the same time, she was telling others of her wish to die. Given the circumstances, both views seem equally convincing. At the funeral, Na Li said that Yai Chit's wish had come true when she died. Having said that, when I interviewed her, she explained her view that Yai Chit did not intend to commit suicide but instead fell into the water while wandering around. The following is an excerpt from our conversation:

> **Ryoko**: Did she tell you she wanted to die?
> **Na Li**: She always said she wanted to die. She was not aware of anything around her. She was dreaming. Her mind was not very clear. She just kept walking around. She walked around all over the place. She told me she wanted to die.
> **Ryoko**: Had she ever tried to kill herself by taking pills?
> **Na Li**: No. She fell into the water. She was walking and stumbled into the water. She drowned and died.
> **Ryoko**: Did she do that on purpose?
> **Na Li**: She was just wandering around. She walked and walked and walked then collapsed.

Na Li did not make a definitive statement about whether Yai Chit had jumped into the water or accidentally fell. She continued:

> I do not know if she had determined to commit suicide. I do not know for sure if that was true or if she fell while wandering around. I have heard people talking about her jumping into the water at Khao Thanan. I heard she died. She had already been removed [from the water] by the time I got there. I heard that she went to Khao Thanan first, but left soon after because there were people around. Then, she went to the back of her house, to the river. There would not be enough water at low tide, so it must have been during high tide. After all, I do not know if she jumped into the water or not. I did not ask. I wonder if she got tired [of life] and followed her heart [into death].

Reporting death is the responsibility of the village chief. If the village chief determines a death is a suicide, the police must be called. In Yai Chit's case, the village chief decided that there was no need to call the police on the grounds that it was a case of "death from old age" and "involved no foul play". A policeman, nevertheless, came to the temple, but it was not to investigate the case but instead to play soccer in the village. The village chief narrated as follows:

> No one pushed her. She fell. I as a village head took responsibility for that decision. Rai (Yai Chit's grandson) is also a volunteer member of the police. He asked me if I was going to report it to the police. There was no need for a report. It would just cause unnecessary trouble. I am in charge of registration.

I conducted the interview with the village chief at Na Chua's house. Na Chua, who was also present during the interview, questioned the village chief about the possibility that it could have been a suicide, telling him that Yai Chit had told her on numerous occasions that she was going to commit suicide. Na Chua also explained to him that she had planned to kill herself at Khao Thanan, but failed because there were too many people around. The following was the village chief's response:

> Elderly people wander around aimlessly. Had it been a younger person, we would have needed to investigate to find the cause. This elderly person walked around and fell. She was old. We can assume that no one would have wanted to push her into the water. We can safely assume that no one would have wanted to kill her.

He recorded on the death certificate that it was "death from geriatric disease" (*tai chiwit lok chara*), rather than an accidental drowning.

In any case, however, neither the village chief, who denies the possibility of suicide, nor Na Chua, who maintains that it was suicide, knows the truth.

> **Village chief**: I do not know what was on her mind.
> **Na Chua**: She always told me [that she wanted to die].
> **Village chief**: She was talking among old people that she was going to kill herself.
> **Na Chua**: But she did not have the courage to put it into action. She did not have the courage to actually kill herself. She said she planned to jump [into the pond] at the Rock (Khao Thanan), but she said that there was too much water and people would save her.
> **Village chief**: No one knows what is on an old person's mind.

The village chief used the word "assume" (*sannitthan*) frequently in his speech. Teacher Phen also used this word when recounting Yai Chit's death. This is because they can only assume, as no one knows the truth.

In contrast, Na Chua was certain that Yai Chit's death was suicide, even after having the aforementioned conversation with the village chief.

> Otherwise, why would she have entered the river? She went down herself. She went there for one purpose. She had decided to drown herself. Yai Chit could not swim. Let's say she was able to swim. Then she would naturally and involuntarily swim herself out of it when she finds herself in deep water. She sank underwater and drowned without a struggle because she could not swim. If she had been able to swim, she would have saved herself in a panic. People of that age cannot swim.

The ambiguity of Yai Chit's death

The assumption that Yai Chit's death was suicide was drawn from the fact that she had repeatedly told others she wanted to die. However, she was wearing a diaper and it was completely exposed when the body was discovered. This may indicate that she was only half conscious at the time. It seems somewhat reasonable to conclude that she physically lacked certain characteristics that are typically observed in people who can bring themselves to commit suicide. Accordingly, her death was treated as a natural death from old age rather than a suicide.

The existence of two different interpretations of Yai Chit's death is essentially a matter of the ambiguity of the intention of the deceased herself. This brings us to the question of what is implied by this ambiguity. Philosophically, her death is neither an ontological death of an individual self, nor a death as a human universal, nor a death as a general situation. Furthermore, the ambiguity of Yai Chit's death lies neither in the physical death of an animalistic being, nor in the death of a human who is capable of deciding for themselves to commit suicide. Yai Chit's death is identified as not belonging singularly to either one of the above-mentioned categories. Rather, it is simply taken as the death of one human being known as Yai Chit, which is open to individuals' situational judgments. People accepted her death without recognizing the absolute contradiction between the claim that she had wanted to die and the official decision that she died a natural death from old age; and therefore they never investigated further to find the truth. It is, however, worth stressing that this was a response to a particular situation, and that Yai Chit was an old woman. Had it been the death of a younger person, the cause of death would have been investigated. The ambiguity of the event of Yai Chit's death is a direct reflection of the uncertainty surrounding the death itself.

Talking point among villagers

The villagers were not particularly interested in whether the old woman's death was a suicide or not. Rather, their focus was on the ethical standards for the survivors that would dictate their posthumous fate, which I will summarize at some length here. The discovery of the drowned body of an old woman was a shocking piece of news, a type of event that would rarely occur in the village. Besides, Buddhism considers suicide a sin. Therefore, I had expected that I would hear certain opinions and discussions on Yai Chit's posthumous life, including whether suicide is really a sin or not and what would be the fate of Yai Chit who had committed such sin. Contrary to my expectation, almost no one brought up the topic—except for Na Chua, who made a brief comment that she did not have to kill herself because she was going to die sooner or later anyway. Instead, whenever people talked about Yai Chit's death, the focus of conversation was on the karma (*wenkam*) of the parent-child relationship. This is related to the fact that many believe that one of the likely causes of her suicide was the unwillingness of her children to look after her.

On one occasion, three Buddhist women were talking about Yai Chit's suicide: the mother of the family I had previously lived with (in her seventies), her daughter Aliya (forty years old) and a Buddhist woman who lives nearby (fifty years old).

The mother had converted from Islam to Buddhism for marriage. The following is an excerpt of the conversation that developed around the topic of how Yai Chit committed suicide as a result of the inattentiveness of her children.

> **Daughter**: That is not an act of a Buddhist (*khon thai*). Buddhists must look after their parents.
>
> **Mother**: Not caring for your parents is a sin (*bap*). It is a terrible sin. If you care for your parents, you will have a better life.
>
> **Daughter**: If you are disrespectful, you will have a miserable life. You will not be successful at work. You will not prosper. You may manage to make a living, but only just.
>
> **Mother**: You will have no extra money.
>
> **Daughter**: That's what we believe. Everything has indeed been this way. If you care for your parents, you live well. Us Buddhists believe in karma. Karma does exist.
>
> **Neighbor**: Karma comes back [to you] from your child. Look at aunt Sin. She mistreated her parents (*mai ao*) and now she is being mistreated by her child.

Aunt Sin is this Buddhist woman's father's sister who had converted to Islam to marry her husband. According to them, her child headed down the wrong path, abusing drugs and even physically harming his mother. This was supposedly due to the fact that she did not look after her parents well.

Similarly, Hamae, a Muslim man in his seventies, also made the following remark regarding Yai Chit's death:

> Our parents gave us the gift of life. We must return the favor. We can do all the things we can do because of our parents. We can think because our parents gave us a brain. Think about that. We must never forget. To anyone, regardless of religion (*satsana*), disrespecting one's parents is a sin.

His unmarried daughter Wai, who is in her forties, then joined our conversation:

> **Father (Hamae)**: Old folks have comfortable lives (*sabai*) here. We can stay with our children or grandchildren (*luk lan*).
> **Daughter (Wai)**: Even if they get sick, their children or grandchildren will look after them. They help each other and care for them.
> (Some lines omitted)
> **Ryoko**: They call it karma in Buddhism.
> **Father**: Same as us. We also have sin, debt and karma in Islam.
> **Daughter**: We are no different.
> **Father**: If you neglect your parents (*mai soncai*), then your children will neglect you. It is fate (*wen*).

Teacher Phen (Buddhist) also told me that elementary school textbooks contain folktales to teach this concept. The following is an example she provided:

> This is a story taught at elementary school. A father was hollowing out a coconut shell. He was carving and sanding until it was all nice and shiny. His son asked him what he was doing with the coconut shell. The father answered "your grandfather is no longer able to work. He is useless so I might as well make that tool (*ai pu*) and [he can] beg on the street". Before long, the grandfather passed and the father aged. Now the child is carving a coconut shell, just like his father. When asked what he is doing, he answers that he is going to put his father on the street. This is a great lesson. It is important that children read this story. Kids these days do not read so we must tell them the story.

As we can see from the above narratives, the deceased individual's religious fate was not much of a consideration for people. Rather, the death of the old woman prompted people to reaffirm a long-established value—the idea of the ideal parent-child relationship. It is therefore safe to conclude that her death had a direct influence on the way of life of as well as the relationships between the survivors.

Suicide and institutions

At the beginning of the chapter, I quoted Imamura's statement: "Humans become specifically human beings only after 'killing' our animality, which is essentially what makes us physically alive". Imamura based his theory on the assumption that humanity is differentiated from other animals through the denial of the conservative maintenance of life of the "self", which he sees as equivalent to the development of self-awareness (Imamura 2007: 155–156).

But how does "death" relate to this? Imamura recognizes that what makes us physically alive is our body, as it is with other animals. He explains that self-awareness arises from the ability to deny the body, or in other words, the ability to cause self-death. Imamura sees that speaking about and understanding suicide with a structured language points to the essence of human beings. The ability to express such concepts in language opens a path to reach others beyond one's self. The notion that we can distinguish humanity from other animals based on the emergence of language as a communicative tool has been repeatedly pointed out in past studies. However, it must be underlined that Imamura's argument's uniqueness is found where he clearly delineates "suicide" as a "possibility for causing self-death". The important assumption to keep in mind here is that a physical body is the fundamental condition of all animalistic life including humans (Imamura 2007: 211).[6]

Now let us return to the paradox mentioned earlier: "Humans should die to be humans; yet at the same time, we cannot die, and we should not die". The key idea for solving this paradox is that suicide "does not originate in isolated individuals, but such choice can only be potentially available through relationships with others … Ending one's own life is proof of being human and evidence of freedom; and such act causes one to be acknowledged by others as being a human being" (Imamura 2007: 211). This notion brings the social dimension into the equation.

Imamura's solution to the paradox is summarized below. First, the phrase "humans should die" can be interpreted as referring to having the courage to risk your life, rather than actually dying. What this implies is that unless you actually die, it is the same as pretending to die. We can extract the elements of "faking" and "pretense" from this reasoning. "Pretense" here is the force that not only allows the continued existence of, but also drives the institutionalization of social relations. Not "faking" or "pretending" to die means actually dying. Hence, "pretense" is indispensible for our survival. Imamura claims that this provides the grounds for all institutions where the struggle to obtain acknowledgement from others by putting one's life on the line is the ritual struggle to solve the contradiction of the possibility and impossibility of self-death (Imamura 2007: 215).

The ultimate form of the struggle to obtain others' acknowledgement, which constitutes the grounds for human society, is the "pretense" of death based on self-denial, fought with one's life on the line. Human society cannot operate without ritualizing or institutionalizing struggles. "The life-or-death struggle for acknowledgement is, at its heart, an institutional theory" (Imamura 2007: 215). In sum, the sociality of human beings itself is established to be specifically human by way of "pretending" to deny the animalistic life; and to Imamura, that is precisely the grounds for institutions.

Imamura associates this "pretense" with a ritual act. He regards the act of faking one's own death as a "rite of passage" (to adulthood).

[It] has been the ritual, or institution, where adolescents demonstrate their courage to end their own life to others ... Candidates must deny their familial (or animalistic) life. And in order to kill such self to flourish in the new adult life, they must pass the ordeal of challenging themselves with their own death. (2007: 214)

He argues that this "faking" is imperative in forming social relations, and in turn, essentially, is "ontologically" critical for the overall existence of human beings.

Imamura stipulates the death of human beings as the death of sociality, as Uchibori points out in Chapter Two. This means that Imamura only argued about "death" (Uchibori's terms), not physically "dying". That is, he deems that institutions emerge at the level of symbolization out of physically dying.

It is worth referring to Tanaka's discussion in Chapter Seven here on institutions in relation to rituals. He identified that ritualization is a common element of practices across many different institutions and defined the main characteristics of ritualization as acts of formality and purposelessness (deprivation of purpose). Tanaka identifies that the difference between animal displays and human institutions is intent. While the former is driven strongly by purposes, the latter is characterized by the very fact that the actor's intent is not necessarily directly linked to the act itself. Imamura's discussion on human institutions, which is built on the notion of "pretense" or denial of specifically human life in the context of relations with others, aimed to understand the meaning of human institutions from a broader perspective, whereas that of Tanaka, which points to the purposelessness of rituals, attached importance to the characteristics of actions. Despite this difference in approach, both seem to take the same perspective that the emergence of human institutions can be attributed to the distortion or denial of physical existence or life, which is essentially the primary element of human institutions.

Back to Imamura, the "dying" of the human being, equating with the "dying" of the self, should be negated to solve the paradox of the emergence of institutions for human beings. As a result, he needed to postulate the "faking" or "pretense" of dying to work it into the discussion of sociality centering on the self. However, I will suggest that the "dying" of others more easily influences sociality, including the self and others. This is exemplified in the case of Yai Chit's death. When confronted with the death, "dying" accurately speaking, of an individual known as Yai Chit, the main concern of the villagers was neither whether it was suicide or not, nor the cause of her death. Discussion centered on the ethical question of how they ought to have interacted with Yai Chit. We may be able to explain our institutional use of the word "ought" as being the result of the process in which a distortion of life, or a "death", an abrupt death in this case, is leveraged as a means to explore the social world—the mechanism of dynamism from "pretense" of the denial of life (discourses around Yai Chit's suicide) to life, in Imamura's words. This may help illustrate the peculiarities of the human species as opposed to animals.

In place of conclusion: People die when their time comes

The villagers' reception of Yai Chit's death suggests the most ultimate resignation pertaining to human life, the acceptance of the fact that people die when their time comes. Everyone, including those who want to kill themselves and those who do not, holds the same view on death. The following is a comment one villager made regarding Yai Chit's death:

> People die when the time comes. You cannot die if it is not your time. She tried to die many times, but she could not because it was not her time yet. Finally the time came for her to die.

Similarly, Yai Chit's daughter Win also said "She was confused. She left home and entered the water. Then she died. The time came for her". Through this process of resignation, the living accepts the deceased, and this acceptance in turn is linked to the death/life relationship. Based on this acceptance, people live side-by-side with others, in this world and the otherworld.

The time of "dying" is uncontrollable for both human beings and animals. So, we can say that human institutions emerge out of the acceptance of the universality of "dying".

18 The Evolutionary Foundations of Institutions: Rule, Deviation, Identity

Suehisa Kuroda

Key ideas

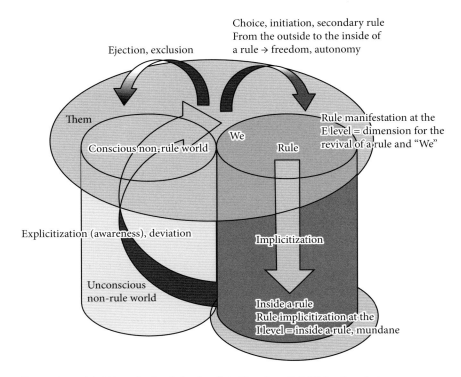

Dynamic model of the rule: A rule has implicit (I) and explicit (E) levels and phenomena surrounding the rule can be described by movements between them.

This conceptual diagram has been formulated around three points: 1) For a rule to be distinguished from stereotypical animal behaviors, the awareness of the rule that "We act according to this" is needed (Explicit (E) level); 2) people normally have internalized rules and act freely within such rules with little awareness (Implicit (I) level); and 3) the E level is brought about by rituals or the signal to start a game as well as the signal at the end and any deviation that arises at the I level, among which deviation in particular suddenly pulls participants up to the E level. These are very much ordinary occurrences, but they form the basic structure for the emergence of rules and institutions and it is possible to clarify many phenomena concerning rules and institutions from here.

"We" are participants who follow rules, which become institutions where these participants constitute an entire sustained social group. Deviation is impossible at the E level where people are supposed to follow the rules consciously. Rather, deviation occurs at the I level where people live inside the implicitized rules. Deviation puts the participants at the E level (new E space) where they are forced to make a choice to either exclude the deviant (splitting "We"), make all members ratify the rules and start over, amend the rules to include the deviation (a secondary rule, expanding "We") or go along with the deviation (dismantling "We"). The maintaining of "We" at this level by returning to the rules or "We" or by altering the rules gives rise to a sense of autonomy and freedom and reinforces their identities. What happens in the new E space can be regarded as the resurrection of rules and "We". It happens because humans cannot live at the E level alone and must return to their primary state of living in implicitized rules. Deviation occurs at this implicit level. Conversely, even some physiological or genetics-based behaviors that are not consciously thought of as rules have the potential to be lifted to the E level and turned into rules or institutions by deviation or the sharing of the illusion of deviation. One example of this is the sublimation of incest avoidance to incest taboo. The E level can be brought into existence suddenly by the appearance of "They" or "Enemy". In this situation, order within "We" disappears and makes way for unification, with the reinforced "We" consciousness, to manifest behaviors that clearly distinguish "We" from "Them". Raiding and war are such examples. These behaviors arise on the E level and therefore take the form of rituals or symbolic acts emphasizing "We". Primitive warfare in chimpanzees can fall under this category of behaviors, albeit in the absence of rituals.

Constraint and deviation, structure and non-structure

What informs members of human social groups that "This is how 'we' should be", or "We should do this, we must not do that" has been given many names, including institution, rule, taboo, norm, ethic, moral, justice, commandment, law, convention, standard and arrangement. Although these terms are given different meanings, they all suggest that human beings collectively regulate and constrain their own actions. These regulations and constraints are thought to form the basis of human society.

People who apparently do not adhere to the behavioral constraints demanded by groups are subjected to, for example, discipline, if they are children, and exclusion if they are adults behaving as thugs or criminals. Humans become members of groups (actors) only when they have been trained to adhere to the relevant institutions and rules (Nakayama 2007), and this process entails shackling themselves to a whole array of explicit and implicit behavioral constraints and internalizing them. However, we are normally unaware that the "actor" comes into existence through the act of self-transformation or self-restraint, and when we have this awareness we actually take pride in it as a mark of belonging to groups.

In this chapter, we use the term "institution" to represent the phenomenon in which members of human groups constrain or control their own actions and do so as if "voluntarily", and examine the social conditions and biological foundations for this phenomenon mainly from the perspective of primate sociology. If the commonly held presumption that language is necessary for institutions to exist is applied to societies of languageless non-human primates (hereinafter referred to simply as "primates"), institutions do not exist there. However, for animals besides humans to form groups, some mechanisms for behavioral control and adjustment to enable coexistence are essential. Several chapters in this publication (Chapter Four by Hayaki, Chapter Six by Nishie, Chapter Seven by Itoh, Chapter Eight by Hanamura and Chapter Twelve by Adachi) have shown from various angles that social intercourse in primate societies is directed and modulated by reciprocal or unilateral self-inhibition or expectations. These discussions on the relationship between behavioral control/adjustment mechanisms and institutions will certainly help further inform and deepen our concepts of institution and rule.

This chapter is an attempt to collate the meaning and structure contained in what we call rules and institutions by reference to the view of institution proposed by J. Itani (1987), while leaving behind the common belief that institutions are exclusively built upon language. Itani identifies a crucial difference between primate and human culture in relation to the formation and maintenance of groups. Primate culture is largely about variation in foraging techniques and is limited to skills and behavioral patterns that manifest in individuals separately, whereas human culture manifests as behavioral constraints accompanying identification with groups, and institutions are amongst the most common manifestations of collective constraints. In the same thesis, Itani argues that institutions come into existence through clear distinction operated by language. Itani's arguments imply the following:

1. that he considers the function of identification with groups as a particularly salient characteristic of institutions,
2. that he does not recognize the existence of institutions in primate societies and
3. that he differentiates institutions from general cultures' constraint on behaviors. Itani (1991) later states in an article entitled "Karuchua no gainen—aidentifikeshon ron sono go" (The concept of monkey culture: After identification theory) that chimpanzees' "infanticide can be considered to be one of their cultures, involved in the formation and sustenance of groups", and argues that chimpanzees also have a form of culture that constrains behaviors and accompanies collective identity.

To begin with, our discussion aims at relativizing Itani's view on the indivisibility of institution and language. I have previously attempted to define institution separately from language and argued for the possibility that some form of institutional distributive system may emerge from food sharing behaviors observed among the genus *Pan* (bonobo and chimpanzee species) (Kuroda 1999). Once we have revised the concepts of rule and institution using such a definition, we will examine the relationship between identities and institutions, as well as culture.

Among primates, members' identification with their groups manifests clearly in inter-group conflict. As the outline of a group becomes clear as members unify with their peers, structure and non-structure simultaneously emerge (Kuroda 2013a). The structure built by institutions and rules cannot exist unless a phase of non-structure, or "deviation", appears. Based on this, this chapter serves as a sequel to my discussion on the maintenance of social structure and communitas-type non-structure (Kuroda 2013a).

Defining "rule" and "institution"

Defining "rule" and "institution" without language

As mentioned, it is commonly held that institutions cannot exist without conceptual language. This is because language is thought to be necessary to establish a clear distinction between right and wrong, or what one should and should not do. A point of view adopted by primate sociology is also compatible with this definition (Itani 1987; M. Kawai 1992). If the definition is accepted literally, however, institutions will fall outside of the scope of primate sociology. Moreover, as language is considered to be an institution, it will lead to the tautology that institutions are actualized by an institution, which prevents us from delving into the question of the formation or origins of institutions. Everything that is deemed characteristic of human society is deeply related to intersubjectivity, representational abilities and symbol manipulation abilities and therefore its relationship with language will eventually become undeniable. Nonetheless, we shall begin with the definitions of rule, norm and institution that minimize the element of language as I attempted previously (Kuroda 1999), in order to understand these phenomena separately from language. Those basic definitions are as follows:

> Rule: A matter with which all members of a group expect that they themselves, as well as others, will comply.
>
> Norm: The expectation of all members of a group that they and others will comply with a certain matter.
>
> Institution: A rule of a sustained social group.

In fact, these definitions have been formulated by simply replacing a verbal stipulation with an "expectation" and removing any reference to punishment that is contained in common definitions, but, most importantly, they are free of the concept of language. These definitions clearly emphasize that rules and institutions are perceptions of one's own and others' actions and at the same time focus on the way rules and institutions emerge through the actor and the relationship between actor and group. These definitions do hide a tautological relation to rules (see the discussion on pp. 403–405), but we will set this issue aside for the moment and begin our discussion.

The object of mutual "expectations" can be something that has been culturally acquired or a behavior that is largely dictated by genetics. The range of members having mutual "expectations" is the group covered by the rule, which is "We" from the actor's perspective. In the case of humans, there can be variety in terms of "We" composition; for example, one can aim one's "expectation" at oneself alone constructing a list of behaviors to constrain oneself, as well as assuming dyadic relations such as between an individual and some divinity, or an individual and a pet. For the purpose of this discussion, however, a group refers to a unit consisting of two or more conspecifics, and any matters that remain within the individual are not regarded as rules. A sustained social group refers to one that remains stable over the long term, albeit with some membership change, and contains male and female members and their offspring. The unit group among primates and social groups on and above the local community level in humans belong to this category.

To "expect" a matter from others, the actor is supposed to "know" or "be conscious" of it, but this definition does not necessarily require the actor's "consistent" consciousness to comply with it in the process of action. In fact, humans have a strong tendency to internalize rules and institutions as "natural/given" and conform unconsciously or semi-unconsciously (this tendency is named "rule implicitization"). In other words, it is normal for humans to "live 'inside' rules" without being conscious of them. However, rules must be made explicit somewhere in some form, as in "This should be done this way" or "Now 'We' do this". Otherwise, most human behaviors cannot be distinguished from animals' stereotypical behaviors such as ants marching in single-file or birds returning to their nests. Accordingly, in the following discussion becoming "aware" of the rules plays a more important role than "knowing" or being "consistently conscious" of them.

It is possible to envisage several different levels of awareness here, ranging from the momentary awareness of an error that slips back into obscurity, to that of the rules of the game when one uses them to achieve victory, the awareness of one's every move in a ritual and the awareness that is self-referential in stipulating what "We" do and brings the actor's identity to the fore. The same can be said about the levels of rule implicitization. The rules and institutions that are repeated daily and form part of life operate at such a deeply implicit "natural/given" level that people cannot think of any other way of doing things. I call such institutions "natural institutions" (Kuroda 1999; see Chapter Fifteen by Omura). The rules of games that are played are less implicit. This distinction will be made when necessary in the following discussion, but the minimum requirement for "awareness" by our definition is the momentary surfacing of a rule to the conscious mind.

As these definitions include subjecting to tacit progression and make no reference to punishment for deviation, stereotypical conventions and communication codes in human groups are also regarded as institutions here. It is possible to regard them as rules covering a whole group because its members not only interact with one another on the assumption of (= expectation) mutual compliance with certain rules, but also believe (= expect) that third parties other than those interacting also rely on the same assumption in interacting with others.

In primate sociology, the interpretation of social phenomena among primates must rely on observable phenomena or those that are highly deducible from observations. Observers interpret the attitude of intensive gazing taken by monkeys as some kind of "expectation", but this cannot be ascertained unless something occurs. Behaviors indicating that the monkey "'had' expectations" are more apparent. In other words, quickness of response or displayed emotion to the other party's action, or a reaction suggesting a sense of betrayal, allows observers to deduce the existence of expectations. This is more or less the same in humans if we consider cases in which rules are operating tacitly (i.e., a majority of cases = rule implicitization). This is because mutual expectations are made explicit only by deviations or accidental errors when parties fail to interact by conventional stereotyped behaviors. In other words, the impact of deviations is to make rules and institutions explicit (see discussion on pp. 405–406). Awareness aroused by deviation triggers emotions and feelings such as surprise, confusion, discontent and antipathy in the parties to a greater or lesser extent (see Chapter 15 by Omura and Chapter 16 by Sugiyama for the link between institutions and emotions). Our position is that this is also the case for primates. Conversely, if a party or individual thinks that a certain action is a deviation from an expected matter, but many others do not react to it, that is, they think nothing of it, then the matter is not a rule or institution.

Application to primate societies

One example where the definition of rule on page 394 is applicable to primates is social play (play with two individuals; incidentally, play involving more than three only occurs briefly—see Chapter Four by Hayaki; Kuroda 2011). Social play in primates is initiated by the displaying of a play face (open-mouth laugh), or patterns of exaggerated action, or approaching or signaling to approach, and is sustained by reciprocal self-control to balance strength between players (Chapter Four by Hayaki). Rough-and-tumble play in Japanese macaque infants is often interrupted suddenly when one player lets out a faint scream and moves away. This is obviously because the other player has inadvertently used excessive force. This breakdown (deviation) suggests the existence of the mutual expectation that the players will moderate the level of force used in play-biting or pinning down (which becomes a rule). In the case of social play in Japanese macaques, players commonly break play and separate from one another, then return to resume play repeatedly. Hayaki (1990) interprets this phenomenon as a technique to reset the level of force used in play. In many cases play is initiated by behaviors that are not dissimilar to normal or aggressive behaviors such as simple approaching, jumping on and turning one's back. One compelling interpretation is that these behaviors develop into play because primate behavioral patterns are ambiguous, leaving the parties free to read each other's intentions (Hayaki 1990; Kuroda 1986). Thus it is possible to deduce from our observations that a play relation is comprised of an apparent "intention" to participate in play, and behaviors suggesting "mutual expectation" of matching strength.

One problematic example of rule- or institution-like cases that are in fact neither rules nor institutions is the existence of the alpha male among groups of chimpanzees in a stable phase (Chapter Eight by Nishie). A dominance order is observed in regard to high-ranking chimpanzees, but it is too unstable to be called a rule because of "politics", with standings often being reversed depending on the presence or absence of allies. This instability is also found in the top rank (alpha male status), which is easily changed when allies desert or a challenger appears. For this reason, the alpha male must try to ensure stability by constantly securing allies and supporters. F. de Waal (1982b) calls the resolution of a power struggle to confirm rank order among male chimpanzees a "temporary agreement". However, some males among groups of chimpanzees in Gombe Stream and Mahale Mountains in Tanzania have been observed to maintain their alpha status consistently for several years. During the stable phase, many other individuals stereotypically exhibit particular behaviors and attitudes toward the alpha male, including greetings. Of course, everyone clearly knows who the alpha is and therefore their attitude towards him is almost a rule. The problem is that some individuals do not exhibit the greeting behavior (Itoh 2013). Moreover, other individuals do not react to such negligence. Accordingly, while this case can be considered a quasi rule-based behavior, excluding the non-greeting individuals, it cannot be regarded as an institution because allowing for such exceptions would render it overly arbitrary.

Nevertheless, rank order among Japanese macaques, and, more generally, some codes of communication among primates have characteristics that are equivalent to those of a rule. For example, the dominance relationship among Japanese macaque females is determined by lineages, and infants acquire their initial ranks by the age of three or so with the support of older individuals from the same matrilineal lineage. Although this dominance relationship is stable and manifests stereotypically in dyadic exchanges, the occasional appearances of individuals who upset this order exposes the fact that it is maintained by self-inhibition on the part of the subordinate. This situation produces friction and conflicts between lineages, and many third-party individuals tend to side with a dominant lineage in case of an offensive. However, this is what happens in disturbances in general, and it is indeterminable as to whether this is specifically pertinent to rank deviation. In the end, the dominance relationship in question can be regarded as a rule in the sense that it characterizes the two-party exchange, but it falls short of qualifying for being called an institution.

Fields in which rules and institutions manifest

When existing primate societies are re-examined by reference to the definitions introduced above, it may be possible to call the rank order that stereotypes play and exchange between individuals a rule, but among primates it is difficult to identify an overarching rule covering a sustained social group as a whole, that is, an institution. This difficulty stems from the *sine qua non* condition for an institution to exist that an underlying rule must cover all members of a sustained social group, not only the expectations of those presently performing an action, or parties to an interaction (a performing subgroup). In fact, for a rule to acquire the status of an institution, observing bystanders must also expect that the parties to the action, or the interaction, will follow or are following the rule. This requirement, which is not necessary for a rule to apply, is the crucial problem when it comes to recognizing institutions.

An example that highlights this problem is the case of mother-son incest. Among primates this is an extremely rare occurrence. In chimpanzees, it has been observed that mothers who were pressed by their sons for incestuous mating attacked their sons, or screamed and fled (Goodall 1986; Nishida 2007). These observations suggest that mothers are averse to such action and consciously avoid it (and in this sense it can be called a rule that appears between mother and son based on the above definition). It is evident from the way chimpanzee and bonobo individuals interact that they do recognize the mother-child relationship among other individuals (Kuroda 1982, 1999). Despite this, there have been no reports of other individuals reacting to the occurrence of incest with any emotional or affective expressions. In short, they do not seem to feel that other individuals should inhibit their incestuous behavior. In fact, for self-inhibition of incestuous behavior—presumably occurring within each individual member of the group— to give rise to a negative reaction toward another individual's violation, it is necessary that the observer project their own self-awareness onto the actions of the transgressor, that is, they feel another's relationship as their own relationship, and the violation of another as a violation of the self. This projection between self and other is considered to be similar to empathy, sympathy or psychological processes such as self-other identification and intersubjectivity. However, these terms carry slightly different meanings and one can detect various levels of intersubjectivity. Anthropoids are known to display sympathetic behaviors not only to their conspecifics, but also to humans (Nishida 2007; de Waal 2010), but it seems that they either do not have sufficiently high levels of intersubjectivity to generate institutions, or do not pay attention to the actions of others to the same degree as humans do, which is perhaps almost the same thing.

However, in a previous study I examined whether food sharing in the genus *Pan* could evolve to be an institutional action without mediation by language and suggested the possibility of another pattern with regard to the relationship between the basic conditions for an institution to arise, on the one hand, and the manifestation of interest in others' actions on the other hand (Kuroda 1999). This means that a situation in which an entire group takes an interest in one matter will give rise, naturally, to the expectation that others will act in the same way as the self, which is effectively equivalent to self-other projection. One such example is the state of excitement that chimpanzees enter as they confront an enemy group (Kuroda 2013a). There cannot be third parties in this situation, including those who retreat out of fear, and all members become psychologically co-focalized. This condition in itself is similar to raiding among pastoralists as described by Kawai (2013; Chapter Ten), which functions as an institution. We shall consider later whether inter-group conflict among chimpanzees can be regarded as an institution.

The structure in which rules and institutions emerge

Consciousness that creates rules

The requirement for "expectation" found in our definitions for rule and institution demands the "awareness" that "This should be done in this way", or "knowing" that "'We' do it in this way". It means that a rule becomes a rule as a consequence of the awareness (or consciousness) that one is complying with it. So does an institution. It can be rephrased in simpler terms as "a rule means being aware of a rule", but this formulation may draw the accusation that it is as tautological as the proposition that "institutions are unthinkable without language", which we tried to avoid earlier. However, nothing can in reality become a rule without the manifestation of explicit awareness, as I stated in our earlier discussion on definitions. This indicates that the minimalistic requirement for a rule to exist lies in the simple collectively induced response that "'We' are complying with such and such" itself. This means that our unequivocal calls to order bereft of conceptual reasoning such as "a rule is a rule; follow it" and "this is how it has always been done", exhortations that so tend to exasperate young people, correctly describe the essence of rule. It also means that when the implicit norm of "complying with 'it'" arises in a group, "it" becomes a rule, or an institution, regardless of what "it" is. In the case of games, "it" does not have to be a set of detailed rules; rather, a sense of complying with the rules (a meta-rule), or a manifestation of compliance. In other words, "awareness of the rule" in itself will bring the rule to the fore.

To this effect, we can rephrase our previous definition of "rule" as "the awareness of the continuity of their actions". Continuity implies affirmation. In this expression, the constraint is orientating actions framed by "Our" relationships and keeping "continuity". The "continuity" can be seamless or intermittent, or the permanence of some prohibition. Based on discussions on pages 400–401 as well as Chapter Four by Hayaki, "members' awareness of the continuity of their actions" is applicable at least to primate social play.

On the other hand, even a very mundane everyday action can turn into a task that triggers a shared consciousness of "'We' do it in this way, or are supposed to do it in this way", and transforms it into a rule or an institution, in particular if every move is made slowly and carefully under the gaze of the group, as noted by Tanaka (Chapter Three) (the following discussion is only applicable to humans). As this is the act of making "the way 'We' normally do it" explicit, "not doing it in a different way" is also implicitly conveyed as exhortation against "not doing it that way". In some instances, the actual performance of a given act could be hindered by the laughter it would provoke. According to Y. Kimura (1983), this is because our mind is unable to bear the burden of continually giving double meaning to a single action and ends up erasing it with laughter. To avoid this situation and bring an extraordinary meaning to an ordinary action that is normally performed unconsciously, "all" participants must pay attention and acknowledge that it is a special extraordinary action disconnected from everyday occurrences.

The "do/do not" division is highlighted more clearly by acts of deviation (see pp. 405–406). This division or rift is the necessary condition for a rule, but as the primary state of a rule is implicit, we normally immediately return to the world of (almost unconscious) compliance with implicit rules, deleting the division in short by confirming and/or modifying the rule. This procedure is called a secondary rule. Viewed in this light, we can understand the privileged nature of an action performed under the consciousness of "'We' do it in this way" from beginning to end, i.e., a ritual. Throughout the course of a ritual the rules remain explicit. In other words, in rituals their rules come to the fore and a division between "do it this way" and "don't do it any other way" is staged; so it may reside in the same dimension as deviation and secondary rules, but in the case of a ritual the rift is not allowed to close. Paradoxically, it is akin to deviation. In a ritual, deviation loses its place and things are performed with a sense of space far from our daily life where the rules remain implicit and the potential for deviation pervades. In this field, the act of laughing that pulls people back to the mundane (living "inside" the rules) is impermissible, and deviation is impossible as well.

Deviation, freedom, secondary rule, "We"

We have so far confirmed that a rule that is followed unconsciously and not remembered is not identified as being a rule. In a game, an awareness of the rules may be sparked at the outset and whenever a rule violation occurs. The initiation of a game is a moment of transition from the non-rule state to the rule state, and a rule violation is the reverse of that. As there is neither a beginning nor an end when stereotyped conventions (natural institutions) are being followed unconsciously, failures and errors, i.e., deviations, are the only times when awareness of the rules arises = when rules and institutions emerge (most of the following discussion is about human society permeated with rules).

The relationship between a deviation and a rule in the above sense brings "freedom" to the surface in a multilayered manner. Firstly, a deviation makes apparent that which is external to the rule. The implicit rule emerges from the background to form a figure with its externality (non-compliance state with the rule), and correspondingly, elicits awareness of being "We" as well as being something else, thus expanding the potentialities of being for the actors. Becoming an "actor" within one's own group means subjecting oneself to the rules and institutions of "We" in the midst of this state. Needless to say, one cannot do so while being immersed in the rules (living "inside" the rules). One must step up the ladder of logical types/levels to make a choice between these potentialities. Even though one cannot exist outside of "We", this structure enables one to fantasize that one has voluntarily made a choice as a free actor.

Because the actual consciousness of "We" stands on a "bundle of rules", deviation from one rule by one individual may not always result in breaking "We", unless such occurrence involves breaking a critical taboo. Rather, it may be possible to mend the tear by altering the rule, as Soga demonstrates in Chapter One. This is another factor contributing to the sense of autonomy and freedom. This type of rule change occurs frequently in the case of relatively "loose rules" or adjustive rules.

As a simple example, we can imagine this occurring when children of different ages play "together" by creating special rules for younger children (Kuroda 1999). The purpose of this type of adjustment in play is not only the performance of a certain game, rather, "playing 'together'", or the sustained generation of "We" consciousness is more important[1].

As mentioned above, the sharing of an action and its reflection, "We", may be seen in different lights. If we classify the difference conceptually, at one end we would have a situation where the focus is solely on the manifestation of "We", in the abstract, without anchoring it in any form of collective actions, and the individual rules creating "We" would lose their peculiar meaning, inviting chaos in which deviation also loses its meaning (i.e., anything goes as long as everyone has fun). At the opposite end would be the situation in which everyone's attention is focused on the "action" manifesting "We" (i.e., doing "it" together is important), where deviation is inconceivable. As I mentioned on page 394, rituals fall under the latter category and, possibly, so do raiding (see Chapter Ten) and warfare. Of course, these two polar opposites are two sides of the same coin and are supposed to be readily convertible.

Generally, the rules of a game are called primary rules and the procedures to change them are referred to as secondary rules (Hashizume 2003). The existence of secondary rules indicates that the "We" consciousness and the underlying rules are flexible and recoverable, i.e., homeostatic, and hence humans thrive living "inside" the rules. In other words, secondary rules provide an adaptive means to return to the "inside" of the rules. Stressing on this, we can broaden the definition of secondary rules as working over the rules to resume the rule state regardless of whether this involves rule change or not.

Rituals also serve as "secondary rules" in the broad sense as above. When deviation regarded as violation of a taboo occurs, the violator appears to bring the outside into the inside of "We" to split it. While "We" may respond by either isolating or expelling this ambivalent being that is and is not part of "We", at the same time "We" will invoke a ritual to mend the "split" in "We" for the reestablishment of community and to return to living "inside" the rules.

In summary, deviation not only unveils a primary rule, but also manifests a secondary rule at the same time. Deviation is an appearance of a division between the non-rule and the rule state. The connection mechanism from non-rule state to rule state becomes a secondary rule. Thus, a rule has a multidimensional structure that includes the dimension of the meta-rule. This is an obvious consequence of defining "rule" in combination with "awareness" (which is a meta-dimension of rule-based action), hypothesizing that the primary state of rules is tacit = implicit. If the aforementioned play in primates is recognized as a rule, it's breaks during play in Japanese macaques that can be regarded as the simplest forms of secondary rules.

Application to the incest taboo

We have concluded that because a rule becomes a rule through awareness, or an actor standing outside of its performing space, the simultaneous existence of the rule's inside and outside is a necessary condition for a rule, and such condition occurs at times of initiation, deviation, interruption. This enables us to deepen our understanding of the incest taboo. The type of rule or institution that lurks in everyday living without initiation or interruption can only manifest itself through deviation (or imagined deviation). In other words, only by deviation could incest avoidance, which may have become physiologically ingrained in the course of evolution at some organismal level, be sublimated into a rule = taboo. It does not matter here if deviation stands for a literal act, or a consciousness (imagining) of violation.

This reasoning reveals that the existing views of the origins of the incest taboo such as "incest is forbidden because it happens 'or' because it rarely happens" are missing the mark. Based on the ontology of "rule", the emergence of incest avoidance as a taboo on the one hand, and the emergence of an awareness of real and/or presumed deviation on the other hand, occur at the same time. The view that the taboo is "for" the exchange of women is also missing the point. An interpretation that is more in line with our argument here is made by Levi-Strauss (Watanabe 2001), who assumes that the "emergence of the rule" of incest taboo is pivotal for the organization of human society. In terms of primate sociology, incest avoidance, which has pre-existed as a natural constraint, is objectified as a social constraint. However, it is not that relationships in human society were structured and connected "for the first time" upon the emergence of rules as Levi-Strauss argues; rather, relationships that had existed from the anthropoid or early human stages, i.e., "pre-existing" relationships, were "socialized" in the course of cultural evolution as shared relationships among the social group. This required the presence of a constitutive cognitive power to give rise to the shared consciousness "'We' who avoid this", as well as the reflective view of self and the intersubjective ability to identify self and other.

On the other hand, the Freudian interpretation that universalizes the temptation of incest (Watanabe 2001) cannot be, or should not be, disregarded, because it also postulates the primordial conditions for incest avoidance to become a rule.

Multidimensional rule structure and third term exclusion

Our discussion so far has clarified that a rule consists of three elements (dimensions); a rule becomes a rule only when it combines with deviation from it = the anti-rule/non-rule dimension, and at the same time it is also joined by an element of another dimension that integrates the two = secondary rule. Transition between the dimensions of non-rule and rule is structured with a beginning and an end, whereas deviation is generally a violent situation in which participants are suddenly made to stand in a transcendental position outside of the rule. Deviation from a rule makes participants confront all the elements of a rule; the "We" consciousness that is otherwise embedded inside and a primary rule, as well as the possibility of choosing between rule, anti-rule and repair simultaneously.

It is worth noting that the position of deviation in the relationship between the above-mentioned three dimensions resembles the non-structure phase ("structured non-structure": Kuroda 2013a) sustaining group structure based on the equality principle, as well as the third term/element in the third term exclusion theory of H. Imamura (1982). Because a rule is the generation and maintenance of order in a group and the producer of the perception of "We", if the generation and maintenance of society always entails the exclusion of the third term (Imamura 1982), something that can correspond to a third term should exist when a rule emerges; this role must be assumed by deviation. If this is the case, the meaning of the third term exclusion theory can be applied to deviation as follows. Deviation is literally the destroyer of a rule and "We", which form the order of the group. However, at the same time, its eruption makes the rule and "We" manifest to be reorganized, so is the same as for order. Thus, deviation is inevitably isolated for exclusion by the agents of order, and thereby it brings the resurrection of order. To use the language of the third term exclusion theory, deviation constitutes the ambivalent third element with a profane (*kegare*) side and a sacred side. Of course, even though it brings about the awareness of order, deviation is swiftly removed and the highlighted rule made tacit and implicit immediately together with its deviation. This is symbolized for instance by the African king cited by Imamura (1982), who is treated as if he were profane at the time of rituals while isolated in daily life, as well as the solitary king referred to by Frazer as living in the grove of Nemi (Frazer 2002).

So what does the secondary rule brought out by deviation compare to? As the secondary rule is a mechanism to turn the chaos of the simultaneous presence of order and anti-order back to order, it can be likened to a pure and clean meta-ordering force that reigns over order and anti-order. This pure and clean force has no profanity and hence does not have to be concealed when it emerges; it can secure a permanent place (a position of emptiness: Imamura 1982) as a collective will or authority. According to Imamura, this is also one of the characteristics of the third term.

The above associations, supported by our argument thus far, are based on Imamura's theory and may enhance the validity of the definitions outlined on pages 397–400. However, Imamura's theory emphasizes the constant action of the ordering movement to push some entity out[2], i.e., stressing the need for violent exclusion. On the other hand, the nature of deviation in this chapter is the manifestation of that which is external to an order formed by a set of rules and our emphasis is on its action to revitalize order and to open up a meta-world (a horizon on which secondary rules or rituals are invoked) that creates opportunities for perceptions of freedom or autonomy.

"We"-type institutions and intersubjective institutions

As the definition of rule we have been using here is coupled with "We" consciousness, we can say that any interaction in which a rule appears is some form of collective identity within a group, but identification in primates does not operate at the same level as the "We" consciousness in humans. For instance, social play with three or more participants is rare even among chimpanzees and bonobos, which are closely related to humans (see Chapter Four by Hayaki; Kuroda 2011). This shows the limitation of their rules as well as the specificity of the "We" coupled with it. It also overlaps with the fact that we have not found any primate social systems that can clearly be labeled institutions. As institutions come into existence when each member expects all other members of the group to behave as they do, a collective identity develops that facilitates self-other identification within the group. This level of "We" consciousness is not found in primates. In terms of a sense of belonging to a group, the "We" consciousness also clearly emerges in the form of collective aggression toward another group at times of intergroup conflict (Kuroda 2013), but these two types of identification are not the same.

For a rule to become institutionalized, violations of it must be perceived not only by those directly concerned or parties to the transgression, but by all members of the group, and it has long been taken for granted that language and the ability for self-other identification, or the presence of intersubjectivity, is the only mechanism allowing the emergence of institutions. However, as mentioned on page 394, certain kinds of actions can become a matter of generalized interest to a group as a whole, even if its members' intersubjectivity remains at a low level, hence creating the possibility of manifesting an institution-like situation. This means that the situation in which an entire group takes a strong interest in one matter will not only give rise to the expectation that others will act the same way as oneself, but also produce the same effect through self-other projection.

In a thought experiment, we can easily imagine that this situation could occur amid group tension or excitement and that one such example would be the scene of confrontation between groups of chimpanzees. Here, virtually no third-party position is available, not even for those who retreat out of fear, and all members psychologically become part of a performer subgroup. In this situation, dominance rank and long-standing rivalries among male chimpanzees disappear and all that exists becomes enemies versus peers ("We"). Even young males, who are usually treated unmercifully by adult males, gain a position by fighting bravely as members of the group (Goodall 1986; Kuroda 2013a). This situation can be regarded as extremely similar to, or the same as, those where all interests are focused on an "action" manifesting "We", referring back to the difference in the manifestation of a rule as opposed to "We" awareness as discussed on pages 405–406. As far as raiding among pastoralists can be regarded as a form of institutionalized action, if one of them can be called an institution, I think it is worth exploring whether and to what degree warring groups of chimpanzees manifest some of the self-same essential traits.

Of course, I have no intention of strongly making such a claim here. I merely wish to draw attention to the points that the scene or the type of action that turns all members into a performer subgroup plays an important role in human and primate societies and that it fulfills a function that is of the same type as that of an institution, despite occurring via different mechanisms. For the sake of clarity, let us make a distinction between "institutions" based on intersubjectivity, which are common institutions that come into existence through self-other projection, and "We-type institutions" appeared by magnifying "We" awareness. In the case of the genus *Pan*, which lacks the ability to declare "This is how we do it", the presence of a "We-type institution" can only be conservatively recognized as a quasi-institution.

The intergroup conflict in chimpanzees described above as a "We-type institution" achieves the maintenance of inter-male solidarity within a group (Itani 1987; Itani's vent hypothesis: Kuroda 2013a), which is interpreted to serve as a structured non-structure that brings about the communitas-like unification of a male group (the non-structure phase for the maintenance of the order structure: Kuroda 2013a). In intersubjective institutions, the institution is an order itself, i.e., a structure, and deviation that rejects it, through its expulsion, is actually instrumental in its re-enforcement. On the other hand, the We-type institution dissolves differences between parties, nullifies order within groups and simply brings to the foreground the distinction between "We" and "Other" together with the action. In a sense, it assumes the same role as deviation in the intersubjective institution. This is also the horizon or role of rituals discussed on page 394. The We-type institution has structurally no room for deviation because it turns all members into a performer subgroup and focuses their attention on a particular action in the same way as seen in rituals. In our examination of the We-type institution in this way, we have realized that it actually overlaps with processes underlying human war and raiding, as well as with patterns of chimpanzees' intergroup conflict behavior, without needing to refer to R. Caillois' discourse on war (Caillois 1974). One of the conclusions that can be drawn from this discussion is that the reason why desertion in the face of the enemy in war is so unforgiveable is not only because such an action weakens fighting spirit, but also even more fundamentally because this type of all-out collective action allows no room for deviation.

I have called the We-type institution in chimpanzees a quasi-institution, not just because the phenomenon happens to be similar to the We-type institution among humans. Some individuals among male chimpanzees are capable of showing cooperative behaviors in order to avoid conflicts that accompany dominance competitions, and sometimes females act as mediators to reconcile quarreling males. Chimpanzees are equipped with a social capacity to huddle together and rejoice when a struggle for dominance has been settled (de Waal 1982b; Kuroda 1999; Hosaka, personal correspondence). The act of food sharing can be regarded as an act motivated by an understanding of others' desire, which implies a certain level of intersubjectivity (Itani 1987; Kuroda 1999). Consequently, one can expect that further studies and analysis of We-type institutions in the genus *Pan* may reveal deep-rooted connections between their formation and these manifestations of social skills and mental states.

War culture complex
Finally, I would like to touch on another We-type institution in chimpanzees. It has been reported that males in long-observed chimpanzee communities engage in the killing and eating of male infants, occurrences that seem to happen once every few years (Nishida 2007; Takahata 1985). Itani hypothesizes that male infants who have escaped such killings perpetrated by adult males grow up to

identify with them amid the extraordinary level of excitement accompanying the endo-cannibalistic situation, and grow up to become infanticidal cannibals themselves, and postulates that infanticide is part of their culture. The excitement of infanticide creates a situation in which members of the group, including juveniles, approach adult males for a share of the meat and watch their every move while acting afraid and nervous. This arouses a sense of identity in them.

There has been no definitive explanation for the killing of male infants. Several opposing views have been put forward. For instance, the victims of infanticide are thought to be the sons of female migrants in their first year in their new communities who are likely to have been sired by males from their previous communities, and it would thus make sociobiological sense to kill them. However, it has also been suggested that they may in some cases have been sired by male members of the current communities. More to the point, according to Itani, among chimpanzees, hostile confrontations between groups are common and solidarity is needed among male members in dealing with such conflicts, but this cannot be achieved if there are too many males in the group; the optimum number is around ten. Furthermore, identification with infanticidal violent males will produce individuals who can make significant contributions in intergroup confrontations. In short, he explains infanticide by associating intragroup violence with intergroup violence. There are occasions on which organized killings occur between groups, and Goodall (1986) called them primitive warfare. After the fashion of Goodall, I call a culture that reproduces these two types of violence a "war culture complex" (Kuroda 1999). It is noteworthy that the complex is comprised of two "We-type institutions".

As the We-type institution is the structured non-structure phase that reinforces group order, what Imamura (1982) calls "violence at the time of the formation of society" can probably be described as a We-type institution. The non-structure phase made by deviation was also built into intersubjective institutions. Thus, at the most fundamental level, all societies, including the anthropoidal ones, are made of structure and non-structure in a nested manner.

What I would like to add in closing is that although many of the non-structure phases discussed here were related to violent situations, the genus *Pan* comprises another species of peaceful anthropoids which are not prone to aggressive behaviors escalating to killings. The existence of bonobos demonstrates the possibility that our own evolution did not necessarily follow a bloodied path of violence. I shall discuss the bonobos' "We-type institutions" on another occasion.

Notes

Introduction

1 These days this tradition is carried on mainly by the field of primate sociology.

2 A social group (troop) structure in which constituent members are ranked linearly in the order of dominance from the top to the nth position. The term "dominance hierarchy" is seldom used today due to its anthropomorphic overtones.

Chapter 2

1 Let us look at a recent episode involving misleading reporting of an observation. It concerns a video and commentary used in a television report entitled "Chimpanzees 'mourn' the dead, too" broadcast on Japan's NHK in 2010. The observational video showed a mother chimpanzee in the wild carrying around the corpse of her dead infant on her back until it became mummified, all the while grooming and flapping away flies just as she would do for a living infant. What is noteworthy here is the commentary accompanying the image that announced that the chimpanzee had feelings for its dead child and cared about it even after its death and the interpretation that this constituted the mother's "mourning (or memorializing) behavior". A number of newspapers reported the event in a similar manner. One newspaper presented the view of a member of the observation team that the chimpanzee "understood (the child) had died" because the way she carried the child on her back was different from the way she carried a living child and suggested the possibility that "the origin of a desire to memorialize the dead" might lie in this behavior (*Asahi Shimbun*, 27 April 2010, evening edition). To put my reasoning in a nutshell, this representation involves misdirection that is akin to the plot of a fairytale in which the question of immediacy and that of meaning are linked in a straight line. As there is a sufficient body of research in primatology about the sustained orientation of feelings towards other individuals, the question we should be asking here concerns how long these feelings are sustained after the death of an individual and the ways in which their contents differ from those towards a living individual. When an individual goes missing, irrespective of whether it is alive or dead, for example, the loss may cause another individual to panic. Can this anxiety turn into a sustained feeling such as grief, and does it apply to a dead body showing signs of lifelessness and decay? I have not found any substantial positive answers, at least to the last question. Thus, in my view it is justifiable

that a majority of technical interpretations in the field of primatology do not recognize "perception of death" in chimpanzees at this stage—in spite of the fact that they define it rather loosely (Nishida 2011; Hosaka et al. 2000; Sugiyama et al. 2013; Nishie's presentation at the Japan Society of Cultural Anthropology, 2012; Inoue's presentation at the Primate Society of Japan, 2012). Their "dying" certainly exists at the pre-institutional level.

2 Let me add to this remark. A commentary at the special exhibition of the Natural History Museum, London, stated that Neanderthals practiced burial involving ceremonies. However, this does not appear to be a common view. The mainstream view identifies ceremonial burial as one of the fifteen AMH traits and considers that Neanderthals practiced burial but not in ceremonial form, as Mellars et al. (2007; also Mellars' lecture given at the National Museum of Nature and Science, Tokyo, November 2011) argue.

3 With respect to language capability, which, together with death, represents the symbolization capacities of AMH, Akazawa (2010) considers that Neanderthals were limited. Although the researchers of Max Planck Institute (Krause et al., 2007) announced the discovery of a language gene in a study of Neanderthal DNA, it is still uncertain how the so-called language gene actually works. Including announcements of these uncertain claims, discussions on the *arche* of language and the *arche* of death are homologous. Judging from some artefacts demonstrating the oldest symbolization capacities of AMH in South Africa, it seems reasonable to say that the most probable estimate of the time of the rapid blossoming of these capacities at this stage is 75,000 years ago. In this context, we have perhaps to adopt the expression of emergent "Cognitively Modern Humans"; that is, CMH as against AMH.

4 Naturally, by the way, the meaning of newly accepting "dying" against the given state of immortality can only be discussed in relation to fiction. It is very interesting to note that the decision and action of "rejection of immortality" taken by two types of robots—Andrew in Asimov's *Bicentennial Man* and Robita in Tezuka's *Phoenix*—are represented in two different ways. Humanity is defined as "the mortal" in the former and the "collectivity of death" of "inhumanity" is portrayed in the latter. The distance between these representations and what Marx (1964[1927]) hinted at in the mid-nineteenth century in terms of death being "a harsh victory of the species over the particular individual" is not so great.

5 Hitoshi Imamura (2007) discusses "indebtedness" to the dead or death that

exists at the *arche* (= birth) of human existence. What he is referring to here is basically the dead of the past. Terashima (2011) also justifiably refers to "indebtedness" in relation to "equality", but he does not devote much space to the significance of "indebtedness" to the dead in particular. While "indebtedness" is something like a basic element of gift-bound existence or reciprocity at the root of human sociality ("collectivity") to Imamura, he does not talk about death as a trigger for "indebtedness" into the future after one has died. Imamura speaks of human death as a self-evidently social death, but his eye to the social death ultimately turns toward one's "own death" as if to follow Becker's lead, perhaps due to what may be called the logical refraction of a social philosopher who came from economic philosophy. In addition, D. Graber (2011), whose goal is a complete history of "debt" (= "indebtedness") from the *arche*, cites the ancient Vedic literature advising on "indebtedness" to others, including Death and the dead, at birth as Imamura does. However, Graber stops at the discussion of the moral sources of economic "debt" instead of attributing the entire human existence to "indebtedness" to the dead. This point highlights a difference in the orientation of his and Imamura's arguments even though they both place the gift-bound and/or gift-driven existence, including "debt", at the *arche* of human society.

Chapter 4

1 Players draw squares in the shape of a scarecrow on the ground, toss a stone into one of the squares and hop on one leg through the squares to pick up the stone.

2 Due to the rapid improvement of information processing technology and Internet access, it is common these days for people to play games on the computer with someone remote to them. This mode of play is outside the scope of our discussion here as we treat play engaged in by the self and others interacting directly at the same place as social play.

3 Pat-a-cake is a game for young children involving two players clapping hands with each other along to a *Mother Goose* nursery rhyme.

4 Tomasello argues that the understanding of others as intentional agents is unique to humans, but various reported cases in many primate species indicate that this is not necessarily true. However, the developmental characteristic of a dramatic increase in triadic interactions coupled with a rapid development of the understanding of others as intentional agents from around the ninth month after birth can be considered unique to humans.

Chapter 6

1 Pant-grunt is defined in Nishida et al. (1999) as follows: "Pant-grunt: Goodall (1989): 'A series of soft or loud grunts functioning as a token of respect given during greeting by submissive chimpanzees and during submissive interactions … A highly fearful individual may utter frenzied pant barks that may be labeled pant-screams'. At Mahale, pant-grunting adult females may <present> to adult males, who may mount the females and show thrusting. In response to pant-grunting by young adult and adolescent males, alpha males may jump on or attack them without being appeased". We must take note that the "meaning of pant-grunt" as a behavioral pattern and the "dominance rank (dominant-subordinate) relationship" as a social relation are circularly defined in this way. This point will be discussed later.

2 Cases in which the alpha male of a chimpanzee group stayed away from many of the members and ranged alone, leading to a change in dominance rank, have been reported in detail at Mahale (Nishida 1981; Uehara 1994; Hosaka and Nishida 2002) and Gombe (Goodall 1986) in Tanzania, and therefore this case is not completely unprecedented. However, I would like to note as a fact in relation to my later analysis that it is certainly not a frequent occurrence— once in several years at most.

3 Mizutani (2005) states, based on "the supremacy of forms in social intercourse (conversation and interaction) (= *Spielform*)" pointed out by G. Simmel in *Fundamental Questions of Sociology*: "Pure forms of social intercourse that manifest in conversations will remain even after abstraction of all contents of the interaction and in this sense constitute a condition for the possibility of interaction in general". "The use of the form of interaction in uncertain social situations" pointed out in this chapter can be considered to correspond to this statement by Mizutani.

4 Based on S. Tambiah's argument on "ritual involution", Uchibori (1989) nominates "excessive repetitiveness" as a characteristic of ritual as a form of expression. He explains that "a ritual is a system of actions incorporating some repetition by nature" and "always contains the possibility of involution due to its very nature" and that "ritual involution" occurs when repetitiveness becomes excessive and "makes a ritual far too ritualistic". Although Uchibori's argument is about "rituals" containing various actions found in human society, it appears to be also applicable to the "ritualistic interactions" ("excessive" grooming and pant-grunts) discussed in this chapter.

5 Of course, the "exaggeration" of actions may be partly caused by the

excitement of "extraordinary encounters", but the perspective I would like to emphasize here is what causes the stability of the stylized behavioral pattern and their strong dependence on it that makes them repeat and "act out" the "familiar way" even in such a state of excitement or panic (i.e., even when faced with such an uncertain situation).

Chapter 7

1 In this chapter, "mode of coexistence" will be used instead of "condition of coexistence".

2 See Itoh (2003) for details.

3 An even more surprising phenomenon was observed at the ex-Great Ape Research Institute of Hayashibara, where I did several years of fieldwork. They were conducting a face-to-face morphometric study on chimpanzees around four times per month in which playtime follows a session of morphometry. Chimpanzees behave differently during playtime and the morphometry session. Environmental conditions such as the combination of human attendants and the equipment and room used do not change, but they can still predict the beginning of play in the course of the experiment.

4 See Hanamura (Chapter Eight) for details of vocal exchanges.

5 Although the function of the food-grunt is still unclear, locally it is called a "delighted voice" because it is uttered at feeding locations when the chimpanzees appear to be delighted.

6 See also Tokoro (Chapter Nine).

Chapter 8

1 In the cases mentioned in this chapter, invisible pant-hoot vocalizers or their sex and age class identified by myself are described as below and used as a reference for the analysis of whether a succession of pant-hoots was produced by the same individual or any of the individuals in a subsequent visible encounter and to what extent the observed chimpanzee was able to identify the vocalizer. If either my research assistant, who is highly capable at identifying chimpanzees, or I was able to identify the vocalizer's identity or sex and age class, these details are noted in parentheses as "presumption". If our identification results were inconsistent or neither of us was able to make an identification, the identity of the vocalizer is not mentioned. The place and direction of a series of pant-hoots are also used as a reference in determining if they were vocalized by the same individual.

2 Sugawara (2004) uses this term in describing that in conversation among the African hunter-gatherer Bushmen, the pattern of "turn-taking" is used with the attitude that simultaneous speech is acceptable where there is no need for cognition. It is different from the usage of this term here that refers to the attitude of "anyone can choose any action any time" using the pant-hoot exchange pattern.

3 Incidentally, the M group of Mahale has a congregating season when many individuals synchronize the general direction of their ranging while continuing frequent meeting and parting, and a dispersing season when they range while separating into smaller parties with a reduced level of meeting and parting. Itoh (Chapter Seven) suggests the possibility that they have been repetitively producing assembly with their mutual anticipation that "everyone gathers on such an occasion" based on the fact that the phenomenon of "assembling", which is sparked by the fruiting of *Ilombo*, has been repeated yearly. While all of the cases in this chapter were observed in the dispersing season, during the congregating season, the frequency of pant-hoot utterances and hearing increases and pant-hoots are exchanged between many different individuals. Under these conditions, it is speculated that chimpanzees may repeat their calls and responses with the mutual expectation that "everyone exchanges pant-hoots on such an occasion" beyond the force of circumstances.

Chapter 9

1 Yeager's argument came to my attention thanks to a presentation given by Toru Soga at one of the Institution Research Project meetings.

2 Institution I emphasizes certain aspects of institution, namely, "organized system" and "systematic functions".

3 While I will not directly address this in the case analysis in this chapter, I can envisage the theoretical existence of institutions at the Institution III level in addition to the aforementioned two. Institution III could include proto-institutions, so to speak, which presuppose the emergence of some kind of normativity even though they do not rely on formal organizations with fixed boundaries functioning as meta-authorities or so-called laws or conventions. It is likely that Institution III will be the main subject of consideration in non-human primates. Nevertheless, the case analysis in this chapter will concentrate on institutions at the I and II levels due to space limitations.

Notes 419

4 Ethnographic studies on geographical and social conditions in the Sulu Archipelago and local ethnic groups such as Sama and Tausug include Nimmo (1972), Kiefer (1986), Sather (1997) and Tokoro (1999, 2011, 2013).

5 *Panglima* is traditionally one of the titles for prominent regional administrators appointed by the sultan of the kingdom of Sulu, but today it often refers to the barangay captain, the head of the smallest administrative unit called *barangay* in the Philippines.

Chapter 10

1 I am familiar with the work of Sagawa (2011), who uses quantitative data.

2 Whilst acknowledging that the five groups—excluding the Ik, Didinga and Acholi—are part of the Teso-Turkana group of Eastern Nilotic languages and that there are differences between them in their use of language, they can understand one another sufficiently well.

3 Accurately speaking, the Acholi farm one to several head of cattle, while there are also cases of the Ik keeping from a few to around ten goats as a result of government and NGO policies to turn them into crop and livestock farmers. However, because the Ik soon end up eating the goats that have been given to them, creating livestock farmers is proving rather difficult. In any case, it is thought that they are not seen as raiding targets because they have too few cattle.

4 It is said that amongst the Bodi of Ethiopia, when a treasured favorite bullock dies, its owner grieves deeply and wails, and when this turns to "anger", he goes and kills someone in an adjacent farming village.

Chapter 11

1 I have learned this way of understanding "meaning" from Osawa (1992, 1994). However, the description here is a substantially revised version that has been made applicable to pre-institutional societies.

2 Luhmann (1993) distinguishes three meaning dimensions—factual, temporal and social—to which these three here correspond.

3 This view originates in ecological perception theory developed by cognitive psychologist J. J. Gibson based on the understanding that "the physical stimuli to the sensory organs are not the only cause of perception" (Sasaki 1994). His successors call their position "ecological psychology". See Reed (2000) for a more comprehensive depiction.

Chapter 12

1 In this chapter, the term "behavior" is used where a certain behavior appears distinct from other behaviors in humans and all other animals. The will or intention of the individual displaying the behavior is irrelevant. On the other hand, the term "action" is used where the individual has an awareness of or an intention to perform the behavior.

Chapter 13

1 This diagram is reprinted through the courtesy of earth and planetary physicist Prof. Toshimichi Otsubo. In his discourse on the two-body problem aimed at university students, he derives Kepler's equation by expanding the polar coordinates (r, f) analytically, then substituting e, v, t_0, and performing integration (Otsubo 2009: 149).

2 To be more exact, Kepler envisaged yielding iteratively (Colwell 1993: 4): $M_0 = E_0 - e \sin E_0$, then $E_1 = E_0 + (M - M_0)$, calculate $M_1 = E_1 - e \sin E_1$, continue to $E_2 = E_1 + (M - M_1)$. Kepler's iteration is detailed in Thorvaldsen (2010).

3 See https://en.wikipedia.org/wiki/Kepler's_laws_of_planetary_motion.

4 $[\forall x(n) (x(n) \in A(n+1) \Leftrightarrow x(n) \in B(n+1))] \Leftrightarrow (A = B)$ and $[\forall x(n+1) (a \in x(n+1) \Leftrightarrow b \in x(n+1))] \Leftrightarrow (a = n)$. n and n+1 denote ranks, A and B are sets and a and b are symmetric polynomials with the same rank.

5 On this point, I was able to put together my argument thanks to the following advice from mathematician Yūji Yamada: "We cannot produce a logic from a logic; we must infuse a soul into a logic first before deriving another logic".

6 A proof is an absolute necessity for mathematicians, but it is not an appealing task. Keith Devlin states that "Only after the mathematician thinks she has solved a problem does she start to work out a logical proof …", then quotes the following words of Fields Medal winner Richard Borcherds: "The logical progression comes only right at the end, and it is in fact quite tiresome to check that all the details really work" (Devlin 2007: 269).

Chapter 14

1 "Mother" can be used in the same argument with some difference. We shall not discuss the difference here as such discussion is bound to deviate to a question at a different level, a cultural level.

2 Our discussion here is about the stage prior to the creation of institutions and therefore religious or ritual institutions such as ancestor worship are not relevant.

Chapter 15

1 Inuit society has been struck by waves of rapid change in all aspects of life since the forced transition from the traditional seasonal migratory lifestyle to sedentary ways of life under the Aboriginal assimilation policy of the Canadian government from the 1950s to the 1960s. Despite their changed circumstances, however, their subsistence activities have not lost their importance as the foundations of the Inuit lifestyle and identity. They actively practice subsistence activities so far as to say that "Inuit who do not engage in subsistence activities are not Inuit" (Stewart 1995). Although people commonly purchase commercial food products with their cash income, wild animal meat is still favored as "'real food' (*niqinmarik*)", which is essential for the preservation of their ethnic identity, and the distribution of this meat continues to function as one of the cornerstones for the maintenance of their social relations (Kishigami 1996, 2007; Stewart 1992; Wenzel 1991).

2 Damasio proposes three states: the state of "emotion" that is an unconscious physiological reaction, the state of "feeling" that is an unconscious expression of this state and the state of "feeling made conscious" that is a perceived feeling state. The latter two states are treated together as "feeling" in this chapter, as there is no need for the distinction for the purposes of discussion, and separating them would make the argument rather cumbersome. While I have used Damasio's concept in this chapter, there has been a wealth of studies on emotion and feeling in the fields of anthropology and psychology and there is a need to organize these concepts put forward in these studies and to position my discussion in this chapter in relation to these study findings. Further, as my discussion here is closely linked to Bowlby's attachment theory (Bowlby 1991), there is a need to consider it in that context. They will be the subjects of my future work.

3 It has been pointed out by Sugawara (2002) that one cannot directly perceive one's own emotion and that perceiving one's own emotion always involves interaction with others. As Takagi (2001) points out based on Vygotski's argument, not only emotion but also the self cannot be cognized directly by the self; interaction with others is essential for the self to be cognized.

Chapter 16

1 There has been much debate on the definitions of feeling and emotion in the fields of psychology, cognitive science and neuroscience, but I refrain from

discussing them in detail here. I shall make this distinction simply in order to consider the manner in which feeling is institutionalized.

Chapter 17

1 I conducted my first stint of fieldwork in the village over a period of one year and four months from 1987 to 1988. I have been visiting the village almost every year for periods of ten days to two months throughout the last twenty-five years. Na Chua who was fifty years old on my first visit is now seventy-six.

2 The term *yai* is used to address maternal grandmothers in Thailand. The term *ya* is used for paternal grandmothers.

3 While purportedly collected for merit making for the deceased (*tambun*), it is commonly understood that the money is to help the host of the funeral financially. It has become mandatory for villagers to attend funerals and give condolence money.

4 If the money donated exceeds the funeral expenses, the family members who bore the expenses share the profit. One villager even went so far as to say that it was like capital investment, albeit acknowledging the inappropriateness of their remarks.

5 In rituals at temples, villagers offer food and pray for the good fortune of the dead.

6 As mentioned at the beginning of the chapter, Uchibori in Chapter Two also noted that the physical dimension that involves the maintenance of individual life is the foundation of all; and when meaning is ascribed to it, it generates a new dimension that could lead to the emergence of institutions. Uchibori calls this "death" as opposed to "dying". Uchibori shares Imamura's view in that he envisages institutions as human cohesion, and hence social events.

Chapter 18

1 From another point of view, this can be interpreted as a game to invoke a secondary rule, i.e., meta-play centering on "We" consciousness such as play to alter play or a rule to change a rule. I call this complexity in terms of logical types/levels within these seemingly simple actions "promiscuity" (Kuroda 2011).

2 It is a highly biotic concept as it can be compared to entropy egestion, excrement or extended phenotypes to maintain an organization.

Bibliography

Adachi, K. (2003) "Kongun to iu shakai" (The society of mixed species associations). In M. Nishida, K. Kitamura and J. Yamagiwa (eds), *Ningensei no kigen to shinka* (Origin and evolution of human nature). Kyoto: Shōwadō, 204–232.

Adachi, K. (2013) "The sociology of anti-structure: Toward a climax of groups". In K. Kawai (ed.), *Groups: The Evolution of Human Sociality*. Kyoto and Melbourne: Kyoto University Press and Trans Pacific Press, 21–41.

Ahern, E. M. (1981) *Chinese Ritual and Politics*. Cambridge: Cambridge University Press.

Akazawa, T. (2010) "Jinrui shi no wakareme—Kyūjin Neanderutāru to shinjin Sapiensu no kōtai geki" (A turning point in human history: Transition from Neanderthals to Sapiens). *Bunka jinruigaku* (Japanese journal of cultural anthropology), 74(4): 517–540.

Anderson, B. (1983) *Imagined Communities: Reflections on the Origin and Spread of Nationalism*. New York: Verso.

Ando, J. (2011) "Kyōikugaku wa kagaku ka shisō ka—Shinka kyōikugaku no shatei" (Is pedagogy a science or a philosophy?: The scope of evolutionary pedagogy). *Tetsugaku* (Philosophy), Keiō Gijuku 150-nen kinen ronbun shū, 127: 87–117.

Anezaki, H. and T. Katayama (2002) *Kuma ni attara dōsuru ka—Ainu minzoku saigo no karyūdo* (What to do if you encounter a bear: The last Ainu hunter). Tokyo: Kirakusha.

Ariès, P. (1962) *Centuries of Childhood: A Social History of Family Life*. New York: Vintage Books.

Asimov, I. and R. Silverberg (2000) *Andrew NDR114*. Japanese translation of I. Asimov and R. Silverberg (1976) *Andrew NDR114*, T. Nakamura (trans.). Tokyo: Sogensha.

Aso, T. (1998) "Naze otona ha kodomo to asobunoka?" (Why do grownups play with children?). In T. Aso and T. Watamaki (eds), *Asobi to iu nazo* (The mystery of play), Series—Hattatsu to shōgai wo saguru (Exploration of development and disability). Tokyo: Minerva Shobō.

Atkinson, M. (1992) *The Art and Politics of Wana Shamanship*. Berkeley: University of California Press.

Azuma, H. (1987) "Manabu koto to oshieru koto" (Learning and teaching). In H. Azuma et al. (eds), *Manabu koto to oshieru koto* (Learning and teaching), Iwanami kōza: Kyōiku no hōhō 1. Tokyo: Iwanami Shoten, 3–28.

Balikci, A. (1989) *The Netsilik Eskimo*. Long Grove: Waveland Press.

Becker, E. (1989) *Shi no kyozetsu*. Japanese translation of E. Becker (1973) *The Denial of Death*, S. Kon (trans.). Tokyo: Heibonsha.

Bell, C. (1992) *Ritual Theory, Ritual Practice*. Oxford: Oxford University Press.

Bloch, M. (1974) "Symbols, songs, dance and the features of articulation: Is religion an extreme form of traditional authority?". *Archives Européenes de Sociologie*, 15: 55–81.

Bloch, M. (1989) *Ritual, History and Power: Selected Papers in Anthropology*. London: The Athlone Press.

Bodenhorn, B. (1989) *The Animals Come to Me, They Know I Share: Inupiaq Kinship, Changing Economic Relations and Enduring World Views on Alaska's North Slope*. PhD thesis: Cambridge University.

Boesch, C. (1991) "Teaching among wild chimpanzees". *Animal Behaviour*, 41: 530–532.

Boesch, C. and H. Boesch (2000) *The Chimpanzees of the Taï Forest: Behavioural Ecology and Evolution*. Oxford: Oxford University Press.

Boesch, C. and M. Tomasello (1998) "Chimpanzee and human cultures". *Current Anthropology*, 39(5): 591–614.

Bohannan, P. (1960) "Introduction". In P. Bohannan (ed.), *African Homicide and Suicide*. Princeton: Princeton University Press.

Bohannan, P. (ed.) (1960) *African Homicide and Suicide*. Princeton: Princeton University Press.

Bourdieu, P. (1988) *Jissen kankaku I*. Japanese translation of P. Bourdieu (1980) *Le Sens Pratique I*, H. Imamura and T. Minatomichi (trans.). Tokyo: Misuzu Shobō.

Bourdieu, P. (1992[1981]) "Rites as acts of institution". In J. G. Peristiany and J. A. Pitt-Rivers, *Honor and Grace in Anthropology*. Cambridge: Cambridge University Press, 79–89.

Bowlby, J. (1991) *Aichaku kōdō—Boshi kankei no riron (1)*. Japanese translation of J. Bowlby (1969) *Attachment: Attachment and Loss Volume One*, J. Kuroda (trans.). Tokyo: Iwasaki Gakujutsu Shuppansha.

Bowles, S. and H. Gintis (2011) *A Cooperative Species: Human Reciprocity and Its Evolution*. Princeton: Princeton University Press.

Boyer, P. and P. Lienard (2006) "Why ritualized behavior?: Precaution systems and action parsing in developmental, pathological and cultural rituals". *Behavioral and Brain Sciences*, 29: 1–56.

Briggs, J. L. (1968) *Utkuhikhalingmiut Eskimo Emotional Expression*. Ottawa: Department of Indian Affairs and Northern Development, Northern Science Research Group.

Briggs, J. L. (1970) *Never in Anger: Portrait of an Eskimo Family*. Cambridge: Harvard University Press.

Briggs, J. L. (1979) *Aspects of Inuit Value Socialization*. Ottawa: National Museum of Canada.

Briggs, J. L. (1998) *Inuit Morality Play: The Emotional Education of a Three-Year-Old*. New Haven: Yale University Press & ISER Books, Memorial University.

Brown, N. O. (1970) *Erosu to tanatosu*. Japanese translation of N. O. Brown (1959) *Life Against Death: The Psychoanalytical Meaning of History*, S. Akiyama (trans.). Tokyo: Takeuchi Shoten.

Bshary, R. (2001) "Diana monkeys, *Cercopithecus diana*, adjust their anti-predator response behavior to human hunting strategies". *Behavioral Ecology and Sociobiology*, 50: 251–256.

Bundo, D. (2010) "Sōgō kōi no porifonī—Baka pigumī no ongaku jissen" (Polyphony of interaction: Musical practices of Baka pygmies). In D. Kimura, M. Nakamura and K. Takanashi (eds), *Intārakushon no kyōkai to setsuzoku—Saru, hito, kaiwa kenkyū kara* (Boundary and conjunction of social interaction: Studies in nonhuman primates, humans and conversation). Tokyo: Shōwadō, 207–226.

Burghardt, G. (2005) *The Genesis of Animal Play: Testing the Limits*. Cambridge: The MIT Press.

Byrne, R. W. (2002) "Imitation of novel complex actions: What does the evidence from animals mean?". *Advances in the Study of Behavior*, 31: 77–105.

Byrne, R. W. and A. Whiten (1989) *Machiavellian Intelligence: Social Expertise and the Evolution of Intellect in Monkeys, Apes, and Humans*. London: Clarendon Press.

Caillois, R. (1974) *Senso ron—Wareware no uchi ni hisomu megami Berona*. Japanese translation of R. Caillois (1963) *Bellone ou la pente de la guerre*, S. Akieda (trans.). Tokyo: Hosei Daigaku Shuppankyoku.

Call, J. and M. Tomasello (2008) "Does the chimpanzee have a theory of mind? 30 years later". *Trends in Cognitive Sciences*, 12(5): 187–192.

Caro, T. M. and M. D. Hauser (1992) "Is there teaching in nonhuman animals?". *The Quarterly Review of Biology*, 67: 151–174.

Chapman, C. A., R. W. Wrangham and L. J. Chapman (1995) "Ecological constraints on group size: An analysis of spider monkey and chimpanzee subgroups". *Behavioral Ecology and Sociobiology*, 36: 59–70.

Chiba, T. (1994) *Nipponjin ha naze seppuku surunoka* (Why Japanese commit self-disembowelment). Tokyo: Tōkyōdō Shuppan.

Colwell, P. (1993) *Solving Kepler's Equation: Over Three Centuries*. Richmond: Willmann-Bell.

Cords, M. (1987) *Mixed-Species Association of Cercopithecus Monkeys in the Kakamega Forest, Kenya*. University of California Publications in Zoology, 117.

Csibra, G. (2007) "Teachers in the wild". *Trends in Cognitive Sciences*, 11(3): 95–96.

Csibra, G. and G. Gergely (2006) "Social learning and social cognition: The case for pedagogy". In Y. Munakata and M. J. Johnson (eds), *Process of Change in Brain and Cognitive Development: Attention and Performance*. Oxford: Oxford University Press, 249–274.

Csibra, G. and G. Gergely (2009) "Natural pedagogy". *Trends in Cognitive Sciences*, 13(4): 148–149.

Csibra, G. and G. Gergely (2011) "Natural pedagogy as evolutionary adaptation". *Philosophical Transactions of the Royal Society B*, 366: 1149–1157.

Damasio, A. (2003) *Muishiki no no jiko ishiki no no*. Japanese translation of A. Damasio (1999) *The Feeling of What Happens: Body and Emotion in the Making of Consciousness*, M. Tanaka (trans.). Tokyo: Kōdansha.

Damasio, A. (2005) *Kanjiru no*. Japanese translation of A. Damasio (2003) *Looking for Spinoza*, M. Tanaka (trans.). Tokyo: Daiyamondosha.

Damasio, A. (2010) *Dekaruto no ayamari*. Japanese translation of A. Damasio (1994) *Descartes' Error: Emotion, Reason, and the Human Brain*, M. Tanaka (trans.). Tokyo: Chikuma Shobō.

Davies, P. (2008) *Kōun na uchū*. Japanese translation of P. Davies (2007) *The Goldilocks enigma*, M. Yoshida (trans.). Tokyo: Nikkei BP sha.

Dawkins, R. (1987) *Enchō sareta hyōgen kei—Shizen tōta no tan'i toshiteno idenshi*. Japanese translation of R. Dawkins (1982) *The Extended Phenotype*, T. Hidaka, T. Endo and A. Endo (trans.). Tokyo: Kinokuniya Shoten.

De Certeau, M. (1987) *Nichijōteki jissen no poietiku*. Japanese translation of M. de Certeau (1980) *L'invention du quotidien*, T. Yamada (trans.). Tokyo: Kōkubunsha.

De Waal, F. (1982) *Chimpanzee Politics: Power and Sex Among Apes*. London: Jonathan Cape.

De Waal, F. (1989) *Peacemaking among Primates*. Cambridge: Harvard University Press.

De Waal, F. (1996) *Good Natured: The Origins of Right and Wrong in Humans and Other Animals*. Cambridge: Harvard University Press.

De Waal, F. (2010) *Kyōkan no jidai he—Dōbutsu kōdōgaku ga oshietekureru koto*.

Japanese translation of F. de Waal (2009) *The Age of Empathy: Nature's Lessons for a Kinder Society*, H. Shibata (trans.). Tokyo: Kinokuniya Shoten.

Devlin, K. (2007) *Sūgakusuru idenshi*. Japanese translation of K. Devlin (2000) *The Math Gene*, A. Yamashita (trans.). Tokyo: Hayakawa Shobō.

Dubreuil, B. (2008) "The cognitive foundations of institutions". In B. Hardy-Vallee and B. Payette (eds), *Beyond the Brain: Embodied, Situated and Distributed Cognition*. Newcastle: Cambridge Scholars Publishing, 125–140.

Dulaney, S. and A. P. Fiske (1994) "Cultural rituals and obsessive-compulsive disorder: Is there a common psychological mechanism?". *Ethos*, 22(3): 243–283.

Dunbar, R. I. M. (1992) "Neocortex size as a constraint on group size in primates". *Journal of Human Evolution*, 20: 469–493.

Dunbar, R. I. M. (1993) "Coevolution of neocortical size, group size and language in humans". *Behavioral and Brain Science*, 16: 681–735.

Eilam, D., R. Zor, H. Hermesh and H. Szechtman (2006) "Rituals, stereotypy and compulsive behavior in animals and humans". *Neuroscience and Biobehavioral Reviews*, 30(4): 456–471.

Elton, C. (1927) *Animal Ecology*. London: Sidgwick and Jackson.

Elton, C. (1966) *The Pattern of Animal Communities*. New York: Wiley.

Endo, A. (1992) "Seibutsu sekai no konouenaku fukuzatsuna sōgo sayō" (The most complex interactions in the world of organisms). In M. Higashi and T. Abe (eds), *Chikyū kyōsei kei towa nanika* (Symbiotic planet). Tokyo: Heibonsha.

Erikson, E. H. (1966) "Ontogeny of ritualization in man". *Philosophical Transactions of the Royal Society of London Series B*, 251: 337–349.

Evans-Pritchard, E. E. (1969[1940)] *The Nuer: A Description of the Modes of Livelihood and Political Institutions of a Nilotic People*. Oxford: Oxford University Press.

Fagen, R. (1981) *Animal Play Behavior*. New York: Oxford University Press.

Fienup-Riordan, A. (1983) *The Nelson Island Eskimo*. Anchorage: Alaska Pacific University Press.

Fiske, A. P. and N. Haslam (1997) "Is obsessive-compulsive disorder a pathology of the human disposition to perform socially meaningful rituals?: Evidence of similar content". *The Journal of Nervous and Mental Disease*, 185(4): 211–222.

Fortes, M. and E. E. Evans-Pritchard (2015[1940]) "Introduction". In M. Fortes and E. E. Evans-Pritchard (eds), *African Political Systems*. New York: Routledge, 1–24.

Foster, M. G. (1972) "The anatomy of envy". *Current Anthropology*, 13(2): 165–202.

Foucault, M. (2010) *Kangoku no tanjō—Kanshi to shobatsu*. Japanese translation of M. Foucault (1977) *Discipline and Punish*, H. Tamura (trans.). Tokyo: Shinchōsha.

Frazer, J. G. (2002) *Kinshi hen*. Japanese translation of J. G. Frazer (1890) *The Golden Bough*, T. Nagahashi (trans.). Tokyo: Iwanami Shoten.

Freud, S. (2007) "Kyōhaku kōi to shūkyō girei". Japanese translation of S. Freud (1907) "Obsessive actions and religious practices", T. Michihata (trans.), in *Furoito zenshū 9, 1906–1909* (Complete works of Freud 9, 1906–1909). Tokyo: Iwanami Shoten, 201–212.

Freud, S. (2009) "Tōtemu to tabū". Japanese translation of S. Freud (1913) "Totem and taboo", N. Sudo and K. Kadowaki (trans.), in *Furoito zenshū 9, 1912–1913* (Complete works of Freud 9, 1912–1913), Tokyo: Iwanami Shoten, 1–206.

Fry, D. (2005) "Rough-and-tumble social play in humans". In A. Pellegrini and P. Smith (eds), *The Nature of Play: Great Apes and Humans*. New York: The Guilford Press.

Fukui, K. (1993) "Tatakai to heijunka kikō—Sūdan nanbu Narimu kachiku ryakudatsu no jirei kara" (Battles and equalisation mechanisms: Cases of livestock looting by the Narim of South Sudan). *Shakai jinruigaku nenpō* (Annual report of the Japanese journal of social anthropology). Tokyo: Kōbundō, 19: 1–38.

Fukui, K. (2004a) "Bokuchikumin ni yoru nōkōmin he no shūgeki to ryakudatsu–Echiopia seinanbu ni oite kurikaesareru tatakai kara" (Attacks on farmers by pastoralists: Repeated attacks in Southern Ethiopia). In H. Fujiki and T. Udagawa (eds), *Kōgeki to bōei no kiseki* (Traces of attacks and self-defence). Tokyo: Tōyō shorin, 210–242.

Fukui, K. et al. (2004b) "Tokushū: Hito wa naze tatakau no ka" (Special edition: Why do people fight?). In K. Fukui (ed.), *Kikan minzokugaku* (Ethnology quarterly), 109: 4–62.

Fukushima, M. (2001) *Anmoku chi no kaibō—Ninchi to shakai no intāfēsu* (Anatomy of tacit knowing: Interface between cognition and society). Tokyo: Kaneko Shobō.

Fuller, R. Buckminster (1992) *Cosmography: A Posthumous Scenario for the Future of Humanity*. New York: Macmillan Publishing Company.

Funabiki, T. (1985) "Himoji komyunikeshon no ba toshiteno girei" (Ritual as a field of nontextual communication). *Bunka jinruigaku* (Japanese journal of cultural anthropology), 1: 40–47.

Funabiki, T. (1987) "Girei ni okeru ba to kōzō" (Field and structure of ritual). In A. Ito et al. (eds), *Gendai no shakai jinruigaku dai 2 kan: Girei to kōkan no kōi* (Contemporary social anthropology vol. 2: Ritual and exchange). Tokyo: Daigaku Shuppankai, 3–29.

Funabiki, T. (2013) "Human groups at the zero-level: An exploration of the meaning, field and structure of relations at the level of group extinction". In K. Kawai (ed.), *Groups: The Evolution of Human Sociality*. Kyoto and Melbourne: Kyoto University Press and Trans Pacific Press, 309–322.

Garvey, C. (1980) *Gokko no kōzō—Kodomo no asobi no sekai* (Play: The developing child). Japanese translation of C. Garvey (1977) *Play*, T. Takahashi (trans.). Tokyo: Saiensusha.

Gause, G. E. (1936) *The Struggle for Existence*. Baltimore: Williams and Wilkins.

Gelfand, S. I., M. L. Gerver, A. A. Kirillov and N. N. Konstantinov (2002) *Sequences, Combinations, Limits*. New York: Courier Dover.

Girard, R. (1971) *Yokubō no genshōgaku—Romantiku no kyogi to romanesuku no shinjitsu*. Japanese translation of R. Girard (1961) *Mensonge romantique et Vérité romanesque*, Y. Furuta (trans.). Tokyo: Hōsei Daigaku Shuppankyoku.

Gluckman, M. (1955) *Custom and Conflict in Africa*. Oxford: Blackwell.

Gomez, J. C. and B. Martin-Andrade (2005) "Fantasy play in apes". In A. Pellegrini and P. Smith (eds), *The Nature of Play: Great Apes and Humans*. New York: The Guilford Press.

Goodall, J. (1971) *In the Shadow of Man*. London: Collins.

Goodall, J. (1986) *The Chimpanzees of Gombe: Patterns of Behavior*. Cambridge: Belknap.

Goodall, J. (1990) *Yasei chinpanjī no sekai*. Japanese translation of J. Goodall (1986) *The Chimpanzees of Gombe: Patterns of Behavior*, Y. Sugiyama and T. Matsuzawa (trans.). Kyoto: Minerva Shobō.

Gosso, Y., E. Otta, M. Morais, F. Ribeiro and V. Bussab (2005) "Play in hunter-gatherer society". In A. Pellegrini and P. Smith (eds), *The Nature of Play: Great Apes and Humans*. New York: The Guilford Press.

Graeber, D. (2011) *Debt: The First 5,000 Years*. New York: Melville House.

Greiffenhagen, C. and W. Sharrock (2006) "Mathematical relativism". *Journal for the Theory of Social Behaviour*, 36(2): 97–117.

Grinnell, J. (1917) "The niche-relationships of the California thrasher". *The Auk*, 34: 427–433.

Hamamoto, M. (2001) *Chitsujo no hōhō—Kenia kaigan chihō no nichijō seikatsu ni okeru gireiteki jissen to katari* (Mechanism for order: Ritual practices and stories in everyday life in the Kenyan coastal region). Tokyo: Kōbundō.

Hanamura, S. (2010a) "Gūyūsei ni tayutau chinpanjī—Chōkyori onsei wo kaishita sōgō kōi to kyōzai no arikata" (Interaction through long-distance calls and mode of auditory co-presence in chimpanzees: Contexts and contingency of hearer's action). In D. Kimura, M. Nakamura and K. Takanashi (eds), *Intārakushon no kyōkai to setsuzoku—Saru, hito, kaiwa kenkyū kara* (Boundary and conjunction of social interaction: Studies in nonhuman primates, humans and conversation). Tokyo: Shōwadō, 185–204.

Hanamura, S. (2010b) "Chinpanjī no chōkyori onsei wo kaishita kōi setsuzoku no yarikata to shikaigai ni hirogaru ba no yōtai" (Long-distance calls by chimpanzees: How they connect actions and organize their social field beyond visual contact). *Reichōrui Kenkyū* (Primate research), 26: 159–176.

Haraway, D. (2000) *Saru to onna to saibōgu—Shizen no sai hatsumei.* Japanese translation of D. Haraway (1991) *Simians, Cyborgs, and Women—The Reinvention of Nature*, S. Takahashi (trans.). Tokyo: Seidosha.

Harris, G. G. (2007) *Casting Out Anger: Religion among the Taita of Kenya.* Cambridge: Cambridge University Press.

Hashizume, D. (2003) *Ningen ni totte hō toha nanika* (What is law for humans?). Tokyo: PHP Shuppan.

Hayaki, H. (1985) "Social play of juvenile and adolescent chimpanzees in the Mahale Mountains National Park, Tanzania". *Primates*, 26: 343–360.

Hayaki, H. (1990) *Chinpanjī no naka no hito* (The human inside the chimpanzee). Tokyo: Shōkabō.

Hayaki, H. (2002) "Asobi no seiritsu" (Emergence of play). In T. Nishida, K. Kawanaka and S. Uehara (eds), *Mahare no chinpanjī—"Pansuroporoji" no 37 nen* (Mahale chimpanzees: The 37 years of "panthropology"). Kyoto: Daigaku Gakujutsu Shuppankai.

Hayaki, H., M. A. Huffman and T. Nishida (1989) "Dominance among male chimpanzees in the Mahale Mountains National Park, Tanzania: A preliminary study". *Primates*, 30: 187–197.

Hayek, F. A. (1967a) "The result of human action but not of human design". In F. A. Hayek, *Studies in Philosophy, Politics, and Economics.* London: Routledge and Kegan Paul.

Hayek, F. A. (1967b) "Dr. Bernard Mandeville". *Proceedings of British Academy*, 52: 125–141.

Hayek, F. A. (1969) "The primacy of the abstract". In A. Koestler and J. R. Smythies (eds), *Beyond Reductionism: The Alpbach Symposium*. London: Hutchinson.

Hayek, F. A. (1973) *Law, Legislation and Liberty, Volume 1: Rules and Order*. Chicago: University of Chicago Press.

Heintz, B. (2003) "When is a proof a proof?". *Social Studies of Science*, 33(6): 929–943.

Hinde, R. A. (ed.) (1972) *Non-Verbal Communication*. Cambridge: Cambridge University Press.

Hinde, R. A. (1974) *Biological Bases of Human Social Behavior*. New York: McGraw-Hill.

Honigman, J. J. and I. Honigman (1965) *Eskimo Townsmen*. Ottawa: Canadian Research Centre for Anthropology.

Horn, H. S. (1966) "Measurement of 'overlap' in comparative ecological studies". *The American Naturalist*, 100: 419–424.

Hosaka, K. (1997) *Mahare sankai ni seisokusuru chinpanjī no shūryō nikushoku kodo* (Hunting and predation in chimpanzees at the Mahale Mountains). PhD thesis: Kyoto University.

Hosaka, K. and T. Nishida (2002) "Osutorashizumu—Arufā osu, murahachibu karano fukken" (Ostracism: Restoration of an alpha male from ostracism). In T. Nishida et al. (eds), *Mahare no chinpanjī—"Pansuroporoji" no 37 nen* (The Mahale chimpanzees: 37 years of "panthropology"). Kyoto: Kyoto Daigaku Gakujutsu Shuppankai, 439–471.

Hosaka, K., A. Matsumoto, M. A. Huffman and K. Kawanaka (2000) "Mahale no yasei chinpanjī ni okeru dōshu kotai no shitai ni taisuru hannō" (Reactions to the dead body of a conspecific individual in wild chimpanzees in Mahale). *Reichorui kenkyu* (Primate research), 16(1): 1–15.

Hume, D. (2007[1739–1740]) *A Treatise of Human Nature*. Two vols., edited by D. F. and M. Norton. Oxford: Oxford University Press.

Humphrey, C. and J. Laidlaw (1994) *The Archetypal Actions of Ritual: A Theory of Ritual Illustrated by the Jain Rite of Worship*. Oxford: Clarendon Press.

Humphrey, N. K. (1976) "The social function of intellect". In P. P. G. Bateson and R. A. Hinde (eds), *Growing Points in Ethology*. Cambridge: Cambridge University Press, 303–317.

Hutchinson, G. E. (1957) "Concluding remarks". *Cold Springs Harbor Symposia on Quantitative Biology*, 22: 415–427.

Hutchinson, S. E. (1996) *Nuer Dilemmas: Coping with Money, War, and the State*. Berkeley: University of California Press.

Huxley, J. (1966) "Introduction to a discussion on ritualization of behavior in animals and man". *Philosophical Transactions of the Royal Society of London Series B*, 251: 249–271.

Ichikawa, M. (1982) *Mori no shuryō min—Mubuti pigumī no seikatsu* (Hunters of the forest: The life of the Mbuti Pygmy). Kyoto: Jinbun Shoin.

Ichikawa, M. (1991) "Byōdō shugi no sinkashi teki kōsatsu" (An evolutionary historical examination of egalitarianism). In J. Tanaka and M. Kakeya (eds), *Hito no shizen shi* (Natural history of humanity). Tokyo: Heibonsha, 11–34.

Ikuta, K. (1987) *"Waza" kara shiru* (Learning from "skills"). Korekushon ninchi kagaku 6, Tokyo: Tokyo Daigaku Shuppankai.

Imamura, H. (1982) *Bōryoku no ontorogī* (The ontology of violence). Tokyo: Keisō Shobō.

Imamura, H. (1989, 1992) *Haijo no kōzō—Chikara no ippan keizai josetsu* (The structure of exclusion: Introduction to the general economics of power). Tokyo: Chikuma Gakugei Bunko.

Imamura, H. (2005) *Marukusu nyūmon* (Introduction to Marx). Tokyo: Chikuma Shobō.

Imamura, H. (2007) *Shakaisei no tetsugaku* (The philosophy of sociality). Tokyo: Iwanami Shoten.

Imamura, K. (2010) *Sabaku ni ikiru onna tachi* (Women living in the desert). Tokyo: Dōbutsusha.

Imanishi, K. (1949) *Seibutsu shakai no ronri* (The logic of living things societies). Tokyo: Mainichi Simbunsha.

Inagaki, K. and G. Hatano (1989) *Hito wa ikani manabu ka* (How people learn). Tokyo: Chūō Kōron Shinsha.

Ingold, T. (2000) *The Perception of the Environment*. New York: Routledge.

Inoue, S., S. S. K. Kaburu and N. E. Newton-Fisher (2012) "Yasei chinpanjī ni okeru shūdan nai arūfa osu goroshi to sono shitai heno hannō—Jirei hokoku" (Killing of the alpha male and reactions to its corpse within a community of wild chimpanzees: A case study). Presented at the 28th Conference of the Primate Society of Japan (7 July, Sugiyama Jogakuen University).

Itakura, S. (1999) "Reichōrui ni okeru 'kokoro no riron' kenkyū no genzai" (The present status of research on "theory of mind" in primates). *Reichōrui kenkyū* (Primate research), 15: 231–242.

Itani, J. (1973) *Takasakiyama no saru* (Japanese monkeys in Takasakiyama). Tokyo: Kōdansha.

Itani, J. (1981) "Kokoro no oitachi—Shakai to kōdō" (The upbringing of the mind:

Society and behavior). *Kōza Gendai no shinrigaku* (Lectures: Contemporary psychology). Tokyo: Shōgakukan.

Itani, J. (1986) "Ningen byōdō kigen ron" (Thesis of the origin and bases of equality among humans). In J. Itani and J. Tanaka (eds), *Shizen shakai no jinruigaku—Afurika ni ikiru* (Anthropology of natural societies: Living in Africa). Kyoto: Academia Shuppankai.

Itani, J. (1987) *Reichorui shakai no shinka* (The evolution of primate society). Tokyo: Heibonsha.

Itani, J. (1991) "Karuchua no gainen—Aidentifikēshon ron sonogo" (The concept of monkey culture: After identification theory). In T. Nishida et al. (eds), *Saru no bunka shi* (The cultural history of primates). Tokyo: Heibonsha.

Itani, J. (1993) *Chinpanjī no gen'ya—Yasei no ronri wo motomete* (The wild life of chimpanzees: In search of logic in the wilderness). Tokyo: Heibonsha.

Itoh, N. (2002) "Mori no naka no tabemono—Chinpanjī no shokumotsu mitsudo to kukan bunpu" (Food in the woods: Food density and spatial distribution for chimpanzees). In T. Nishida et al. (eds), *Mahare no chinpanjī—"Pansuroporojī" no 37 nen* (The Mahale chimpanzees: 37 years of "panthropology"). Kyoto: Kyoto Daigaku Gakujutsu Shuppankai, 77–100.

Itoh, N. (2003) "Matomaru koto no mekanizumu" (Mechanism of assembling). In M. Nishida, K. Kitamura and J. Yamagiwa (eds), *Ningensei no kigen to shinka* (Origin and evolution of human nature). Kyoto: Shōwadō, 233–262.

Itoh, N. (2004) *Mahare Sankai Kokuritsu Kōen no shokubutsu fenolojī to chinpanjī no rigo shūsansei* (The plant phenology and fission-fusion social system in chimpanzees at the Mahale Mountains National Park). PhD thesis: Kyoto University.

Itoh, N. (2013) "A group of chimpanzees: The world viewed from females' perspectives". In K. Kawai (ed.), *Groups: The Evolution of Human Sociality*. Kyoto and Melbourne: Kyoto University Press and Trans Pacific Press, 111–119.

Itoh, N. and D. Muramatsu (2015) "Patterns and trends in fruiting phenology: Some important implications for chimpanzee diet". In M. Nakamura, K. Hosaka, N. Itoh and K. Zamma (eds), *Mahale Chimpanzees: 50 Years of Research*. Cambridge: Cambridge University Press, 174–194.

Itoh, N. and M. Nakamura (2015a) "Diet and feeding behavior". In M. Nakamura, K. Hosaka, N. Itoh and K. Zamma (eds), *Mahale Chimpanzees: 50 Years of Research*. Cambridge: Cambridge University Press, 227–245.

Itoh, N. and M. Nakamura (2015b) "Mahale flora: Its historical background and long-term changes". In M. Nakamura, K. Hosaka, N. Itoh and K. Zamma (eds),

Mahale Chimpanzees: 50 Years of Research. Cambridge: Cambridge University Press, 150–173.

Itoh, N. and T. Nishida (2007) "Chimpanzee grouping patterns and food availability in Mahale Mountains National Park, Tanzania". *Primates*, 48(2): 87–96.

Itoh, N., K. Zamma, T. Matsumoto, H. Nishie and M. Nakamura (2015) "Appendix II: Dietary list". In M. Nakamura, K. Hosaka, N. Itoh and K. Zamma (eds), *Mahale Chimpanzees: 50 Years of Research*. Cambridge: Cambridge University Press, 717–739.

Jensen, C. (2011) "Introduction: Contexts for a comparative relativism". *Common Knowledge* (Special issue: "Comparative relativism: Symposium on an impossibility"), 17(1): 1–12.

Kakeya, M. (1983) "Netami no seitaijinruigaku" (Ecological anthropology of envy). In R. Otsuka (ed.), *Gendai no jinruigaku I, seitai jinruigaku* (Anthropology of today I, ecological anthropology). Tokyo: Shibundō, 229–241.

Kakeya, M. (1987) "Netami no seitaigaku" (Ecology of anthropology of envy). In *Sōzō no sekai* (World of creation), vol. 6. Tokyo: Shōgakukan, 56–83.

Kakeya, M. (1994) "Yakihata nōkō shakai to heijunka kikō" (Shifting cultivation society and the leveling mechanism). In R. Otsuka (ed.), *Kōza chikyū ni ikiru (3), shigen eno bunka tekiō* (Lectures on living on the Earth (3), cultural adaptation to natural resources). Tokyo: Yūzankaku Shuppan, 121–145.

Kamei, N. (2010) *Mori no chiisana "hantā" tachi—Shuryō saishūmin no kodomo no minzokushi* (Little "hunters" of the forest: An ethnography of hunter-gatherer children). Kyoto: Daigaku Gakujutsu Shuppankai.

Kani, T. (1944) "Keiryūsei konchū no seitai—Kagerō, tobikera, kawagera sonotano yōchū ni tsuite" (Ecology of stream-living insects: Mayfly, caddis fly, stonefly and other aquatic insect larvae). *Nippon seibutsu shi* (The Japanese journal of biology), 4, konchū jōkan. Tokyo: Kenkyusha.

Kawai, K. (2004) "Dodosu ni okeru kachiku no ryakudatsu to rinsetsu shūdan kan no kankei" (Dodoth cattle looting, raiding and relations with adjacent neighboring ethnic groups). In J. Tanaka, S. Sato, K. Sugawara and I. Ohta (eds), *Yudomin (nomaddo): Afurika no genya ni ikiru* (Nomads: Living on the African fields). Kyoto: Shōwadō, 542–566.

Kawai, K. (2006) "Kyanpu idō to chō uranai: Dodosu ni okeru rinsetsu shūdan to no kankei wo meguru shakai kūkan no seisei kijo" (Animal camp migration and intestinal divination rituals: Dodoth mechanisms creating social space around relations with neighboring groups). In R. Nishii and S. Tanabe (eds), *Shakai kukan no jinruigaku: materiaritī, shūtai, modaniti* (The

Anthropology of social spaces: Materiality, agents and modernity). Kyoto: Sekai Shisōsha, 175–202.

Kawai, K. (2007) "Dodosu no chō uranai: bokuchikumin no yūdō ni kakawaru jōhō to chishiki shigen no keisei wo megutte" (Dodoth intestinal divination: The formation of information and knowledge resources concerning the nomadic ways of pastoral peoples). In C. Daniels (ed.), *Chishiki shigen no in to yō* (The positives and negatives of knowledge resources). Tokyo: Kōbundō, 29–71.

Kawai, K. (2013) "Forming a gang: Raiding among pastoralists and the 'practice of cooperativity'". In K. Kawai (ed.), *Groups: The Evolution of Human Sociality*. Kyoto and Melbourne: Kyoto University Press and Trans Pacific Press, 167–186.

Kawai, K. (ed.) (2013) *Groups: The Evolution of Human Sociality*. Kyoto and Melbourne: Kyoto University Press and Trans Pacific Press.

Kawai, M. (1992) *Ningen no yurai* (Human origins). Tokyo: Shōgakukan.

Kawanaka, K. (1991) "Fukei shūdan no osu tachi—Chinpanjī no osu no shakaiteki seichō" (Males in patrilineal groups—Social development in male chimpanzees). In T. Nishida et al. (eds), *Saru no bunka shi* (Simian culture). Tokyo: Heibonsha, 217–239.

Keesing, R. M. (1975) *Kin Groups and Social Structure*. New York: Holt, Rinehart and Winston.

Kiefer, T. (1986) *The Tausug: Violence and Law in a Philippine Moslem Society*. Illinois: Waveland Press.

Kimura, D. (1991) "Tōtekiteki hatsuwa—Bongando no 'aite wo tokutei shinai ōgoe no hatsuwa' ni tsuite" (Casting talk-addressee-unspecified loud speech of the Bongando). In J. Tanaka and M. Kakeya (eds), *Hito no shizenshi* (Natural history of humanity). Tokyo: Heibonsha, 59–88.

Kimura, D. (2003) *Kyōzai kankaku: Afurika no futatsu no shakai ni okeru gengoteki sōgo kōi kara* (Sense of co-presence: Verbal interaction among two African societies). Kyoto: Kyoto Daigaku Gakujutsu Shuppankai.

Kimura, Y. (1983) *Warai no shakaigaku* (A sociology of laughter). Kyoto: Sekai shisōsha.

Kishigami, N. (1996) "Kanada kyokuhoku chiiki ni okeru shakai henka no tokushitsu ni tsuite" (Characteristics of social changes in the Canadian Arctic). In H. Stewart (ed.), *Saishū shuryō min no genzai* (The gatherer-hunters today). Tokyo: Gensōsha, 13–52.

Kishigami, N. (2007) *Kanada Inuitto no shoku bunka to shakai henka* (Food culture of the Canadian Inuit and social change). Kyoto: Sekaishisōsha.

Kishigami, N. and H. Stewart (1994) "Gendai Neturikku Inuitto shakai ni okeru shakai kankei ni tsuite" (Indigenous social relations in a contemporary Canadian Inuit society). *Kokuritsu minzokugaku hakubutsukan kenkyū hōkoku* (Bulletin of the National Museum of Ethnology), 19(3): 405–448.

Kitamura, K. (1982) "Insesuto pazuru no kaihō—Reichōruigaku kara mita Revi-Sutorosu riron" (Solving the incest puzzle: Lévi-Strauss' theory from a primatological perspective). *Shisō* (Thought), 693: 56–71.

Kitamura, K. (1986) "Pigumi chinpanjī—Atsumari ni okeru 'kari' no sekai" (Pygmy chimpanzees: "Temporary" worlds of gathering). In J. Itani and J. Tanaka (eds), *Shizen shakai no jinruigaku—Afurika ni ikiru* (Anthropology of natural societies: Living in Africa). Tokyo: Academia Shuppankai, 43–70.

Kitamura, K. (1992) "'Kurikaeshi' wo megutte—'Kankei' wo tēma tosuru komyunikēshon" (On repetition of an action: Communication themed on relationships). Hirosaki Daigaku Jinbun Gakubu (ed.), *Bunkei rongō* (Studies in humanities: Humanities), 27: 23–51.

Kitamura, K. (1996) "Shintai teki komyunikēshon ni okeru 'kyōdō no genzai' no keiken—Turukana no 'kōshō' teki komyunikēshon" (The experience of the "collective present" in physical communication: "Negotiative" communication among the Turkana). In K. Sugawara and M. Nomura (eds), *Komyunikēshon to shiteno karada* (Body as a means of communication). Tokyo: Taishukan Shoten, 288–314.

Kitamura, K. (2003) "Kazoku kigen ron no saikōchiku—Revi-Sutorosu riron tono taiwa" (Reconstructing family origin theory: Dialogue with Lévi-Strauss' theory). In M. Nishida, K. Kitamura and J. Yamagiwa (eds), *Ningensei no kigen to shinka* (Origin and evolution of human nature). Kyoto: Shōwadō, 2–30.

Kitamura, K. (2004) "'Hikaku' ni yoru bunka no tayōsei to dokujisei no rikai—bokuchikumin Turukana no ninshikiron (episutemorojī)" (An understanding of the diversity and distinctiveness of culture through "comparisons": The epistemology of Turkana pastoralists). In J. Tanaka, S. Sato, K. Sugwara and I. Ohta (eds), *Yūdōmin (nōmaddo)—Afurika no genya ni ikiru* (Nomads: Living on the African fields). Kyoto: Shōwadō.

Kitamura, K. (2007) "Komyunikēshon no seitaigaku ni mukete (1)" (Toward an ecology of communication (1)). *Okayama Daigaku bungaku bu kiyō* (Bulletin of the faculty of literature, Okayama University), 47: 25–45.

Kitamura, K. (2008a) "'Shakaitekinaru mono' toha nanika?—Tasha tono kankeizuke ni okeru 'kettei fukanōsei' to 'sōzōteki taisho'" (What is "social"?—"Undecidability" and a "creative coping" in the process of making relations with others). *Reichōrui kenkyū* (Primate research), 24: 109–120.

Kitamura, K. (2008b) "Komyunikēshon no seitaigaku ni mukete (2)" (Toward an ecology of communication (2)). *Okayama Daigaku bungaku bu kiyō* (Bulletin of the faculty of literature, Okayama University), 49: 1–11.

Kitamura. K. (2013) "From whence comes human sociality? Recursive decision-making processes in the group phenomenon and classification of others through representation". In K. Kawai (ed.), *Groups: The Evolution of Human Sociality*. Kyoto and Melbourne: Kyoto University Press and Trans Pacific Press, 59–77.

Klein, R. G. and B. Edgar (2002) *The Dawn of Culture*. New York: John Wiley & Sons.

Kline, M. (1953) *Mathematics in Western Culture*. Oxford: Oxford University Press.

Kojima, S., A. Izumi and M. Ceugniet (2003) "Identification of vocalizers by pant hoots, pant grunts and screams in a chimpanzee". *Primates*, 44: 225–230.

Krause, J. et al. (2007) "The derived FOXP2 variant of modern humans was shared with Neanderthals". *Current Biology*, 17: 1908–1912.

Krebs, C. J. (1989) *Ecological Methodology*. New York: Harper & Row.

Kurimoto, E. (1996) *Minzoku funsō wo ikiru hitobito—gendai Afurika no kokka to mainoritī* (People living ethnic conflicts: Modern African states and minorities). Kyoto: Sekai Shisōsha.

Kurimoto, E. (1999) *Mikai no sensō, Gendai no sensō* (Primitive warfare, modern warfare). Tokyo: Iwanami Shoten.

Kuroda, S. (1982) *Pigumī chinpanjī—Michi no ruijinen* (Pygmy chimpanzee: Unknown ape). Tokyo: Chikuma Shobō. Second edition published in 1999, Tokyo: Ibunsha.

Kuroda, S. (1986) "Zentai kara bubun he" (Whole to part). In A. Asada et al. (eds), *Kagakuteki hōhō toha nanika* (What are scientific methods?). Tokyo: Chūkō Shinsho.

Kuroda, S. (1999) *Jinrui shinka saikō—Shakai seisei no kōkogaku* (A reconsideration of human evolution: Archeology of the emergence of the hominid society). Tokyo: Ibunsha.

Kuroda, S. (2011) "Reichōrui shakai ni okeru mono no shakaika" (Socialization of objects in primate societies). In I. Tokoro and K. Kawai (eds), *Mono no jinruigaku* (Anthropology of objects). Kyoto: Kyoto Daigaku Gakujutsu Shuppankai.

Kuroda, S. (2013a) "Collective excitement and primitive war: What is the equality principle?". In K. Kawai (ed.), *Groups: The Evolution of Human Sociality*. Kyoto and Melbourne: Kyoto University Press and Trans Pacific Press, 273–292.

Kuroda, S. (2013b) "Revealing the non-structured nature of social groups: From the field of Primatology". In K. Kawai (ed.), *Groups: The Evolution of Human Sociality*. Kyoto and Melbourne: Kyoto University Press and Trans Pacific Press, 323–328.

Laing, R. D. (1966) "Ritualization and abnormal behaviour". *Philosophical Transactions of the Royal Society of London Series B*, 251: 331–335.

Lancy, D. F. (2010) "Learning 'from nobody': The limited role of teaching in folk models of children's development". *Childhood in the Past*, 3: 79–106.

Lancy, D. F., J. Bock and S. Gaskins (eds), (2010) *The Anthropology of Learning in Childhood*. Lanham: Altamira Press

Lave, J. and E. Wenger (1991) *Situated Learning: Legitimate Peripheral Participation*. New York: Cambridge University Press.

Lawson, E. T. and R. N. McCauley (1990) *Rethinking Religion: Connecting Cognition and Culture*. Cambridge: Cambridge University Press.

Lee, R. B. and I. De Vore (eds), (1968) *Man the Hunter*. Chicago: Aldine.

Leslie, A. M. (1987) "Pretense and representation: The origins of 'theory of mind'". *Psychological Review*, 94(4): 412–426.

Lévi-Strauss, C. (1962) *The Savage Mind*. London: Weidenfeld & Nicholson.

Lévi-Strauss, C. (2000) *Shinzoku no kihon kōzō*. Japanese translation of C. Lévi-Strauss (1949) *Les structures élémentaires de la parenté*, K. Fukui (trans.). Tokyo: Seikyūsha.

Lewis, I. M. (1985) *Ekusutashī no jinruigaku—Hyōi to shāmanizumu*. Japanese translation of I. M. Lewis (1971) *Ecstatic Religion: An Anthropological Study of Spirit Possession and Shamanism*, T. Hiranuma (trans.). Tokyo: Hōsei Daigaku Shuppankyoku.

Lienard, P. and P. Boyer (2006) "Whence collective rituals?: A cultural selection model of ritualized behavior". *American Anthropologist*, 108(4): 814–827.

Livingston, D. (1986) *The Ethnomethodological Foundations of Mathematics*. London: Routledge & Kegan Paul.

Luhmann, N. (1993–1995) *Shakai shisutemu riron 1 & 2*. Japanese translation of N. Luhmann (1984) *Soziale Systeme. Grundriß einer allgemeinen Theorie*, T. Sato (trans.). Tokyo: Kōseisha Kōseikaku.

MacArthur, R. H. and E. O. Wilson (1967) *The Theory of Island Biogeography*. Princeton: Princeton University Press.

Majima, I. (1997) "Danane chihō nanbu Dan zoku no shinwa-rekishi denshō gun: 45 no jirei" (Myths/historical traditions of the Dan people in southern Danané area: 45 cases). *Monogatari to minshū no ninshiki sekai: Monogatari no hasseigaku* (Stories and people's world of perception: Embryology of stories), 1: 119–237.

Marx, K. (1964) *Keizaigaku tetsugaku sōkō.* Japanese translation of K. Marx (1932) *Oekonomische-philosophische Manuskripte aus dem Jahre 1844,* N. Shirotsuka and K. Tanaka (trans.). Tokyo: Iwanami Shoten.

Maurer, B. (2006) *Mutual Life, Limited.* Princeton: Princeton University Press.

McGraw, W. S. (2000) Positional behavior of *Cercopithecus petaurista. International Journal of Primatology,* 21: 157–182.

McGrew, W. C. (1992) *Chimpanzee Material Culture: Implications for Human Evolution.* New York: Cambridge University Press.

Mellars, P., K. Boyle, O. Bar-Yosef and C. Stringer (eds), (2007) *Rethinking the Human Revolution: New Behavioural and Biological Perspectives on the Origin and Dispersal of Modern Humans.* Cambridge: McDonald Institute for Archaeological Research, Cambridge University.

Meltzoff, A. N. (1988) "Infant imitation after a 1-week delay: Long-term memory for novel acts and multiple stimuli". *Development Psychology,* 24: 470–476.

Meltzoff, A. N. and M. K. Moore (1977) "Imitation of facial and manual gestures by human neonates". *Science, New Series,* 198(4312): 75–78.

Metcalf, P. (1983) *A Borneo Journey into Death.* Philadelphia: University of Pennsylvania Press.

Mima, T. (2012) *Risukuka sareru shintai* (Body seen as a risk). Tokyo: Seidosha.

Miyawaki, Y. (2006) *Henkyō no sōzōryoku—Echiopia kokka shihai ni kōsuru shōsū minzoku Horu* (The imaginative power of the frontier: Hole, the small ethnic group defying the Ethiopian state). Kyoto: Sekai Shisōsha.

Miyazaki, H. (2010) *Kibō toiu hōhō* (The method of hope). Tokyo: Ibunsha.

Mizuhara, H. (1986) *Sarugaku saikō* (Primatology revisited). Tokyo: Gunyōsha.

Mizutani, M. (1997) "Dentatsu, taiwa, kaiwa—komyunikēshon no metashizenshi ni mukete" (Transmission, dialogue and conversation: Toward meta natural history of communication). In Y. Tani (ed.), *Komyunikēshon no shizenshi* (Natural history of communication). Tokyo: Shinchōsha, 5–30.

Mizutani, M. (2005) "Komyunikēshon to rinrigaku (ge)" (Communication and ethics (Part 2)). *Tetsugaku kenkyū* (The journal of philosophical studies), 580: 109–129.

Morin, E. (1973) *Ningen to shi.* Japanese translation of E. Morin (1951) *L Homme et la mort dans l'histoire,* Y. Furuta (trans.). Tokyo: Hōsei Daigaku Shuppankyoku.

Morishita, M. (1959) "Measuring of interspecific association and similarity between communities". *Memoires of the Faculty of Science Kyushu University Series E (Biology)*, 3: 65–80.

Morita, M. (2009) *Haieku no shakai riron—Jiseiteki chitsujo ron no kōzō* (Hayek's social theory: The structure of spontaneous order theory). Tokyo: Nihon Keizai Hyōronsha.

Myowa, M. (2004) *Reichōrui kara jinrui wo yomitoku—Naze "mane" wo surunoka* (Understanding humans through primates: Why do we "imitate"?). Tokyo: Kawade Shobō Shinsha.

Myowa, M. (2009) "Ningen rashii asobi toha?—Hito to chinpanjī no asobi ni miru kokoro no hattatsu to shinka" (What is human play?: Mental development and evolution in play in humans and chimpanzees). In N. Kamei (ed.), *Asobi no jinruigaku kotohajime* (Introduction to the anthropology of play). Tokyo: Shōwadō.

Nakamura, M. (2003a) "'Gatherings' of social grooming among wild chimpanzees: Implications for evolution of sociality". *Journal of Human Evolution*, 44: 59–71.

Nakamura, M. (2003b) "Dōji ni 'suru' kezukuroi—Chinpanjī no sōgokōi kara miru shakai to bunka" (Grooming at the same time: Society and culture viewed from chimpanzee culture). In M. Nishida, K. Kitamura and J. Yamagiwa (eds), *Ningensei no kigen to shinka* (Origin and evolution of human nature). Kyoto: Shōwadō, 264–292.

Nakamura, M. (2009) *Chinpanjī—Kotoba no nai karera ga kataru koto* (Chimpanzees: What they say without language). Tokyo: Chūkō Shinsho.

Nakamura, M. (2015) "Home range". In M. Nakamura, K. Hosaka, N. Itoh and K. Zamma (eds), *Mahale Chimpanzees: 50 Years of Research*. Cambridge: Cambridge University Press, 94–105.

Nakamura, M. and N. Itoh (2015) "Seeds from feces: Implications for seed dispersal and fecal analyses". In M. Nakamura, K. Hosaka, N. Itoh and K. Zamma (eds), *Mahale Chimpanzees: 50 Years of Research*. Cambridge: Cambridge University Press, 259–273.

Nakamura, M. et al. (2013) "Ranging behavior of Mahale chimpanzees: A 16 year study". *Primates*, 54: 171–182.

Nakamura, M., N. Itoh and T. Sakamaki (1999) "Chōsa chi shōkai: Mahare Sankai Kokuritsu Kōen (Tanzania Rengo Kyowakoku)" (Site report: The Mahale Mountains National Park, Tanzania). *Reichōrui kenkyū* (Primate research), 15(2): 93–99.

Nakayama, G. (2007) *Shikō no yōgo jiten* (Dictionary of philosophical terms). Tokyo: Chikuma Shobō.

Nimmo, A. H. (1972) *The Sea People of Sulu*. San Francisco: Chandler Press.

Nishida, M. (1986) *Teijū kakumei* (Settlement revolution). Tokyo: Shinyōsha.

Nishida, T. (1968) "The social group of wild chimpanzees in the Mahali Mountains". *Primates*, 9: 167–224.

Nishida, T. (1970) "Social behavior and relationships among wild chimpanzees of the Mahali Mountains". *Primates*, 11: 47–87.

Nishida, T. (1973) *Seirei no kodomo tachi* (Children of spirits). Tokyo: Chikuma Shobō.

Nishida, T. (1977) "Mahare sankai no chinpanjī (I)—Seitai to tan'i shūdan no kōzō" (The chimpanzees in the Mahale Mountains (I): The ecology and unit-group structure). In J. Itani (ed.), *Chinpanjī ki* (Monographs of chimpanzees). Tokyo: Kōdansha, 543–638.

Nishida, T. (1981) *Yasei chinpanjī kansatsu-ki* (The world of wild chimpanzees). Tokyo: Chūōkōronsha.

Nishida, T. (1990) "A quarter century of research in the Mahale Mountains: An overview". In T. Nishida (ed.), *The Chimpanzees of the Mahale Mountains*. Tokyo: University of Tokyo Press, 3–35.

Nishida, T. (2007[1999]) *Ningensei wa doko kara kitaka—Sarugaku karano apurōchi* (Where has human nature come from? An approach from primatology). Kyoto: Kyoto Daigaku Gakujutsu Shuppankai.

Nishida, T. (2011) *Chimpanzees of the Lakeshore: Natural History and Culture at Mahale*. Tokyo: Cambridge University Press.

Nishida, T. and K. Hosaka (2001) "Reichōrui ni okeru shokumotsu bunpai" (Food sharing in primates). In T. Nishida (ed.), *Hominizēshon* (Hominization) (kōza seitai jinruigaku 8). Kyoto: Kyoto Daigaku Gakujutsu Shuppankai, 255–304.

Nishida, T., T. Kano, J. Goodall, W. C. McGrew and M. Nakamura (1999) "Ethogram and ethnography of Mahale chimpanzees". *Anthropological Science*, 107: 141–188.

Nishie, H. (2010) "Sōgokōi ha owaranai—Yasei chinpanjī no 'jōchōna' yaritori'" (Never-ending interaction: "Redundant" interaction among wild chimpanzees). In D. Kimura, M. Nakamura and K. Takanashi (eds), *Intārakushon no kyōkai to setsuzoku—Saru, hito, kaiwa kenkyū kara* (Boundary and conjunction of social interaction: Studies in nonhuman primates, humans and conversation). Tokyo: Shōwadō, 378–396.

Nishie, H. (2012) "Ningen sokkuri—Chinpanjī no shi wo meguru episodo kara" (Almost human: From an episode surrounding the death of a chimpanzee). Presented at the 46th Conference of the Primate Society of Japan (23 June, Hiroshima University).

Nishimura, K. (1989) *Asobi no genshōgaku* (Phenomenology of play). Tokyo: Keisō Shobō.

Nishizaka, A. (2008) *Bunsan suru shintai—Esunomesodorojī teki sōgokōi bunseki no tenkai* (Distributed bodies: An essay in ethnomethodological interaction analysis). Tokyo: Keisō Shobō.

Niwa, F. (1993) *Nihonteki shizenkan no hōhō—Imanishi seitaigaku no imi suru mono* (Methodology of the Japanese view of nature: The meaning of Imanishi's ecology). Tokyo: Nōson Gyoson Bunka Kyōkai.

Notman, H. and D. Rendall (2005) "Contextual variation in chimpanzee pant hoots and its implications for referential communication". *Animal Behaviour*, 70: 177–190.

Nuttall, M. (1992) *Arctic Homeland*. Toronto: University of Toronto Press.

Oates, J. F. (1986) "Food distribution and foraging behavior". In B. B. Smuts et al. (eds), *Primate Societies*. Chicago: University of Chicago Press, 197–205.

Odling-Smee, J. F., K. N. Laland and M. W. Feldman (2003) "Niche construction: The neglected process in evolution". *Monographs in Population Biology* 37. Princeton: Princeton University Press.

Ohsawa, M. (1990) "Komyunikēshon to kisoku" (Communication and rules). In H. Ichikawa et al. (eds), *Kōkan to shoyū* (Exchange and ownership). Tokyo: Iwanami Shoten, 51–128.

Ohta, I. (1986) "Turukana zoku no goshūsei" (Reciprocity among the Turkana). In J. Itani and J. Tanaka (eds), *Shizen shakai no jinruigaku—Afurika ni ikiru* (Anthropology of natural societies: Living in Africa). Kyoto: Academia Shuppankai, 181–215.

Omiya, M. (2008) *Hisenkei hadō no koten kaiseki* (Classical analysis of nonlinear waves). Tokyo: Morikita Shuppan.

Omoda, S. (2011) *Misheru Fukō—Kindai wo ura kara yomu* (Michel Foucault: Reading modernity from the other side). Tokyo: Chikuma Shobō.

Omura, K. (2008) "Kakawariaukoto no yorokobi—Kanada inuitto no kankyo no shirikata to tsukiaikata" (The pleasures of getting involved: The Canadian Inuit's ways of knowing and ways of associating with the environment). In Y. Yama, A. Furukawa and M. Kawada (eds), *Kankyō minzokugaku* (Environmental folklore). Kyoto: Shōwadō, 34–57.

Omura, K. (2011) "Nijū ni ikiru—Kanada Inuito shakai no seigyō to seisan no shakaiteki fuchi" (Dual ways of life: Social constellation of subsistence and production in the Canadian Inuit society). In K. Matsui et al. (eds),

Gurōbarizēshon to "ikiru sekai" (Globalization and "living world"). Kyoto: Shōwadō, 65–96.

Omura, K. (2012) "Gijutsu no ontorogī—Inuito no gijutsu fukugō shisutemu wo tōshite miru shizen = Bunka jinruigaku no kanōsei" (The ontology of technology: Considering the potentiality of natural-cultural anthropology through an analysis of the Inuit technological-complex system). *Bunka jinruigaku* (Japanese journal of cultural anthropology), 77(1): 105–127.

Omura, K. (2013) "The ontology of sociality: 'Sharing' and subsistence mechanisms". In K. Kawai (ed.), *Groups: The Evolution of Human Sociality*. Kyoto and Melbourne: Kyoto University Press and Trans Pacific Press, 123–142.

Ortner, S. (1984) "Theory in anthropology since the sixties". *Comparative Studies in Society and History*, 26(1): 126–166.

Osawa, M. (1992) *Kōi no daisūgaku—Supensā-Buraun kara shakai shisutemu ron he* (Algebra of action: From Spencer-Brown to social systems theory). Tokyo: Seidosha.

Osawa, M. (1994) *Imi to tashasei* (Meaning and otherness). Tokyo: Keisō Shobō.

Otsubo, T. (2009) "Tentai no kido undō" (The orbital motion of the celestial body). In T. Fukushima and M. Hosokawa (eds), *Tentai no ichi to undō* (The position and motion of the celestial body). Tokyo: Nippon Hyōronsha, 135–177.

Paradise, R. and B. Rogoff (2009) "Side by side: Learning by observing and pitching in". *Ethos*, 37(1): 102–138.

Premack, D. and G. Woodruff (1978) "Does the chimpanzee have a theory of mind?". *The Behavioral and Brain Sciences*, 1: 515–526.

Premack, D. and A. J. Premack (1994) "Why animals have neither culture nor history?". In T. Ingold (ed.), *Companion Encyclopedia of Anthropology: Humanity, Culture and Social Life*. New York: Routledge, 350–365.

Premack, D. and A. J. Premack (2003) *Original Intelligence: Unlocking the Mystery of Who We Are*. New York: McGraw-Hill.

Rakoczy, H., K. Hamann, F. Warneken and M. Tomasello (2010) "Bigger knows better: Young children selectively learn rule games from adults rather than from peers". *British Journal of Developmental Psychology*, 28: 785–798.

Rancière, J. (1991) *The Ignorant Schoolmaster: Five Lessons in Intellectual Emancipation*. Translated, with an Introduction, by K. Ross. Stanford: Stanford University Press.

Reed, E. S. (2000) *Afōdansu no shinrigaku—Seitai shinrigaku heno michi* (Psychology of affordances: Toward an ecological psychology). Japanese translation of E.

S. Reed (1996) *Encoutering the World: Toward an Ecological Psychology*, N. Hosoda (trans.). Tokyo: Shinyōsha.

Reice, S. R. (1994) "Nonequilibrium determinants of biological community structure". *American Scientist*, 82: 424–435.

Richards, A. I. (1950) *Bemba Witchcraft*. Rhodes-Livingstone papers 34. Manchester: Manchester University Press.

Riles, A. (2000) *The Network Inside Out*. Ann Arbor: University of Michigan Press.

Riles, A. (2011) *Collateral Knowledge*. Chicago: University of Chicago Press.

Rousseau, J. J. (1978[1755]) *Ningen fubyōdō kigen ron*. Japanese translation of J. J. Rousseau (1755), in Y. Hara (trans.), *Rusō zenshū dai 4-kan* (Complete works of Rousseau, vol. 4). Tokyo: Hakusuisha.

Sagawa, T. (2011) *Bōryoku to kantai no minzokushi—Higashi Afurika bokuchiku shakai no sensō to heiwa* (An ethnography of violence and hospitality: War and peace in East African pastoral societies). Kyoto: Shōwadō.

Saito, K. (2012) "Imanishi Kinji no 'sumiwake' hakken to gengoka" (Kinji Imanishi's discovery of "habitat segregation" and verbalization). In T. Yokoyama (ed.), *Kotoba no chikara—Aratana bunmei wo motomete* (Power of language: In search of a new civilization). Kyoto: Kyoto Daigaku Gakujutsu Shuppankai, 289–320.

Sakamaki, T. (2005) "Yasei chinpanjī no fukujūteki hassei kōdō, pantoguranto no kenkyū" (Submissive vocalization behavior in wild chimpanzees, a study of pant-grunt). PhD thesis: Kyoto University.

Sakumichi, S. (2001) "'Tsurasa' wo tegakari ni shita fīrudo rikai no kokoromi—Hokusei Kenia Turukana ni okeru fīrudo wāku kara" (Some notes for ethnography as emotion talk: Coping with Turkana nakinai (begging) in the northwestern part of Kenya). In Hirosaki Daigaku Jinbun Gakubu (ed.), *Jinbun shakai ronsō—Jinbun kagaku hen* (Collected papers in humanities and sociology: Humanities volume), 5: 77–109.

Sakumichi, S. (2004) "Turukana ni okeru tasha no 'ikari'" ("Anger" of others in Turkana). In I. Ohta (ed.), *Yudomin* (Nomads). Tokyo: Shōwadō, 492–514.

Sakurai, K. (2000) "Disupurei to komyunikeshon" (Display and communication). In T. Hidaka (ed.), *Dobutsu no kodo to shakai* (Animal behavior and society). Tokyo: Hoso Daigaku Kyoiku Shinkokai, 37–49.

Sannomiya, M. (ed.) (2008) *Meta ninchi* (Metacognition). Kyoto: Kitaoji Shobō.

Sasaki, M. (1994) *Afodansu—Atarashii ninchi no riron* (Affordances: A new cognitive theory) (Iwanami kagaku raiburari). Tokyo: Iwanami Shoten.

Sather, C. (1997) *The Bajau Laut: Adaptation, History, and Fate in a Maritime Fishing Society of South-eastern Sabah*. Oxford: Oxford University Press.

Schmidt, M. F. H., H. Rakoczy and M. Tomasello (2011) "Young children attribute normativity to novel actions without pedagogy or normative language". *Developmental Science*, 14(3): 530–539.

Searle, J. R. (1995) *The Construction of Social Reality*. London: Penguin Books.

Searle, J. R. (2005) "What is an institution". *Journal of Institutional Economics*, 1(1): 1–22.

Seiyama, K. (1995) *Seido ron no kōzu* (A composition of institution theory). Tokyo: Sōbunsha.

Seton, E. T. (1994) *Seton Doubutsuki*. Tokyo: Shūeisha.

Shepher, J. (1971) "Mate selection among second generation Kibbutz adolescents and adults: Incest avoidance and negative imprinting". *Archives of Sexual Behavior*, 1(4): 293–307.

Shiobara, T. (2012) "Seido" (Institution). *Nippon daihyakka zensho* (Encyclopedia Nipponica). Shogakukan. http://100.yahoo.co.jp/detail /%E5%88%B6%E5%BA%A6/ (accessed 11 July 2012).

Simonse, S. (1998) "Age, conflict and power in the Monyomiji age system". In E. Kurimoto and S. Simonse (eds), *Conflict, Age, and Power in North East Africa: Age Systems in Transition*. Oxford: James Currey, 51–78.

Soga, T. (1996) "Fubyōdo na kachiku sōzoku seido—Rakuda bokuchiku min Gabura no oya to ko no katto" (Inequitable livestock inheritance system: Parent-child conflicts among the camel pastoralist Gabra). In J. Tanaka et al. (eds), *Zoku shizen shakai no jinruigaku* (Anthropology of natural society, second series). Tokyo: Academia Shuppan, 215–242.

Soga, T. (1998) "Rakuda no shintaku ga umu kizuna—Kita Kenia no bokuchikumin Gabura ni okeru rakuda no shintaku seido" (Ties created by the camel trust system: The camel trust system among the pastoralist Gabra in northern Kenya). *Afurika kenkyū* (Journal of African studies), 52: 29–49.

Soga, T. (2002) "Kokka no soto kara uchigawa he—Rakuda bokuchikumin Gabura ga keikenshita senkyo" (From outside to inside of the state: The impact of an election on the camel pastoralist Gabra). In S. Sato (ed.), *Yuboku min no sekai* (The world of nomadic peoples). Kyoto: Kyoto Daigaku Gakujutsu Shuppankai, 127–174.

Spencer-Brown, G. (1969) *Laws of Form*. London: George Allen and Unwin.

Statistics Department, Ministry of Finance and Economic Planning (1994) *The 1991*

Population and Housing Census (National Summary) Uganda. Entebbe: The Republic of Uganda.

Sterelney, K. (2003) *Thought in a Hostile World: The Evolution of Human Cognition*. Malden: Blackwell Publishing.

Stewart, H. (1991) "Shokuryō bunpai ni okeru danjo no yakuwari buntan ni tsuite" (Sexual division of labor and world view of Netsilik Inuit reflected in food sharing practices). *Shakai jinruigaku nenpō* (Annual report of social anthropology), 17: 115–127.

Stewart, H. (1992) "Teijū to seigyō—Netsurikku Inuitto no seigyō katsudō to shoku seikatsu ni miru keishō to henka" (Sedentarism and subsistence activities: Continuity and change of traditional Netsilik Inuit subsistence and foodways). *Dai 6-kai hoppō minzoku bunka shinpojiumu hōkokusho* (Proceedings of the 6th International Abashiri Symposium). Hokkaido Museum of Northern Peoples, 75–87.

Stewart, H. (1995) "Gendai no Netsurikku Inuitto shakai ni okeru seigyo katsudo" (Subsistence activities in contemporary Netsilik Inuit society: Physical survival, cultural survival). *Dai 9-kai hoppo minzoku bunka shinpojiumu hokokusho* (Proceedings of the 9th International Abashiri Symposium). Hokkaido Museum of Northern Peoples, 37–67.

Strathern, M. (1988) *The Gender of the Gift*. Berkeley: University of California Press.

Strauss, S., M. Ziv and A. Stein (2002) "Teaching as a natural cognition and its relations to preschoolers' developing theory of mind". *Cognitive Development*, 17: 1473–1487.

Sugawara, K. (1993) *Karada no jinruigaku* (Anthropology of the body). Tokyo: Kawaide Shobō Shinsha.

Sugawara, K. (1998) "Ecology and communication in egalitarian societies: Japanese studies of the cultural anthropology of Southern Africa". *Japanese Review of Cultural Anthropology*, 1: 97–129.

Sugawara, K. (2002) *Kanjō no enjin = hito* (Emotional hominids = humans). Tokyo: Kobundō.

Sugawara, K. (2004) *Busshuman toshite ikiru—Genya de kangaeru kotoba to karada* (Living as Bushmen: Thinking words and body in the wilderness). Tokyo: Chūkō Shinsho.

Sugiyama, Y. (2004) "Kieta mura, saisei suru mura: Bemba no nōson ni okeru noroi jiken no kaishaku to ken'i no seitosei" (Village that disappears, village that revives: The interpretation of witchcraft cases in the rural villages of Bemba and the legitimacy of authority). In H. Terashima (ed.), *Byōdō to fubyōdō wo meguru jinruigakuteki kenkyū* (Anthropological study on equality and inequality). Kyoto: Nakanishiya Shuppan, 134–171.

Sugiyama, Y. (2013) "The small village of 'We, the Bemba': The reference phase that connects the daily life practice in a residential group to the chiefdom". In K. Kawai (ed.), *Groups: The Evolution of Human Sociality*. Kyoto and Melbourne: Kyoto University Press and Trans Pacific Press, 239–260.

Sugiyama, Y., H. Kurita, T. Matsui, S. Kimoto and T. Shimomura (2009) "Carrying of dead infants by Japanese macaque (Macaca fuscata) mothers". *Anthropological Science*, 117(2): 113–119.

Suzuki, T. (2002) "'Kokoro no riron' towa nanika" (What is theory of mind?). *Kagaku tetsugaku* (Philosophy of science), 35(2): 83–94.

Takagi, K. (2001) *Vigotsukī no hōhō* (Vygotsky's approach). Tokyo: Kaneko Shobō.

Takahata, Y. (1985) "Adult male chimpanzees kill and eat a male newborn infant: Newly observed intragroup infanticide and cannibalism in Mahale National Park, Tanzania". *Folia Primatologica*, 44: 161–170.

Tambiah, S. J. (1985) "A performative approach to ritual". *Culture, Thought, and Social Action: An Anthropological Perspective*. Cambridge: Harvard University Press, 123–166.

Tanabe, S. (2010) *"Sei" no jinruigaku* (Anthropology of "life"). Tokyo: Iwanami Shoten.

Tanaka, J. (1971) *Busshuman* (Bushmen). Tokyo: Shisakusha.

Tanaka, J. (1978) *Sabaku no karyūdo* (Hunters of the desert). Tokyo: Chūkō Shinsho.

Tanaka, M. (1989) "Kari megami no henbō—Suri ranka Tamīru gyoson ni okeru sonraku saishi" (Transformation of the goddess Kali: A village ritual in a Tamil fishing community in Sri Lanka). *Kokuritsu minzokugaku hakubutsukan kenkyū hōkokusho* (Bulletin of the National Museum of Ethnology), 13(3): 445–516.

Tanaka, M. (2012) "Girei" (Ritual). In H. Hoshino et al. (eds), *Shūkyōgaku jiten* (Encyclopedia of religious studies). Tokyo: Maruzen, 64–65.

Tanno, T. (1991) "'Wakachiai' toshite no 'bunpai'" ("Distribution" as "sharing"). In J. Tanaka and M. Kakeya (eds), *Hito no shizen shi* (Natural history of humanity). Tokyo: Heibonsha, 35–57.

Terashima, H. (2007) "Karada no shigensei to sono kakuchō" (Resource potential of body and its expansion). In K. Sugawara (ed.), *Shintai shigen no kyōyū* (Sharing of body resources). Tokyo: Kōbundō, 29–58.

Terashima, H. (2011) *Byodo ron—Reichōrui to hito ni okeru shakai to byōdōsei no shinka* (Equality: Evolution of society and equality in primates and humans). Kyoto: Nakanishiya Shuppan.

Terborgh, J. (1983) *Five New World Primates: A Study in Comparative Ecology.* Princeton: Princeton University Press.

Tezuka, O. (2004) *Hi no tori (mirai hen, fukkatsu hen)* (Phoenix (future, resurrection)), (Tezuka Osamu manga zenshū (Collected works of Osamu Tezuka)). Tokyo: Kōdansha.

Thomas, E. M. (1979) *Yūboku no senshitachi.* Japanese translation of E. M. Thomas (1965) *Warrior Herdsmen*, M. Mukai and J. Tanaka (trans.). Tokyo: Shisakusha.

Thorvaldsen, S. (2010) "Early numerical analysis in Kepler's New Astronomy". *Science in Context*, 23(1): 39–63.

Toda, M. (2007[1992]) "Kanjō—Hito wo ugokashiteiru tekiō puroguramu (shinsō ban)" (Emotions: Adaptation program that runs the humans (special edition)), *Korekushon ninchi kagaku* (Cognitive science collection) 9. Tokyo: Tokyo Daigaku Shuppankai.

Tokoro, I. (1999) *Ekkyō—Suru kaiiki sekai kara* (Border crossings: From the world of the Sulu maritime world). Tokyo: Iwanami Shoten.

Tokoro, I. (2011) "Fukusū no jikan, jūfukusuru kioku—Suru kaiiki sekai ni okeru sōki to bōkyaku" (Multiple times, overlapping memories: Remembering and forgetting in the Sulu maritime world). In R. Nishii (ed.), *Jikan no jinruigaku* (Anthropology of time). Tokyo: Sekai Shisōsha, 278–300.

Tokoro, I. (2013) Violence and the autopoiesis of groups: From the ethnography of pirates and feuds. In K. Kawai (ed.), *Groups: The Evolution of Human Sociality.* Kyoto and Melbourne: Kyoto University Press and Trans Pacific Press, 143–167.

Tomasello, M. (1999) *The Cultural Origins of Human Cognition.* Cambridge: Harvard University Press.

Tomasello, M. (2006) *Kokoro to kotoba no kigen wo saguru.* Japanese translation of M. Tomasello (1999) *The Cultural Origins of Human Cognition*, T. Ohori et al. (trans.). Tokyo: Keisō Shobō.

Turner, V. (1957) *Schism and Continuity in an African Society: A Study of Ndembu Village Life.* Manchester: Manchester University Press.

Turner, V. W. (1969) *The Ritual Process: Structure and Anti-Structure.* Chicago: Aldine.

Turton, D. (1997) "Introduction: War and ethnicity". In D. Turton (ed.), *War and Ethnicity: Global Connections and Violence.* Rochester: New York University of Rochester Press, 1–45.

Uchibori, M. (1984) "The enshrinement of the dead among the Iban". *Sarawak Museum Journal*, 23(54): 15–32.

Uchibori, M. (1989) "Girei no henshitsu—Naisen to ibento ka" (Degeneration of ritual: Involution and event-making). *Hitotsubashi ronsō* (The Hitotsubashi review), 101: 182–197.

Uchibori, M. (1997) "Shiniyuku mono heno girei" (Rituals for the dying and the dead). *Girei to pafōmansu* (Ritual and performance), Iwanami cultural anthropology series, vol. 9. Tokyo: Iwanami Shoten, 71–104.

Uchibori, M. (2013) "Assembly of solitary beings: Between solitude and 'invisible' groups". In K. Kawai (ed.), *Groups: The Evolution of Human Sociality*. Kyoto and Melbourne: Kyoto University Press and Trans Pacific Press, 43–57.

Uchibori, M. and S. Yamashita (2006[1986]) *Shi no jijruigaku* (Anthropology of death). Tokyo: Kōbundō/Kōdansha.

Uchida, T. (2005) *Sensei wa erai* (The teacher is great). Tokyo: Chikuma Shobō.

Uehara, S. (1994) "Mahare sankai kokuritsu kōen de kansatsu sareta chinpanjī no osu no tandoku seikatsu" (Lone male chimpanzees in the Mahale Mountains National Park, Tanzania). *Reichōrui kenkyū* (Primate research), 10: 281–288.

Watabe, S. (2010) "Kōdo jōhōka jidai ni okeru 'kyōiku' saikō—Ninchi kagaku ni okeru 'manabi' ron karano apurōchi" (Reconsidering "education" in the advanced information age: Cognitive scientific approach to "learning"). *Kyōikugaku kenkyū* (Japanese journal of educational research), 77(4): 14–25.

Watanabe, K. (2001) "Gensō to genjitsu no hazama no insesuto tabū" (Incest taboo between fantasy and reality). In J. Kawada (ed.), *Kinshin seiko to sono tabū* (Incest and incest taboo). Tokyo: Fujiwara Shoten.

Weber, M. (1960) *Shihai no shakaigaku 1 Keizai to shakai* (Sociology of domination 1: Economy and society). Japanese translation of M. Weber (1922), K. Sera (trans.). Tokyo: Sōbunsha.

Wenzel, G. (1991) *Animal Rights, Human Rights*. Toronto: University of Toronto Press.

Willmott, W. (1960) "The flexibility of Eskimo social organization". *Anthropologica*, N.S. 2: 48–59.

Woodburn, J. (1982) "Egalitarian societies". *Man* (New Series), 17(3): 431–451.

Wrangham, R. and D. Peterson (1998) *Otoko no kyōbōsei ha dokokara kitaka* (Demonic males: Apes and the origins of human violence). Japanese translation of R. Wrangham and D. Peterson (1996) *Demonic Males: Apes and the Origins of Human Violence*, A. Yamashita (trans.). Tokyo: Mita Shuppankai.

Wrangham, R. W., J. L. Gittleman and C. A. Chapman (1993) "Constraints on group size in primates and carnivores: Population density and day-range as assays of exploitation competition". *Behavioral Ecology and Sociobiology*, 32: 199–209.

Yamagiwa, J. (1993) *Gorira to hito no aida* (Between gorillas and humans). Tokyo: Kōdansha Gendai Shinsho.

Yamagiwa, J. (1994) *Kazoku no kigen—Fusei no tōjō* (Origins of the family: Establishment of paternity). Tokyo: Tokyo Daigaku Shuppankai.

Yamagiwa, J. (2012) *Kazoku shinka ron* (Evolutionary history of the human family). Tokyo: Tokyo Daigaku Shuppankai.

Yeager, T. (2001) *Shin seido ha keizaigaku nyūmon—Seido, ikō keizai, keizai kaihatsu*. Japanese translation of T. Yeager (1999) *Institutions, Transition Economies, and Economic Development*, S. Aoyama (trans.). Tokyo: Tōyō Keizai Shimpōsha.

Yoon, J. M. D., M. H. Johnson and G. Csibra (2008) "Communication-induced memory biases in preverbal infants". *PNAS*, 105(36): 13690–13695.

Name Index

Ahern, E. M., 68
Becker, E., 52
Bell, C., 69
Bloch, M., 68
Bourdieu, P., 68
Bowlby, J., 421
Briggs, J. I., 336
Brown, N. O., 53
Damasio, A., 343, 421
de Certeau M., 57
Dunbar, R., 31
Freud, S., 75
Funabiki, T., 49
Goodall, J., 44
Graber, D. 415
Hume, D., 9
Humphrey, C., 70
Huxley, J., 73–74
Imamura, H., 6, 329–330
Imanishi, K., 4, 278, 329
Itani, J., 3, 5, 329

Kani, T., 278
Kawai, M., 4
Kitamura, K., 342
Kuroda, S., 3, 223, 237, 329, 338, 340, 346
Laidlaw, J., 70
Laing, R. D., 75
Lévi-Strauss, C., 251
Marx, K., 330
Metcalf, P., 50
Morin, E., 44
Seton, E.T., 44
Soga, T., 41
Sugawara, K., 421
Takagi, K., 421
Tambiah, S. J., 68
Thomas, E. M., 221, 235
Tomasello, M., 340
Vygotski, L., 421
Warhol, A., 63
Yamagiwa, J., 4

Subject Index

absence, 282, 285

accident, 381

action, 369

  action selection, 148, 150, 156, 161–162

    see also "behavioral choice"

  conventional action, 132

  center of action, 281

  habitual action, 10

adat, 204, 206–208, 210, 215

affordance theory, 247

agreement, 9

aim of raiding, *see* "raiding"

ajore, 221 *see also* "raiding"

alpha male, 123–124

ambivalence toward coexistence, 343

  see also "coexistence"

analogy, 289

Anatomically Modern Humans
  (AMH), 45

ancestral spirit, 362

anger, 231, 352, 356

  anger incident, 356, 369

  anger story, 370

  expression of anger, 357

  unspoken anger, 365

animal, 388–389, 421

animality, 373 *see also* "humanity"

anthropology

  anthropology of feelings, 348 *see also*
    "feeling"

  ecological anthropology, 1

  social/cultural anthropology, 1

appropriateness/inappropriateness,
  243

arrangement, 226

assembly of pastoral peoples, 234

asymmetry, 297

attachment, 338, 341, 343, 421

Australopithecus, 45

automatic, 28–29

awareness, 399 *see also* "self-
  awareness"

  awareness of restrictions, *see*
    "restriction"

"be", 194

begging, 29–30

behavior

  behavioral choice, 277 *see also*
    "action selection"

  behavioral constraint, 396

  behavioral practice, 226

Bemba, 353

bidirectionality, 298

Bodi, 230–231, 419

body ornamentation, 229

bonobo, 253

Buddhist, 377, 386

Bushman, 22, 25

call-response, 171, 195

camaraderie, 338

cattle

  cattle as the pragmatic existence, 234

Cattle Complex, 235
center of action, 281 *see* "action"
chat, 193
child, *see* "infant"
chimpanzee (*Pan troglodytes*) , 85, 143, 168, 235, 253
circular decision making, 245
close relationship, *see* "relationship"
coexistence
  ambivalence toward coexistence, 343
  condition of coexistence, 143
  conflicts and uncertainties surrounding coexistence with others, 345
  desire for coexistence with others, 339–340, 342–344, 347
  mode of coexistence, 143–144, 150, 154–158, 161–162
cognitive capacity, 34 *see also* "Dunbar number"
collective approach, 243
communality, 51
community size, 31 *see also* "Dunbar number"
community structure, 270
competition, 273
complex, 251
condition of coexistence, *see* "coexistence"
conflict, 345, 351
  conflicts surrounding coexistence with others, 345
conscious, 399
  consensus formation, 284
constitutive rule, *see* "rule"
contingency, 175, 198, 200, 211

contingent nature, 184
control, 314
convention, 9–10, 23, 65, 88, 132–133, 138, 157–159, 161–162, 168, 191
  conventional action, 132
  conventional rule, 136 *see also* "rule"
cooperation, 332
co-presence, 283, 352 *see also* "coexistence"
coronation, 65
cultural institution, 116 *see* "institution"
cultural transmission, 100
custom, 8, 10
  customary practice, 9–10

Daasanetch, 228, 231
dead, the, 43
death, 373 *see also* "dying"
definition of "rule" and "institution" without language, 397 *see also* "rule" and "institution"
desire for coexistence with others, *see* "coexistence"
de-subjectivization, 72
development of self-awareness, 344
deviation, 192, 404–405 *see also* "freedom", "secondary rule", ""We""
Diana monkey, 268
Didinga, 224
dietary menu, 268
display, 74
disturbance, 273
Dodoth, 221, 224
domestication, 334

dominance order/rank, 23, 123, 134, 401
  dominant-dependent relationship, 334 *see also* "relationship"
Dunbar number, 31–34 *see* "cognitive capacity", "community size", "group size"
dyadic interaction, *see* "interaction"
dying, 42, 373, 390–391 *see also* "death"

East African pastoral society, 221
ecological anthropology, 1, *see also* "anthropology"
ecological niche, *see* "niche"
education, 97
  education as cultural institution, 116 *see also* "institution"
  education without teaching, 105 *see also* "teaching"
  formal education, 115
Efe Pygmies, 99
emotion, 343–344, 421
  hidden emotion, 360
  internal emotion, 353
empathy, 26
emulation, 111
encounter, 167, 189
  non-face-to-face encounter, 172, 174, 179, 189
environment, 271, 280
  environmental niche, *see* "niche"
envy, 351, 365 *see also* "jealousy"
  hidden envy, 362
  internal envy, 370
  past envy story, 369
equality, 332

equality and inequality principle, 7
equilibrium, 272
  non–equilibrium, 272
Eros (life), 53
established practice, *see* "practice"
ethnic group
  Bemba, 353
  Bodi, 230–231, 419
  Bushman, 22, 25
  Daasanetch, 228, 231
  Didinga, 224
  Dodoth, 221, 224
  Efe Pygmies, 99
  Gabra, 29, 34–37
  Hoor, 229, 231
  Iban, 51
  Inuit, 421
  Jie, 224
  Matheniko, 224
  Mbotgote, 318
  Pari, 231
  Pokot, 234
  Pygmy, 22, 25
  Sama, 199, 201–208, 213, 217
  Taita, 367
  Toposa, 224
  Turkana, 224, 233, 367
ethnic identity, 227
"everyone", 148–150, 159, 162
"everyone (will) does so", 144, 150, 160
evolution
  evolution of human sociality, 1, 238 *see* "sociality"
  evolution of institution, 223 *see* "institution"
  human evolution, 234 *see* "human"
excessiveness, 133

exchange of women, 251
exogamy, 251
expectation, 398
expert, 370
expression of anger, *see* "anger"
extended family group, 331
Extended Phenotype, 280
external frame of reference, 27, 29

face-to-face, 21 *see also* "non-face-to-face encounter"
facial expression, 23, 34
fear, 33
  fear of isolation, 343
  fear of rejection and alienation, 339
  generalized fear, 37
feedback, 277
feeding competition, 274
feeding niche, *see* "niche"
feeling, 13, 343–344, 351, 421
  anthropology of feelings, 348
  hidden feeling, 361
  institutionalization of feeling, 348
festival, 67
field, 174, 184, 187, 277, 283 *see* "interaction"
fishing, 332
fission-fusion, 143–144, 155–156, 161, 168–169
folivore, 270, 275
food separation/segregation, 272, 274
food sharing, 234, 237, 253, 330 *see also* "rule"
form, 132–133, 416
formal education, *see* "education"
formality, 65, 71
formalized forms of play, 88

freedom, 405
frugivore, 270, 275
functional niche, *see* "niche"

Gabra, 29, 34–37
gathering, 332
gender, 68
generalized fear, *see* "fear"
genesis of language, 340 *see* "language"
gift/ gifting, 253, 306
goal-oriented behavior, 100 *see* "process oriented convention"
great ape, 1
greeting, 260
grooming
  hand-clasped grooming, 192, 259
  intense grooming, 127–128, 133
group size, 31 *see* "Dunbar number"
Groups: The Evolution of Human Sociality, 2, 11
guarantee function, 319
gun, 225

habitat niche, *see* "niche"
habitat segregation, 272, 278
habit, 8, 10
habitual action, 10 *see* "action"
hand-clasped grooming, 192, 259 *see* "grooming"
hazard-precaution system, 77
here and now, 353
heterogeneous, 267
heterospecific, 268
hidden "envy", *see* "envy"
hidden emotion, *see* "emotion"
hidden feeling, *see* "feeling"

Hindu, 66
holospecia, 278
homesickness, 339
Hoor, 229, 231
hostile relation, 224, 232 *see* "non-
    hostile relation"
human, 373, 388–389
  human culture, 396
  human evolution, 234 *see* "evolution"
  present-day human, 1
humanity, 388
hunter-gatherer society, 237
hunting, 332

Iban, 51
identity, 227
image, 48, 49
imaginative play, 89
imitation, 101
immediacy, 42
immortality, 54
incest, 33
  incest avoidance, 407
  incest taboo, 251, 407
  mother-son incest, 402
incohesiveness, 11
incurring, 33
infancy, 347
infant, 338, 343, 347
injunction, 290
insectivore, 276, 270
institution 1, 112, 137–138, 143, 157–159,
    162, 167, 193, 195, 284
  institutional order formation, 29
  institutional performance, 304
  cultural institution, 116 *see also*
    "education"

definition of "institution" without
    language, 397
evolution of institutions, 223, 289
intersubjective institution, 409
natural institution, 4–5, 92, 223, 329,
    345–347, 399
no need for institution, 32
post-institution stage, 256
pre-institution, 41, 56, 256
rite of institution, 68
"We"-type institution, 409
institutionalization, 346, 370
  institutionalization of feeling, 347–
    348 *see also* "feeling"
institutionalized play, 91
intense grooming, *see* "grooming"
intention, 290
  intentional agent, 90
  interaction, 283, 337–338, 344–345,
    421
  interaction system, 249
  interactive behavior, 10
  dyadic interaction, 82–83
  field of interaction, 174, 178
interest, 195
internal emotions, *see* "emotion"
internal envy, *see* "envy"
interpretation, 290
interspecific competition, 272–273 *see*
    "niche"
intersubjective institution, 409 *see*
    also "institution"
intersubjectivity, 403
Inuit, 421

Japanese macaque, 85
jealousy, 33 *see also* "envy"

Jie, 224
joint attentional frame, 83

karma (*wenkam*), 386–387
kibbutz, 33
kiku, 3–5, 9 *see* "norm"
"killing" mentality, 229
king, 35

language, 193, 299, 336, 340, 342
  language acquisition, 340
  "languageless institution" theory,
    329
  genesis of language, 340
laughter, 404
learning, 98 *see* "teaching"
  learning in chimpanzees, 98
  learning in traditional performing
    arts, 111
  social learning, 100
legitimacy, 30
legitimate peripheral participation,
  105
legitimization, 290
lifeform, 279
liminal space, 256
linguistic imagination, 335
linguistic representation, 336
loneliness, 286
long-distance vocalization, *see* "pant-
  hoot"
loose rule, 405 *see* "rule"
loud announcement, 358

M group, 169
Mahale (Tanzania), 143, 169
marriage, 64

master-apprentice relationship, *see*
  "relationship
mathematical proof, 289
Matheniko, 224
matrilineal kin, 353
mayfly, 278
Mbotgote, 318
meaning, 42, 244
mediator, 314
mental agent, 91
metacognition, 110
metarepresentation, 113
mixed species association, 268, 270,
  274, 282
mode of coexistence, 143–144, 150,
  154–155, 156–158, 161–162 *see*
  "coexistence"
monkey study, 3
morality, 347–348
moral, 13
mother-son incest, *see* "incest"
mounting, 260
multiple representation, 113
murder, 230
Muslim, 377, 387

natural institution, 4–5, 92, 223, 329,
  347, 399 *see also* "institution"
  natural institution of the extended
    family group rule, 346
  natural institution surrounding
    coexistence with others, 345
  primordial natural institution, 342,
    345, 347
natural pedagogy, 104
natural selection, 248
Neanderthal, 45

negotiative and performative creation of order, 29
neocortex, 31
ngulu (mediums'), 362
niche, 266–267, 270, 275–276, 283
  niche construction, 279
  niche measurement, 273
  niche overlap, 272–273
  niche separation, 272
  niche theory, 271
  ecological niche, 248
  environmental niche, 271
  feeding niche, 268
  functional niche, 271
  habitat niche, 271
  role niche, 271
no need for institution, 32 *see* "institution"
non-equilibrium, 272 *see also* "equilibrium"
non-face-to-face encounter, 172, 174, 179, 189 *see also* "face-to-face"
non-hostile relation, 224–225, 227, 232 *see also* "hostile relation"
non-human primate, 1 *see* "primate"
non-structured assemblage/gathering, 6, 355
norm, 398
normative example, 10

obsessive-compulsive disorder (OCD), 75
omission, 285
ontogenetic nature of the human species, 347
ontogeny, 348
orderliness, 65

others, 8, 14, 101
"ought", 390

Pan, 253
pant-grunt, 124, 134, 416
pant-hoot, 169
Pari, 231
party, 314
past envy story, *see* "envy"
pastoral value-sharing sphere, 234, 236
pattern = order, 137
pattern of action connection, 167, 171, 189
"pay attention", 28–29
peer, 249
performative order formation, 29
performer, 307
performing subgroup, 402
Philippines, 199, 201–202, 216
phylogeny, 348
place of living, 279
play, 193
  play institution, 92 *see also* "institution"
  play-fighting, 84
  pretend play, 89
Pokot, 234
positive feeling about being with others, 344 *see also* "coexistence"
possession, 76, 255
post-institution stage, 256 *see* "institution"
practice, 10
  behavioral practice, 226
  customary practice, 9–10
  established practice, 10

Subject Index

pre-institution, 41, 56, 256 *see* "institution"

present-day human, 1 *see* "human"

pretend play, 89 *see* "play"

pretense, 389–390

Pretense, 389

pretense of death, 373

primate *see also* "human"

  primate culture, 396

  primate society, 24

  non-human primate, 1

primate sociology, 1, 413

primordial natural institution, 342, 345, 347 *see also* "natural institution"

problem, 155–156, 160–162

process of self-awareness and self-projection, 345 *see* "self-awareness", "self-projection"

process-oriented convention, 192, 194 *see* "goal-oriented behavior"

prohibitive rule, *see* "rule"

projection between self and other, 330, 402

public information, 148–149

pursuit party, 227

Pygmy, 22, 25

raiding, 221–222 *see also* "ajore"

  raiding group, 227

  aim of raiding, 225

rain-making ritual, 66

rank order, 401

"real food" (*niqinmarik*), 421

"reason" (*ihuma*), 336

reciprocal relationship, 332 *see* "relationship"

recursivity, 300

  recursive relationship, 266 *see* "relationship"

  recursive repetition, 266

redefinition, 368

reinterpretation, 368

relationship

  relationship of trust and equality, 334 *see* "equality ", "trust"

  close relationship, 366

  dominant-dependent relationship, 334

  master-apprentice relationship, 109

religiosity, 65

repetitiveness, 65

  representational ability, 7

reproducible, 244

resignation, 391

resource, 243

  resource shortage, 272–273

restriction, 330, 337

  awareness of restrictions, 339

retaliation, 230–231

retell, 369

retrospection, 65

revenge, 230–231

rite of institution, *see* "institution"

rite of passage, 67

ritual, 67, 139, 389

  ritual rule, 245

  ritualistic act, 132, 138–139

ritualization, 69, 71, 73, 133, 139

role, 266–267, 276

  role niche, *see* "niche"

  rule, 8, 81, 137, 193

  rule implicitization, 399

  rule of may, 193

rules of sustainable social groups, 329

constitutive rule, 112

conventional rule, 136

definition of "rule" without language, 397

extended family group rule, 346

food-sharing rule, 335

loose rule, 405

prohibitive rule, 245

secondary rule, 405

sharing rule, 335, 341

trust rule, 334–335

sacrifice, 66

Sama, 199, 201–208, 213, 217

sanction, 337

sansamuka, 355

saru-gaku (primatology), 3

school lesson, 192

secondary rule, 406 *see also* "rule"

segmentary lineage system, 27

seido (institution), 9 *see also* "institution"

self-awareness, 330, 340, 342, 347
  development of self-awareness, 343

self-inhibition, 87

self-projection, 342, 347
  self-projection on others, 339–340
  self-projection, 343

self-regulate, 345

self-restraint, 396

sense, 356

sharing, 243, 351
  sharing rule, 335, 341 *see* "rule"
  shared value, 284, 286 *see also* "value"

sign, 132, 138, 322–323

signification, 133

signified, 139

social, the, 6
  social intelligence, 114
  social interaction, 8
  social learning, 100 *see also* "learning"

social/cultural anthropology, 1 *see also* "anthropology"

social group, 143, 150, 157–158, 162
  sustained social group, 399

sociality
  evolution of human sociality, 1, 238

society without government, 26

sorcery, 35, 352

speech, 33

spontaneous order, 134, 136

Sri Lanka, 66

status function, 112

structural-functionalism, 67

subsistence, 421
  subsistence skill, 332
  subsistence system, 331

suicide, 53, 373, 375, 380–381, 383, 385, 388

Sulu Archipelago, 199, 201–202

sustained social group, *see* "social group"

symmetry, 303

sympatric, 268, 279

tabula rasa (blank slate), 106

Taï National Park, 268

Taita, 367

teacher and learner, 115

teaching *see* "learning"

"teaching" in non-human animals, 102

education without teaching, 105

tease, 340–341

  teasing game, 341

teleological approach, 64

Thanatos (death), 53 *see also* "the dead","death"

theory of mind, 91, 110

third party, 21–22, 35, 178, 184, 317–319, 322

third term exclusion, 408

Toposa, 224

traditionalism, 65

trapping, 332

trial and error, 248

trust, 332, 334, 336

  trust rule, 335 *see also* "rule"

  trust system, 35, 36

Turkana, 224, 233, 367

unidentified others, 37

unidirectionality, 303

unknown people, 30

unspoken anger, *see* "anger"

unstable relation, 224

value, 248

  value judgment, 284

  shared value, 284, 286

very small society, 25

violence, 24

War culture complex, 411

ways of action connection, 167, 172, 179, 188–189, 191

"We", 398

  "We"-type institution, 409

"why we are doing so", 157

"what we do", 149, 157–160, 162

wild animal, 331

witchcraft, 361, 365

worldview, 331–332, 335, 340

Yu'pik, 331

Zambia, 353